Demystifying Economic Regulation

A Practitioner's Guide: Theory, Methods and Practice

.

Demystifying Economic Regulation

A Practitioner's Guide: Theory, Methods and Practice

Insight and Guidance for Sector Ministers,
Senior Regulators, Policy Makers and Students

H. Sama Nwana

Visiting Professor
Department of Electronic & Electrical Engineering
University of Strathclyde
Glasgow, Scotland, UK.

First edition published in August 2024 by Strathclyde Academic Media.

The author and publisher of this book have made best efforts to contact copyright holders to seek permissions where appropriate. The book also benefits from copyright owners' waivers for "fair use" including from:

Ofcom UK (https://www.ofcom.org.uk/about-ofcom/website/copyright);

UK Government (https://www.nationalarchives.gov.uk/doc/open-government-licence/version/3/).

In the event of any omissions or errors, please get in touch via the above email address, and corrections will be made for future editions.

The full text of this book has been peer-reviewed to ensure high quality academic standards.

Edited by Louise Crockett.

Demystifying Economic Regulation: A Practitioner's Guide

H Sama Nwana

Paperback ISBN: 978-1-7395886-1-8

Hardback ISBN: 978-1-7395886-2-5

Ebook ISBN: 978-1-7395886-3-2

Regulation is one of the five key drivers of any sector of the economy, along with Technological changes, Consumer behaviour, Industry and the Macroeconomy. Best practice Regulation needs to weave from the evidence of all these other drivers along with much more, e.g., the state of sector competition amongst market players, wholesale and retail prices, regions of the country with no services, Government policies, etc. – making it nuanced, complex and much misunderstood. However, it can be and should be demystified.

"Never tire to study – and to teach others."
Confucius

Contents

Dedication

To the memory of *Iain R. Williams (1964 – 2024)* who inspired, co-founded and ran the Cenerva Telecommunications Regulatory Master Classes (TRMC) programme[1] so expertly. Without this spark, this book would never have been written.

To the memory of my late mother *Odilia Mantan Nwana (1942 – 2021)* whose values, to-do lists, diligence, hard-work, persistence and outcomes-focus clearly rubbed off on me – much more so than I thanked her during her lifetime for 'transmitting' these traits unto me. Her spirit urged me on, as I wrote this book.

---

[1] Regulatory TRMC - Cenerva – Telecommunications Regulatory Master Classes - https://cenerva.com/regulatory-training/regulatory-trmc/

Acknowledgments

This book draws on my experiences as a senior network industry regulator in the UK (at Ofcom), and more than a decade ever since of training and conducting consultancy engagements with Sector Ministers, Senior Regulators, Industry Operators and Policy Makers from across the world.

I am indebted to all fellow Cenerva Ltd and University of Strathclyde colleagues, associates and collaborators who train on various aspects of regulation, for the education they have also afforded me too. Their knowledge and works have guided some of how I chose to articulate many concepts in this book. I thank them very much. They are James Wild, Dr Charles Jenne, Prof William Webb, Chris Taylor, Andrew Gorton, Peter Seymour, Dr Jibirila Leinyuy, Phil Dunglinson, Simon Perkins, Dr Martin Koyabe, Johan David Michels, Prof Bob Stewart, Graham Butler, Dr Dimitra Kamarinou, Dr Divine Anye, Dr Sara Silva, Prof Geoffrey Myers, Fraser Graham, Steve Day and more. They will see in this book how much I have learnt from them.

I am exceedingly grateful for very helpful [and very detailed] peer-review comments on the manuscript that evolved into this book from Prof Geoffrey Myers (of the London School of Economics), Dr Jibirila Leinyuy, Dr Fabrizio de Francesco (of the University of Strathclyde) and one other reviewer who wants to be anonymous. Prof Myer's and Dr Leinyuy's feedback in particularly have greatly increased the accuracy and scholarship of this book. I am also so much indebted to my Cenerva colleague Steve Day who helped produce many of the figures and tables in this book.

Dr Jibirila Leinyuy in particular – an absolutely brilliant economist who works for the UK's Department for Science, Innovation and Technology (DSIT) - without knowing, prompted me to author this book. I deeply appreciate him allowing me to learn from his expert lecture slides that he developed and used whilst teaching Economic Regulation at City, University of London over several years.

There are so many scholars I cite in this book that I am in awe of – and I acknowledge them all for the education they have afforded me through their published works. I only hope I have done them justice in distilling from their scholarships.

Most importantly, there is much distillation of my experience and views of the art and science regulation in these pages, particularly in Chapter 5. Chapter 5, on Demystifying Economic Regulation, is truly *individual* and *personal* – it is largely my viewpoint. So, I therefore acknowledge that some experts on regulation may take different views to mine. I see this as germane to academic scholarship. I have already modified some of my positions on the bases of comments I received during critical reviews of this book and discussions with peers. I encourage other experts on regulation to improve on my efforts.

Lastly, I thank Strathclyde Academic Media (SAM) for adding this book to its published portfolio. In this vein I acknowledge Dr Louise Crockett – who so expertly edited the book - and Professor Bob Stewart who invited me to publish the book through SAM. Both Dr Crockett and Professor Stewart are fulltime staff of the University of Strathclyde, Glasgow, Scotland.

All remaining errors are therefore of course my own.

Preface - Regulation is both complex and nuanced

My aim of authoring this book is rather **bold** – to demystify the Regulation of *Network*[1] Industries and Economic Regulation through introducing the reader to [hopefully] simpler-articulated theories, methods and practices of Regulation. I emphasise "Network Regulation" because, more generally, there is a range of regulators out there worldwide who are not economic regulators, e.g., *technical regulators*, *medical regulators*, *ethical regulators* and more. We[2] teach and train regularly on [Telecoms] Economic Regulation practice, and our trainees feedback to us all the time that they do *not* have relatively simple texts or books that articulate the art and science of regulation in a relatively 'accessible' manner. They want a book that demystifies regulation as we try and do on our courses.

However, the truth is that Good economic regulation is complex, nuanced, idiosyncratic to the local country context and *not* one-size-fit-all across countries. Regulation cannot be one-size-fit-all at all: e.g., regulating the telecoms sector in Hong Kong with a geographical area size, population and GDP per capita respectively of 1,108 km^2, 7.6M people and USD $49,801 will be very different from regulating of the similar sector in Nigeria with a geographical area size, population and GDP per capita respectively of 923,770 km^2, 220M people and USD $2,200 [3].

Our experience is that practicing policy makers and regulators tend to want regulation to be the opposite: believing (or wanting) regulation to be simple, unnuanced, non-idiosyncratic and one-size-fit-all. Sadly, it is not and would never be. And the costs of poor regulation to a country are just humongous.

---

[1] The academic field of regulation is much broader as Koop, Christel and Lodge, Martin (2017) elaborate on.

[2] Cenerva (www.cenerva.com) – a boutique training-led consultancy. We also have a partnership with the University of Strathclyde, Glasgow through which some of our trainees can register for certifications on Economic Regulation.

[3] These statistics are estimated 2021 numbers which are very representative of Hong Kong and Nigeria.

Regulation is complex partly because it is one of the five key drivers of any and every sector of the economy: i.e., *technology changes, consumer behaviour, industry, macroeconomy* and *regulation* itself (Nwana, 2014). Good policy and regulation in any local country should 'weave' from the evidence of all these other drivers and much more, e.g., the state of competition in the sector amongst market players, wholesale and retail prices, regions of the country with no services, etc.

Regulation is ultimately about *control*. Good economic regulation derives from the *Law* and statutes setting up the regulator or regulatory agency – without these, no regulators and no regulation! The laws and statutes must be fit-for-purpose and up-to-date too because the world continues to change around regulators. If they are not, there is extraordinarily little the best qualified people within the regulators or agencies can do to control the sector properly with out-of-date laws and statutes.

Good economic regulation employs *Economics* and good economic methods and principles. At its core, economics is the study of how society uses its limited resources, e.g., hospitals and hospital beds, roads, radio spectrum, airport runways, fresh water, forests, installed electricity power generation capacity, etc. Economics also covers the production, distribution, and consumption of goods and services in the economy.

Good economic regulators employ economists/economics because it is about pre-empting and preventing *market failures*, an example of which is when a monopolist player emerges and sets unaffordable prices or rates for their services and products, leaving no choice for the buyers other than for them to purchase their overpriced goods/services - or go without. Every situation in which the demands of consumers and citizens (or more broadly the 'demands of society') are not matched by the supply of the amount of goods and services – which leads to *inefficiency* – is termed a market failure. The reader should look around their local economies – particularly in less developed, developing and emerging countries – and observe market failures in their electricity/power sector (nowhere near enough generation capacity and/or distribution networks to meet demand), in their health sector (not enough hospitals, doctors, nurses and outdated equipment), in their transportation sector (not enough and poor roads leading to inefficient trading of good and services intra the country), in their banking sector (a low percentage of citizens being banked and hence they are not truly participating in the economy), in their telecoms/finance sectors (with services in urban areas only, but not in rural areas), etc. Such market failures abound in these countries and it is the job of regulators [and Governments] to ameliorate them.

Good economic regulation controls the power of dominant firms in the sector so that they *do not abuse their dominance*. This is easier said than done because such firms do not become so big in the first place without the legal and lobbying power to protect their dominant positions. Observe how difficult it is to regulate the big technology firms in the world today: Facebook/Meta, Google/Alphabet, Amazon, Apple, etc., - as well some of the biggest firms in your own country. They have an army of lawyers, lobbyists, inhouse and external consultants[4] to counter any regulator, Governments and even a supranational organisation like the European Union (EU).

Good economic regulation employs many *methods of regulation*, e.g., Access Regulation, Price Regulation, Universal Access Regulation, Quality Regulation, Safety Regulation, Risks Regulation, Rate of Return Regulation, Price Cap Regulation, SMP Regulation and more. These methods require legal, technical and economic analyses to underpin their use.

Good regulation requires *minimum political interference* – something we do not see in many emerging markets/countries with politicians' fingerprints all over many 'independent' regulators' 'decisions'.

Good economic regulation also typically involves *Technology* and technologists. Technology innovation is constant in every sector of the economy. New innovative technologies provide cheaper, more and better-quality options and choices for consumers and citizens. For example, newer and more fuel-efficient airplanes provide better experience to air passengers, longer routes, more destinations and *cheaper* fares[5] than older airplanes. Newer [technology] hospital X-ray/MRI image[6] machines are able to provide cheaper, more plentiful (i.e., more patients being scanned) and more detailed pictures of areas inside the body – leading doctors and medical specialists to make more efficient conclusions as to whether surgery is needed for example. The older machines are less efficient.

---

[4] Including me in some countries – *mea culpa*.

[5] Particularly, when inflation is taken into account

[6] An image obtained by magnetic resonance imaging.

Therefore, regulation should *encourage and incentivise innovations*, new technology, new products and services rather than protect old dying industries. Where would the world be today if old [PSTN] telecoms companies [who served miniscule numbers of subscribers in society with super-expensive fixed line phones] were protected by regulation at the expense of mobile/cellular companies serving billions around the globe today?

Good economic regulation also must be built on real contemporary *evidence* from the local country market (urban, peri-urban and rural). The Rwanda telecommunications market is very idiosyncratic/unique and vastly different from the Singapore telecommunications market – no matter how much Rwanda may rightly be striving to be the next Singapore of Africa.

And Good economic regulation is also both an *art and a science*. We could go on.

The point of these latter many paragraphs is that Good economic regulation is indeed complex and nuanced, detailed but with much common sense, and there are many dense academic textbooks and numerous peer-reviewed papers on the subject. However, as I note earlier, most of our trainees and students find these books and papers *impenetrable* or just too difficult to understand. We find that the trainees and students are not even truly aware of the benefits of Good economic regulation. So, they are prone to agree with the last or favourite consultant they talk to – consultants who *often* lazily bring solutions from other markets not 'fit for purpose' for their clients' local markets – and, sadly, the clients are none the wiser to challenge such proposals.

Regulation is far too important for many sectors in developing and emerging markets to be caught in this mire – of it being done so badly because it is complex, nuanced, thoroughly misunderstood and considered as just another civil service job. The results are clear, bad and sad: (i) poor and non-existent services across the country (ii) observable market failures and (ii) dominant players abusing their positions in these markets, at the expense of consumers and citizens of the sectors – with regulators *seemingly* unaware of such challenges, and even if they are, seemingly not sure on what to do about them.

We believe the market failures in many sectors of developing economies including in energy, telecoms, water, transportation, health, aviation, education, banking, etc. are – in a large part – due to the failure of regulation. And the political class we observe in many of these countries do *not* appreciate why regulators need to be left *independent*[7] - whilst the regulator class have become truly lazy to the task of regulation because it is hard, nuanced and complex, and in many cases caught in webs spun by dominant sector players. Truly independent regulation is rare but incredibly priceless when implemented (Stern, 1997).

We believe this challenge calls for *more education and awareness of the true importance of regulation,* as well as *demystifying* it as much as possible. This is the challenge of this book.

If only *some* Sector Ministers, leaders of regulatory agencies and other [senior and middle-level] policy makers leaf through these pages – just to make themselves *more aware* of the key importance of Good economic regulation – then it would have been worth all the effort writing it. If what this book does is to help instigate these especially important sector leaders/ministers to understand better the role and importance of regulation, and then they seek to educate themselves on the subject more – even better. Ideally, Ministers should better appreciate their roles as policy makers and the separation [and complementarity] of policy making from regulation. I believe that senior and other industry leaders will also find this book valuable, in addition to all students with an interest in regulation.

All hyperlinks in this book were active on 30th June 2024.

H Sama Nwana
June 2024

---

[7] A reviewer of this book correctly highlights the distinction between *formal* and *informal* independence. Formal is what the statute says, while informal is what actually happens. The type of independence I am referring to in this paragraph is informal independence which I believe is arguably more important. This is because whatever the statute says, politicians have levers they can pull to interfere. I see this this in a range of countries.

Graphical Summary Narrative of Book

I am a trained engineer. So, I find it natural to take complexity, disassemble it as best as I can, and start putting it back together in order to construct more explicable and repeatable solutions. This process allows for both science and art to be used to reconstruct and explain complexity. I make no apologies for adopting this approach in the writing of a book to explain the complexity of 'Good Economic Regulation' as captured below in the graphical summary of the contents of this book on regulation.

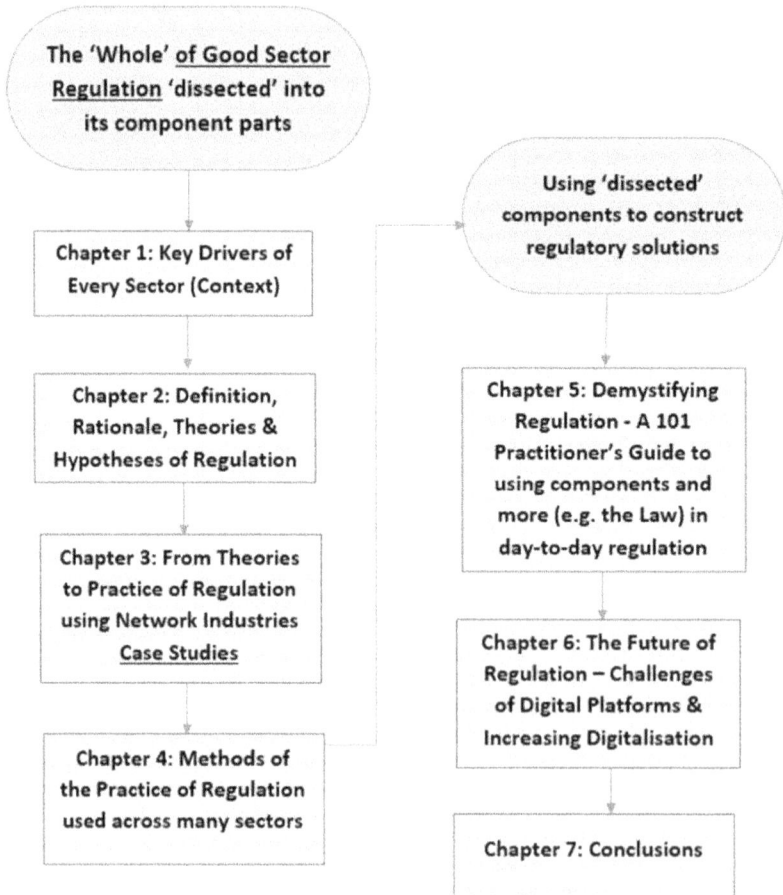

The 'Whole' of Good Sector Regulation 'dissected' into its component parts

Chapter 1: Key Drivers of Every Sector (Context)

Chapter 2: Definition, Rationale, Theories & Hypotheses of Regulation

Chapter 3: From Theories to Practice of Regulation using Network Industries Case Studies

Chapter 4: Methods of the Practice of Regulation used across many sectors

Using 'dissected' components to construct regulatory solutions

Chapter 5: Demystifying Regulation - A 101 Practitioner's Guide to using components and more (e.g. the Law) in day-to-day regulation

Chapter 6: The Future of Regulation – Challenges of Digital Platforms & Increasing Digitalisation

Chapter 7: Conclusions

About the Author

H Sama Nwana[8], CITP, FBCS, FIET, CEng, BSc (Hons), MSc (Dist.), PhD, MA (Cambridge), MBA (Dist.) (London Business School)

H Sama Nwana is Managing Partner of Cenerva Ltd[9], a boutique UK-based training-led consultancy based in London (UK) on Telecoms, Media, Technology (TMT), Digital Economy and General Cross-Sector Regulatory issues, with an emphasis on developing and emerging markets.

He is Full Visiting Professor at the University of Strathclyde (UK), and has held similar roles in the past at the Universities of Bristol (UK) and Brunel University (UK). Nwana has published other relevant authoritative books including *Telecommunications, Media & Technology (TMT) for Emerging Economies: How `to make TMT Improve Developing Economies for the 2020s* – published in April 2014; and a follow-on book (April 2022) entitled *The Internet Value Chain & the Digital Economy: Insight and Guidance on Digital Economy Policy and Regulation*. In fact, he is the author/editor of 8 books and more than 120 refereed papers in journals, conferences and industry publications. He is a heavily cited

---

[8] (99+) H Sama Nwana | LinkedIn - https://www.linkedin.com/in/h-sama-nwana-bbb0742/?originalSubdomain=uk

[9] www.cenerva.com

author according to Google Scholar with an i10-index of 46 and more than 8000 citations.

As a senior executive board member, former senior regulator at Ofcom UK, ex-industry MD, multiple award-winning technologist, and thought leader, he regularly consults[10] and delivers C-level trainings for the likes of IFC, World Bank, Meta/Facebook, Microsoft, MTN, USAID, as well as Governments, network regulators, competition authorities, venture capital firms and telecoms operators across the Caribbean, Middle East, Europe, South East Asia and Africa. Hailing from Cameroon, and hence being African, he is passionate about connecting Africa's/ASEAN's millions of unconnected through a combination of entrepreneurial, commercial, regulatory and policy instruments. In February 2024, he joined the Board of the Global Cyber Alliance (GCA)[11].

---

[10] Or has done in the past.

[11] https://globalcyberalliance.org/

List of Definitions

4IR	4th Industrial Revolution
AI	Artificial Intelligence
ADR	Alternative Dispute Resolution
ADSL	Asymmetric Digital Subscriber Line
AEDT	Automated Employment Decision Tools
ANS	Airspace Navigation Service
ANSP	Air Navigation Service Provider
ASEAN	Association of Southeast Asian Nations
B2B	Business to Business
B2C	Business to Consumer
BST	Base Station Transmitter/Transceiver
BSV	Broader Social Value
BU-LRIC	Bottom-Up Long Run Incremental Cost
CapEx	Capital Expenditure
CBA	Cost-Benefit Analysis
CEER	Council of European Energy Regulators
CFPB	Consumer Financial Protection Bureau (USA)
CISA	Cybersecurity Infrastructure Security Agency (USA)
CLEC	Competitive Local Exchange Carrier
CMA	Competition and Markets Authority (UK)
COP	Conferences of the Parties (COP)
CPI	Consumer Price Index
CNI	Critical National Infrastructure
CPNP	Calling Party Network Pays
CCSR	Call Completion Success Rate
CSP	Cloud Service Provider
CSSR	Call Setup Success Rate
DCR	Dropped-Call Rate
DGA	Data Governance Act (EU/EC)
DMA	Digital Markets Act (EU/EC)
DRCF	Digital Regulation Cooperation Forum (UK)
DSA	Digital Services Act (EU/EC)

DSL	Digital Subscriber Line
DTT	Digital Terrestrial Television
DOCSIS	Data Over Cable Service Interface Specification
EAD	Emergency Airworthiness Directive
EBDS	European Board for Digital Services
EBR	Evidence-Based Regulation
EC	European Commission
ECPR	Efficient Component Pricing Rule (ECPR)
ECTEL	Eastern Caribbean Telecommunications Authority
EECC	European Electronic Communications Code
EEOC	Equal Opportunity Employment Commission (USA)
ETF	Evaluation Task Force (UK)
FAAAM	Facebook [Meta], Amazon, Alphabet, Apple and Microsoft
FAANG	Facebook [Meta], Amazon, Apple, Netflix and Google
FANGAM	Facebook [Meta], Amazon, Netflix, Google, Apple & Microsoft
FCA	Financial Conduct Authority (UK)
FCC	Federal Communications Commission (USA)
FIR	Flight Information Region
FRND	Fair, Reasonable and Non-Discriminatory
FSOC	Financial Stability Oversight Council (USA)
FTC	Federal Trade Commission (USA)
FWA	Fixed Wireless Access
GDP	Gross Domestic Product
GDPR	General Data Protection Regulation (EU)
GSM	Global System for Mobile Communications
GSMA	GSM Association
HCN	High-Capacity Network
HFC	Hybrid Fibre Coaxial
HMT	Hypothetical Monopolist Test
HSE	Health and Safety Executive (UK)
IA	Impact Assessment
ICAO	International Civil Aviation Organization
ICO	Information Commissioner's Office (UK)
ICT	Information & Communications Technologies
ILEC	Incumbent Local Exchange Carrier
IMDA	The Infocomm Media Development Authority (Singapore)
IMF	International Monetary Fund

IMT	International Mobile Telecommunications
IP	Internet Protocol
IT	Information Technologies
ITU	International Telecommunications Union
IVC	Internet Value Chain
KPI	Key Performance Indicator
KSA	Kingdom of Saudi Arabia
LDC	Least Developed Countries
LLM	Large Language Models (for Generative AI)
LLU	Local Loop Unbundling
LNG	Liquified Natural Gas
LRIC	Long Run Incremental Cost
LTE	Long Term Evolution (a 4G mobile standard)
MFS	Mobile Financial Services
MNO	Mobile Network Operator
MNP	Mobile Number Portability
MTBF	Mean Time Between Failures
MTTR	Mean Time to Repair
MoU	Memorandum of Understanding
MVNO	Mobile Virtual Network Operator
NTSB	National Transportation Safety Board (USA)
OPEX	Operational Expenditure
NGN	Next Generation Network
NGO	Non-Governmental Organisation
NIS	Network and Information Systems (Directive) - EU
NP	Number Portability
NRA	National Regulatory Authority
OECD	Organisation for Economic Cooperation and Development
Ofcom	Office of Communications (UK)
Ofgem	Office of Gas and Electricity Markets (UK)
Ofwat	Office of Water Services (UK)
OpEx	Operational Expenditure
OS	Operating System
OTT	Over The Top [Services]
PBR	Principles-Based Regulation
PSTN	Public Switched Telecommunications Networks
RAG	Red, Amber, Green

RAN	Radio Access Network
RIA	Regulatory Impact Assessment
RPC	Regulation Policy Committee (UK)
RPI	Retail Price Index
RPI-X	Retail Price Index net "productivity offset"
SDG	Sustainable Development Goals (of the UN)
SDSL	Symmetric Digital Subscriber Line
SMP	Significant Market Power
SMS	Short Messaging Service
SoC	Standards of Conduct
SOE	State Owned Entity
SSNIP	Small but Significant Non-transitory Increase in Pricing
T&Cs	Terms & Conditions
TCT	Three Criteria Test
TDM	Time Division Multiplex
TELRIC	Total ELement Long Run Incremental Cost
TMT	Telecommunications, Media & Technology
TSLRIC	Total Service Long Run Incremental Cost
UKRN	UK Regulators Networks
UNFCCC	United Nations Framework Convention on Climate Change
UPU	Universal Postal Union
USF	Universal Service Fund
USO	Universal Service Obligation
VLOPs	Very Large Online Platforms
VLOSEs	Very Large Online Search Engines
Wi-Fi	Wireless Fidelity
WHO	World Health Organization
WLA	Wholesale Local Access
WLR	Wholesale Line Rental
WRC	World Radio Conference

List of Figures, Tables & Images

List of Figures

List of Tables

List of Images

Chapter 1

Introduction to Market Sector Drivers and Regulation

Every sector of the economy is driven by five key factors, and in the Preface of this book I note what they are: *technology changes, consumer behaviour, industry, macroeconomy* and *regulation* (Nwana, 2014). I note that Regulation is complex partly because it is just one of the five key drivers of any sector. In this Chapter, I expound on these drivers more, and why they all impact the regulation of any sector in any country context.

There are five main drivers of note, and they are shown in Figure 1.1, the macroeconomy of the country, technological changes happening, consumers' behaviours and needs, industry changes, and regulation[1]. Together, they truly shape any sector. We look at them in turn, using examples from several sectors drawing from Nwana (2014).

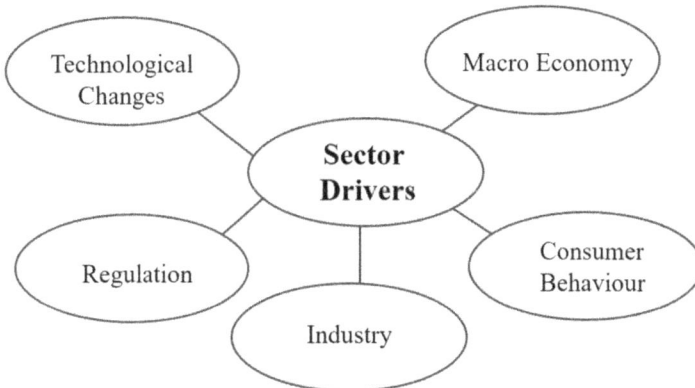

Figure 1.1 - Key Factors that Drive any Sector of the Economy

---

[1] More accurately, policy and regulation.

1.1 Macroeconomy

The macroeconomy clearly is a key driver of any sector of the economy, as is the case with many other sectors of the economy. If there is low economic growth or even a recession or high inflation, people are less prone to wanting to spend on anything but essential services. Telecommunications is evolving to become an "essential" service in most countries during the 2020s.

The online Encyclopaedia Britannica defines macroeconomics as the:

> "study of the behaviour of a national or regional economy as a whole. It is concerned with understanding economy-wide events such as the total amount of goods and services produced, the level of unemployment, and the general behaviour of prices... macroeconomists also utilize aggregate measures such as gross domestic product (GDP), unemployment rates, and the consumer price index (CPI)"[2].

1.1.1 Illustrating why Macroeconomy is a key driver to any sector

Let us illustrate why macroeconomy is important to how a sector would be regulated using some recent [2023] macroeconomic data from the country of Ghana as shown in Table 1.1.

In the GSMA Report[3], Ghana is aptly described as a lower middle-income country, according to the World Bank income classification[4], projected to grow at 2.8% of GDP in 2023 (lower than the figure for 2022 shown in Table 1.1).

---

[2] https://www.britannica.com/topic/macroeconomic

[3] *Ibid.*

[4] https://blogs.worldbank.org/opendata/new-world-bank-country-classifications-income-level-2022-202

GHANA's DEVELOPMENT INDICATORS

Total population (million)*	32.1
Proportion of adults 15+ (%)	62.7
Rural population (%)	42.0
GDP growth (%)*	3.6
GNI per capita, Atlas method (current US$)	2,280
GDP per capita (current US$)	2,369
Financial inclusion	68.2
Net bilateral aid flows from Development Assistance Committee (DAC) donors, total (current US$)	672,169,996

Source IMF World Economic Outlook 2023, World Development Indicators 2021. Data for 2021. Data for 2022 indicated by *
Financial inclusion is measured by Account ownership at financial institution or with mobile-money-service provider (% of population ages 15+)
The DAC has 24 members: Australia, Austria, Belgium, Canada, Denmark, the European Union, Finland, France, Germany, Greece, Ireland, Italy, Japan, South Korea, Luxembourg, the Netherlands, New Zealand, Norway, Portugal, Spain, Sweden, Switzerland, the United Kingdom, and the United States.

Table 1.1 – Ghana's (2023) Macroeconomic Development Indicators[5]

This is because Ghana has been experiencing [for many consecutive years] some global economic headwinds as well as domestic issues affecting macroeconomic stability. Some of these issues are illustrated in Figure 1.2.

Looking at the *top* graph of Figure 1.2, the reader can clearly see how the Government gross debt in Ghana (i.e., the lower curve) has grown steadily from circa 2006 to exceed General Government revenue in 2022. Looking at the *bottom* graph of Figure 1.2, the reader can note how inflation (the higher line) has consistently since 2002 outstripped real GDP annual percentage growth. The combination of the debt pile exceeding revenues on the top graph of Figure 1.2 and the inflation spike (to greater than 25%) and poorer growth in 2022 in Ghana resulted in a macroeconomic crisis in Ghana in 2022/23 leading to the Government of Ghana reaching an agreement with the IMF for a USD 3 billion extended credit facility that would go with an economic reform program in Ghana[6].

---

[5] Source: Based on GSMA Report - https://www.gsma.com/publicpolicy/wp-content/uploads/2023/03/E-Levy-Ghana-Economic-Impact-Assessment.pdf

[6] https://www.imf.org/en/News/Articles/2023/05/17/pr23151-ghana-imf-executive-board-approves-extended-credit-facility-arrangement-for-ghana

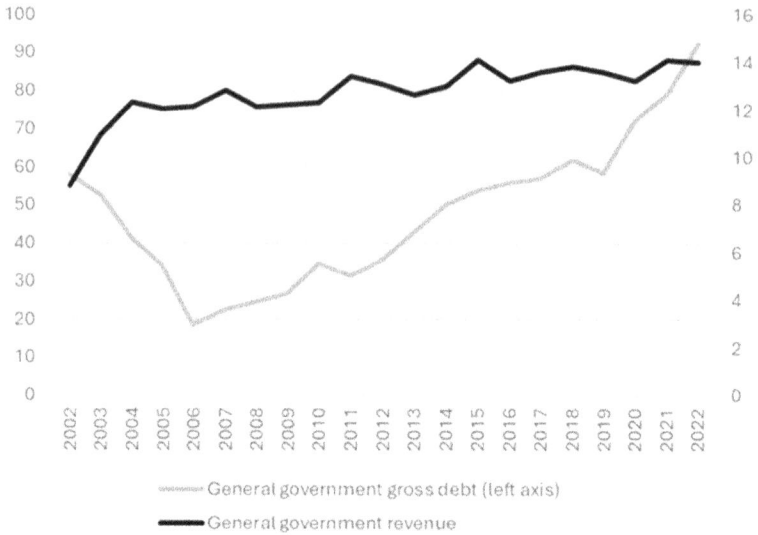

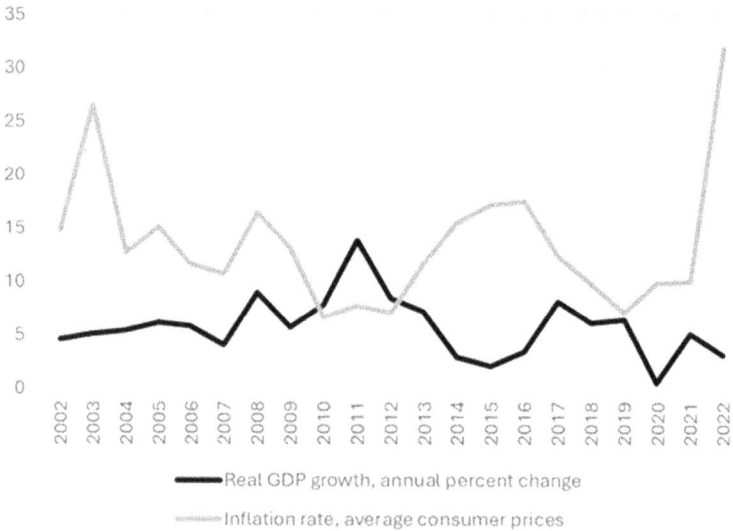

Figure 1.2 – Some Macroeconomic headwinds for Ghana in 2023[7]

(Reproduced with permission of the GSMA)

[7] Source – based on GSMA Report: https://www.gsma.com/publicpolicy/wp-content/uploads/2023/03/E-Levy-Ghana-Economic-Impact-Assessment.pdf

1.1.2 Why Macroeconomy matters to policy and regulation

The point of the previous section on illustrating macroeconomic challenges using the country of Ghana is *not* to pick on this country that I really love, but to relate it to regulation – the subject of this book.

The reader should consider (him/herself) questions like these:

1. Would *international* investors invest in a country where there is likely to be distress in the country paying its international debt obligations (see top graph of Figure 1.2)? The answer is unlikely.

2. Would *international* investors invest in Ghana (and sectors in the country) where inflation is at 25% per year (see bottom graph of Figure 1.2) and growth at less than 3%? Almost certainly No. Turning to another African country, after years of hyperinflation[8], the annual inflation rate in Zimbabwe was still 57.5% in April 2024[9] still keeping international investors aways. The history of hyperinflation has partly contributed to the country rolling out a new gold-backed currency called the ZiG in a concerted effort to mitigate the currency instability and hyperinflation that has plagued the country for decades, leading many international investors to flee Zimbabwe.

3. Would even *national* investors who have borrowed in USD dollars invest in businesses in a country with inflation at 25% annually? The answer is very unlikely.

4. Would even *national* investors who have borrowed in Ghanaian local currency – or even local banks - invest in businesses in a country with inflation at 25% annually? The costs of money, i.e. the interest rates to borrow locally, would have to be remarkably high. Therefore, the answer is very unlikely too.

5. I could go on.

Regulating any sector in an economy with the macroeconomic challenges as shown in Figure 1.2 is simply hard. Regulators and policy makers in

---

[8] "Hyperinflation is an extreme case of monetary devaluation that is so rapid and out of control that the normal concepts of value and prices are meaningless" – Source: https://www.investopedia.com/ask/answers/061515/what-are-some-historic-examples-hyperinflation.asp

[9] https://tradingeconomics.com/zimbabwe/inflation-cpi

such contexts cannot ignore these realities. Policy makers/Ministers would have to employ policy instruments such as fiscal (e.g., reducing sector taxes) and monetary policies[10] to encourage foreign investors to come invest against such headwinds, including concessions as required. Regulators may have to allow higher price increases operators than they would like to [with such high inflation] in order for operators to improve their profitability and/or not go bankrupt. Regulators may have to accept that operators would not invest and innovate until they see profitability in their sights. And even if operators decide to invest (e.g., a telco investor investing in fibre), the regulator may have to allow much higher regulated returns in the earlier years in order to help de-risk the investment in long term assets like fibre.

Therefore, it must be pointed out that political and macroeconomic stability in addition to microeconomic reforms are key reasons for unleashing growth in any sector of the economy and emerging economies over the last fifteen years.[11] Other microeconomic reforms that are needed cover trade policy, credit regulation, labour market regulation, business regulation, strengthening the courts, etc. So, firstly, Governments should continue to do more positive macroeconomic reforms. Secondly, the growth of sectors in the economy relies on many of these macro- [and microeconomic] factors being managed in the right way in the economy. Thirdly, macroeconomic factors can and do have other drastic impacts on any sector as shown in Figure 1.2. Lack of access to bond markets would hold back investment in networks in the electricity or telecoms sectors. Lack of financial incentives and access to credit would spell danger for any emerging production and media sectors. Fourthly, weak courts discourage investment in the event business disputes emerge, and they would aplenty in the developing economies. Levy & Spiller (1996) argue that the judicial endowment of an independent judiciary is necessary for credible commitment to provide an environment for investment in expensive sunk costs needed for network industries like telecoms. The other endowments the authors mention include legislative, norms affecting use of government power, and administrative capability. To have an

---

[10] Inflation well into in the double-digits for several years would like lead to tightening of monetary policy. In theory, tightening monetary policy would make credit more expensive, which in turn would reduce consumption and investment in the economy, which in turn lowers inflation as companies adjust prices.

[11] *Lions on the move: The progress and potential of African economies,* McKinsey & Company: McKinsey Global Institute, June 2010.
mgi_lions_on_the_move_african_economies_exec_summary.ashx (mckinsey.com)

independent regulator making flexible discretionary decisions, a country needs to have or to develop sufficiently on all four endowments. This latter is difficult to find in most emerging market countries I have come across.

The point is clear – Good economic regulation [and regulators] must take into consideration macroeconomic factors in their day-to-day consultations and decision making.

1.2 Technology Changes

No sector of the economy is immune to the forces of technological changes. Indeed, no sector of the economy is immune to the influence of technology. The one thing that is constant about technology is change itself—and this is a blessing, but is sometimes seen as a curse. A blessing because technology ushers in efficiency, reduces costs, and introduces innovation and new ways of working. It changes industry value chains too (Nwana, 2022). A curse because humans instinctively resist change, and if the rate of change is too fast, where you continually have to keep up with modern technologies, it becomes costly, at least in the short term.

1.2.1 Illustrating why Technology is a key driver to any sector

In the Preface, I note that technology innovation is constant in every sector of the economy. I note that newer and more fuel-efficient airplanes provide better experience to air passengers, longer routes, more destinations and *likely* cheaper fares[12] than older airplanes. I note that newer [technology] hospital X-ray/MRI image[13] machines are able to provide cheaper, more plentiful (i.e., more patients being scanned) and more detailed pictures of areas inside the body – leading doctors to make more efficient conclusions as to whether surgery is needed for example. The older machines are less efficient. Let me continue to illustrate in a bit more detail why technology changes are important to how a sector would be regulated using the ICT/TMT Sector (Nwana, 2014).

---

[12] Particularly, when inflation is taken into account.

[13] An image obtained by magnetic resonance imaging.

Imagine the headache (i.e., costs) that mobile operators have of maintaining three (or four) generations of networks at the same time: 2G networks for voice, 3G networks and 4G networks for data – and now they need to build 5G networks too in order to address the exponential growth of data. This is *roughly* akin to having the vinyl record disks, cassette tapes, CDs, DVDs, Blu-ray disks,[14] and MP3[15] formats of your music all existing at the same time. We typically try and retire some of these formats and move on—and so will the operators have to retire certain technologies at some time and at significant costs to themselves.

Below is a short, non-exhaustive list of some of the technological changes over the last two decades in the ICT/TMT sector:

- mobile: 1G[16] to 2G[17] to 2.5G EDGE networks[18] to 3G[19] to 4G[20] to 5G – with 6G on the horizon
- broadband: DSL to cable to FTTC to FTTH[21]
- digital storage: CD to DVD to PVR (personal video recorders) to home servers to cloud services
- digital broadcast: standard TV (SDTV) to high-definition TV (HDTV to 3DTV (three-dimensional TV) to on demand TV

---

[14] Blue-ray disk is a new storage disc format which supersedes the DVD and CD formats.

[15] MP3 is an abbreviation for "MPEG Layer 3"—a compressed digital sound format that is ideal for downloading music from the Internet.

[16] 1G is first-generation mobile. Now obsolete, it was analogue and offered only 9.6kb/s.

[17] Second generation (2G) systems, in contrast, are digital and enable cross-border "roaming." Standardization of frequency use was absolutely vital. Otherwise, we all would be using different phones/devices operating on different frequencies in different countries—a recipe for unmitigated chaos. Europe agreed on a system called the Global System for Mobile communications (GSM), whilst the United States adopted two 2G standards: CDMA and Digital AMPs (D-AMPS). Japan's 2G system was called Personal Digital Cellular (PDC). However, GSM is by far the largest 2G system, with most operators across the African continent and other emerging markets having GSM. CDMA lost out.

[18] Like GSM but with speeds from circa 56 to 115 kb/s.

[19] 3G is third generation. It is really a "catchall" term to describe faster access, which includes digital video, and it is also called UMTS. Speeds start from at least 200 kb/s and go up to 42 Mbps and higher.

[20] 4G is fourth generation. It is an all Internet protocol (IP) network with speeds from 100 Mbps up to 1 GB/s. Africa and emerging markets still have to deploy these networks.

[21] DSL is digital subscriber line. Cable is usually two or more metal wires running side by side. Optical fibre uses glass and transmits light between the two ends of the fibre carrying vast amounts of data. FTTC is fibre to the curb, whilst FTTP is fibre to the premises or to the home (FTTH).

- navigation: analogue paper maps to digital satellite navigation (SatNav) systems
- books: analogue paper books to digital e-books and e-readers like the Amazon Kindle) (you may be reading this book as an e-book)
- bookshops: brick-and-mortar bookshops in towns/cities to digital online stores like Amazon
- TVs: from CRT (analogue cathode ray tubes) to plasma and LCD liquid crystal display) TVs to 3DTVs to ultra-high-definition TV to flexible and stretchable screens, etc.
- Devices: more powerful by the year in terms of speed of processing, storage capacity, able to deal with more technologies (e.g., Wi-Fi, 2G, 3G, 4G, Bluetooth, etc.) and able to deliver multiple services

What the list begins to illustrate is the juggernaut of technology evolution driven largely by packets of data, addressed according to the Internet protocol TCP/IP[22] that are sent to the destination in any order, along multiple network routes. Upon arrival, the recipient computer recompiles the data into the intended order. Networks are designed in such a manner that there are multiple routes available to the data, thereby ensuring there is no single point of weakness. The increasing use of IP is a major driver of change in the TMT sector leading to the Internet Value Chain (Nwana, 2022). Internet protocol fundamentally changes the economics of many a value chain, resulting in significant innovations, as has happened in the books and music retailing sectors. I acquire most of my music and books now digitally, by purchasing and downloading them online.

1.2.2 Why technology changes matters to policy and regulation – Mobile money emerged from the telecom sector

The previous Section 1.2.1 *implicitly* answers this question. How can any regulator [or policy maker] ignore all such technology changes happening out there? Good policy making must embrace such technological renewals

---

[22] Transmission control protocol/Internet protocol—the communications protocol developed to enable computers of all kinds to share services and communicate directly as if part of a seamless network.

ushering in new efficiencies[23] (see later in Chapter 5) in addition to giving consumers what they want – not what the companies can offer. Increased efficiencies may be due to (i) reducing costs (productive efficiency) and/or (ii) improving quality or introducing new products and services (allocative efficiency, see Section 2.2 and 5.4).

Here are three good summary reasons why technology changes matters to policy and regulation.

Firstly, technology change is a *constant* in all sector sectors, more so in some like ICT/TMT than others. Learning to manage a sector undergoing so much change is vital, and the skills required to manage such an important sector of the economy are unique. Putting the economy in the hands of modern-day Luddites[24] and naysayers to change is a positively suboptimal thing to do. Those who run the ICT/TMT policy and sectors of our economies must be comfortable with change, and not many are.

Secondly, many emerging markets countries have the benefit of learning from the mistakes of the Western nations. Hardly any of these countries implemented 1G analogue mobile technology—and most rightly went straight into 2G. They now have to make similar choices on TV and radio broadcast technologies, on ICT infrastructure, on types of regulation, etc. More informed choices can and should be made in these markets which drive efficiency, economic growth, innovation, and value for money for its citizens. The policy makers need to be well advised on such choices.

Thirdly, convergence is truly real today in all sectors of the economy – thanks to the Internet Protocol (IP) and the Internet Value Chain. It drives certain sectors for example to having ever larger and larger operators; e.g., Safaricom in Kenya is not only into mobile but arguably the biggest banking operator in the country. Big is sometimes good, but in the main, it is not. Monopolies in the long term are not in the best interests of consumers and citizens, and they must therefore be regulated firmly but fairly.

---

[23] Allocative, productive and dynamic efficiencies.

[24] Luddites were nineteenth-century English textile workers who refused to embrace and protested against more efficient time- and labour-saving machinery being introduced then into the textiles sector between 1810 and 1820. They failed.

A classic example of how technology change in telecoms industry has resulted in significant innovation to another sector across Africa and other markets is that of mobile money. As of June 2013, only 20-25% of Africans had bank accounts and mobile money begun filling the gap in providing some modicum of banking-type services to the then-75 percent unbanked on the continent (Nwana, 2014). The whole area of mobile money transfers was literally invented in Africa (notably Kenya), making it a true area of African innovation. Safaricom's M-Pesa is a mobile phone-based digital wallet and money transfer service widely used in Kenya. Nowhere in the TMT sector on the continent is the aphorism "necessity is the mother of invention" truer than with mobile money.

In 2020, it was reported by the Central Bank of Kenya (CBK) data that M-Pesa mobile money transactions accounted for more than 50% of Kenya's GDP[25]. This means Kenyans transacted half the equivalent of Kenya's GDP through their mobile phones' digital wallets in 2019. And according to Safaricom's May 2023 Investor Presentation, the company

> "grew our 30-day active M-PESA users by 7.2Mn in the last three years. Grew M-PESA chargeable transactions / customer from 12.9 to 23.5 the last three years" Source: [26].

And this is why Kenya's Safaricom is now the biggest banking institution in the country as of 2024. Indeed, as of September 2023, M-PESA had a 97% share of m-money subscriptions in Kenya, while Airtel Money has 2.9%, while T-Kash has just 0.1%[27].

The 50% of [Kenyan] GDP turnover for M-pesa for 2019/20 would be much higher now in 2024. The specific number today matters less. For the purposes of this section, suddenly – thanks to technology changes - mobile network operators (MNOs) are now in the sphere of regulation by Central Banks, in addition to telecoms regulators. Who would have thought that

---

[25] https://www.paymentscardsandmobile.com/mobile-money-transactions-half-of-kenyas-gdp/ - Mobile money transactions equivalent of half of Kenya's GDP (paymentscardsandmobile.com)

[26] FY23 Investor Presentation_3 May 2023 FINAL (safaricom.co.ke).

[27] https://www.telcotitans.com/vodafonewatch/rumours-linking-safaricoms-m-pesa-outage-to-kenyan-tax-agency-denied/7651.article - Rumours linking Safaricom's M-PESA outage to Kenyan tax agency denied | Public Affairs | TelcoTitans.com

twenty years ago? The CBK[28] is the prudential regulator of Safaricom today in Kenya whilst the Communications Authority[29] (CA) remains as the telecoms regulator. Therefore, to regulate any sector properly requires a great understanding of and embracing of technology changes – they are inevitable in most sectors, and the rate of change is just getting higher.

The Kenya Safaricom/M-pesa story is a textbook example of why technology changes matters to policy and regulation – a telecoms company officially launched and licenced to provide mobile telecoms services in October 2000 has now evolved to become the most important financial institution in the country transacting much more than 50% of the country's GDP. Policy and regulation have had to adapt, whether it is financial inclusion policy or CBK regulation of a telecoms company.

1.3 Consumer Behaviour (Demand-Side)

The legendary former long-time CEO of General Electric [Jack Welch] once remarked that "when the rate of change on the outside [of Electric] exceeds the rate of change inside, the end is near." This speaks to accepting change before the change is thrust on you – hence, companies become obsolete if they do not innovate.

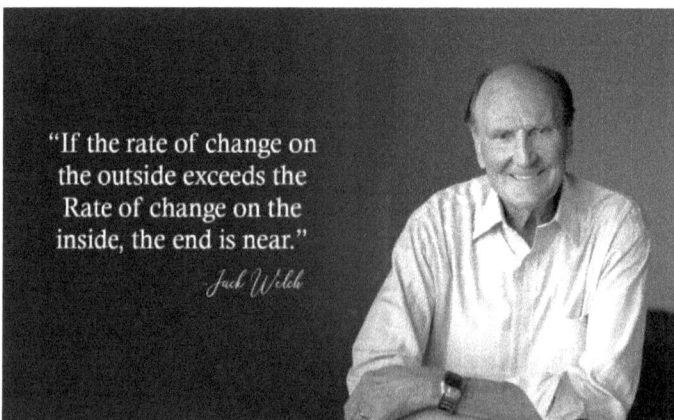

Image 1.1 – Jack Welch Quote on Rate of Change

---

[28] https://www.centralbank.go.ke

[29] https://www.ca.go.ke/

12

Similarly, policy makers and regulators need to accept and adapt to change, and yes the change is probably driven by technology covered earlier – but also by consumers themselves too. In January 2007, Apple Founder [the Late Steve Jobs] changed the ICT World with the first iPhone which ushered in the era of smartphones. Since 2007, consumers have decided with their purses what they want – with ever increasing smartphones over the then Telco-industry preferred feature phones. Consumers' behaviour won because the first iPhone changed the world in 2007 (Nwana, 2022, p. 121).

1.3.1 Illustrating why Consumers are key drivers to any sector

Just consider the following in addition to how the iPhone changed the world:

- How many Millennials and Gen-Zs would tolerate fixed line-only phones tethering them to where the phones are like my generation (Boomers II/Gen X) endured?
- How many of them would tolerate accessing their banking services only during 9-3.30pm, Monday to Friday?
- How many of them would give up their smartphones (mobile phone) in preference to keeping their TV if forced to give up one? Ofcom UK used to publish responses to a similar question by age group as depicted in Figure 1.3. It clearly shows that, overall, 51% of UK citizens in 2018 will keep choose their mobile phones over their TV – whilst 77% of 16-24 year olds will retain their mobile phones in preference to just 5% choosing to keep their TVs. Note the generational divide too in how 65% of the 75+ will retain their TVs over 8% keeping their mobiles. This illustrates the stark differences amongst consumers' choices too.
- What proportion of mobile money users in emerging market countries would give up person-to-person mobile money transfers willingly and return to sending fiat paper cash to remote villages through people they may not trust?
- Etc.

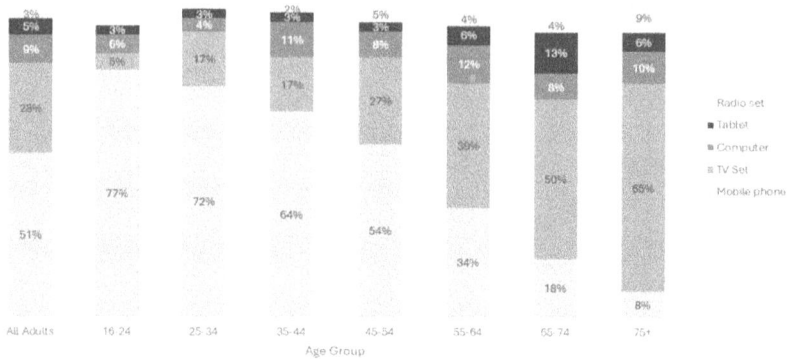

Radio set
■ Tablet
■ Computer
▣ TV Set
Mobile phone

All Adults | 16-24 | 25-34 | 35-44 | 45-54 | 55-64 | 65-74 | 75+
Age Group

A5. Which of these things you use would you miss the most if it was taken away? (prompted responses, single coded)
Base: All adults aged 16+ (1882 aged 16+, 246 aged 16-24, 256 aged 25-34, 322 aged 35-44, 272 aged 45-54, 309 aged 55-64, 221 aged 65-74, 256 aged 75+ in 2018)
Showing responses by >2% of all adults

Figure 1.3 – Most Missed Device in the UK, by age: 2018

Source: Ofcom UK [30]

1.3.2 Why consumers and citizens are the key driver stakeholders for whom regulation exists

The answers to this rhetorical question in my section heading are obvious – and they tell us consumer behaviour is a key driver of any sector.

Consumers want value-for-money services; they demand new, better, and "shinier: technology—particularly the Gen-Zs and Millennials who want "cool" and cooler devices and services.

Consumers want interactivity with their peer groups via TikTok, Instagram and Facebook. They want the "portal of me," i.e., services to their tastes or more personalised services, and to be always on if possible. Their smartphones with the chosen apps provide their "portal of me" – not a portal of services chosen for them by some supplier. They seek entertainment via Netflix, Instagram, TikTok, YouTube, movies, and music, and they care less about the intricacies of technology behind them. Even your grandmother just wants her phone to work and *not* some

---

[30]https://www.ofcom.org.uk/__data/assets/pdf_file/0025/149146/online-nation-report.pdf
- Online Nation (ofcom.org.uk)

14

convoluted explanation of how great the technology is. Just like she does not want to know how electricity or water gets to her premise or home – she just wants these services working. They want all of these for less, i.e., "more for less" and with superior quality of service for all these services. Justifiably so, too, as they do not have that that much disposable income to spend on more of more communication, electricity or water services.

So, demand-side consumer behaviour forces a continuous set of changes to service providers' offerings to meet evolving consumer needs. Consumer groups fragment into different segments who have dissimilar needs: teenagers, Millennials/Gen-Zs, the over fifty-fives, women, baby boomers, business users, etc. These groups all require different offerings that service providers must offer. They also want their privacy, and for the services to be safe and functional.

Therefore, policy makers and regulators must be able to specify and enable these consumer needs to emerge, and other Government and industry stakeholders must be able to "size" this demand by consumers/citizens, and supply their demand needs accordingly. Consumers are sovereign, a notion Lodge & Stirton (2010) describe as *Consumer Sovereignty*, in just the same way as these authors promote the *Citizen-consumer Empowerment* perspective, demanding direct accountability through their participation. Consumers and citizens are the very *primary* stakeholders that regulation and regulators are legislated for. The reader must never forget this. By the way, the reader should know the subtle difference between consumers and citizens: all consumers are citizens. However, not all citizens in society are consumers to a certain service for a variety of reasons: affordability, non-availability where they live or they may not like the service in the first place. Therefore, consumer and citizen policy are not completely distinct – they overlap.

1.4 Industry (Supply-Side)

Thanks to changes in technology (Section 1.2) and consumer behaviour (Section 1.3) above, Industry operators have to respond and adapt to meet demand as required.

1.4.1 Illustrating why Industry is a key driver to any sector

Just consider the following examples:

- The Airline Industry must expand annually and innovate (through more airplanes, more airports being built, more airport terminals, more runways being built at airports, more entertainment like movies, more connectivity like in-plane Wi-Fi, etc.) in order to meet the increasing demand by air travellers – the globe is getting smaller and smaller.

- The Energy Industry must innovate away from fossil fuels into cleaner forms of energy in order to address climate change, cleaner cities, consumer demands – leading to more use of nuclear, solar or greener forms of energy.

- The Banking Industry must innovate and drive more inclusion for the billions of unbanked still in the world without having to build expensive branches in unprofitable regions through Internet banking and Mobile Financial Services (i.e., mobile banking plus mobile money transfers plus mobile payments) – see Nwana (2014, p. 504).

- The Drug Industry continues to innovate – in 2020 and 2021, drug industry operators like Pfizer, Moderna and Astra Zeneca innovated new drugs in record time to alleviate the Covid-19 pandemic. The race to develop covid-19 vaccines was truly a matter of life and death for consumers and citizens across the globe. Millions of lives were saved by these vaccines.

- The ICT/TMT Industry is having to contend with and compete with Over the top (OTT) players – thanks to the Internet Value Chain (see Nwana, 2022). Take Skype for example as an "over the top" service. If one uses a handset connected to a Wi-Fi hot spot to Skype-call someone else, Skype is *not* paying for the use of operators' infrastructure though the user may in fact be paying for the use of infrastructure such as through their broadband subscription. Worse, by them using such an OTT service, they are not using the operator's (e.g., Vodacom's or Orange's) service. Google Search is another OTT service in which Google does not pay operators to host on their networks.

I could go on. Industry is clearly and unarguably a key driver to any sector.

1.4.2 Why Industry [and its value chains] really matter to Regulation and Regulators

The examples of Section 1.4.1 are clear on one key thing – that Industry provides the *supply-side* of services to consumers/citizens' demand-side needs. Encyclopaedia Britannica defines Industry as follows:

> "group of productive enterprises or organizations that produce or supply goods, services, or sources of income. In economics, industries are generally classified as primary, secondary, tertiary, and quaternary; secondary industries are further classified as heavy and light"[31].

True indeed. Industry produce and supply goods and services for the benefit of providing sources of incomes to their employees and shareholders, whether it is the Airline Industry, the Energy Industry, the Banking Industry, the Pharmaceutical Industry or the ICT/TMT Industry. Sector Regulation and Regulators desire and need to enable a thriving and healthy industry which both delivers on the needs of their consumers/citizens and generates sources of incomes for their shareholders and employees.

Industry is truly invaluable – just recall what the Pharma Industry achieved towards addressing the Covid-19 pandemic or what the Big Tech Industry Big 5 or Big 6 (FAAMG, FAAAM or FANGAM[32]) has achieved for most consumers and citizens today. These six companies are household names across the ICT/TMT, IVC and cloud value chains – and most of them are amongst the top twenty most valuable companies in the world measured by stock market valuation as Image 1.2 attests.

Indeed, Big Tech's Apple and Microsoft were still the top two most valuable companies in the world as of January 2024 according to CompaniesMarketCap[33].

---

[31] https://www.britannica.com/money/industry - Industry | Definition, Sectors, & Facts | Britannica Money

[32] Facebook/[Meta], Amazon, Netflix, Google (Alphabet), Apple and Microsoft

[33] https://companiesmarketcap.com/ - Companies ranked by Market Cap - CompaniesMarketCap.com

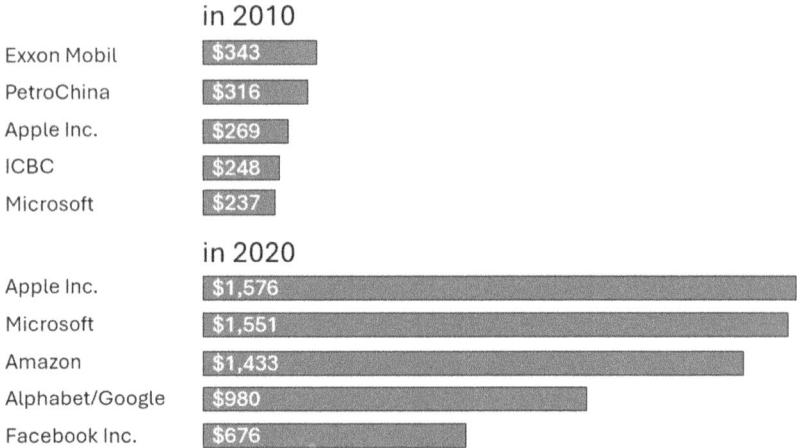

in 2010

Exxon Mobil	$343
PetroChina	$316
Apple Inc.	$269
ICBC	$248
Microsoft	$237

in 2020

Apple Inc.	$1,576
Microsoft	$1,551
Amazon	$1,433
Alphabet/Google	$980
Facebook Inc.	$676

Largest companies in terms of market capitalisation.
All figures in 2020 billion US dollars; 2020 companies as of 1st July 2020

Image 1.2 – The five largest companies (2010 vs. 2020)[34]

Big Telco and Big Tech are a discussion topic nowadays because of convergence – or more specifically because of the Internet Protocol (IP) and the Internet Value Chain (Nwana, 2022).

And this mention of 'value chains' is critical to Industry. Industry value chains largely help define the Industry and its participants, whether they are wholesale, retail or just ancillary players, etc. Industry value chains also change/adapt, sometimes by small evolutions as in the Airlines Industry - but sometimes radically as in the case in the ICT/TMT sector with the Internet Value Chain of Figure 1.4 'overrunning' the erstwhile simpler PSTN-led value chain of the old Telco Industry of the 1980s to circa 2007.

[34] Source: Ycharts.com, adapted from
https://www.reddit.com/r/dataisbeautiful/comments/hy8k1z/the_five_largest_companies_in_2010_vs_2020_oc/?rdt=41340

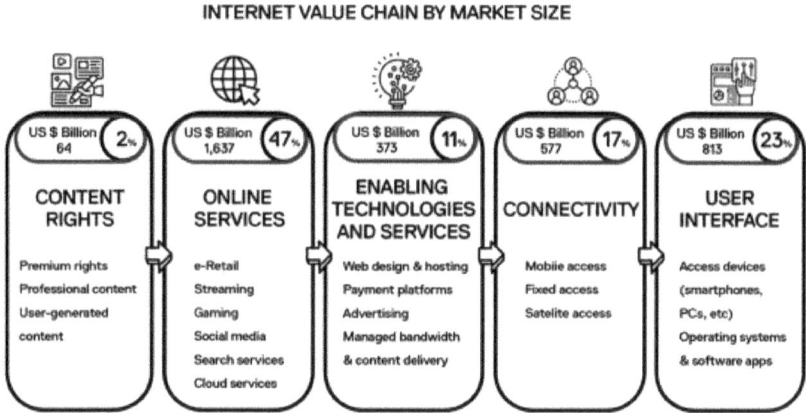

INTERNET VALUE CHAIN BY MARKET SIZE

CONTENT RIGHTS	ONLINE SERVICES	ENABLING TECHNOLOGIES AND SERVICES	CONNECTIVITY	USER INTERFACE
US $ Billion 64 — 2%	US $ Billion 1,637 — 47%	US $ Billion 373 — 11%	US $ Billion 577 — 17%	US $ Billion 813 — 23%
Premium rights	e-Retail	Web design & hosting	Mobile access	Access devices
Professional content	Streaming	Payment platforms	Fixed access	(smartphones,
User-generated	Gaming	Advertising	Satelite access	PCs, etc)
content	Social media	Managed bandwidth		Operating systems
	Search services	& content delivery		& software apps
	Cloud services			

Figure 1.4 – A Simplified Version of the GSMA 2015/2022[35] IVC

I wrote in 2019 that:

> "There was a period pre the Iphone (2007) when the telecommunications [mobile] value chain was just the simple classic vertically integrated 3-layer one of the TDM services layer (voice/SMS services), the network layer and the equipment layer. Then the IP-based Internet and its content-led value chain came along with its attractive devices, numerous online services, thousands of apps and unlimited content that wows subscribers – completely "over-running" the erstwhile mobile telecoms 3-layer value chain. These positive benefits for consumers and citizens also include social media apps like WhatsApp, Facebook, Viber, etc. Indeed, all the "Online Services" in the Internet value chain of [Figure 1.4] are all OTT services, and perhaps blowing away the first myth: OTT is not equal to social media apps! E-Retail, streaming, gaming, search and cloud services apps (and more) all also run over-the-top. Rich interactive apps and great devices along with fantastic content which telcos can never produce are being lapped up by subscribers, driving more network demand, but also driving the need for enhanced networks. Mobile operators have suddenly found themselves delineated to the connectivity layer/segment of the Internet value chain whilst other players dominate other layers. The Internet value chain has "supplanted"

[35] https://www.gsma.com/publicpolicy/wp-content/uploads/2022/05/Internet-Value-Chain-2022-1.pdf

parts of the erstwhile telecoms one with OTTs sitting in a different segment (Online Services) whilst operators sit in the connectivity segment. There goes another myth: the different segments should be looked at by regulators differently." Nwana (2019)[36]

Industry changing [due to technology evolutions/revolutions] responding to legitimate consumers' demands is a good thing – and regulation *should not* stand in its way bar pre-empting market failures and/or protecting consumers' interests.

Big Telco vs. Big Tech is a big topic of debate in the ICT/TMT sector as of 2023/24 with the 'Fair Share' debate[37]. This is because of the pains of a radically evolved new value chain shown in Figure 1.4 which has brought with it humongous positive benefits to consumers and citizens with services like TikTok, Instagram, Google and Facebook – whilst on the other hand brought with it numerous negative externalities like Internet scams, fake news, misinformation, disinformation, cybercrime and much more (see Nwana, 2022). Recall earlier Skype and Google not paying for use of the telco infrastructures they "ride on", though I also emphasise – as I note earlier - that consumers may be paying for use of infrastructure. Big Telco operators tend to deliberately omit this important detail in their 'Fair Share' debate arguments.

If anything, the role of regulation and regulators has just exponentially increased in the ICT/TMT sector as is evidenced by the emergence of a new class of regulators like Data Protection Offices (DPOs), Cybersecurity and Cybercrime Agencies, Artificial Intelligence (AI) agencies, etc.

This speaks to Policy Makers and Regulators accepting change too before the change is thrust on them, in just the same way as Jack Welch in Image 1.1 is clear that "when the rate of change on the outside [of Electric] exceeds the rate of change inside, the end is in sight." In this quote, he is speaking of Industry companies like General Electric. However, the same applies to Regulators and Regulation: when the rate of change on the

---

[36] Internet Security Primer-research-190701 (itu.int) - https://www.itu.int/dms_pub/itu-d/oth/07/1a/D071A0000070001PDFE.pdf

[37] https://www.cnbc.com/2023/02/28/big-tech-vs-big-telco-top-eu-official-says-theres-no-battle-over-network-funding.html - Big Tech vs. Big Telco: Top EU official says there's no 'battle' over network funding (cnbc.com)

outside [of the Regulator] exceeds the rate of change inside, the end of the Regulator too is in sight. Indeed, it is worse because the company in the case of Jack Welch's quote would just ossify and die, whilst the ossified regulator would just hold back the growth of the sector with out-of-date regulations and rules. Therefore, policy makers and regulators need to accept and adapt to change, and yes the change is driven by technology, industry value chains and consumers' demands covered earlier.

1.5 Regulation (and Policy)

Regulation (and Policy) is the fifth and arguably most important driver of any sector of the Economy. At its best, regulation truly helps 'wield together' from the other drivers of the macroeconomy, technology, industry (supply side) and consumers/citizens (demand side) to enable a healthy, growing and thriving sector full of competition, low prices, more consumer choice, more inclusion, safe services, etc.

1.5.1 Illustrating why Regulation (& Policy) is a key driver to any sector of the economy

Just imagine the following examples:

- Imagine an Airline Industry *without* an Aviation Regulator – typically some equivalent of a Civil Aviation Authority (CAA) in the UK[38]. The safety of flying passengers in airplanes is a paramount function and objective of any Aviation regulator. It would be inconceivable and incredibly careless for a country/jurisdiction not to have such an equivalent agency or authority – whilst encouraging increased airplanes in its skies. With respect to the other drivers, Aviation regulators (and Government Policy) had to also step in to protect the Aviation sector during the Covid-19 macroeconomic shock by paying salaries for Airline staff who were at home – called the Furlough

---

[38] https://www.caa.co.uk/

Scheme[39] which costed USD/Euros/Sterling billions to European Governments. This is an example of how the Regulation/policy driver works hand in hand with the Macroeconomy, Consumers (i.e., air passengers) and Industry drivers.

- Imagine a Finance Industry in your country *without* a Prudential Banking Regulator – typically the Central Bank of the country or some form of Prudential Regulatory Authority (PRA). The Central Bank is typically responsible for *prudential regulation*, i.e.. ensuring banks, insurers and large investment firms (e.g., investment banks) are prudent (and cautious) with the hard-earned assets of their customers, i.e., simple consumers and citizens. "Put simply, prudential regulation is a legal framework focused on the financial safety and stability of institutions and the broader financial system"[40]. Can the reader imagine the hard-earned monies in a widow grandmother's bank account are all lost due to the collapse of the bank? This would likely 'kill' the poor widow. So, a prudential regulator implements prudential rules that ensure all banks hold enough reserves to be able to cover up unto a certain amount. For example, in the UK as of January 2024, the Bank of England (BoE) mandates a Depositor Protection "withdrawal right" on deposit transfer of up to £85,000 lump sum to another bank, in the case the current bank fails and goes bankrupt. This would almost certainly consumer-protect the widow/grandmother's savings. This protection is invaluable to her. This is another example of how the Regulation/policy driver works hand in hand with the Macroeconomy, Consumer (e.g., the widow) and Industry drivers.

- Imagine an Energy Industry in your country *without* an Energy Regulatory Authority or Agency? Electricity and Gas are amongst the most basic utility services for daily living in developed countries. If these large energy companies choose *not to properly hedge* their wholesale electricity and gas prices leading to significantly higher costs for retail suppliers who sell into consumers' households? This would be terrible for the average householders to see their monthly energy costs suddenly triple or quadruple. This happened in some European countries like the UK due to the Russia-Ukraine war [that started in early 2022] which

---

[39] This is a period of time when an employee is told not to come to work and is either paid or not paid (see https://www.britannica.com/dictionary/furlough).

[40] https://www.apra.gov.au/what-prudential-regulation - What is prudential regulation? | APRA

affected oil supplies into several European countries. The UK Energy Regulator and the Government (through Government Policy) both had to step in with billions of pound sterling in subsidies in order to protect consumers and households[41].

- Imagine the Telecom Industry's regulator in Kenya, Communications Authority[42] (CA), had intervened *to stop* the technological innovation of Mobile Monies and Mobile Financial Services by the country's telecom giant called Safaricom. As I noted earlier, today, Kenya's Safaricom is now the biggest banking institution in the country. The 50% of [Kenyan] GDP equivalent turnover for M-pesa for 2019/20 would *not* have materialised – it would have wrongly been stopped in its tracks at birth by archaic regulations. Today in 2024, Safaricom in Kenya provides more connectivity and financial inclusion than any other equivalent Industry company in other African countries. As noted earlier the CBK[43] is the prudential regulator of Safaricom today in Kenya whilst the Communications Authority[44] (CA) remains as the telecoms regulator. This is classic example of how the Regulation/policy driver works hand-in-hand with the Macroeconomy driver (>50% of Kenyan GDP), Consumers (i.e., Kenyans), Technology (e.g., mobile monies) and Industry drivers.

I hope the reader can see from these examples the close interrelationships between the five drivers to any sector, i.e., the macroeconomy, industry, technology, consumers and regulation/policy.

1.5.2 Why regulation (and policy) and regulators truly matter

The examples in the previous sub-section (Section 1.5.1) hopefully start shining a light on the key role Regulation (and policy) plays in any Sector. As I note earlier, it is arguably the most critical. The reason is because – as clearly covered above - regulators' primary raison d'être for their

---

[41] As one reviewer of this book aptly points out, this example shows the limits and role of the regulator vs. politicians. The UK Gas regulator Ofgem's price cap reflecting wholesale energy costs was *not* sufficient to protect consumers from the cost-of-living crisis. The situation required the UK Government to provide subsidies which the regulator (rightly) did not either have the funds or authority to provide, but it did assist in the implementation.

[42] Homepage | Communications Authority of Kenya - https://www.ca.go.ke/

[43] CBK | Central Bank of Kenya - https://www.centralbank.go.ke/

[44] Homepage | Communications Authority of Kenya - https://www.ca.go.ke/

existence is for the benefits of consumers and citizens. This makes regulation (and good Government policy)—whether carried out by independent regulators or by arms of Governments—a key driver of every sector.

Consider how regulation (and policy) has transformed the Telecoms Sector over the past 25 years in most countries:

- **Liberalisation and Competition**: Telecommunications across the Caribbean, Africa and emerging markets have changed incredibly and become very dynamic because telecoms markets were liberalised, i.e., many constraints, including only local national companies holding national licenses, were swept away. Imagine if those rules still existed ensuring that MTN, being a South African–headquartered company, could *not* enter Nigeria, Ghana, Uganda, Rwanda and a dozen other countries. What if Digicel did not enter into the many Caribbean markets they are in? Where would these countries' telecoms sectors be today?

- **Spectrum Management**: The efficient allocation of spectrum airwaves can only happen with good regulation. Markets which have been liberalised, opened up to competition, and who issued several spectrum licenses to new entrant mobile operator brands have seen competition thrive, leading to mobile prices plummeting in recent years. Ethiopia (in Africa) has been opening up its telecoms market over the past 3 years (since 2021) with the set-up of the 'independent' Ethiopian Communications Authority (ECA)[45]. As a result, the ECA as of 2023/24 has since liberalised and licensed in new MNO entrant into the market (Safaricom Ethiopia) and will licence at least one more in 2024/25. These new entrants have (or would have) access to the necessary spectrums to compete with incumbent Ethio Telecom.

- **Telecommunications Bottlenecks**: Telecommunications is mired with many bottlenecks, be they at the last mile that get into premises, at interconnection points into international gateways, at exchanges, at ducts, at poles, etc. Ducts and poles which connect fixed cables such as optical fibre or other communication wires to

---

[45] Home - ECA - https://eca.et/

homes and offices clearly need access rights established, or else one company could dominate an entire market to the detriment of consumers. There must be an entity that regulates access to such bottleneck assets, and this is typically the regulator, though not always necessarily. Otherwise, new entrants will never be able to get into the market, and weaker incumbents may be crushed by the bigger ones who control access to such bottleneck assets.

- **Interconnection**: Terminating mobile/PSTN calls is a natural monopoly element of a network. Call origination may be competitive, i.e., you may dial from a fixed line or from one of several mobile operators' networks (or lines) or maybe even a Skype call. However, for that individual calling your number, only your network provider can terminate that call on your phone device. This gives it immense monopoly power, and this operator can charge as it likes unless it is regulated. Regulators have to regulate such mobile termination rates to be as close as possible to that of a virtual equally efficient operator (EEO) - a synthetic virtual operator which a regulator creates and models to work out and arrive at what the efficient true costs should be.

Clearly, regulation would remain a mainstay of the ICT/TMT sector[46] and one of its key drivers. A market which is *not* regulated properly will not attract investments and will lead to higher prices, inferior quality of service, poor innovation, poor competition, no new entrants, and fewer jobs. Why would you want to guarantee such outcomes? A rhetorical question, but an important one, nonetheless. As one of the reviewers of this manuscript highlights, this question is not rhetorical at all. This is because there has been academic research on the positive impact of independent regulators *which have good governance* on outcomes such as investment or technology adoption, especially in electricity and telecoms sectors in developing countries (Stern, 2007). Citing from Stern (2007):

"It is regularly found that the precision of the estimates of the impact of regulation is greatly improved when an index of regulatory characteristics is used and when more index elements are included. The general results from these single equation, 'reduced form' models is that, *controlling for other relevant*

---

[46] As well as in other network industries that I cover in this book.

variables (e.g. per capita GDP, relative prices, etc) regulation does have a significant positive impact on infrastructure industry and efficiency which may be reinforced by competition and/or privatisation"[47].

1.6 Why these five drivers *collectively* matter daily to Regulators

The title of this book is *Demystifying Economic Regulation: Theory, Methods and Practice*: It therefore seeks to expound on the art and science of regulation as practiced by the best statutory regulators in the world. I was both lucky and honoured to have worked at one of the best telecoms regulators at Ofcom[48] (UK), and worked with some incredibly bright colleagues on the art and science of regulation, including its underlying theories, methods and day-to-day practice.

The five main drivers of every sector shown of Figure 1.1 that have just been elaborated on in some detail in this chapter truly matter to regulators and day-to-day regulation. The reasons include the following. First, the narrative of each of the drivers above in this chapter explains why these drivers individually matter. Second, the rest of the four drivers (i.e., the macroeconomy of the country, technological changes happening consumers' behaviours and needs and industry changes) all provide the background context 'environment' in which Good economic regulation is *practiced* daily by regulators using sound theories and methods of regulation. I have observed in many emerging market countries where regulations and rules are being promulgated almost devoid of any considerations of these other drivers. The best-in-class regulators in the world would never do this. Therefore thirdly, any consultation produced and published by a regulator must research and take into account all these drivers before making the proposals in the consultation document. For example, it would be nonsensical to make proposals on increases in tariffs which bear no relationship to existing inflation rates. Fourthly, investments in the sector that would be enabled by regulation would always be based *inter alia* on all these factors including regulation itself.

---

[47]https://www.city.ac.uk/__data/assets/pdf_file/0013/81031/stern_regulatory_institutions.pdf - CCRP Working Paper Series (city.ac.uk)

[48] www.ofcom.org.uk

Lastly, senior policy makers and senior regulators who do not have a good understanding of these drivers in their markets would almost certainly be short-changing their consumers and citizens with the proposals, policies and regulations. This should not happen.

1.7 Breakdown of the Rest of the Book and How to Read the Book

Even though I write "how to read the book" in this section title, I cannot truly in all honesty prescribe one way to read this book. Nonetheless I try below.

1.7.1 Breakdown of the Book

Following is a breakdown of the rest of the book. It consists of seven Chapters:

Chapter 1 (Introduction to Market Sector Drivers and Regulation) – this chapter – covers the five main drivers of note of every sector of the economy, because, together, they truly shape any sector. One cannot properly regulate any sector without understanding their fundamental underlying drivers, in the same way one cannot regulate firms without an understanding of their incentives and interests.

Chapter 2 (Theories of Regulation) – covers a hopefully simplified but comprehensive 101 introduction to some definitions, history, rationale, theories and hypotheses for [economic/social] regulation. The chapter also covers regulatory failures and regulatory risks, defining what they are and providing many examples. It is a desired outcome of Good economic regulation to pre-empt regulatory risks and failures.

Chapter 3 (From Theories to the Practice of Regulation) - starts with an overview of the regulation models, approaches and examples of regulatory institutions out there in our economies, and why they are designed the way they are. It then proceeds to overview sector market structures because different market structures present distinctive characteristics leading to different approaches to their regulation. It then proceeds to overview the typical practical implementation considerations [of regulation] across several network industries, whilst linking as much as possible to the theories and hypotheses of Regulation of Chapter 2.

Chapter 4 (Methods of the Practice of Regulation): to achieve statutory goals, regulators and Governments employ a combination of many methods of [economic] regulation, with each method targeting various aspects of activities in the sector. This is admittedly an exceptionally long chapter. This chapter overviews - in significant detail using examples - circa sixteen mostly-used methods of regulation. These methods of regulation apply across most sectors, though the details of their implementations may/would differ sector to sector.

Chapter 5 (Demystifying Economic Regulation: a 101 Practitioner's Guide): this chapter lends its title to the entire book. It attempts to take a step-by-step 'peeling of the onion and adding the peels back' approach to demystifying the art and science of day-to-day practical regulation. It draws from the experience of my practice of regulation both as a full-time regulator and as an industry consultant over 15 years. It starts by my presenting distillations of practical day-to-day regulation as 'formulae'. It proceeds to reveal more of the complexity and nuance towards the end of the chapter. As I note in the Preface of this book, Good economic regulation is complex and nuanced, but it can be demystified. So, Chapter 5 reports on my approach to Demystifying Economic Regulation.

Chapter 6 (The Future of Regulation) starts by introducing the challenges of regulating Digital Platforms (e.g., Google and Amazon) that are increasingly dominating modern living. Additionally, it discusses the challenges to regulating current sectors with all the increasing digitalization happening in them. It revisits the roles of the different models of regulation (of Chapter 3) with increasing digitalization too. Drawing from latter, the chapter goes on to discuss how the growing area of Mobile Financial Services (MFS) in Developing and Emerging Markets should be regulated, e.g., via Regulatory Networks, and how this would work. Penultimately, it briefly overviews regulatory approaches to the increasing employment of Artificial Intelligence (AI), Machine Learning and Cloud Computing technologies across our economies. Finally, it also briefly overviews the issues involved in the regulation of Cloud Computing.

Chapter 7 (Conclusions) concludes the book with some brief reflections of the journey of this book. Even though, I title this chapter 'Conclusions', perhaps 'Reflections' or 'Postscript' (or all three) is (are) more apt.

1.7.2 How to read the book

Regarding how you may choose to read the book – if I may venture, I suggest the following.

1. First, I recommend you start by reading my Preface. It spells out all my initial motivations and biases in equal measure. I also recommend reading and appreciating my Graphical Summary Narrative of this book. It tells you the reader about how the book was 'constructed'. You may be one of those readers who want to read my concluding Chapter 7 at this stage. It is some 'version' of an Executive Summary of the entire book.

2. Second, I am a huge fan of the structure and/or the Table of Contents of any book I write should be able to tell the reader much of *my* story narrative details. So, I recommend you the reader scan the 'narrative' story which 'jumps out' to you from the Table of Contents – chapter by chapter. *I deliberately use (very) long Section Headings to help with this – I do not apologise for this at all.* We are all terribly busy these days to read books fully, so if I can help you get *some* measure of the book from its Table of Contents, so be it. Just try to spend some time digesting the story of the book from the Table of Contents. I strongly believe it would help. This should only take twenty to thirty minutes (max) and should give you the measure of my messages in this book.

3. With these prior two suggestions, I believe the reader would be best advised to read Chapters 1 to 6 sequentially – though this should by no means be taken as mandatory. However, one reviewer of this book noted that each of the chapters can be read as standalone or individually.

4. Chapter 6 can be read relatively independently.

5. Chapter 7 is a brief concluding chapter. As I note earlier, some readers may even choose to read this concluding chapter because it could be considered as a sort of 'Executive Summary' for the book.

In summary, I would be honoured that the reader reads any portions of the book. It would have been well worth writing it.

Chapter 2

Theories of Regulation

The true long form title of this chapter is 'Definition, History, Rationale, Theories of Regulation, Regulatory Failures and Risks.' So, this chapter provides a simplified 101 introduction to some definitions, history, rationale, theories and hypotheses of economic & social regulation. It also covers what regulatory failures and risks are, and why they matter to regulating better by pre-empting them as much as possible.

2.1 Defining Regulation & History of Regulation

What is Regulation? Before one even gets to a definition of 'Economic Regulation or 'Social Regulation', it is arguably apt to commence with a simple definition of the 'regulation' itself. The Cambridge English Dictionary defines the noun 'regulation' as

"an official rule or the act of controlling something:
- Safety/health/traffic/fire/security regulations;
- The correct procedure is laid down in the rules and regulations;
- Government regulation of inflation"[49].

The Cambridge Dictionary definition of regulation above clearly emphasises 'controlling' something including societal issues like safety, health, traffic, fire and security. It then proceeds to noting that "the correct procedure [to controlling for these issues] is laid down in the rules and regulations," as well as notes an example of Government regulation of inflation. Summarising then from this definition, *regulation is about the laid down rules of controlling something.*

---

[49] https://dictionary.cambridge.org/dictionary/english/regulation - REGULATION | English meaning - Cambridge Dictionary

Logically then, 'Economic Regulation' concerns the laid down [economic] rules of controlling a sector of the economy towards certain desired outcomes.

However, I am no economist and would rather cite a real one like Robert Litan[50], who writes on regulation:

> "Regulation consists of requirements the government imposes on private firms and individuals to achieve government's purposes. These include better and cheaper services and goods, protection of existing firms from "unfair" (and fair) competition, cleaner water and air, and safer workplaces and products. Failure to meet regulations can result in fines, orders to cease doing certain things, or, in some cases, even criminal penalties."

2.1.1 Economic Regulation vs. Social Regulation

Being a real economist, Robert Litan is more authoritative when he also writes that Economists distinguish between two types of regulation: economic and social,

> " "Economic regulation" refers to rules that limit who can enter a business (entry controls) and what prices they may charge (price controls). For example, taxi drivers and many professionals (lawyers, accountants, beauticians, financial advisers, etc.) must have licenses in order to do business; these are examples of entry controls. As for price controls, for many years, airlines, trucking companies, and railroads were told what prices they could charge, or at least not exceed. Companies providing local telephone service are still subject to price controls in all states.

> "Social regulation" refers to the broad category of rules governing how any business or individual carries out its activities, with a view to correcting one or more *"market failures."* A classic way in which the market fails is when firms (or individuals) do not take account of the costs their activities may impose on third parties...

---

[50] Regulation - Econlib - https://www.econlib.org/library/Enc/Regulation.html

32

When this happens, the activities will be pursued too intensely or in ways that fail to stem harm to third parties. For example, left to its own devices, a manufacturing plant may spew harmful chemicals into the air and water, causing harm to its neighbors. Governments respond to this problem by setting standards for emissions or even by requiring that firms use specific technologies (such as "scrubbers" for utilities that capture noxious chemicals before steam is released into the air)"[51] (*the author's emphases*).

Robert Litan's more expansive definition of Regulation above (i.e., economic and social regulation) provides for the simplest definitions I could find. His definitions highlight the economic regulation notions of laid down rules like *entry controls* (rules that limit who can enter a business through *licencing*), *price controls* (rules controlling what prices operators can charge and *market failures* (when firms and individuals do not take into account the costs their activities may impose on third parties like customers, the environment or society).

In summary now, Economic/Social Regulation concerns Government *controls* of various aspects of sectors of the economy in order to realise desired outcomes: to pre-empt and prevent market failures, to promote efficiency, fairness, non-discrimination, stability, to protect consumers/citizens and the protection of other public interests including aspects like the environment. These controls involve the definition and enforcement of laid down [economic/social] rules, laws, and policies that govern and constrain the behaviour and conduct of individuals (i.e., consumers and citizens), businesses, and organisations operating within a specific industry or sector.

In the interest of scholarship, an expert economist reviewer of this book noted that Litan's distinction between economic and social regulation is not that clear to him conceptually, noting that price controls are usually used to address market failures, and that both categories affect economic activity. The reviewer also notes that Litan's definition of social regulation seems very narrow, e.g. "many people would think of social regulation as including issues at the edges of, or beyond, economic activity such as

---

[51]*Ibid.*

33

human fertilisation where broader values are in play such as ethics, justice or public value"[52]. I agree with this reviewer.

Baldwin et *al.* (2012, p.3) point out that the word 'regulation' is typically used in the following senses:

- *As a specific set of commands*: where regulation concerns the promulgation of a laid-down binding set of rules, e.g. a health and safety at work statute from a Health and Safety agency;
- *As a deliberate Government or State influence*: wherein regulation concerns a broad sense of Government actions that influences business or social behaviour, e.g. Government's use of taxes or subsidies to control economic incentives;
- *As all forms of social or economic influence*: this sense of regulation assumes all mechanisms affecting behaviour – whether they are Government actions - or - market actions, professional/trade bodies, self-regulators, etc. are all considered regulatory. This broad usage of the term 'regulation' emphases the fact that regulation need not necessarily be carried out by Government institutions, because other non-State actors can affect behaviour;

Baldwin et *al.* (2012, p.3) make a crucial point to conclude their answer to 'What is regulation?' when they aptly write:

> "As a final comment on the concept of regulation, it should be noted that regulation is often thought as an activity that restricts behaviour and prevents the occurrence of certain undesirable activities (a 'red light' concept). The broader view is, however, that the influence of regulation may also be *enabling* or *facilitative* ('green light') as, for example, where the airwaves are regulated so as to allow broadcasting operations to be conducted in an orderly fashion, rather than left to the potential chaos of an uncontrolled market."

---

[52] Source: an expert economist reviewer of this book. March 2024.

2.1.2 A Brief History of Regulation

How did regulation emerge in the first place? The history of regulation is clearly incredibly old and complex. There can hardly be a smooth functioning society of any kind without some form of regulation, i.e. laid down rules that are defined and enforced, albeit explicitly through enacted societal laws or implicitly via *de facto* rules. Therefore, it is fair to note that Regulation dates back to ancient civilizations, from the moment societies started forming and norming. As part of societal norming, rules had to be laid down to maintain social order and protect public interests. If we consider the five main eras/periods of history[53] – Prehistory (to 600 B.C), the Classical Era or Ancient Times (600 B.C. to 476 A.D.), the Middle Ages (476 A.D. to 1450 A.D.), the Early Modern Era (1450 A.D. to 1750 A.D.) and the Modern Era (1750 A.D to Present) – laws and regulations have prevailed in all of them.

Take the *Prehistory* era for example, the Babylonian Code of Hammurabi was established during this period. These were laws and regulations dating back close to 1800 years before Christianity. According to Encyclopaedia Britannica[54], the Hammurabi Code is/was

> "the most complete and perfect extant collection of Babylonian laws, developed during the reign of Hammurabi (1792–1750 BCE) of the 1st dynasty of Babylon. It consists of his legal decisions that were collected toward the end of his reign and inscribed on a diorite stela set up in Babylon's temple of Marduk, the national god of Babylonia. These 282 case laws include economic provisions (prices, tariffs, trade, and commerce), family law (marriage and divorce), as well as criminal law (assault, theft) and civil law (slavery, debt). Penalties varied according to the status of the offenders and the circumstances of the offenses."

From the mid Ancient Times through the Middle Ages to the Early Modern era, Christianity and other religions like Islam were established and reigned. This led to regulations that were mainly concerned with maintaining religious and moral codes/standards. For example, the

---

[53] https://study.com/learn/lesson/time-periods-eras-world-history.html
[54] https://www.britannica.com/topic/Code-of-Hammurabi - Code of Hammurabi | Summary & History | Britannica

Catholic Church exerted significant regulatory control over individual's lives, regulating matters such as marriage and education.

Come the Modern Era (1750 A.D to Present) with the Industrial Revolution of the 18th and 19th centuries, regulation started becoming more sophisticated through the advent of economic and social regulation due to more significant changes to society. This was partly because increasing industrialisation 'forced' Governments to introduce *social regulation*, i.e. to regulate to protect workers and control/tackle other social issues arising from rapid industrialisation like safety, health, fires, security, pandemics, etc. This era also ushered in *economic regulations*, such as factory acts, labour laws, and minimum wage regulations.

However, circa the 16th to 18th centuries, *Mercantilism* prevailed in Europe in particular driven by Colonial accumulation of wealth enriching European countries at the expense of their colonies. Mercantilism involves heavy state control and regulation, which required Governments to maximise exports and trade of finished products whilst also maximising imports of raw materials and precious metals like gold and silver. These two factors maximised wealth accumulation. Mercantilism was implemented through laws and regulations including imposed tariffs, the creation of (super) monopolies like the English East India Company[55], and the imposition of strict controls over all colonial trade. *Capitalism* that later emerged eschewed mercantilism because it promotes minimum State control and regulation, whilst also building profits for private individuals and corporations.

As mercantilism waned during the late 19th century [in the United States in particular], large capitalist corporations and monopolies emerged such as the Bell Telephone Company[56]. Such monopolies possessed large market concentration, and coupled with much unfair competition, led to the passage of antitrust laws or pro-competition laws, such as the Sherman

---

[55] "The East India Company was probably the most powerful corporation in history. At its height, it dominated global trade between Europe, South Asia and the Far East, fought numerous wars using its own army and navy, and conquered and colonised modern day India, Pakistan, Bangladesh and Burma" – source https://www.nationaltrust.org.uk/discover/history/what-was-the-east-india-company.

[56] https://www.britannica.com/topic/Bell-Telephone-Company - Bell Telephone Company | American corporation | Britannica

Antitrust Act of 1890 and the Clayton Antitrust Act of 1914. These laws promote competition and prevent monopolistic practices.

Come the 20th century, there was a proliferation of more *capitalist* economic and social regulations across various sectors of the economy, e.g. aviation, health, transportation, education, finance, pharmaceutical, telecommunications, etc. These proliferation of regulations from circa the 1930s responded public concerns and market failures, leading Governments to enact laws and regulations to protect consumers, pre-empt market failures, promote competition, maintain workplace health and safety, pre-empt discrimination, and preserve the environment. In the United States, regulatory agencies like the Food and Drug Administration (FDA) emerged, which regulates/controls for the safety and efficacy of drugs. So, from the 1930s onwards and past the war, new licensing regulations emerged for goods, foods, civil aviation, transportation, television and much more.

Financial regulation[57] became quite prominent during the 20th century following the Great Depression of the 1930s and the global financial crisis of 2008. Governments found themselves forced to lay down new rules (e.g., in the USA, Dodd-Frank, CFPB, FSOC[58]) to safeguard the stability of financial systems, to further regulate banks and financial institutions, and to further protect investors. Paradoxically, these increased regulations came about because the global financial crisis of 2008 revealed the risks associated with excessive deregulation in the Banking and Finance Sectors. Deregulation and liberalisation of many sectors of the economy had dominated the 1980s and 1990s across Western countries under the pretext that regulations were just 'red tape' adding a burden to economic activity. This was after Governments (e.g. Prime Minister Margaret Thatcher's government in the UK and President Ronald Reagan's in the USA) began reducing regulations in various sectors, including finance, banking, telecommunications, etc., with the goals of releasing market forces to drive more efficiency and innovation – and hence more GDP growth. This neo-liberal approaches introduced more risks which has reignited post world

---

[57] Governments regulate financial institutions and markets to assure and ensure stability and to prevent systemic risks. This covers rules and regulations on banking, securities trading, insurance, and other financial activities.

[58] https://www.investopedia.com/ask/answers/063015/what-are-major-laws-acts-regulating-financial-institutions-were-created-response-2008-financial.asp - Major Regulations Following the 2008 Financial Crisis (investopedia.com);

war II Keynesian economics government intervention approaches to promote stability and economic growth.

More recently in the 2020s, Technology Regulation is arguably the focus today with new areas like the Digital Economy, Artificial Intelligence, Big Data, Cybersecurity, Cybercrime, OTT challenges, E-Commerce and much more (Nwana, 2022). New laws, regulations and regulators have been developed and are being developed and established to govern these new telecommunications-related areas.

In summary, the history of economic/social regulation spans millennia from the Prehistoric era to date, and reflects an ongoing process of the needs of society forming, norming, performing and storming to new heights (e.g. astronauts going to the moon, long distance aviation, sub-millisecond financial trading, 4th Industrial Revolution, etc). The history of regulation and deregulation also demonstrates a dynamic interplay between neoliberal letting market forces prevailing on the one hand, and Keynesian Governmental interventions on the other – in order to balance stability of sectors and the protection of consumers. This dynamic is bound to continue.

2.2 Rationale of Regulation

What then is the rationale for Regulation? In order words, what are the reasons for regulation? The previous section has already made multiple allusions to some of them, including 'market failure,' monopoly, public interests (e.g. the environment, pollution, etc.) and consumer protection rationales. The rationales speak to why Government and/or Regulatory Agencies may choose to intervene or control/constrain the choices that rational economic agents (corporations, businesses or individuals) can apply to specific business parameters, e.g. prices (via price controls), revenues (via taxes), quantity and quality. The controls may also apply to the overall integral market parameters, e.g. entry or exit controls, market design, etc. These controls could apply to any sector of the economy including public utilities, electricity, gas, water, transport, telecoms, postal services, banking and more.

The rationales for regulation include the following key ones (Leinyuy, 2013):

(i) Natural monopoly rationale
(ii) Market failures rationales (including public good rationales and miscellaneous other objectives like universal service, vulnerable consumers and affordability): this category is arguably providing the most exhaustive set of reasons for regulation.
(iii) Legal, Institutional, Historical or Rights-Based Rationales

We briefly cover these rationales for regulation in turn over the following sub-sections.

2.2.1 The Natural Monopoly Rationale for Regulation

We have to start with the questions: 'What is a natural monopoly'? Indeed, what is a monopoly? Why do these matter? Let us start with what is a monopoly. Simply, a monopoly describes a market scenario wherein one firm produces and supplies for the entire market or industry. More elaborately, Britannica notes that monopoly and competition are:

> "basic factors in the structure of economic markets. In economics, monopoly and competition signify certain complex relations among firms in an industry. *A monopoly implies an exclusive possession of a market by a supplier of a product or a service for which there is no substitute.* In this situation the supplier is able to determine the price of the product without fear of competition from other sources or through substitute products. It is generally assumed that a monopolist will choose a price that maximizes profits"[59] (*the author's emphasis*).

Following on from the definition of a monopoly above, a natural monopoly is a type of monopoly in any sector or industry which exhibits extremely high barriers to entry into the sector due to extremely high start-up costs. This naturally prevents any rivals from entering and competing leading to

---

[59] https://www.britannica.com/money/monopoly-economics - Monopoly and competition | Definition, Structures, Performance, & Facts | Britannica Money

a sector with only one efficient operator – the natural monopoly company. This player would typically be the only provider of a service or products for an entire geography (region, state, province, etc.) if not the entire industry.

A good example of a natural monopoly is your local water company. To supply water to your local village or town requires an extremely sizeable upfront investment (or fixed costs) for all the water pipe works infrastructure into every home and business, digging up all the roads as well as the company controlling the supply of the water [from a reservoir, waterfall, etc.] in order to meet the village/town demand. It would be *unnatural* and most inefficient for my home to be supplied by one company [Company X] using X's dug-in pipes and its own water source whilst my neighbour's house is supplied by Company Y, using Y's laid dug-in pipes from its own water supply. Two or three companies independently digging in water pipes on my street would not only be wasteful duplicating the other's digging, but would also be crazy - and it makes sense for one *natural* monopoly firm to do it all. These same arguments apply to other natural monopolies like railways, gas or electricity companies where laying separate networks of rails, gas or electricity cables would be most inefficient.

2.2.1.1 Demystifying the natural monopoly equation – and economies of scale, scope and density

Drawing from these prior naturally monopoly examples, let me digress a bit to try and demystify defining a natural monopoly more formally, and ditto for the concepts of economies of scale, economies of scope and economies of density. Many students/trainees are scared by economic equations – you [the reader] really should *not* be. They look scarier than they really are. See if you agree at the end of this brief section of this book.

William J Baumol in his classic 1977 paper *On the Proper Cost Tests for Natural Monopoly in a Multiproduct Industry* (Baumol, 1977) was the first to formally define a natural monopoly. He identified two key criteria: a single firm is a natural monopoly given EITHER:

i.   That single firm can produce output to supply the entire market at a lower per unit cost than two or more firms can produce.

Mathematically, this is referred to as the *subadditivity of the cost functions*; OR

ii.   That single firm operates in an industry to which new entrants are not naturally attracted and would *not* survive, even when there are no predatory measures on the part of the incumbent monopolist. This criteria is called the *sustainability of monopoly*.

Baumol (1977) provides a precise mathematical representation of the subadditivity concept as follows (for a cost function of the firm represented by C and an aggregate output represented by X):

$$C(x) \leq C(x^1) + C(x^2) + C(x^3) + ... + C(x^n) \quad - \textbf{ Equation 1}$$

For any set of n firms' outputs of $x^1, x^2, ..., x^n$ such that
$$\sum x^i = x \text{ for all i (from 1 to n)}$$

Do not be put off by such mathematical equations which you would see in most economic textbooks. Equation 1 basically states that:

- If there are n potential active firms in the industry who all have access to the same technology;
- and so, they all have a similar cost function C;
- For a monopoly scenario, the cost of one firm $C(x)$ producing the entire output x to satisfy the demand for the industry would be less than or equal to the sum of all the individual costs of the n potential active firms producing smaller outputs to x, i.e., x^1, x^2, x^3, etc., to x^n;
- such that the sum of these latter smaller outputs from the potential active firms would sum up to the output x demanded by the industry.

In summary, this *subadditive cost function* equation states that production of output is accomplished at least cost by a single monopoly firm. Furthermore, this subadditive cost function generally depends on the existence of both economies of scale and economies of scope.

$$C(\beta x) < \beta C(x); \beta > 1 \qquad - \textbf{ Equation 2}$$
$\Rightarrow$ i.e., decreasing average cost (Economies of Scale)

$$C\ (x^1 + x^2) < C\ (x^1,\ 0) + C(0,\ x^2) \qquad \text{– \textbf{Equation 3}}$$
$$\text{(Economies of Scope)}$$

Equations 2 and 3 define economies of scale and economies of scope mathematically (for an average cost function C and demand output x). Once again, do not be put off by such equations.

- Equation 2 states that the average cost of producing a positive number quantity (β) of output x <u>combined</u> is less than the average costs of producing one <u>individual</u> output x multiplied by the same positive number of outputs demanded (β). This is akin to setting a production line to produce one output product, then setting it up again to produce another, etc. This is called the economies of scale equation because the average costs decreases with increasing quantity produced, and explains why it makes sense for a single natural monopoly firm to produce and supply for the entire demand of some sectors of the economy.

- Equation 3 states that the average costs of producing two output products ($x^1 + x^2$) <u>combined</u> (sharing fixed production costs) is less than the average costs of producing them <u>separately</u>. This is called the economies of scope formula, showing it makes sense for one firm to manufacture or even to sell *multiple* products. This formula explains the ever-growing mega supermarkets we see around the world selling tens of thousands of products – they have massive economies scope, as well as economies of scale. Falling marginal prices stimulates more consumption, which stimulates construction of larger lower-unit-cost mega-supermarkets or production plants.

Returning from the minor digression into a mathematical precision of a natural monopoly, economy of scale and scope - why do these questions of a natural monopoly, economies of scale and scope even matter to regulation? The brief answer is that natural monopolies exhibit the significant characteristic of *economies of scale*. What is economies of scale? Economies of scale is simply a reduction in long run average cost (LRAC) as output increases. Think about it intuitively for a few seconds, and it make sense. Industries like water, rail or electricity that exhibit extremely high fixed costs and low marginal costs experience economies of scale. This means that the average cost of producing units decreases as the firm produces more. The declining LRAC of service/product stems from the fact that the cost of serving a new customer is less than the average cost. This sort of cost structure leads to a situation where a larger firm can produce and deliver goods or services at a lower cost per unit than smaller competitors. Note that economies of scale are characterised by declining average cost. This does not require marginal cost to be declining, just that the marginal cost is below the average cost.

For distribution networks like electricity, water, posts, railways, gas and water, the main explanation for declining costs is due to what is termed *economy of density*. This means it is cheaper – on a per household basis – for just a single network distributor company to deliver water, gas or mail/parcels to all the houses than to have two competing distribution networks serving half of the households each. This is because a single distribution network avoids the unnecessary duplication of a key part and extremely expensive part of the value chain of the network industry. For electricity networks, the high voltage national distribution infrastructure costs of pylons and high-tension electricity cables and buried cables are not sensitive to the megawatts of electricity transmitted. So, duplicating this infrastructure is not economically efficient.

Then add to the economies of scale and economies of density, the other benefits of *economies of scope*. As seen earlier, economies of scope happens when it is cheaper for a single firm to produce two or more related products or services, than for them to be produced separately by two separate firms. This is often seen in network industries like telecoms where a single firm more efficiently provides broadband Internet, voice services and the distribution[60] of video entertainment services combined.

When the economies of scale available in the production or distribution process are so massive that the market in question can be served by only one company, then a natural monopoly has essentially been observed. However, here is the even greater problem dynamic. There is usually a tendency for such network firms to enjoy all three of *economies of scope, economies of scale and economies of density* – leading to an ever more pronounced natural monopoly challenge. If a company is in a position of a such natural monopoly, it presents significant risks of higher prices, reduced output and maximising the profitability of the company at the expense of consumers' welfare. This is clearly not good. I emphasise the

---

[60] Not content creation, I hasten to add.

distinction here between *prices* and the *costs* which are the focus of the discussion above - the natural monopolist may have such a large cost advantage over potential competitors that it can set its prices a long way above its own costs.

For this reason, regulation of a natural monopolies like water, railway and electricity companies is logical. Competition is *not* necessarily the right intervention or response here because competition would be socially costly (i.e., costs accrue to society) for reasons I note above (e.g., three separate railway networks being rolled out in the same geography by different companies). With competition ruled out, we are left with regulation of access, prices, quality as well as output of the natural monopoly. Regulation would seek to set prices close to incremental or marginal costs, i.e., the costs of producing an additional unit of output that quasi-reflects what competition would have achieved. Such price regulation also transfers and therefore balances wealth from the monopoly firm to consumers.

It is not for nothing that we hear the oft-mentioned expression: *competition is the best regulator*. This expression speaks to the 'truism' covered later in Chapter 3 that unregulated monopolies are almost immune to offering customers the key benefits of competition of low prices, better quality, more choice, more innovation, etc. The lack of these yields less consumer welfare. I write 'truism' because I essentially make the argument earlier above that competition is *not* the best regulator in the case of a natural monopoly, and instead that access/price/quality regulation is the best approach.

2.2.1.2 Using revenue and cost curves to demystify why to regulate a natural monopoly

Permit me another minor digression or segue way into illustrating the natural monopoly regulation rationale using economics curves as shown in Figure 2.1. I confess to being a bit of a nerd of maths concepts because they are so much more precise than words.

Once again, the reader should not be put off by such diagrams as Figure 2.1. Economists use them to illustrate some incredibly useful concepts. Essentially, Figure 2.1 depicts four important curves with (Price/Cost on the Y-axis vs. Quantity on the X-axis): long run average costs curve

(LRAC), long run marginal cost curve (LRMC), the classic Demand or Average Revenue (AR) and lastly, the Marginal Revenue (MR) curve. Let us interpret Figure 2.1 and some of its key concepts some more as follows:

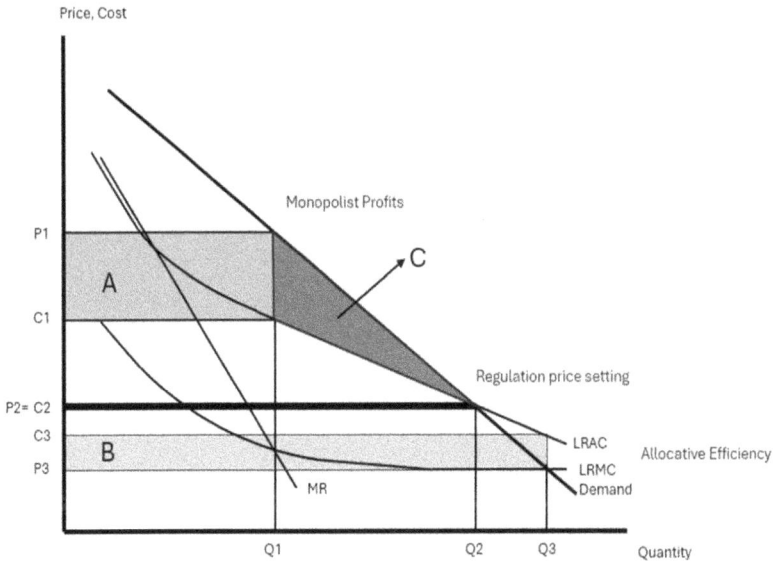

Figure 2.1 – Illustrating the Regulation of a Natural Monopoly using Revenue and Cost Curves
(Adapted from this Educational Source: [61])

- **Cost Curves**: A natural monopoly with massive upfront costs enjoys huge economies of scale. These are reflected by the downwards sloping LRAC and LRMC cost curves. However, as I note above, declining average cost is the defining characteristic of economies of scale, not declining marginal cost. This makes sense because as the company manufactures more quantity of output, the long run average costs per unit of output falls (or reduces). Note that the LRMC curve is below the LRAC because the *marginal* costs of producing an additional unit would typically be less than the average costs across all units produced.

---

[61] https://assignmentpoint.com/natural-monopoly-a-monopoly-in-an-industry/ - Natural Monopoly - a monopoly in an industry - Assignment Point

- **Revenue Curves**: the Demand or Average Revenue (AR) curve also slopes downwards because as the price of the product increases, demand will fall (or consumers will consume less). The average revenue is defined as the revenue that a firm obtains by selling a unit of their output. However, there is also a final revenue curve called the Marginal Revenue (MR) curve. Marginal revenue describes the additional revenue *increase* generated from the sale of <u>one additional</u> unit of output. The MR curve will also typically be lower than the Demand (AR) curve because average revenue is simply Total Revenue/Total Quantity. Put another way for the trained economists reading this paragraph, MR < AR typically because, the lower marginal revenue reflects the price for an additional sale less the loss of revenue on units from the new lower price on previous ('inframarginal') units when an additional unit is sold, due to the downward-sloping demand curve.

- **Monopoly Profit Maximisation**: the monopoly firm will maximise its profits by producing at the point where its marginal costs (LMRC) equal its Marginal Revenue (MR). The firm will know this LRMC costs and MR revenues profiles. Figure 2.1 shows the intersection of these two curves at quantity Q1. So, a monopoly firm would *rationally* choose to produce just quantity Q1 and charge average price/revenue P1. The average cost of manufacturing quantity Q1 is shown on Figure 2.1 at C1.

- **Supernormal Profits**: the area/rectangle A then shows the supernormal profits of the monopoly firm. As shown, the firm will rationally choose to manufacture *less* output Q1 in order to maximise its profits, even if Q1 is much less than the demand needed by society.

- *Enter Regulation* - **Regulation to the Socially Optimal Quantity (Allocative Efficiency)**: the Regulator will clearly *not* be happy with the monopoly firm producing well below demand required by society in order to maximise its profits by rectangle A. The regulator will want higher quantities and lower prices. So, it will force the private natural monopoly to change production to the socially optimum point, i.e., the point at which price or average revenue (AR) equals marginal cost (LRMC). Figure 2.1 shows this socially optimum quantity as Q3. This is the point of *allocative efficiency*, i.e., because it optimises the level of output produced at a price equivalent to the marginal cost of production. That is, where the value of an additional unit, as reflected in the demand or AR curve, equals the cost to society of producing that unit (in the absence of externalities). Reading from Figure 2.1, we see the price is now at P3. This makes sense from the point of view of the regulator: low price P3 (vs. P1 earlier) and more quantity Q3 (vs. Q1 earlier).

- **Subnormal Profits/Subsidy**: however, *there is a problem now* for the monopoly firm producing at quantity Q3 and price P3. The cost of manufacturing at Q3 reading from the LRAC is at C3. Can the reader spot the problem? C3 is greater than P3, i.e. costs are higher than revenues, which arises because of the economies of scale (marginal cost is below average cost). The monopoly firm will not like what the regulator is forcing it to do by producing (quantity Q3) and pricing below its costs (C3). This is bad business. So, the area of the B rectangle is called *subnormal profits*. The rational natural monopoly will demand a subsidy equivalent to area B to cover these losses and take the firm back to normal profit levels so they can continue producing over the long run.

- **Alternative Regulatory Price Setting at price P2 and Quantity Q2**: the regulator may choose *not* to implement a subsidy and settle for the private natural monopoly to produce a lower quantity than the allocative efficiency quantity Q3. As seen in Figure 2.1, this happens at the point where the price (AR or Demand curve) equals average cost (LRAC) at quantity Q2 and cost C2. The regulator may now impose a price being equal to average costs, i.e., P2.

- **The benefits of regulatory intervention**: at price P2, the natural monopoly firm is producing at much larger quantities Q2 than it would have otherwise produced, i.e. Q1. Recall the rational monopolist would have produced at much lower Q1 quantities whilst charging much higher prices at P1, leading to the firm enjoying the supernormal profits of area A. Regulatory intervention has eliminated these supernormal profits – good for consumers and society.

- **Deadweight Loss**: the regulator setting the price at P2 has however introduced some significant inefficiencies which economists term a *deadweight loss*. A deadweight loss is a cost borne by society which is created by market inefficiency. Such inefficiency occurs when supply and demand are out of kilter or out of equilibrium. Returning to Figure 2.1, the supply and demand equilibrium occurs when the consumption (demand curve) and the allocation of goods match, i.e., the efficient equilibrium is (Q3,P3) as explained above, since the marginal cost curve is the efficient supply curve. Recall that (Q1, P1) is the monopolistic outcome. So regulation that forces the natural monopoly to the outcome (Q2, P2) moves output and price closer to the efficient outcome, thereby improving efficiency and reducing the deadweight loss compared to unregulated monopoly. This has now resulted in the area above the LRAC curve but below the Demand curve – the area marked C – which is called a deadweight loss. Shifting manufacturing from Q1 to Q2 has created this area, which otherwise would not have existed. Area C is effectively a measure of the reduction in deadweight loss from regulation compared to unregulated monopoly, i.e. the area marked 'C'. Deadweight loss is much used in economics, and it essentially refers to any welfare loss (also see Decker [2023] diagram reproduced at Figure 4.3 and labelled 'Welfare loss') caused by an inefficient allocation of resources away from the equilibrium. In summary, a deadweight loss is the part of the potential economics surplus (at the social optimum) which is lost because it is captured neither by consumers nor by producers.

Returning from the segue way into using revenue and cost curves of Figure 2.1 – and their interpretations – I hope this segue way or diversion has demystified (to a significant degree) the use of such economic curves to in order to further illustrate the rationale for regulation.

In summary, the natural monopoly rationale for regulation strives to balance the efficiency advantages of a single monopoly firm whilst protecting the interests of consumers and citizens. Natural monopolies were recognised as far back as the 19th century as potential sources of market failure. John Stuart Mill [62] therefore advocated Government

---

[62] British philosopher John Stuart Mill (1806-1873) was one of the most influential thinkers in the history of liberalism who contributed widely to social theory, political theory and

regulation of natural monopolies to make them serve the public good. By regulating natural monopolies, Governments strive to ensure that essential services (e.g., water, electricity, railways) and goods are provided efficiently, at reasonable prices to consumers, and in the public interest.

2.2.2 Market Failures Rationale for Regulation

Arguably, the most cited rationales for regulation are 'market failure' rationales. In the Preface of this book, I 'define' market failure by noting an example where a monopolist player sets unaffordable prices for their services and products leaving no choice for the buyers other than for them to purchase their overpriced goods/services or go without. Earlier on this chapter whilst defining regulation, I note another example of 'market failure' as when firms and individuals do not take into account the costs their activities may impose on third parties like customers, the environment or society. What this tells us is that there are several to many forms of market failures that need to be regulated.

Simplistically, a market failure is therefore a scenario where free markets fail to allocate resources efficiently. As seen earlier, a market failure can occur due to several reasons, e.g., monopoly scenarios (higher prices and less output), negative externalities (over-consumption and costs to third party like consumers or the environment) and inadequate public services goods (not provided by a free market).

Baldwin et *al.* (2012, p.17-24) list the following key scenarios where markets fail, necessitating the need for regulation I briefly explain what these economic concepts are, and why their existence would and should likely trigger the need for regulation.

Windfall profits distribution: a firm earns a windfall (aka economic rent or excess profit) where it is handed a significant cheaper source of supply than that available in the rest of the market. Imagine – as it has happened in several countries I know – that the regulator or Government assigned some radio airwaves spectrum resource (e.g., 1800MHz) at some nominal annual price to some local firm (Company X) decades ago back in 2003

---

political economy. https://en.wikipedia.org/wiki/John_Stuart_Mill - John Stuart Mill - Wikipedia

say. Let us say the Company X pays USD $500,000 a year to the regulator for the rights to use this spectrum. At that time [in 2003] this spectrum could only be used using one technology: 2G second generation voice technology, and the regulations stipulated so because we did not have technology neutral regulations back then too. Company X has used the spectrum to provide 2G voice services for the past two decades. In the intervening decades too, the drivers of *technology* [e.g., new tech standards] and *industry* ecosystem drivers led to the innovation of new devices and RAN equipment capable of using the same 1800MHz spectrum - not only for 2G voice services - but for 3G, 4G and even 5G technologies. And the regulator has liberalised the use of the 1800MHz spectrum giving Company X the rights to be able to use this spectrum with whatever technology they choose to use the spectrum for, i.e., 2G, 3G, 4G, 5G or even some combination of some of these.

This means the spectrum value has appreciated in the hands of Company X in three ways at least: a much bigger ecosystem of equipment for 1800MHz than 20 years ago, more technology options now exist for the spectrum (3G, 4G, 5G) and increased rights from the regulator to use the spectrum as Company X sees fit compared to two decades ago. *None of this increased value of the spectrum is due to any actions of Company X at all.*

Imagine Company X is now approached by Company Y, and the latter proposes to buy this spectrum off Company X for USD 100M two decades afterwards [i.e., after 2003]. $100M divided by $500K (that Company X pays the regulator annually) = 200 times. If allowed, Company X will bank these completely unearned windfall profits over the trade of a State asset from Company X to Company Y, with none of these profits shared with the Government – the ultimate owners of spectrum airwaves on behalf of the people. This is a clear scenario – not necessarily of a market failure – but of a distributional issue challenge, which necessitates some regulatory intervention to secure deserved public dues from such windfall profits. Many economists would say that there is no market failure here at all because there is no distortion of output or resource allocation. In effect, the technology change created a surplus and the 'failure' here is about how the gains that should be shared with Government (a distributional issue). Look around your country – particular in emerging market countries – and you may/would see examples of such market failure scenarios in several sectors of the economy.

Externalities: externalities could be positive or negative. Positive externalities concerns goods/services which give benefit to third parties, e.g. building a new train station in a town which increases the average price of homes in that town. Negative externalities refers to goods/services which impose costs on a third party, e.g. building a smelly polluting plant in another town that also increases traffic leading to reductions to the average price of homes in that town. Consider the negative externalities associated with plastic bags that are obtained free or quite cheaply at supermarkets whilst shopping. The bags eventually are dumped in city dumps, rivers and oceans with significant costs to the ocean/rivers environment and their ecosystems. The Government eventually pays for the clean-up of the rivers. This means there is a market failure because the true and full costs of producing the plastic bags were not borne by the producers and consumers – and they have passed other costs to third parties, in this case the State. Regulation is warranted and this explains why – in Western countries at least – there are hardly any more free plastic bags at checkouts at supermarkets. They have to be paid for, and this has significantly changed consumers' behaviours.

Information adequacies/failures & Demerit goods: Information failures abound in many sectors of our economies where there is a lack of information for consumers to make an informed choice. Competitive markets truly thrive on consumers being sufficiently informed and educated about the choices present to them. Without such information, markets frequently fail for consumers – e.g., what is the point of telecom or electricity companies never informing their current customers on cheaper tariffs provided to new customers to attract them? This happens often.

These are market failures which lead to regulatory interventions, including labelling on cigarette packets (Image 2.1), labelling on the alcoholic content of drinks, labelling on calorific content of foods, etc. may also have positive externalities Society typically underestimates the costs of demerit goods like cigarettes. They come with significant negative externalities as seen on the packaging of Image 2.1.

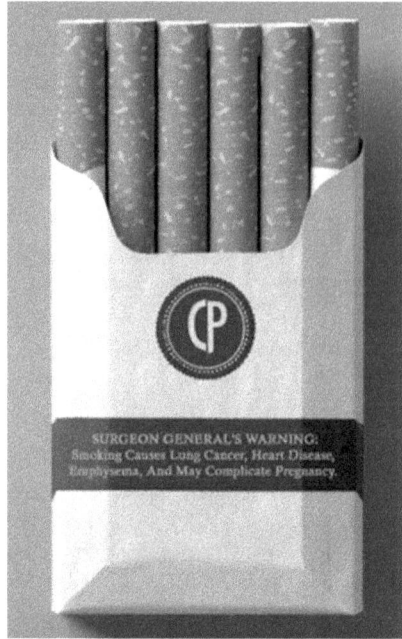

Image 2.1 – Regulatory labelling on cigarette packets[63]

Merit goods – It still amazes this me how many Governments of developing economies underestimate the benefits of merit goods, e.g. education, good intra-country roads to connect regions in a country or railways for mass-transportation. The free market would never provide for all citizens for such services due to market failures, necessitating regulatory intervention through subsidies or long term 'investments' to provide such merit good services.

Continuity and availability of service: In many sectors, the market would not provide socially-desired levels of essential services, e.g. libraries, bus services into rural areas or having telecoms services in rural areas being priced the same as in urban areas. These scenarios and more the reader can imagine would lead to market failures requiring regulatory intervention. So, telecoms is regulated such that profits from urban customers subsidise for more expensive rural connectivity. Ditto, rail

---

[63] Adapted from Source - https://journalistsresource.org/environment/warning-labels-causal-language-cigarettes/ - Strong causal language on product warning labels more effective (journalistsresource.org)

pricing too, etc. Regulation is considered justified to produce socially-desirable outcomes.

Anti-competitive and predatory pricing: some markets fail because competition is not just well refereed in them leading to some [typically larger and more profitable] firms reducing their prices (below their true costs) with the hope of driving out their competitors. When the competitors exit, they can then raise the prices again, unconstrained by any competition. This is not only anti-competitive, but this scenario is called predatory pricing. This is an obvious example of market failure, and regulation using antitrust and/or competition laws must stop this from happening.

Public goods/services and moral hazards: Public goods/services are goods which are non-rival[64] and non-excludable[65] – e.g. health, police, national defence services. Public goods/services are often not provided in a free market. These are market failures which Governments regulate and intervene to provide. Moral hazard refers to when firms/individuals have incentive to change their behaviours when others take the risk. For example, if the health service is free at the point of use like in the UK, there is a risk of citizens overusing and misusing it: drunks on the Friday night and weekends who get into fights and end up filling up Emergency Services rooms at hospitals at the expense of real patients who need these services. Some other Governments intervene/regulate and ensure such patients are charged handsomely for misusing the services. Ditto for missed appointments at Public Health Doctors practices which are/were typically free, and many patients do not bother to show up. Governments are regulating for these increasingly by getting patients to pay for missed appointments. Another moral hazard example is what arguably happens typically when banks are insured by the Government – leading bankers to take risky decisions which can cause bank losses, knowing fully well they Government would bail them out. Many Western Governments bailed out banks during the 2008 banking crisis, and the moral hazard in those bailouts forced the re-regulation of increasingly deregulated banks. Moral hazard scenarios present market failure risks.

Inequality & Unequal bargaining power: Inequality exists in all societies when there is unfair distribution of resources in free markets, e.g.

---

[64] Non rival', where consumption by one person does not diminish the amount available for other to consume, e.g., a television broadcast.

[65] Where consumers of the service cannot be excluded even if they do not pay.

some experiencing poverty and homelessness Such parts of society that experience inequality typically have little to unequal bargaining power leading to market failures. Governments then have to regulate in order to protect the interests of the weak and vulnerable with such market failures.

Scarcity and rationing: Imagine scenarios of shortages of some essential commodity services in your country like electricity, gas or petrol leading to clear market failure due to the inefficient allocation of resources if only the rich individuals and firms can buy up all the limited resources at increased prices. This is a clear market failure. The Government would typically intervene and regulate (via rationing), perhaps to ensure a priority list of society users like hospitals, ambulances, fire services, etc. are given priority access to such scarce resources too.

Rationalization, Planning and coordination: In many scenarios, coordination market failures arise because it is too costly for individuals or small firms to negotiate private contracts in an efficient ways with large providers say. Imagine all individual consumers or small firms in your country having to negotiating individual water or electricity contracts with their large monopoly providers. A regulator may rationalise some sectors like Agriculture which are often subject to market failure, due to volatile prices, fluctuating weather, fertilizer prices and other externalities. These sectors are typically very fragmented in developing markets replete with poor subsistence farmers. To minimise the risks of famine in this scenario, coordination of these fragmented groups of farmers by Government is very logical. Such regulated planning and coordination efforts may include agricultural education, higher quality seeds, guaranteeing the prices of fertilizers all year round, better irrigation practices, etc.

Long term Planning: there are other public interests market failures that are required for the future of society, e.g. environmental protection, protecting the quality of our air in cities by minimising pollution, reducing amount of carbon dioxide (CO_2) emissions, etc. These sort of failures need long term planning and intervention, e.g., many Western countries are fading out diesel cars in cities and promoting electric cars through a combination of regulatory interventions of taxes and other incentives.

These market failure rationales (or reasons) for regulation are not necessarily exhaustive, but I am convinced they are representative.

2.2.3 Historical, Legal, International Standards, Institutional & Rights-Based Rationales for Regulation

The examples in this section can more accurately be characterised as responses to market failures. So, this presents section an alternative way to think about the rationale for regulation, rather than reasons which are truly additional to the market failure rationale above.

Historical Rationale for Regulation: Some regulations emerge from historical events and the lessons learned from past failures. For example, after the Great Depression, the United States enacted the Glass-Steagall Act of 1933[66] in order to separate commercial and investment banking, aiming to prevent a recurrence of the financial crisis.

Legal Rationale for Regulation: as I note earlier about the history of regulation, as mercantilism waned during the late 19th century, large capitalist firms emerged such as the Bell Telephone Company[67]. They possessed large market concentration (and with much unfair competition on their part) led to the passage of antitrust laws or pro-competition laws, such as the Sherman Antitrust Act of 1890 and the Clayton Antitrust Act of 1914. These laws promote competition and prevent monopolistic practices. The set up and regulation of the postal sector is largely driven by a legal rationale, as it may otherwise not have emerged at all.

International Treaties, Standards and Agreements: many regulations are frankly dictated and influenced by international/regional treaties, standards and agreements, particularly in areas such as telecommunications (via the ITU), aviation (via ICAO), international trade, intellectual property and environmental protection. These harmonized regulations facilitate and enable global industries, cooperation and promote fair competition for businesses.

Institutional Rationale for Regulation: as I cover earlier relating to sectors dominated by natural monopolies, Regulatory bodies are

---

[66] https://www.investopedia.com/articles/03/071603.asp - Glass-Steagall Act of 1933: Definition, Effects, and Repeal (investopedia.com)

[67] https://www.britannica.com/topic/Bell-Telephone-Company - Bell Telephone Company | American corporation | Britannica

established to regulate and control sectors or industries. These institutions are responsible for reducing inefficiencies in the roll out of networks (cutting out unnecessary duplications), resolving disputes, enforcement, monitoring compliance, etc.

Rights-Based Rationale for Regulation: Another type of rationale is rights-based, e.g. consumer rights that I cover in Section 4.6. For example, the right to privacy and protection of personal data is at the heart of the historical rationale for data protection.

2.3 Theories & Hypotheses of Regulation

What exactly does 'Theory of Regulation' refer to? What are the key hypotheses of regulation?

2.3.1 What is Theory of Regulation?

Leinyuy (2013) and Baldwin et *al.* (2012, p.40/65-67) collectively note that that this refers to key questions including:

(i)   Who gets the benefits or burdens of regulation?
(ii) What are the intended and unintended outcomes of regulation by Government on economy and society?
(iii) What forms do regulation take? How do regulatory agencies design effective policies and regulations to achieve their desired outcomes?
(iv) Which industries are most likely to be regulated?
(v)   In fact, why are certain sectors/industries regulated by Governments whilst others are not? Why are some sectors regulated *ex-ante* whilst some are only regulated *ex-post*[68]?
(vi) How do the distinct types of regulation function and, indeed, what are the different types of regulations?
(vii) How does the Government and/or regulatory agencies balance the interests of stakeholders, including the public (i.e., citizens),

---

[68] ex-ante means "before the event" whilst ex-post means "after the fact."

consumers, businesses, and non-Governmental organisations (NGOs)?

Therefore, 'Theory of Regulation' refers to understanding and analysing *who, what, why, when* and *which* ways (i.e., *how*) Governments and/or other regulatory agencies that Governments set up intervene in various sectors of the economy – in order to achieve certain publicly desired outcomes, particularly in instances where the market would fail to deliver these outcomes. These outcomes typically include – as seen in Section 2.2 on the rationale for regulation or in the section on the history of regulation - to protect consumers, pre-empt market failures or monopolies, promote competition, maintaining market stability, maintain workplace health and safety, pre-empt discrimination, preserve the environment, and addressing negative externalities like pollution or other negative social outcomes.

2.3.2 Some Key Hypotheses underpinning Theory of Regulation

The Britannica Dictionary defines the word 'hypothesis' as "an idea or theory that is not proven but that leads to further study or discussion"[69]. Britannica proceeds to provide an example hypothesis - that watching excessive amounts of television reduces a person's ability to concentrate – and how an experiment to prove the hypothesis was inconclusive because its results did not support/confirm the hypothesis. The 'Theory of Regulation' of any sector would have one or several underpinning hypotheses, i.e., unproven theory or theories that underpin why regulation of the sector is deemed necessary [by the Government]. Understanding such clear hypotheses are truly key, not least because each hypothesis describes and helps articulate a clear philosophical, economic and/or public interest theory underpinning regulation of the sector.

What then are some of the key hypotheses underpinning theory of regulation? Leinyuy (2013) and Baldwin et *al.* (2012, p.41-67) collectively note the following key hypotheses (they are collated from previous sections, so they will not be exactly new to the sequential reader).

---

[69] https://www.britannica.com/dictionary/hypothesis - Hypothesis Definition & Meaning | Britannica Dictionary

2.3.2.1 Hypothesis 1: Market Failure Theory

The Market Failure Theory (e.g., natural monopoly or other externalities like pollution) can be summarised normatively and positively[70] as follows:

Normative[71]: as covered in the previous section on rationale for regulation, regulation is clearly justified and should occur on the theory that <u>unconstrained</u> competition fails (or would fail) consumers and citizens.

Positive: regulation does (or will) occur when unconstrained competition does not work.

A simple illustration of the theory of how unconstrained competition would *almost certainly* fail consumers and citizens is shown in Figure 2.2 which relates to the interconnection market of telecommunications network operators.

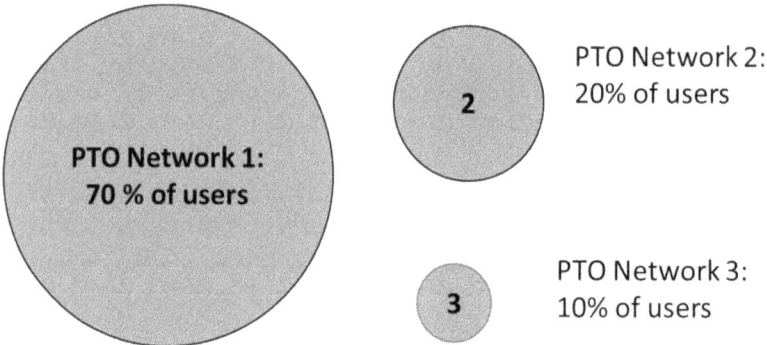

PTO Network 2:
20% of users

2

PTO Network 1:
70 % of users

PTO Network 3:
10% of users

3

Figure 2.2 – Example Interconnection of Telecommunications Networks
(PTO = Public Telecommunications Operators)

Interconnection is the linking of public communications networks to enable users to communicate, e.g., consumers of the smallest Network 3 (with only 10% of subscribers in the country) need to be able to call the subscribers on the dominant Network 1 (with 70% of the market). Clearly

---

[70] In economics, *normative* refers to what should happen whereas *positive* is what does happen.

[71] i.e., based on what is considered to be the usual or correct way of doing something (source: the Britannica Dictionary).

and rationally, there is limited incentive for Network 1 to interconnect with the smaller networks. With unconstrained competition, Network 1 would *rationally* choose to (at best) frustrate interconnection and (at worst) not interconnect at all. This would lead in short order to a clear market failure of the two smaller network operators, leading to one monopoly operator (Network 1) along with monopoly profits due to higher prices. If this happens, this will prove the market failure theory that <u>unconstrained</u> competition fails (or would fail) consumers and citizens. For this reason, in the telecoms sector, regulation of interconnection is deemed warranted and *ex-ante*[72] interconnection rules are established and imposed on all operators to interconnect in a timely and efficient fashion. This is a clear example of the hypothesis of the market failure theory which underpins many other examples of *ex-ante* regulation in the telecoms and other sectors of the economy.

The telecoms example shown in Figure 2.2 clearly illustrates the Market Failure theory of this section with interconnection. Hopefully, it clearly illustrates that regulation is needed where there is (or would be) a market failure, i.e., where competition fails.

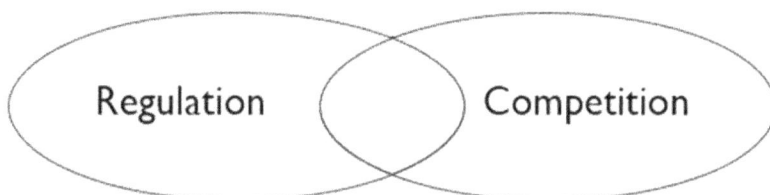

Figure 2.3 – Regulation vs. Competition 'Toolboxes'

This is shown in Figure 2.3 which denotes that – in order to seek to achieve positive outcomes for consumers and citizens that do <u>not</u> arise naturally from market *competition* [on the right of Figure 2.3], i.e. a market failure – *regulation* [on the left of Figure 2.3] becomes necessary to bring net benefits. Figure 2.3 shows that if competition is working fine, there is no need for regulation. Suffice to state now that the 'interplay' of competition and regulation is at the core of the market failure theory, and also especially important to economic regulation in general – the subject of this book. Therefore, the intersection between the two ovals in Figure 2.3 also

---

[72] As noted earlier, 'ex-ante = before the event', i.e., in this case before such a catastrophic set of events as the exit of the two smaller operators of Figure 2.2.

represents the fact that regulation may be needed to facilitate competition, as in the interconnection example above of Figure 2.2.

2.3.2.2 Hypothesis 2: Regulatory Capture Theory

The Regulatory Capture Theory (Stigler, 1971) can be summarised normatively and positively as follows:

Normative: Stigler (1971) argues that Regulation may be actively sought or demanded by the industry for their benefits. Unfortunately, in some instances, it leads to regulatory capture. According to Stigler, regulation with this hypothesis seeks largely to promote private interests. This is because political institutions create incentives for politicians to promote industry's interests over those of the public – hence, the hypothesis of 'regulatory capture'. Regulatory capture is undesirable, promoting private interests over the public interests.

Positive: Regulation is designed and operated to promote industry profits.

Stigler (1971, p.3) makes the core case for this hypothesis that: "as a rule regulation is acquired by the industry and is designed and operated primarily for its benefit". The regulated sector has an incentive to influence regulation so as to benefit from 'economic rent', i.e., the excess amount of money earned above what is economically or socially necessary. A very fragmented millions of consumers and citizens will not be able to mobilise their interests efficiently. This heightens the risks that when politicians are faced with a choice of courting voters during elections vs. significant political campaign budgets from powerful industry players/trade bodies/unions for regulatory protections, they [politicians] tend to err towards powerful industry lobby interests.

This is the basis of the Regulatory Capture hypothesis, and this explains the genesis of 'independent' regulators who are independent of industry, Government and third sector players – whilst being pro competition and consumers. Regulatory capture is a reality in many sectors of the economy of developing countries.

2.3.2.3 Hypothesis 3: Economic Theory of Regulation

The Economic Theory of Regulation hypothesis arguably has two key flavours as would be observed by the end of this section: that of Stigler, (1971) and that of Peltzman (1989). The hypothesis is summarised normatively and positively later. In order to understand this hypothesis, a critique of Stigler's (1971) regulatory capture-focussed version of the 'Theory of Economic Regulation' hypothesis helps. The renowned Economist Adam R. Brown argues that

> "Stigler's theory had problems. It would not explain why Congress passes regulations that hurt big businesses, or why protectionism is sometimes reduced" [73].

So, Adam R Brown notes that, in order to obtain more realistic conclusions, Peltzman modifies the theory beginning with three main premises [captured in the normative narrative following]:

Normative:
   (i) Regulation should redistribute wealth;
   (ii) Regulators (legislators) desire to remain in office - so legislation will always be written to maximize political support. Regulation should take cognizance of this reality;
   (iii) Interest groups compete by offering political support in exchange for favourable legislation. Regulation should take cognizance of this reality too.

Positive: A political equilibrium presenting a balanced theory of both supply and demand of regulation is important.

Peltzman's (1989) flavour of the Economic Theory of Regulation hypothesis sought to address the 'regulatory capture' concern of Stigler's flavour which reigned in many sectors in developed countries between the

---

73

https://adambrown.info/p/notes/peltzman_toward_a_more_general_theory_of_regulation
#:~:text=Peltzman%27s%20theory%2C%20then%2C%20presents%20a,bend%20to%20
producers%27%20demands). Summary of Peltzman: Toward a more general theory of regulation -- Adam Brown, BYU Political Science

1970s to the mid-1980s. The point of regulation here [according to Peltzman's flavour of the Economic Theory of Regulation hypothesis] is to incentivise companies to redistribute their wealth (e.g., via price regulation) as well as getting rid of economic rents – thereby returning the sector to the position before regulation was necessary in the first place, *potentially* obviating the need of having continued regulation (Peltzman, S. & Keeler, T., 1984). If profits are fairly distributed between producers and consumers through fair pricing and there are no economic rents, light-touch regulation or even *deregulation* may be preferable than continued regulation. This Peltzman flavour of the Economic Theory of Regulation hypothesis (Peltzman, S. & Keeler, T., 1984) explains the deregulation and liberalisation of many sectors of the economy that dominated the late 1980s and 1990s across Western countries[74]. This came under the pretext that continued regulations were just 'red tape' adding a burden to economic activity in sectors which had already been regulated down to little or no economic rents and fair prices. However, as Baldwin et *al.* (2012, p.43) also articulate:

> "The *economic theory of regulation* builds on the assumption that actors are inherently self-regarding and oriented at maximizing their own (material) interest. It assumes that all parties involved in regulation seek to maximise their utility (self-interest) (politicians, for instance, seeking votes to maximize their cash incomes); it assumes that all parties are as well informed as possible and learn from experience; and it also assumes that regulation is costless (hence overall efficiency will not be affected by levels of regulation)." *The authors' emphases.*

The failure of the assumptions in the quote above also explain why – according to Stigler's (1971) version of the economic theory of regulation hypothesis – where there is a monopoly or a failure of competition, monopoly profits would accrue (and monopolists start seeking regulatory protections for their rents), potentially leading Governments to set up regulators to get rid of the economic monopoly rents. The self-interest assumption risks arguably were ignored by regulators in the late 1980s and 1990s which led to deregulation in the banking industry and the eventual global financial crisis of 2008 in the Banking and Finance Sectors.

---

[74] Mentioned in the History of Regulation Section earlier.

This is why even Peltzman (1989) himself raises a key challenge with his version of the Economic Theory of Regulation hypothesis - that of "the design of institutions and their adaptability", p. 40. Were the *design*s of the regulatory institutions set up for the Banking and Finance sectors in the late 1980s to 1990s *adaptable* enough to pre-empt the global financial crisis of 2008? This question is clearly rhetorical because Banking and Finance regulation obviously missed the self-interests risks. As noted earlier in this chapter, Governments were forced to lay down new rules (e.g., in the USA, Dodd-Frank, CFPB, FSOC[75]) to further safeguard the stability of financial systems, to further regulate banks and financial institutions (i.e., adding more 'red tape'), and to further protect investors. It is interesting to observe the regulation-deregulation-regulation merry go round with this economic theory of regulation hypothesis.

2.3.2.4 Hypothesis 4: Interests Groups Theory

The Interests Groups Theory hypothesis – Competition between Interests Groups (Becker, 1983; Baldwin et *al.*, 2012, p.43-49) – follows on from the Economic Theory of Regulation hypothesis of the prior section. It maintains that regulatory developments are "driven not by the pursuit of public interest but by the particularistic concerns of interest groups" (Baldwin et *al.*, 2012, p.43). This hypothesis can be summarised normatively and positively as follows.

Normative: According to Becker (1983), politicians, political parties, voters transmit the pressure of the various interest groups. Regulation should therefore be used to increase the welfare of more influential interest groups. Interest groups compete with one another on influencing politicians, political parties and voters.

Positive: As Adam R Brown notes:

"Central to Becker's model is competition between interest groups, not interactions between interest groups and legislators per se. What matters is how much (lobbying) pressure each group applies; thus, each group's relative problem with free riding is what matters, not free

---

[75] https://www.investopedia.com/ask/answers/063015/what-are-major-laws-acts-regulating-financial-institutions-were-created-response-2008-financial.asp - Major Regulations Following the 2008 Financial Crisis (investopedia.com)

63

riding itself. Each group's equilibrium level of pressure depends on the amount of pressure applied by the other group"[76].

Essentially Becker (1983) - as the main proponent of this hypothesis – holds that monopoly rents will ultimately *not* survive in most sectors because other interest groups would mobilise to eliminate them by contesting the acquired rents of the monopoly player(s). The obvious problem here is the following – do all the interests groups have equal abilities to mobilise their interests against monopoly rents? In many sectors of the economy in many countries, the answer to this question is obviously No. Political equilibrium requires the regulator to balance the needs of consumers and the industry.

2.3.2.5 Hypothesis 5: Public Interest Theory

The Public Interest Theory hypothesis (Baldwin et *al.*, 2012, p.40-43) centres on the notion that that regulatory developments are done in pursuit of public interest-related outcomes, in contrast to group, industry or individual self-interests. This hypothesis can be summarised normatively and positively as follows.

Normative: Regulator should act to achieve certain publicly desired outcomes, particularly where the market and competition would fail to realise them.

Positive: Regulator acts in pursuit of public rather than private interests as with Regulatory Capture theory. The regulator is disinterested, dispassionate and expert.

The proponents of regulation – under this hypothesis – are seen as benevolent agents for public interests. Baldwin et *al.* (2012, p.41) summarises the 'public interest' worldview as follows:

76

https://adambrown.info/p/notes/becker_a_theory_of_competition_among_pressure_group
s_for_political_influence - Summary of Becker: A theory of competition among pressure
groups for political influence -- Adam Brown, BYU Political Science

"The 'public interest' world is a world in which bureaucracies do not protect or expand their turf, in which politicians do not seek to enhance their electoral or other career prospects, in which decision-making rules do not determine decisions, and a world in which business and other interests groups do not seek special exemptions or privileges. In short, this is a world of few transaction costs and institutional biases. Instead, regulation is based on some form of dispassionate expertise and objective standards."

This hypothesis clearly has several concerns. What is 'public interest' with many competing public interest groups? For example, is it in the 'public interest' to regulate or to deregulate? Who constitutes the 'benevolent agents' for public interests? Regulators? Government? As a senior ex-regulator, I[77] know first-hand that these are hard public policy questions. It takes much *artistry* in addition to the science of regulation to address such questions.

2.3.2.6 Hypothesis 6: Power of Ideas Theory

The Power of Ideas Theory hypothesis (Baldwin et *al.*, 2012, p.49-53) is an interesting one – one that acknowledges that changing ideologies in the public policy and regulation literature over time shapes approaches to regulation. This hypothesis can be summarised normatively and positively as follows.

Normative: Governments/Legislatures should make certain changes to regulatory approaches, not triggered or driven by the lobbying from private sector interests, but from "the force of ideas" or "power of ideas" (Baldwin et *al.*, 2012, p.49).

Positive: Regulator acts in pursuit of new progressive ideas steering regulatory developments.

The "force of ideas" or "power of ideas" hypothesis is recognisable in many sectors of the economy. The Ronald Reagan (USA) and Margaret Thatcher (UK) administrations of the 1980s ushered in new intellectual

---

[77] The author was a senior regulator at Ofcom UK (www.ofcom.org.uk)

conceptions on how and why Governments should control business. For example, Derthick & Quirk's (1985) book on the Politics of Regulation makes the case strongly for the "force of ideas" hypothesis. Baldwin et *al.*, (2012,) provide an excellent articulation of Derthick & Quirk's (1985) core thesis when they write:

> "For Derthick and Quirk, for example, regulatory reform in the US was one product of a change in intellectual climate... this intellectual climate could be summed up as hostility to existing regulatory regimes with their characteristics of capture, weak enforcement by agencies, red tape, juridification, bureaucratization, high compliance costs and ineffectiveness. Accordingly, deregulation, as seen in the United States in the Reagan area, was driven not by interest-group pressures but by an intellectually guided process of economic rationalism that managed to benefit dispersed consumer groups at the expense of concentrated producer interests" (Residential consumers, the evidence was said to indicate, benefitted from deregulation" Baldwin et *al.*, (2012, p.49/50).

The 'power of ideas' hypothesis is well articulated in the above quote. An intriguing quote from Vietor (1994) in his book *Contrived Competition: regulation and Deregulation in America* seems apt here when he opines: "regulatory and deregulatory booms are due to a fundamental change in people's perception of how an economy and its government interact". Arguably therefore, citizens as voters demand from their politicians (or rather 'buy' from them through their votes) the force of ideas/powers of ideas. American and British voters certainly "bought" some powerful ideas during the Ronald Reagan and Margaret Thatcher years of the 1980s. A key challenge is how one separates the force of ideas from the role of economic interest groups trying to maximise their interests.

2.4 Why Theories and Hypotheses of Regulation Matter

As the reader has gleaned so far in this chapter, theories and hypotheses of regulation truly matter. They are essential for understanding, analysing, and improving regulatory approaches and systems within countries and economies.

They matter because of the following:

66

- **Effective Regulatory Design across Sectors of the Economy whilst Balancing Interests**: the previous section covers why we need theories of regulation. It notes that they are meant to address questions such as the following [which are very worth repeating here].

  o Who gets the benefits or burdens of regulation? What are the intended and unintended outcomes of regulation by Government on economy and society? What forms do regulation take?
  o How do regulatory agencies design effective policies and regulations to achieve their desired outcomes?
  o Which industries are most likely to be regulated? Why are certain sectors/industries regulated by Governments whilst others are not?
  o Why are some sectors regulated *ex-ante* whilst some are only regulated *ex-post*[78]? How do the different types of regulation function and, indeed, what are the different types of regulations?
  o How does the Government and/or regulatory agencies balance the interests of stakeholders, including the public (i.e., citizens), consumers, businesses, and non-Governmental organisations (NGOs)?

Theories and hypotheses of regulation help with effective regulatory design across different sectors of the economy by addressing such questions as above. A good theoretical foundation enables the design of regulations that are targeted, efficient, and effective. Good theories and hypotheses help balance competing interests. This is because regulations often involve balancing between various stakeholders' interests, e.g. Government, industry, consumers and the environment.

- **Identify Market & Regulatory Failures:** regulation tries to address market failures where competition fails. Theories and hypotheses help identify what the likely regulatory and/or market failures are. Is it a case of regulatory capture? Is it a case of Public

---

[78] ex-ante means "before the event" whilst ex-post means "after the fact."

Interest Failure? Markets sometimes fail to efficiently allocate resources or produce socially desirable outcomes as shown in Figure 2.1. Such failures need to be understood. Such understandings are crucial for identifying and defining the appropriate failures, designing appropriate regulatory frameworks, and preventing future market or regulatory failures.

- **Prediction**: Theories and hypotheses help predict outcomes of regulatory interventions. Recall how natural monopoly theory of Figure 2.1 helps predict the level of subsidies that regulation would need to offer a natural monopoly firm for the latter to produce for the long term.

- **Guidance**: Theories and hypotheses, by definition, guide. The Market failure theory would yield a different predicted regulatory guidance and outcome from a Public Interest theory. So, theories and hypotheses provide guidance by guiding legislatures and policy makers by providing insights on how regulations can be designed, implemented, and evaluated in order to realise the intended outcomes, such as lower prices, addressing externalities like pollution, etc.

- **Regulatory Explanation & Adaptation**: as is noted earlier in this chapter, regulation of sectors of the economy adapt over time, resulting in the merry go round of regulation-deregulation-regulation cycle of the banking sector from the 1980s to the 2008 banking crisis and beyond. Theories and hypotheses help explain and guide any 'corrections' required. For example, the Power of Ideas theory/hypothesis explains the deregulatory actions in the finance and banking sector of the Ronald Reagan/Margaret Thatcher years of the 1980s, whilst the Economic Theory of Regulation and Public Interest theories arguably guided the new rules that emerged from the Banking crisis. Theories and hypotheses of regulation help policymakers adapt existing regulatory frameworks and regulations to new market contexts, thereby ensuring that regulatory frameworks remain relevant and effective.

These reasons for theories and hypotheses are not meant to be exhaustive, but more to help the reader understand why much of what has been covered in this chapter are both relevant and important. They truly are.

2.5 Regulatory Failures & Risks

The theories and hypotheses of regulation *portend* to regulatory failures and regulatory risks, i.e., the theories and hypotheses foreshadow signs or warnings that (something, especially something momentous or calamitous) is likely to happen[79]. What then are regulatory failures and regulatory risks? What do they look like? Are they easy to spot?

2.5.1 Regulatory Failures: What are they?

Regulatory failures broadly cover scenarios wherein Government and/or the regulator's actions [regulatory processes, systems, rules and mechanisms] in a particular sector of the economy fail to achieve their intended outcomes, on in some cases backfire and even yields negative results. The reasons can be many and varied ranging including (the following are representative but not exhaustive):

- **Regulatory Capture**: no amount of good regulatory making would escape regulatory capture by key industry incumbents. In many developing market economies in Asia, Africa and the Caribbean, regulation of key sectors (telecoms, electricity, water, etc) and/or weak regulators are sadly captured by loss-making dominant incumbents leading to horrible outcomes for consumers and citizens.

- **Rationale**: Is the entire rationale for regulation (Section 2.1) appropriate? Perhaps, it is not. Unnecessary regulation may end up disrupting the market which would otherwise work better. Regulation may backfire in such contexts.

- **Theory/Hypothesis:**: adopting the 'wrong' theories/hypotheses for the regulatory challenge (Section 2.3) would be problematic.

---

[79] Borrowing and adapting from the Oxford Online Dictionary's definition of the word portend.

Deciding on the 'right' theory/hypothesis requires much judgment which carries risks. The intended regulatory outcomes would be missed here.

- **Poorly designed rules & regulations:** Even if the right theory/hypotheses is adopted, the rules and regulations may be poorly designed leading to suboptimal outcomes.

- **Lack of or inadequate enforcement:** Even when the regulations designed appropriately designed, there may be a failure of enforcement or inadequate enforcement. This is quite common, particularly in developing economies with weak laws, weak powers of enforcement and limited resources to conduct enforcement. Criminals gravitate to markets where the risk of enforcement is low.

- **Adaptability**: regulation and regulators need to be adaptable to the changing environment and drivers of every sector. Chapter 1 covers the other key drivers that regulation must respond to namely macroeconomy, technology, industry and consumer behaviour. Many a time, regulation and/or regulators yield terribly negative outcomes because of lack of adaptation to the changing environment rendering regulations ineffective.

- **Lack of [qualified] Resources**: many regulators I have come across are woefully under-resourced for the objects or mandates put on them by Government - and even when the resources are there, they are typically not qualified to do deep economic and social regulation. This inevitably leads to poor outcomes.

- **Lack of Coordination with other Agencies and/or Government**: typically, for regulation to achieve its desired outcomes requires much coordination with agents outside a specific regulatory agency itself. As a regulator, I had to oversee major regulatory projects coordinating effectively with branches of Government [in the UK] and with major sector players. These were not trivial. In many countries, such coordination between regulators and other external stakeholders, either just do not happen or happen opportunistically leading to poor regulatory outcomes.

- **Inefficient Regulations:** if the compliance costs for businesses and other stakeholders are too burdensome, this will lead to poor efficiencies in the sector and therefore poor outcomes.

- **Unintended Outcomes**: sometimes, regulations lead to unintended outcomes not predicted by policy makers due to the complex nature of regulatory systems and how stakeholders/consumers would react. Many times, in Africa, tax regulations or rules intended to increase tax intake by Governments frequently yield the opposite outcome.

- **Failure to follow due processes leading to challenges**: if regulators do not follow due processes (legal ones and procedures set by the regulator itself), it would find itself [rightly] challenged in the courts, tribunals or elsewhere leading at best to delayed decisions and at worst to poor regulations prevailing. When this happens, consumers and citizens suffer negative effects and outcomes from of regulation.

- **Under-Regulation/Over-Regulation**: Under-regulation results from a lack of information gathering on the risks (and those who create them) that could impact the realisation of regulatory mandates – and acting on those risks to mitigate them. Over-regulation – by definition – leads to inefficiencies due to excessive compliance costs on sector stakeholders, and these costs are passed on to consumers.

2.5.2 Identifying and Remedying Regulatory Failures – and 'Good' Regulation

Having listed the above likely reasons for regulatory failure, the reader would be forgiven for believing now that they [regulatory failures] are easy to identify, yet alone explaining and remedying them. Far from it. As Baldwin et al., (2012, p.68/69) ask, "What constitutes a regulatory failure? … Failure compared to what"? Typically, there are no easy counterfactuals, unless one compares to other failing sectors or economies. Hence, such questions are not easy to answer.

It may be easy and uncontroversial to identify 'obvious' regulatory failures like those which led to outcomes like the Financial Market Crisis of 2008[80] (stock market and housing market crashes), or extremely high energy prices in 2022/23 to UK consumers necessitating the UK Government to intervene post the Russia/Ukraine macroeconomy shock or crisis break out. The World Bank (2009) estimated that as a result of the 2008 Financial

---

[80] https://www.investopedia.com/articles/economics/09/subprime-market-2008.asp - The Fall of the Market in the Fall of 2008 (investopedia.com)

crisis 89 million people lived in extreme poverty (below $1.25 a day) by the end of 2010 in sub-Saharan Africa alone, and that the number of infant deaths was expected to increase by 30 to 50 thousand. According to Investopedia[81], the 2008 Financial Crisis sent the world into a great recession with 8.8 million jobs lost, unemployment spiking by 10% by October 2009, 8 million home foreclosures, USD 19.2 Trillion household wealth wiped out and much more. This was no little regulatory failure.

Another example of smaller but still incredibly significant regulatory failure – in my opinion - is the UK Energy Markets 'Crisis[82]' of 2022. The UK Parliament's Public Accounts Committee (PAC) concluded that Ofgem's[83] failures "come at considerable cost to energy billpayers"[84]. The PAC scathingly concluded:

> "Since July 2021, 29 energy suppliers have failed, affecting around 4 million households. Customers have been left to pay the £2.7 billion cost of supplier failures. This means an extra £94 per household, at a time when energy prices are already at a record high…. Ofgem's failure to effectively regulate the energy supplier market has cost households an estimated £2.7 billion, with further costs expected".

> Ofgem "did not strike the right balance between *promoting competition* in the energy suppliers market and *ensuring energy suppliers were financially resilient…*. The price cap is providing only extremely limited protection to households from increases in the wholesale price of energy … It is *unacceptable* that many vulnerable customers, on top of having to pay higher energy prices, face extra challenges working with energy suppliers and accessing benefits designed to help people with their energy bills.

---

[81] https://www.investopedia.com/news/10-years-later-lessons-financial-crisis/ - Over 10 Years Later, Lessons From the Financial Crisis (investopedia.com)

[82] The author's characterisation.

[83] https://www.ofgem.gov.uk/ - the UK's independent Energy regulator (Office of Gas and Electricity Markets)

[84] https://committees.parliament.uk/committee/127/public-accounts-committee/news/174285/pac-ofgem-failures-come-at-considerable-cost-to-energy-billpayers/ - PAC: Ofgem failures "come at considerable cost to energy billpayers" - Committees - UK Parliament

<u>Vulnerable customers</u> are most exposed to the rise in energy prices and some also face additional cost"[85]. *The author's emphases.*

I provide this above-cited UK Energy crisis account for three reasons. Firstly, in order to provide an 'obvious' and clear example of regulatory failure, arguably identified and recognised after the fact or occurrence. Secondly, to provide some of the identified reasons for the regulatory failure, i.e., in this case the regulator is accused of not having struck the right balance between *promoting competition* in the energy suppliers market and *ensuring energy suppliers were financially resilient.* Thirdly and perhaps most importantly, this brief excerpt from the PAC's scathing report shows regulatory accountability. Most UK regulators like Ofgem are ultimately accountable to the UK Parliament (beyond their Boards). Ofgem cannot fail to act on such a scathing report. So, Ofgem has responsibly been doing more on financial resilienc[86]. How many regulators in most markets including your own [the reader] are subject to such scrutiny? Such scrutiny is good – indeed, incredibly good. As a senior regulator at Ofcom UK, I always felt 'on my toes' because I knew that all I led was (or would come under at some point) scrutiny. One 'ups his or her game' in such situations, and I am saddened to see so many regulators in emerging markets feel no scrutiny at all. This leads to many lazy regulators across the globe at significant costs of consumers and citizens.

Returning to issue of *identifying* regulatory failures, the two examples above covering the Financial Market Crisis of 2008 and the UK Energy Market 'Crisis' of 2022 were easy to recognise. They were big market failures that affected millions of citizens as the evidence shows. However, most regulatory failures are not so clear cut at all. The absence of favourable 'outcomes' in many regulatory regimes does not mean there is regulatory failure. This is because most regulatory mandates are necessarily flexible and open to interpretation. Ofgem in the example above achieved a significant pro-competition landscape in the UK Energy Markets and arguably avoided *over regulation* until a market macroeconomic shock [Russia/Ukraine war] revealed that the energy

---

[85] https://committees.parliament.uk/publications/31575/documents/177114/default/ - UK House of Commons Committee of Public Accounts, *Regulation of Energy Suppliers*, Twenty-Fifth Report of Session 2022-23, 31 October 2022, Regulation of energy suppliers (parliament.uk)

[86] From a quick search, examples of Ofgem taking action on financial resilience are: https://www.ofgem.gov.uk/publications/raft-new-measures-boost-financial-resilience-energy-sector and this press report https://www.bbc.com/news/business-66310852

suppliers were not financially resilient, leading to 29 energy suppliers failing just between July to October 2022. Was this a case of *under-regulation*? It arguably was indeed a case under-regulation which results from a lack of information gathering on the risks (and those who create them) that could impact the realisation of regulatory mandates – and acting on those risks to mitigate them. Were these risks *foreseeable*? Ofgem argued that they foresaw these risks, but not the *scale* of them.

Can such risks then be mitigated? The short answer is Yes, but it will require *identifying* them soon, being able to *explain* what they are and lastly being able to remedy them. Baldwin et *al.*, (2012, p.69-77) argue that it is best to start pre-empting such regulatory failures with understanding the theory of regulation underpinning the regime. Each theory has a typical 'failure mechanism' and such a failure mechanism would have its appropriate remedy. A couple of examples from Baldwin et *al.*, (2012, p.77) would suffice:

- A regime underpinned by a Public Interest Theory hypothesis or the Economic Theory hypothesis (see Hypotheses 3 and 4 in Section 2.3) carries the 'failure mechanism' risk of "collective action problem leads to regulation in favour of particular concentrated interests". The remedy they suggest is that of enhancing interest group participation and contestation to remedy this typical failure mechanism.

- A regime underpinned by a Power of Ideas (and Cultural) Theory hypothesis carries the failure mechanism risk "of inherent blackspots in any single or 'elegant' approach [that] has side-effects and will be exploited by the opposition." The remedy here is to use hybrid solutions.

The essence of this 'methodology' is one of anticipating typical failure mechanisms of the theory/theories underpinning a regime [since such theories account for regulatory failures], and being clear on the appropriate remedies that would apply. The typical regulatory remedies include better coordination, organisational reform, learnings from other regulatory institutions and hybrid solutions which employ more than one theory/hypothesis of regulation to underpin the organisation design, enabling better stability.

In summary, regulatory failure can, at best, only be clearly identified against a clear counterfactual of the alternative of what *'good' regulation* would have yielded. Otherwise, foreseeable risks with every theory underpinning the regulatory regime would have to be explained, pre-empted and remedied as suggest above. This brings up the question of what good regulation is. Baldwin et *al.* (2012, p.69) suggest, whilst discussing 'good' regulation and regulatory failure, that

> "regulators will 'fail' when they do not produce (at reasonable cost) the outcomes that are stipulated in their mandates or when they do not serve procedural or representative values properly."

The authors identify five criteria or tests for *good regulation* namely (p.27):

- *Legislative mandate*: Is the action or regime or regime supported by legislative authority?
- *Accountability*: Is there an appropriate scheme of accountability?
- *Due Process*: Are procedures fair, accessible and open?
- *Expertise*: Is the regulator acting with sufficient expertise?
- *Efficiency*: Is the action of the regime efficient?

By implication, if any or more of these five tests are *not* met by a regulatory regime, the risks of regulatory failure are heightened. These can already be observed in Section 2.5.1 above on the reasons for regulatory failures. On the other hand, regulatory failures could still accrue even if all these five tests of good regulation are met because of challenges like not adapting to environmental conditions or lack of sufficient resources to enforce regulations, etc.

2.5.3 Regulatory Risks: What are they?

Risk is typically defined as the probability of a certain suboptimal outcome or event happening along with its consequent severity of impact of such a particular outcome. Risks are typically quantifiable, unlike uncertainty which are inherently almost impossible to measure. Therefore, regulatory risks refer to the potential negative outcomes or externalities that regulatory decisions and actions can have on consumers, citizens, businesses and on society as a whole. If these risks materialise, they will almost certainly lead to regulatory failures too (such as those identified in Section 2.5.1), in addition to additional risks on the regulator itself.

Typical regulatory risks include the following (including why they matter).

- **Legal:** the risks of legal challenges by industry and sector stakeholders on the part of the regulator. On the part of regulated entities, this would involve regulatory violations of the current rules and regulations with almost certain penalties from the regulator.

- **Market Investment Appetite/Confidence**: I have been involved in many (> fifteen) potential investments across emerging markets which failed because of the potential investor's perception of regulatory risks in the market. If their perceptions of these risks are high, they usually have little confidence and choose not to invest.

- **Competition, Growth & Innovation**: In many developing economies, current extant regulations and laws effectively stifle effective competition, growth and innovation. The entrepreneurs in such countries are typically not be able to innovate due the rules and regulations not providing an enabling environment for them to do so. Antiquated laws and regulations protect bankrupt State-Owned Entities (SOEs)[87] at the expense of new competitive entrants. If the laws and regulations of a country do not permit the emergence of a Digital Economy in that country, such an economy would never emerge (Nwana, 2022).

- **Public Interest**: Effective regulations and rules protect society, albeit public safety, public health, public hygiene, the environment, what children can see on TV before the watershed time of when they are expected to be in bed, etc. If such societal rules which norm society are changed carelessly, there would be negative outcomes on individuals and society.

- **Access/Inclusion**: Effective regulation seeks to include as many as possible of society in the participation in every sector of the

---

[87] A state-owned enterprise (SOE) is a legal entity that is created by a government in order to partake in commercial activities on the government's behalf. It can be either wholly or partially owned by a government and is typically earmarked to participate in specific commercial activities- Investopedia.

economy, albeit telecoms, banking, utilities, etc. Creating such social equity is truly key for the stability of societies.

- **Financial**: regulatory risks also accrue to regulated companies, e.g., the potential of financial losses to sector stakeholders or negative economic outcomes due to fines, legal fees, loss of revenues, etc.

- **Reputational/Trust in Institutions**: once a regulator loses its hard-earned currency of reputation, it may be exceedingly difficult to regain it. The negative perceptions that come with lost reputation on the part of the regulator may lead to non-compliance of industry regulations or outright disrespect of the regulator as the industry referee. On the part of regulated entities, loss of reputation would lead to significant brand diminution, along with almost certain loss of customers and revenues. Regulatory risks and failures erode trust in institutions.

- **Operational**: all regulations lead to changes in business processes and systems on the part of regulated entities as well as the regulator itself. Regulatory risks affect businesses by increasing or decreasing costs, impacting operations, and influencing market operation.

2.5.4 Defining, Assessing and Remedying Regulatory Risks – Regulatory Risk Registers

Discussing defining, assessing and remedying risks in the context of regulation is key because - as can be surmised from the prior section on identifying and remedying regulatory failures (Section 2.5.2) – regulation can be seen

> "as inherently about the control of risks, whether these relate to illnesses caused by the exposure to carcinogens, inadequate utility services, or losses caused by incompetent financial advice" Baldwin et *al.*, (2012, p.83).

For this reason, every best-in-class regulator must hold and update active *Regulatory Risk Registers* which they act on – for every function of the regulator. Such risk registers define and identify regulatory risks, their perceptions, their classification and the likely severity of their impact if the risks materialise. The red or reddest risks must have clear mitigations and be escalated to the Board of the Regulator, who must be aware of these risks and lead on their mitigation. I come across so many regulators in emerging markets with acute "time bomb" risks that the Board of the Regulators are completely clueless on. The consequences have included significant exits of major industry brands from the telecoms sector in many countries across South East Asia, Africa and the Caribbean leading to the emergence of *de facto* monopolies across some of their telecom sectors – i.e., clear regulatory failures.

In conclusion – for this section on Regulatory Failures and Risks - understanding, being able to explain via theories/hypotheses and remedying regulatory failure and regulatory risks are key to a well-functioning regulatory regime that promotes public welfare, maximises public and private value, drive economic growth and stability whilst minimizing negative externalities.

2.6 Chapter Summary

This chapter has covered in some detail the history, rationale, theory and hypotheses of regulation - hopefully in a simpler way - than many textbooks and/or peer reviewed articles written by economists or social science or political science experts do. It also overviews - in some considerable detail - regulatory failures and risks which are key to any well-functioning regulatory regime.

For readers who desire a deeper understanding of the subject matters of this chapter, Baldwin *et al.* (2010) and Baldwin *et al.* (2012) are two excellent texts to start from.

Chapter 3

From Theories to the Practice of Regulation

Karl Marx (1819-1883) is famously reputed to have said: "Practice without Theory is blind; Theory without Practice is sterile." This chapter learns from this maxim.

The real long form title of this chapter is 'Types and Examples of Regulatory Institutions, Networks Industries Market Structures & Regulating Network Industries'. This chapter starts with an overview of the regulatory approaches and examples of regulatory institutions out there in our economies, and why they are designed the way they are. It then proceeds to overview sector market structures because different market structures present different characteristics leading to different approaches to their regulation. Specifically, it overviews network industries' market structures because such industries[88] that dominate the essential services invaluable to modern living. These network industries clearly need to be regulated for the benefits of most if not all citizens of our countries, *using a combination of tools from both regulation and competition toolboxes*. The chapter then proceeds to overview [by providing brief sector overviews] the typical practical implementation of the *regulation vs. competition dynamic* across several network industries, whilst linking as much as possible to the theories and hypotheses of Regulation of Chapter 2. It is important to this book to link the rationales and *theories* for regulation as much as possible to *practice* across several sectors in the hope that the reader appreciates just how nuanced and complex they typically are. Often, I have witnessed trainees [regulators and operators] during training sessions observe aloud something to the effect of – "Aha – this is why we do 'this'[89]". I see this as powerful.

---

[88] E.g., electricity, rail, water and wastewater, gas, sewage, telecoms, etc.

[89] 'This' – typically refers to some *ex-ante* activity that the regulator does, e.g., rules on interconnection, providing consumer information, encouraging switching, driving inclusion and more access, etc. – activities they would not have linked to supply or demand side market failures which regulation seeks to mitigate.

3.1 Types, Models & Examples of Regulatory Approaches

In Chapter 2, the Cambridge Dictionary's definition of regulation is provided which clearly emphasises the concept of 'controlling' something including societal issues like safety, health, traffic, fire and security. The dictionary then proceeds to noting that "the correct procedure [to controlling for these issues] is laid down in the rules and regulations". Therefore, there are many rules and regulations of society that are overseen and enforced by different types of 'regulatory' institutions, be they Police Forces, Customs Agencies, Courts, Trade Associations, Statutory Regulators, Churches, etc. All these institutions 'regulate' or 'control' in some way because they have laid-down rules and regulations which they enforce.

The above narrative speaks to the fact that there are different types of regulatory models in society today. What are the existing types [classification] of regulators doing the 'regulating' and Why?

There are six broad types or models [in a classification] of regulatory institutional approaches as shown in Figure 3.1.

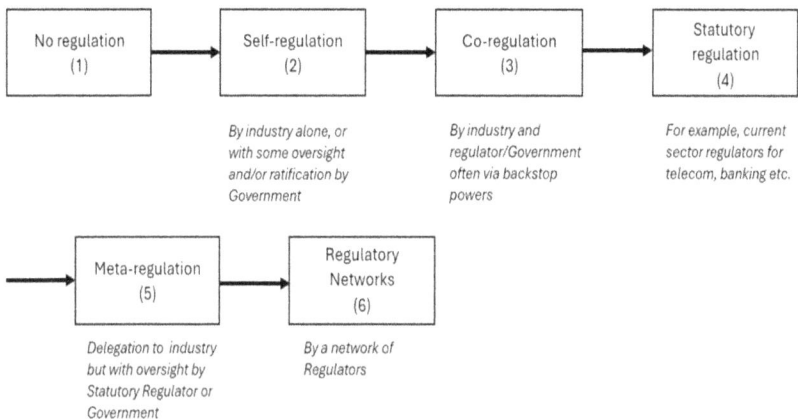

Figure 3.1 – A Classification of Regulatory Approaches

In general, regulation is conducted either by State or non-State entities. The six broad approaches (or models) to regulation as shown in Figure 3.1 includes No Regulation, Self-Regulation, Co-regulation, Statutory

Regulation, Meta-Regulation and Regulatory Networks. These refer to the various different approaches or layers of regulatory control used by Governments, Industries, and other Organisations to 'control' various aspects of societal behaviour, standards, compliance and enforcement.

They are overviewed next, including why each approach is relevant alongside key illustrating examples. Each of these models has its strengths and limitations, and their effectiveness depends on the context in which they are applied. However, it is the responsibility of Government and/or established regulators to consider the context that requires regulation carefully, and decide which of the following model of regulation is most optimal. In order to do so, striking the right balance between Government/Regulator intervention, industry responsibility, and societal interests is key for achieving desired regulatory outcomes.

3.1.1 No Regulation

The 'No Regulation' approach does *not* mean 'no controls'. It essentially refers to an approach where there are no *formal* rules and regulations laid down by Government or by a Legislature in a particular area of activity. There are usually (or there may be) some informal or unwritten rules at play in such areas of activity. In such contexts, citizens or organisations go about their activities without any external regulatory oversight by Government. Why – the reader may wonder – should some areas of activities in society be out of scope for formal regulations? A clear simple example answer is that of areas of activity relating to citizens' personal privacy and liberty.

The right to privacy is enshrined in many international and national laws/declarations.

1. Article 12 of the UN's 1948 Universal Declaration of Human Rights (UDHR) speaks to the right of protection to any individual, his/her family or home against "arbitrary interference", "nor any attacks upon his honour and reputation. Everyone has the right to the protection of the law against such interference or attacks"[90].

---

[90] https://www.un.org/en/about-us/universal-declaration-of-human-rights - Universal Declaration of Human Rights | United Nations

81

2. Article 17 of the UN International Covenant on Civil and Political Rights enshrines similar rights like the UDHR's Article 12 above[91].
3. Article 7 of the EU Charter of Fundamental Rights stipulates "-"Everyone has the right to respect for his or her private and family life, home and correspondence"[92].

Thanks to such basic Laws, certain areas of activities of our daily lives must be off formal regulation. For example, no Government typically[93] regulates or controls how many children a [married] couple can have. No Government would stipulate that an unmarried couple should not have children. Governments do not dictate where citizens must live as in which cities, towns or villages. Governments do not dictate how children are brought up by their parents. Etc. These are all judged by society not to be areas of activity that the Government should be concerned about. Governments *may* also choose not to formally regulate in other areas of activities of societal life, e.g., how often citizens see their physicians/GPs, whether and where citizens can smoke, whether people walk on the left-hand side of the street or on the right hand side, whether you vote at elections or not. For example, it is compulsory to vote in Australia whilst it is not in most other Western countries.

The 'No Regulation' model is obviously related to the cultural norms of the society or country concerned, and Governments must remain sensitive *not to regulate* where they should not.

This approach has its concerns, e.g., lack of consumer/citizen protection (which may lead to children being abused inside their homes by their parents until it may be too late or abuse of housemaids), citizens drinking unlimited amounts of alcohol in their homes leading to later societal costs, environmental pollution/degradation and other societal risks where there are no laid down rules to ensure responsible behaviour by individuals or organisations.

---

[91] https://www.ohchr.org/en/instruments-mechanisms/instruments/international-covenant-civil-and-political-rights - OHCHR | International Covenant on Civil and Political Rights

[92] text_en.pdf (europa.eu) - https://www.europarl.europa.eu/charter/pdf/text_en.pdf

[93] Except China and perhaps a few other countries the author is not aware of.

3.1.2 Self-Regulation

Following on from an example mentioned in the No Regulation model, Self-Regulation would typically govern how many children a couple may choose to have. So, self-regulation takes place when individuals, a company or a group of companies exert control over its membership and their behaviours. This happens because they *voluntarily* create and adhere to their own rules, codes of conduct and regulations. Professional bodies, trade associations, public interest groups, business partnerships (e.g., the big 4 accountancy partnerships of KPMG, PWC, Deloitte & E&Y), an exclusive Golf club, etc. are all self-regulating organisations. In many Western countries, advertising agencies, insurance companies and even the Press self-regulate. Many private organisations self-regulate purely in pursuit of the private benefits of their membership, e.g. a golf club. Others including the Press self-regulate for the benefits of themselves, their customers (i.e. readers, viewers, listeners, browsers, etc.) and broader society. In this context (i.e., Press in some countries like the UK), one can also define self-regulation as when industry designs and enforces its own rules and regulations in order to address a particular activities without the formal oversight or participation of the regulator or Government. In particular, there is no *ex-ante* legal backstop in a self-regulatory scheme to function as the ultimate guarantor of enforcement. For instance, the Motion Picture Association of America's (MPAA[94]) rating system governs and helps restrict children from seeing films with adult content without any Government involvement.

However, in some cases, self-regulation is constrained by Governmental (or a nominated Regulator's) oversight and/or ratification. In this context, it may/would be governed by the Courts too.

Why self-regulate? Self-regulatory solutions are perceived to allow for:

1. **Expertise***:* Self-regulators typically possess niche and higher levels of expertise that is difficult to develop and efficiently use in broader-mandate regulators. The knowledge and expertise of all parties is used more effectively, and they can be more flexible, adaptable and innovative.

---

[94] https://www.motionpictures.org/film-ratings/ - Film Ratings - Motion Picture Association (motionpictures.org)

2. **Efficiency:** Self-regulation would be more efficient and effective, targeting specific problems for them to receive greater focus than a broader regulator can efficiently manage. For example, rating Films as the MPAA does is quite niche and specialist, and with all the innovations with immersive movies, animations, etc., it is best left to self-regulator like the MPAA. Funding can be better targeted at those issues causing problems and generating the most concerns, and with greater promptness and flexibility in responding to changing market conditions.

The challenges of self-regulation relate to concerns about their mandates, accountability and fairness.

3. **Mandates:** Private self-regulators would have self-written mandates, even though their constituency is much broader beyond their members, e.g. the Press. Is it okay that the 'mandates' of Press self-regulation are not subject to democratic legitimacy? In many Western countries like the USA, the Press is seen as the fourth and independent estate in addition to the Executive, Legislature (Senate & Congress) and Judiciary. So, Western society appears to be fine with the Press self-regulating.

4. **Accountability***:* who are self-regulators accountable to beyond their membership? The public may not trust self-regulators. A classic ongoing example is the current ongoing self-regulation by Big Tech firms (Twitter/X, Meta/Facebook, Google, Instagram, TikTok, etc.), of their social media activities. Many politicians and significant fractions of society are sceptical about the accountability of these Big Tech companies as self-regulators of the content on their platforms.

5. **Fairness of Procedures**: self-regulation may not have explicit and well-defined processes and procedures to seek redress. It relies on the assumption self-regulators will behave responsibly to maintain their reputation and avoid negative outcomes. However, self-regulation can sometimes be ineffective if procedures and processes are based on such self-interest. What procedures do social media giants based in the USA put in place for citizens of Nigeria or Papua New Guinea being unfairly defamed on these platforms? Can they get redress in 24 to 48 hours and the offending content expunged? Do they even have the incentive to do so when defamatory and controversial content drives more traffic, and hence advertising revenues (see Nwana, 2022, p. 188-196)?

6. **Enforced self-regulation**: involves subcontracting regulatory functions to regulated firms. The functions that are subcontracted vary by the context which could include monitoring of compliance.

3.1.3 Co-Regulation

Co-regulation is really an extension of self-regulation that involves both Industry and the Government (or the Regulator) designing rules/regulations and enforcing them in a variety of combinations for a variety of activities. In particular, a scheme classified as co-regulatory will need to be clear on the role of the Government (or the regulator) with respect to the role of Industry:

1. either *ex-ante* with respect to operation of the particular activity to be regulated;
2. or where the activity is required to interpret and enforce a statutory regime, *ex-post*.

Therefore, co-regulation is by definition *collaborative* wherein Government authorities and industry stakeholders work together to design and implement regulations. It combines elements of both Government oversight and Industry self-regulation.

For example, in the UK, the Advertising Standards Authority (ASA[95]) is the country's specialist independent regulator of advertising across all media. It is an excellent example of the notion that co-regulation is really an extension of self-regulation. Self-regulation in the ASA case means that the advertising industry has *voluntarily established and paid for its own regulation*. Co-regulation sees the ASA given responsibility on a day-to-day basis for regulating the content of broadcast (TV and radio) ads under contract from statutory media regulator Ofcom[96]. The ASA is the public face for all advertising regulation which has evolved into a comprehensive one-stop shop for regulating marketing communications, both broadcast and non-broadcast, with expertise that Ofcom would have found it hard to hire and retain. It has continuously been adapting its self-regulatory system,

---

[95] https://www.asa.org.uk/ - Home - ASA | CAP

[96] www.ofcom.org.uk

constantly reviewing both the content of its codes and its remit, particularly recently with respect to digital media and the challenges presented by the growth of online marketing communications.

Why co-regulation? The reasons are similar to those of self-regulation above. Co-regulation recognizes that deep and niche industry expertise in shaping regulations while ensuring Government/Regulator oversight to protect the public interest. Therefore, this model tries to balance between expertise and efficiency on the one hand, and mandate, accountability and fairness on the other hand.

3.1.4 Statutory Regulation

The most traditional and direct model of regulatory governance is statutory regulation. It allows Governments to set clear rules, standards and regulations and enforce their compliance. This model of regulation is employed in critical areas such as telecoms, water, energy, rail, financial markets, health, public safety, environmental protection, and competition regulation.

Statutory Regulation is rooted in an absolute legal basis, i.e., rooted in statutes. The Britannica Dictionary defines the word 'statute' as either a written law that is formally created by a government, or a written rule or regulation. In this section, the former is more relevant. The legislature of the country (e.g. Parliament, Senate, Presidential Decrees, etc.) craft laws and statutes, including those that establish public bodies like regulatory agencies. Telecoms and media regulators like Ofcom[97] (UK) or FCC[98] (USA), a water regulator like Ofwat[99] (UK), energy regulators like Ofgem[100] (UK) or WERA[101] (Saudi Arabia), etc., are all statutory regulators or regulatory agencies. Sometimes, the regulator and its legal basis emanate from a singular piece of statute or legislation, e.g. the

[97] www.ofcom.org.uk

[98] https://www.fcc.gov/ - Federal Communications Commission | The United States of America (fcc.gov)

[99] https://www.ofwat.gov.uk/ - Home - Ofwat

[100] https://www.ofgem.gov.uk/ - Welcome to Ofgem | Ofgem

[101] https://erranet.org/member/sera-saudi-arabia/ - Water and Electricity Regulatory Authority - Kingdom of Saudi Arabia (my.gov.sa)

Nigerian Communications Act of 2003 which founded and established NCC[102] as an independent regulator of telecoms in Nigeria. Sometimes, a regulator is created by one statute (Act) but its legal basis derives from multiple other statutes or pieces of legislation, e.g., Ofcom (UK) was created by the UK Communications Act[103] (2003), but its legal basis derives from the latter and at least eight other statutes including the Wireless Telegraphy Act (2006), Broadcasting Acts (1990, 1996), Competition Act (1998), Enterprise Act (2002), Postal Services Acts (2000, 2011) and the Digital Economy Acts (2010, 2017).

In summary, statutory regulation refers to the *formal* establishment of rules, standards and regulations by Government through legislation, regulations that carry the force of law and are enforced by regulatory institutions or Government agencies.

Why this model of regulation? This is the traditional and direct model that gives 'regulation' its name. It seeks to address the natural monopoly problem, market failures, other regulatory failures and more using theories/hypotheses of regulation. Indeed, much of what is covered in this book, particularly in much of the previous chapter (Chapter 2) and other chapters, concerns such traditional/direct models of regulatory governance. Practically all of the regulatory approaches to the network industries overviewed in this chapter are of the statutory nature.

3.1.5 Meta-Regulation

Baldwin *et al.* (2012, p.147) note that the term 'meta-regulation' refers to "processes in which the regulatory authority oversees a control or risk management system, rather than conducts regulation directly – it 'steers rather than rows'". In this context, the primary 'control' duties of regulation are conducted within the risk management systems of Industry corporations leaving the meta-regulator with the roles of auditing, monitoring and incentivising these systems. Baldwin *et al.* (2012) cite the

---

[102] https://www.ncc.gov.ng/ - Nigerian Communications Commission (ncc.gov.ng)
[103] https://www.legislation.gov.uk/ukpga/2003/21/contents - Communications Act 2003 (legislation.gov.uk)

example of the USA's Environmental Protection Agency (EPA[104]) as an example meta-regulator.

Why meta-regulation then? One look at the example EPA's overly broad mandate areas of responsibility starts answering this question. It covers environment topics including the Air, climate change, environmental justice, land (waste and clean-up), pesticides, water topics, bed bugs, emergency response, greener living, lead, radon, chemicals and toxics, health, mould, environmental information by location, etc. The EPA's legal mandate is thus extremely broad, and the most efficient way for it to carry out its duty is by encouraging the use of Environmental Management Systems (EMSs) that implement intra-corporation policies, rules, management processes and regulations designed to control risks to the environment. The meta-regulator (EPA) provides scrutiny and oversight of all the control policies and processes implemented ranging from the voluntary/self-regulated model to the firm-hand meta-regulated model. The use of certifications and standards are typically key to this meta model of regulation by meeting strict EMS standards set by trade associations or strict regulatory requirements.

The advantages here of such clear delegation of regulation down to corporations are clearly numerous in terms of expertise, efficiency and costs of regulation. Each of the hundreds - if not thousands of corporations - can design their own rules and regulations specific to the context of the firm, but these rules are scrutinised by the meta-regulatory agency. This delivers more efficient environmental controls at lower compliance costs.

In summary, meta-regulation involves the meta-regulator (typically an agency of Government) setting broad principles and guidelines for industry self-regulation or co-regulation policies, processes and systems. Rather than dictating mandatory rules from the centre (as a statutory regulator would do), the meta-regulator focuses on setting and implementing risk control frameworks that encourage responsible behaviour and effective self-monitoring by the regulated companies. Environmental protection regulators across the world tend to use this model of regulation.

---

[104] https://www.epa.gov/ - U.S. Environmental Protection Agency | US EPA

However, this model requires *active* monitoring of industry practices with a readiness for firm, strong-hand statutory-type regulation as needed. For example, if some regulated environmental firms start dumping raw sewage into public waters, the meta-regulator needs to be very alive to these and intervene in timely manner if self-regulation/co-regulation fails to achieve their desired outcomes.

3.1.6 Regulatory Networks

Regulatory Networks are increasingly making more sense and becoming more relevant. The underlying theory is that the most optimal regulatory outcomes will typically involve "mixtures" from regulatory institutions and regulatory instruments. Some authors, e.g. Gunningham & Grabosky (1998), have referred to this as *Smart Regulation* which the authors have proposed in the context of environmental policy. The crucial policy and regulatory questions are how, and in what contexts and combinations, can the main policy instruments and regulatory institutions be used to achieve the optimal policy and regulation mixes? This is non-trivial to achieve in my experience.

However, the regulation of some emerging areas like Mobile Financial Services (Mobile Monies, insurance products, lending products, savings products, etc.) – particularly in emerging economies in Africa, the Caribbean and South East Asia – require a *regulatory network* model of at least two regulators and their statutory instruments, i.e. the telecoms regulator and the banking regulator (typically the Central Bank). The core 'regulatory network' in this context is that of the telecoms and prudential banking regulator who form an *informal* collaboration[105], and conduct interactions amongst themselves and other regulatory agencies (e.g., competition agencies, data protection agencies, cybersecurity agencies, etc.), industry and stakeholders. Such a network facilitates the exchange of key information across both/multiple regulators, 'mixes' best practices from both telecoms and prudential banking regulation, and coordinates across different the different sectors. The network also involve "mixtures" from both or more regulatory institutions and regulatory instruments, e.g., prudential regulation instruments from the banking regulator and numbering instruments from the telecoms regulator to aid identification,

---

[105] Typically via an informal Memorandum of Understanding (MoU).

etc. This is happening in Kenya today amongst the CBK[106] (the prudential regulator) and the Communications Authority [107] (CA), the telecoms regulator.

There is another 'flavour' of regulatory networks worth mentioning which include ACER[108] (Agency for the Cooperation of Energy Regulators in Europe) and BEREC[109] (Body of European Regulators for Electronic Communications). ACER and BEREC respectively contribute to the development and better functioning of the European energy internal market and the internal market for electronic communications networks and services. For example, BEREC is an independent EU regulatory entity established with the aim to assist telecoms regulatory authorities in EU member states, as well as the European Commission, in implementing the EU regulatory framework on electronic communications. The BEREC network is a most efficient regulatory network model of coordinating, *harmonising,* sharing best practice and implementing shared regulations derived from the EU regulatory framework. As Baldwin *et al.* (2012, p.459) note, the BEREC regulatory network model here [of all EU telecom regulators] "represents an ingenious attempt to corral the regulators of the EU, the national regulatory agencies or NRAs, down the path of normalization – allowing them, however, to proceed at their own speed (but within the uniform framework necessary for the EU's common or internal market)". This is a clear and another good example of regulatory networks.

---

[106] CBK | Central Bank of Kenya - https://www.centralbank.go.ke/

[107] Homepage | Communications Authority of Kenya - https://www.ca.go.ke/

[108] https://european-union.europa.eu/institutions-law-budget/institutions-and-bodies/search-all-eu-institutions-and-bodies/agency-cooperation-energy-regulators-acer_en - Agency for the Cooperation of Energy Regulators | European Union (europa.eu)

[109] https://www.berec.europa.eu/en | BEREC (europa.eu)

3.2 Regulatory Institutions & Institutional Design

Drawing from the prior section, the following is a non-exhaustive summary of typical regulatory institutions and agencies in most economies.

- Sector specific regulators (Statutory Regulators)
  i. Individual National or Regional Regulators
  ii. UK examples include Ofcom, Ofwat, Ofgem,[110] etc.
- Meta-regulators
  i. An example from the USA is the Environmental Protection Agency (EPA[111])
- Self-Regulators and Co-Regulators
  i. A US example is the Motion Picture Association of America's (MPAA[112]).
  ii. A UK example is the Advertising Standards Authority (ASA[113]).
- Cross-Economy Regulators
  i. There are other cross-economy regulators such as data protection agencies like the UK's Information Commissioner's Office (ICO)[114]. I have kept them apart here, but other authors may include them as meta-regulators above.
- Regulatory Networks
  i. This involves the hypothesis that the most optimal regulatory outcomes will typically involve "mixtures" from regulatory institutions and regulatory instruments, e.g., a collaboration amongst a telecom regulator, a banking regulator and even a data protection regulator in order to control an activity like mobile financial services.

---

[110] www.ofcom.org.uk; https://www.ofwat.gov.uk/; https://www.ofgem.gov.uk/

[111] https://www.epa.gov/ - U.S. Environmental Protection Agency | US EPA

[112] https://www.motionpictures.org/film-ratings/ - Film Ratings - Motion Picture Association (motionpictures.org)

[113] https://www.asa.org.uk/ - Home - ASA | CAP

[114] https://ico.org.uk/ - Information Commissioner's Office (ICO)

ii. Other flavours of regulatory networks include (i) ACER[115] (Agency for the Cooperation of Energy Regulators in Europe) and (ii) BEREC[116] (Body of European Regulators for Electronic Communications)

- Competition Authorities
    i. National Competition Authorities, e.g. the UK's Competition & Markets Authority (CMA[117])
    ii. DG Competition[118] (the EU Competition Regulator)
- Courts
    i. National Courts
    ii. Supra-National Courts, e.g., the European Court of Justice[119]
- Industry
    i. National Industry Associations
    ii. Trade Associations
    iii. Professional Bodies
    iv. Regional Industry Associations, e.g., ENTSO-E [120] (European Network of Transmission System Operators for Electricity)
- Legislators
    i. National Governments/National Parliaments
    ii. EU Council / EU Parliament / EU Commission

---

[115] https://european-union.europa.eu/institutions-law-budget/institutions-and-bodies/search-all-eu-institutions-and-bodies/agency-cooperation-energy-regulators-acer_en - Agency for the Cooperation of Energy Regulators | European Union (europa.eu)

[116] https://www.berec.europa.eu/en | BEREC (europa.eu)

[117] https://www.gov.uk/government/organisations/competition-and-markets-authority - Competition and Markets Authority - GOV.UK (www.gov.uk)

[118] https://commission.europa.eu/about-european-commission/departments-and-executive-agencies/competition_en - Competition (europa.eu)

[119] https://www.europarl.europa.eu/factsheets/en/sheet/26/the-court-of-justice-of-the-european-union# - The Court of Justice of the European Union | Fact Sheets on the European Union | European Parliament (europa.eu)

[120] https://www.entsoe.eu/ - Home (entsoe.eu)

How are these regulatory models used in institutional design of regulatory institutions in the first place? As noted earlier, each of these models has its strengths and limitations. How do Governments choose whether no regulation, self-regulation, co-regulation, statutory regulation, meta-regulation or regulatory networks is most optimal to a regulatory situation at hand? The following are some suggested steps and rules-of-thumbs that may help.

1. Articulate and understand the strengths and weaknesses of these regulatory models: as covered in the previous section.

2. Single Sector Statutory Regulators are needed for Network Industries: As noted, statutory regulation is the most traditional and direct model of regulatory governance, which is applied in critical areas such telecoms, water, energy, rail, financial markets, health, public safety, environmental protection, and competition regulation. Therefore, in most countries, statutory regulators would be set up for each of these activity/sector areas.

3. *Multi-Sector Statutory Regulators* make sense in certain contexts: Alternatively, to point 2 above, some [typically smaller] countries may choose to set up multi-sector regulators, e.g. Jamaica's Office of Utilities Regulation (OUR[121]), Bahamas' Utilities Regulation and Competition Authority (URCA [122]) or Rwanda Utilities Regulatory Authority (RURA[123]). The argument for multi-sector regulators is one of efficiency and low costs, particularly in the regulation of sectors that share broadly similar regulatory 'exam questions', e.g., a multi-sector Utility regulator covering electricity, water and waste – or even gas. Multi-sector regulators

---

[121] https://our.org.jm/ - Home - Office Of Utilities Regulation (our.org.jm) - The Office of Utilities Regulation (OUR) was established by an Act of Parliament in 1995 to regulate the operations of utility companies. Operations began in January 1997

[122] https://urcabahamas.bs/ - URCA Bahamas - Improving lives through effective utilities regulation - The Utilities Regulation and Competition Authority (URCA) is the independent regulatory authority with responsibility for the Electronic Communications Sector (ECS) and the Electricity Sector (ES) in the Bahamas.

[123] https://rura.rw/index.php?id=44 - Background (rura.rw) - RURA was initially created by the Law n° 39/2001 of 13 September 2001 with the mission to regulate certain public Utilities, namely: telecommunications network and/or Telecommunications services, electricity, water, removal of waste products from residential or business premises, extraction and distribution of gas and transport of goods and persons.

also pool expertise instead of fragmenting it across separate even smaller regulators. Setting up such multi-sector regulators truly requires strong and *expert* accountability and scrutiny. I have seen several very sub-optimal multi-sector regulators, not quite achieving most of their intended outcomes in the several sectors they regulate. However, the OUR in Jamaica is generally regarded as relatively successful multi-sector regulator overall.

4. Allow for co-regulation/self-regulation: whilst establishing either single or multi-sector regulators, it is advised that Governments can or should ensure the statutes or laws to set up the regulator allows or approves specific requirements to set up specific co-regulatory schemes. For example, the UK's Communication Act of 2003[124] which set up telecoms and media regulator Ofcom promotes the development and use of self- and co-regulation. Specifically, the Act specifies requirements to approve two specific co-regulatory schemes:

   a.   approval of dispute resolution procedures for consumers dealing with electronic communications service providers, and

   b.   approval of code for premium rate services[125] (PRS).

5. Self-regulation or co-regulation lend themselves to areas of regulatory activities with *niche and deep expertise*: where such a model can bring significant efficiency benefits. These benefits need to be balanced against the risks of possibly 'biased' mandates [towards their members mostly], accountability and fairness risks.

6. No regulation tends to apply to basic law areas like *personal liberty and privacy*: as covered earlier.

7. *Regulatory Networks* have their places: regulatory networks increasingly apply to cross-sectoral activities like Mobile Financial Services covering traditional telecoms services

---

[124] https://www.legislation.gov.uk/ukpga/2003/21/contents - Communications Act 2003 (legislation.gov.uk)

[125] Premium rate services (PRS) use telephone numbers for such services as competitions, TV voting, horoscopes, chat lines, adult lines, recorded information, professional advice services (for example, computer support help lines) and directory enquiries.

combined with banking insurance products, lending products, savings products, etc. Regulatory networks like BEREC provide for a most efficient model of coordinating, harmonising, sharing best practice, and implementing shared regulations derived from the EU regulatory framework. They can be applied across other region consisting of many countries.

Ultimately, the effectiveness of any institutional design depends on the context in which they are applied. However, it is the responsibility of Government and/or established regulators to consider the context that requires regulation carefully, and decide which of the following model of regulation is most optimal. In order to do so, striking the right balance between Government/Regulator intervention, industry responsibility, and societal interests is key for achieving desired regulatory outcomes.

3.3 Network Industries Sector Market Structures

This section overviews key network sector market structures to our economies because different market structures present different characteristics leading to different approaches to their *statutory* regulation. This is because – as is noted in Section 3.1 – statutory regulation is the most traditional and direct model of regulatory governance which allows Governments to regulate critical areas of our economies such telecoms, water, energy, rail, financial markets, health, public safety, environmental protection, and competition regulation. Most, if not all, of these sectors of our economies are *network industries*. This means that much statutory regulation involves network industries, which in turn means we must understand their characteristics and challenges.

3.3.1 Network Industries & their Generic Structures: starting the journey from theory to practice

Network industries are sectors or industries that supply goods or services to their customers that depend on a vast network of interconnected nodes or points, e.g., water, gas, electricity, telecoms, postal services, etc. Network industries enjoy all of *economies of scale, economies of scope* and *network effects*.

Recall Chapter 2 defines economies of scale as simply a reduction in long run average cost (LRAC) as output increases, i.e., that the cost per unit in production and consumption decreases as the output or demand increases. Economies of scope describes scenarios where producing or offering two or more goods together results in a lower marginal cost than producing them separately. Network effects[126] on the other hand means that the value of a good or service increases as more people use it. The regulation challenges clearly grows as network industries with increasing customers, see exponentially increasing economies of scale, scope and network effects. This is because these effects entrench the [natural] monopoly problem significantly increasingly market failure risks – and market failures are key justifications for regulation.

Importantly, there are three generic industry structures that network industries typically approximate (Decker, 2023, p.71-74 – Figures 3.2, 3.3 and 3.4 are sourced and adapted from these pages):

1. **Vertically integrated monopoly structure**: such as that depicted by the Postal Industry example of Figure 3.2. The vertically integrated monopoly operates all of the upstream, core network and downstream activities. Royal Mail (UK) was formerly just such a vertically integrated monopoly operator in the UK Postal Industry[127];

2. **Vertically separated structure with competition in upstream and downstream activities**: such as that depicted by the Gas Industry example of Figure 3.3. The upstream activity of Gas Extraction is typically competitive, whilst core network activity of Gas Transmission and Distribution is typically not, i.e., the latter is typically monopolistic. The downstream Gas Retailing is typically competitive too like is the case with the upstream Gas Extraction.

---

[126] The network effect—sometimes known as network externality—refers to phenomenon wherein the value of a product or service is dependent on the number of people using the service. A world with only one telephone is pretty useless—no one else to phone! A world with a thousand telephone lines is more valuable as each can telephone 999 others. This is clearly more valuable. A network of tens of millions telephone users is clearly exponentially more valuable—this is the essence of the network effect.

[127] Royal Mail - https://www.royalmail.com/

3. **Vertically separated structure with competition in some activities**: such as that depicted by the Telecoms Industry example of Figure 3.4. The monopoly Local Access Network (LAN) with copper lines into every home like former telecoms monopoly BT (UK) had been 'unbundled' such that BT's competitors were/are able to use those lines to provide services like broadband and/or voice into customers' premises.

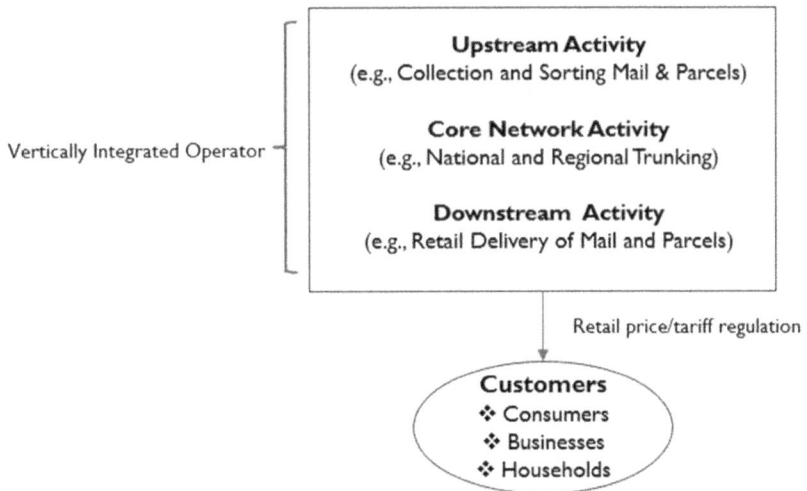

Figure 3.2 – A Vertically Integrated Monopoly (using the example of a Vertically Integrated Monopoly in the Postal Industry)

(Source: significantly adapted from Decker, 2023, p.72; nevertheless, updated diagram printed with written permission of the original author, Prof. Christopher Decker and Publisher)

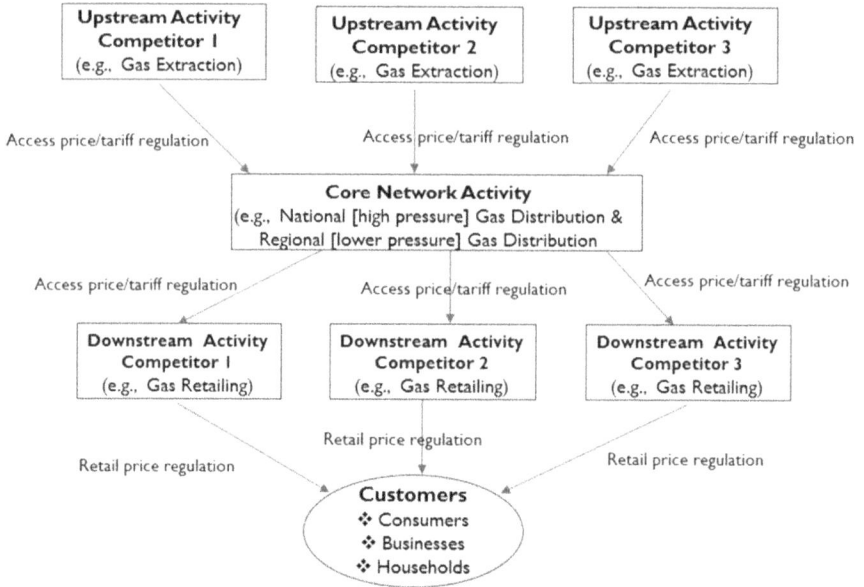

Figure 3.3 – A Vertically Separated Structure with Competition in Upstream and Downstream Activities (using the example of the Gas Industry) - *(Source: adapted from Decker, 2023, p.73; nevertheless, updated diagram printed with written permission of the original author, Prof. Christopher Decker and Publisher)*

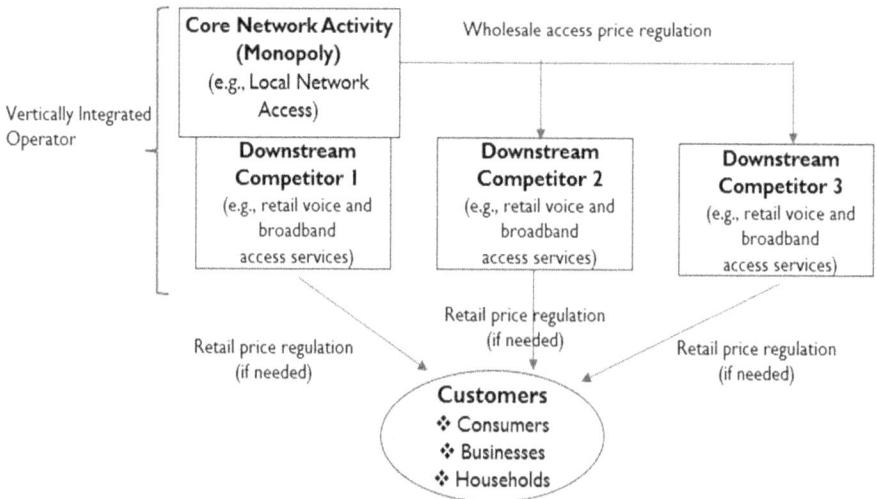

Figure 3.4 – A Vertically Integrated Structure with Competition in some Activities (using the example of the Telecom Industry)

(Source: Decker, 2023, p.74; reproduced with written permission of the original author, Prof. Christopher Decker and Publisher)

All these example network industries of Figures 3.2, 3.3 and 3.4 (i.e., the Postal, Gas and Telecoms industries) are overviewed later in this chapter in more detail. What is important now is the fact that, if a network industry approximates any of these different types of network industry structures then that industry structure will dictate the types of theories and hypotheses of regulation that would underpin the rationale(s) to any interventions of the regulator – as well as the type of tasks and methods of regulation (see Chapter 4) that the regulator would employ. For example, the Figure 3.4 'template' employs the methods of 'wholesale access price regulation' and 'retail price regulation' [as needed]. This is enormously important because it also helps starts translating theory of regulation into practice.

3.3.2 A Brief Introduction to Network Theory and how they help characterise the 'unbundling' of Network Industries

In order to characterise or describe Network Industries, academics like Aldous & Wilson (2000) and Wasserman & Faust (2008) have evolved a discipline called *network or graph theory*. Once again, the reader should not be put off by this brief diversion into network or graph theory. Since network industries consist of networks (as observed with the three generic industry structures of the previous section), network theory is therefore applicable to characterise these industries. Using network theory to characterise these network industries starts the process depicting how these industries that exhibit natural monopoly attributes can start being 'unbundled[128]' in order to mitigating any likely future market failures through regulation.

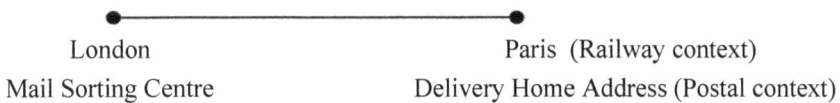

London	Paris (Railway context)
Mail Sorting Centre	Delivery Home Address (Postal context)

Figure 3.5 – A Simple Two-node Network

In essence, network/graph theory holds that a network is a graph, and that graph-based representations can simplify the analysis of complex network systems. This is because there are two elements to a graph: nodes and

---

[128] Or separated into some other logical set of sub-activities that <u>may</u> be done by other firms.

edges (or arcs). Entities are nodes and the edges (arcs) are the interactions between nodes. The simplest network is a two-nodes network.

Figure 3.5 is a graph representation that could depict a simple railway track connecting two cities, with London and Paris as the nodes, and the single edge as the link (interaction) between the two cities. The simple two-node network may also depict the two nodes being a mail sorting centre and a delivery home address, whilst the arc/edge represents the delivery relationship from the sorting centre to the specific unique home address on the letter. Of course, in reality postal delivery men and women deliver letters and parcels to many unique homes daily.

The basic concepts of the simple 2-node network graph can be 'extended' to describe or characterise network industry models as graphs. For example, electricity, gas or cable TV network business can be characterised by the graph shown in Figure 3.6. Why? This is because we would have multiple nodes at both A (gas extraction) and C (retailing).

This is because – as shown in Table 3.1 – Figure 3.6 could easily be the graph depictions of the electricity, gas or cable TV industries.

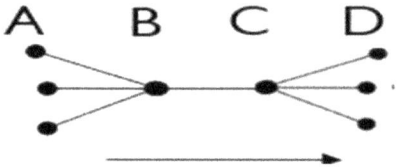

Figure 3.6 – Graph Model Depiction of Electricity, Gas and Cable TV Industries

Taking just the example of the electricity industry, Node A would represent a company/companies conducting Generation Activities, Node B for high-voltage transmission and/or regional distribution, Node C for Retailing activities whilst Node D represents the constellation of retail addresses (through the 'fanning out' to multiple addresses from Node C). These nodes depict options of 'unbundling' the value chain of the industry.

Network Industry	Node A represents	Node B represents	Node C represents	Node D represents
Electricity	Generation Activity agents	High-Voltage transmission & Regional Distribution Activities agent	Retailing Activities agent	Multiple Retail Addresses
Gas	Extraction Activity agents	National and Regional Distribution Activities agent	Retailing Activities agent	Multiple Retail Addresses
Cable TV	Headend Content Aggregation Activity agents	National and Regional Content Distribution Activities agent	Retailing Activities agent	Multiple Retail Addresses

Table 3.1 – Possible Explanation of nodes of Figure 3.6 for different Network Industries

Table 3.1 shows the different activities that would take place in Nodes A, B, C and D of Figure 3.6 for different network industries. It can be seen from a combination of the graph depiction of Figure 3.6 and Table 3.1's description of the nodes that representing network industries as a graph makes the regulatory analysis of the sector/industry value chain much simpler because it shows the system of interacting node agents and the topology of their interactivity. This means that sometimes, only a single agent activity node may connect to the node (e.g. Node B to Node C of Figure 3.6), whilst in other cases an activity node branches out to many other nodes (e.g., Node C to Node D of Figure 3.6).

Let us look at the graphs of a few more network industries to emphasise and clarify the concepts some more.

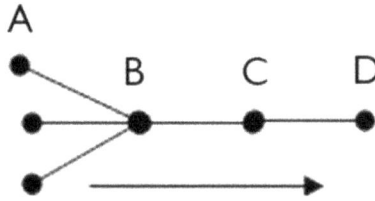

Figure 3.7 – Graph Model Depiction of Garbage Collection Industry

Figure 3.7 roughly depicts a classic graphical depiction of the 'unbundling' of the Garbage Industry.

In this case, as shown in Table 3.2, Node(s) A represents millions of homes from which garbage is generated whilst Node B represents the Waste Collection/Handling. Node C represents Energy Recovery activities whilst Node D represents Final Disposal activities including open dumping or landfilling.

Network Industry	Node A represents	Node B represents	Node C represents	Node D represents
Garbage Collection Industry	Household Waste Generation activities agent	Waste Collection & Handling (Soring & Recycling) Activities agent	Energy Recovery (e.g. Waste-to-Energy or Waste-to-Fuel) agent	Final Disposal Activities agent

Table 3.2 – Possible Explanation of Nodes of Figure 3.7 for Garbage Collection Industry

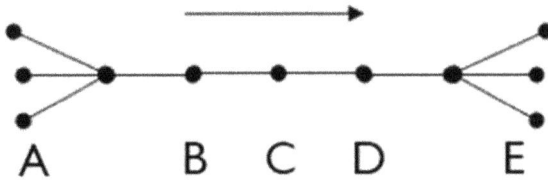

Figure 3.8 – Graph Model Depiction of Postal and Telecom Industries

Figure 3.8 depicts a possible graph model for the Postal and Telecoms industries, along with the elaborations of the various nodes in Table 3.3.

Network Industry	Node A represents	Node B represents	Node C represents	Node D represents	Node E represents
Postal Industry	Household/Businesses Collection Activities and Consumers agent delivering letters to centres, e.g., Post Offices	Sorting Activities agent	National Trunking[129] Activities agent	Regional Trunking Activities agent	Retail Delivery Activities agent
Fixed Telco Industry	Households Local Network Call Initiation Activities agent	Local Exchange	National & International Trunking or Transit[130] Activities agent	Local Exchange	Retail Telco Call Termination Activities agent

Table 3.3 – Possible Explanation of Nodes of Figure 3.8 for the Postal and Telecoms Industries

---

[129] Trunking means the transportation of posts between sorting offices, either to regional sorting offices or to local ones.

[130] The core switches in a telecoms network are called Trunk or *Transit Switches* (TS) and they are all interconnected. Transiting (Trunking) refers to the switching and routing of traffic destined for termination outside of the local area, typically regional or national or long-distance traffic switching and routing to another terminating local network household or business.

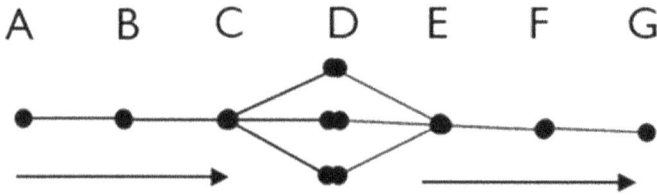

Figure 3.9 – Graph Model Depiction of the Water and Wastewater Industry

Figure 3.9 depicts a possible 'unbundling' graph model for the Water and Wastewater industry, along with the elaborations of the various nodes in Table 3.4.

Node A	Node B	Node C	Node D	Node E	Node F	Node G
Water Abstraction [131] Activities agent	Water Storage & Treatment Activities agent	Water Distri bution agent	Water Retailing Activitie s agent	Wastewater Collection & Transport ation Activities agent	Wastewater Treating Activities agent	Waste Disposal Activities agent

Table 3.4 – Possible Explanation of Nodes of Figure 3.9 for the Water and Wastewater Industry[132]

---

[131] Water abstraction (water extraction) or groundwater abstraction is the process of taking water from any source, either temporarily or permanently. Most water is used for irrigation or treatment to produce drinking water. Source: - http://www.environmentdata.org/ - Water abstraction | environmentdata.org

[132]https://www.allianceforwaterefficiency.org/resources/financing-sustainable-water - Lessons from the UK on Water Efficiency Through Retail Competition for Water Services | Financing Sustainable Water

In summary about these graphs [and tables], the reader should take away the following:

(i) Network industries graphs are structures that are used to isolate interesting and important aspects of the industry. They are interesting because they identify significant domain-specific aspects of the industry, their key players and activities.

(ii) Indeed, the graphs also depict the significant value chains of these industries.

(iii) Perhaps most importantly as covered next, the graphs help identify the various sub-chains which make up the entire value chain of the industry, and which of them are natural monopolies which need active *regulation* in contrast to those that lend themselves to *competition*.

3.4 Regulation vs. 'Effective Competition' with Network Industries using 'Unbundling': from Theory to Practice

Continuing on from the last sentence, recall from Chapter 2 how Figure 2.3 denotes the need to seek to achieve positive outcomes for consumers and citizens that do not arise naturally from market *competition* [on the right of Figure 2.3/Figure 3.10]. That is a market failure exists, and *regulation* [on the left of Figure 2.3/Figure 3.10] becomes necessary to bring in such net benefits. Figure 3.10 provides an elaborated version and more 'toolbox' details not shown in Figure 2.3. Recall too from Chapter 2 that the intersection between the two ovals in Figure 2.3/Figure 3.10 also represents the fact that regulation may be needed to facilitate competition.

Figure 3.10 (like Figure 2.3) depicts that if competition is working fine, there *may be* no need (or less need) for regulation. I emphasise 'may be' because I am referring to a subset of the rationales for regulation set out in Section 2.2. Lack of competition is integral to only a few of the rationales listed in that section such as natural monopoly and market power more generally. Competition 'working fine' does not resolve other rationales for regulation such as externalities (e.g., environmental and climate change regulation).

Figure 3.10 diagrammatically overviews two main regulatory toolboxes which *statutory* economic regulators have at their disposal – on the one hand, tools which are mainly "regulatory" in nature. On the other hand, there are tools under "competition law". There is this key 'interplay' of competition and regulation which is at the core of the market failure theory, which is especially important to economic regulation in general – particularly for network industries.

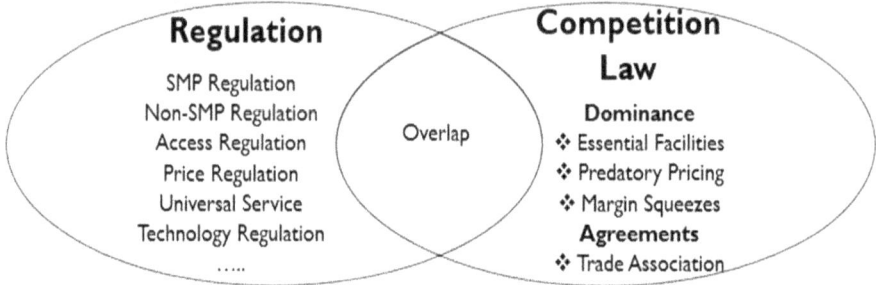

Regulation

SMP Regulation
Non-SMP Regulation
Access Regulation
Price Regulation
Universal Service
Technology Regulation
.....

Overlap

Competition Law

Dominance
❖ Essential Facilities
❖ Predatory Pricing
❖ Margin Squeezes
Agreements
❖ Trade Association

Figure 3.10 – Regulation vs. Competition 'Toolboxes' (Elaborated version of Figure 2.3) – the overlap Regulation/Competition areas include SMP/Dominance, Price Controls/Collusive agreements and Access/Essential Facilities respectively

In this section, drawing from the industry model graphs of the previous section – and from the generic industry models that the sector in question may approximate (see Section 3.3.1) - we proceed to doing an introduction into some details of the regulation vs. competition dynamic with different network industries.

Figure 3.10 is pivotal to the regulation of network industries, i.e. using regulation, competition or a mixture of both. How – the reader may wonder – can a mixture of both be used? This is covered next.

Competition encourages a rivalry for customers' business amongst suppliers across the service dimensions of choice [as much as possible], price [as low as possible], quality [as high as possible], innovation, etc. As Professor Stephen Littlechild wrote in his report for the UK Government [on price controls for BT] in 1983:

> "The main purpose of *regulation* is to protect domestic and small business subscribers against BT's dominant market position. ...

106

Competition is by far the most effective means of protection against monopoly. Vigilance against anti-competitive prices is also important. *Profit regulation* is merely a 'stop-gap' until sufficient competition develops. There is always a danger that regulatory authorities will be 'captured' by incumbent suppliers and influenced against new entry" (Littlechild, 1983, page. 1)[133]. *The author's emphases.*

Professor Littlechild wrote this in the context of the then fully-monopoly British Telecommunications *before privatisation*, but his pronouncements above apply to all network industries. This clearly speaks to the fact that the regulation of a monopoly that faces no competition is just almost impossible because it has so many disadvantages. For examples, the monopoly would be under little pressure – even if the regulator regulates prices - to innovate or to offer more new products and choices to customers. The introduction of new rivals anywhere across the monopoly's value chain would see these rivals pricing more innovative services more efficiently – hence driving more consumer welfare or benefits. *Consumer welfare* refers to the difference between what consumers would have been willing to pay for a good or service and what they actually had to pay. It is the 'consumer surplus' that consumers get from buying a good or service that is also referred to as consumer welfare.

Therefore, the introduction of 'effective competition' – rather than 'ineffective competition' - is crucial with network industries because it would drive up consumer welfare. Ineffective competition can happen when too many small firms enter a market which is best served by a single large firm. As for effective competition, Figure 3.10 alludes to it as the absence *of market dominance*. Market dominance simply refers to the control of an economic market by a firm. What 'effective competition' means in Sector A would be different for Sector B, for Country A would be different for Country B, etc

The approach to achieving effective competition with network industries often involves breaking down the value chain – or unbundling - into separate distinct components, and posing the questions of each of the components: which components are potentially competitive and which remain monopolistic. This process of breaking down the value chain is

---

[133] S.-Littlechild_1983-report.pdf (cam.ac.uk) - https://www.eprg.group.cam.ac.uk/wp-content/uploads/2019/10/S.-Littlechild_1983-report.pdf

called *unbundling*, and is a process that was applied to British Telecommunications (BT) after its privatisation in 1984. The potentially competitive unbundled components are liberalised and opened up to new entrants – enabling competition. Even the components that still remain monopoly bottlenecks are subject to mandatory *regulation*, where the owners of these monopoly assets are forced by regulation to open up access to their competitors at regulated input costs to their *competition*. For example, BT still owns most – if not all – of the physical fixed telephony lines to households in the UK. This is a clear monopoly bottleneck. So, BT was regulated to open up (i.e., grant access through *access regulation*) these 'last mile' distribution networks to its competitors, such that other retailers like BskyB, Telefonica, and even the Post Office's telecoms arm could provide telephony services using their brands – without consumers having to deal with BT who owns the lines.

Returning to Figure 3.10, hopefully the reader now understands how pivotal this simple picture is to the regulation of network industries, i.e. using regulation, competition or a mixture of both. The reader can see from the last several paragraphs how the toolboxes of regulation and competition of Figure 3.10 can be used to massively increase consumer welfare/benefits with natural monopoly network industries, first via unbundling and liberalising new entry for the potentially competitive components (thereby enabling *competition*), and secondly, via regulation of the *monopoly* bottleneck components through access regulation and price regulation/controls. This is the 'interplay' in action of competition and regulation at the core of the market failure theory covered in Chapter 2 [Section 2.3], and also very much at the core to *economic regulation* in general.

One last area of Figure 3.10 that we have not covered so far - the overlap. As is covered with the overview of several network industries later in this chapter, the overlap area also represents the ongoing regulation vs. competition dynamic that is ever present with the regulation of network industries. I am positing explicitly that in the overlap areas, there is a debate over whether to use the regulation or competition toolbox. The Regulation v. Competition overlap area respectively includes 'dynamic duos' such as SMP versus Dominance, Price Controls versus Collusive agreements and Access versus Essential Facilities. Significant Market Power (SMP) is the regulatory 'equivalent' to Dominance with competition, the regulatory equivalent of Access is Essential Facility, etc. These themes/concepts dynamic recur frequently later in this chapter as it explores the regulation versus competition dynamic across several key-to-modern society network industry sectors.

3.4.1 Summary Characteristics of Network Industries

We now know from Section 3.3 that network industries provide products or services through a network industry infrastructure. The last section has graphically depicted (using Figures 3.6, 3.7, 3.8 and 3.9) using graph/network theory several to many network industries that are replete in our economies. Each of these graphical industry models provide an implied value chain of the network industry. However, most of these network industries share the following features and characteristics, which have been covered earlier but worth summarising next.

Vital Importance to Economies (justifying Government Policy Interventions): all these network industries are really those that economies cannot do without. They are *de facto* effective critical national infrastructures (CNIs) that practically – in many cases – the whole population needs, i.e., spilling over from individual users to the entire economy. Imagine switching off a country's rail network or electricity network. This is at the core of why there are almost always policy interventions with network industries leading to follow up regulations.

Sunk Costs & Non-duplicable Networks (see later in Chapter 5): Network industries, as natural monopolies, exhibit high sunk costs and non-duplicable networks. These are yet clear reasons why they should be subject to regulations on both access to the network by competing players as well as pricing. This clearly applies to cases with transmission and distribution networks in energy, telecoms (backbone, backhaul, transit and last mile) and transport infrastructures (like railways, roads, seaports and airports).

Supply-Side Economies of Scale: these network industries all enjoy supply-side economies of scale, i.e., the cost per unit in production and consumption decreases as the output or demand from consumers increases.

Supply-Side Economies of Scope: network industries exhibit this economic concept [benefit] where producing or offering two or more goods together results in a lower marginal cost than producing them separately. This means large monopoly-type firms are favoured supplying many services together., specifically location-specific demand. We see this daily with supermarkets[134] - a major supermarket chain that sells petrol also sells everyday household commodities/needs like bread, milk, newspapers, non-alcoholic beverages, etc. This explains the emergence of ever bigger megastores.

Consumption Network Effects: in contrast to the latter two characteristics, network effects are sometimes referred to as demand-side economies of scale and scope. It is already worrying enough that these network industries already have all these supply-side benefits, but they also naturally benefit on the demand side too. These effects ensure that that the value of a good or service to consumers increases as more people use it. Think for a minute how the value of the Meta/Facebook platform has continuously increased to you as an individual (or another Facebook use you know) as more family members join the platform.

Separable Production Processes: this is a different type of characteristic of network industries that also gives them significant natural monopoly-type advantages. Separable production processes refers to those that can be split into distinct further stages. Each further stage produces and supplies a different output that can be sold or used for further processing downstream. – this way the network industry is benefitting from even more spinoff products. Oil refining is a classic separable production process because it involves separating crude oil into various fractions such as petrol/gasoline, diesel and kerosene – valuable spinoff products in their own right.

Graph Theory: finally, the reader should recall that network graph can be used to describe or characterise network industry models as graphs as covered earlier. These graphs also help characterise distinct characteristics of network industries.

---

[134] I acknowledge that it may read odd to some readers to use supermarkets as an example here, because it is not a regulated network industry. I use it in the spirit of using an everyday example to illustrate supply-side economies of scope.

3.4.2 These Characteristics of Network Industries spell [Economic] Regulation

Hopefully, the reader can see from these afore-listed characteristics of network industries why there are almost always Government policy interventions with these industries leading to follow-up sector regulations.

In addition, there are other key legitimate concerns/risks with network industries:

- Abuse of monopoly power, e.g., excessive pricing to customers;
- Departure from economic efficiency (e.g., the exclusion of competitors by dominant network firms);
- Equity and Inclusion issues (Universal Service Obligations, Specific pricing for particular social groups, etc.);
- Dynamic issues, e.g. their incentives to invest and innovate.

With all these natural monopoly and infrastructure management challenges with network industries, tough questions such as the following accrue (Baldwin *et al.,* 2012; Leinyuy, 2013).

(i)   Should network industries be regulated as public monopolies or regulated private monopolies?

(ii)   Should the network monopolist be allowed to be one of the users?

(iii)   Should there be structural separation of monopoly components from competitive components?

(iv)   Where should behavioural remedies be applied or Competition Law?

(v)   Where should *ex-ante* sector specific regulation be applied?

(vi)   What price should competitors pay to have access to network controlled by a dominant firm?

(vii)   What are the non-discrimination requirements on a vertically integrated dominant firm?

These are some of the challenging questions that different countries have to confront with the regulation of network industries. The OECD as far back as 2001 provided an excellent and still relevant general recommendation to Governments of OECD Member States thus:

"When faced with a situation in which a regulated firm is or may in the future be operating simultaneously in a non-competitive activity and a potentially competitive complementary activity, Member countries should carefully balance the benefits and costs of *structural* measures against the benefits and costs of *behavioural* measures. The benefits and costs to be balanced include the *effects on competition, effects on the quality* and *cost of regulation, the transition costs of structural modifications* and *the economic and public benefits of vertical integration, based on the economic characteristics of the industry in the country under review.* The benefits and costs to be balanced should be those recognised by the relevant agency(ies) including the competition authority, based on principles defined by the member country. This balancing should occur especially in the context of *privatisation, liberalisation or regulatory reform*"[135], p.94 and 95 - *the author's emphases.*

There are major challenges in achieving such balance with any and every sector. The OECD recommendation above is also a long-winded but particularly important way of stipulating that regulating network industries in two countries or two sectors of the same country can never be identical.

However, it is unarguable that the starting position [theory and hypothesis] is that most *network infrastructures* [e.g., electricity, telecoms, water, sewage, gas, postal services, cable TV, etc. – see last section] are natural monopolies, and therefore subject to regulation, whilst the *services* are subject to competition. Next, we explore more details on addressing such economic regulation challenges across several sectors. Some of these afore-posed questions are addressed in the narratives of the sectors that follow in the next several sections.

Recall from Section 2.4 (Chapter 2) that the theories and hypotheses of regulation truly matter in practice because they are essential for understanding, analysing, and improving regulatory approaches and systems within the sectors. These characteristics of network industries spelt out in this section all speak to the potential (and likely) market and regulatory failures that would ensue in the following network industries – absent *ex-ante* regulation interventions to mitigate them. The theories and hypotheses of regulation of Chapter 2 (e.g., market failure theory, public

---

[135] http://www.oecd.org/regreform/sectors/19635977.pdf

interest theory, regulatory capture theory, etc.) all help to predict what would happen with these following network industries, and therefore guide the regulatory designs across the sectors overviewed next.

3.4.3 The Ordering of the Network Industries discussed next

The next sections in this chapter detail the regulation vs. competition dynamic in a range of network industries: electricity, gas, water, post, telecoms, rail, and aviation – in this order. The order is *not* completely random. I had the choice to discussing them in an order guided by several competing criteria, e.g., smaller to greater unbundling, the extent of 'success' of this regulation vs. competition dynamic across these sectors, the extent of my knowledge and expertise across these sectors, or the importance of these sectors to developing countries *as of 2024*. The reality is I chose the last, i.e., the importance of Good economic regulation to these sectors in developing economies across Asia, Latin America, the Caribbean and Africa as of 2024. So, the order reflects my view of the order of priority of *initiating* and/or *reinvigorating* Good economic regulation efforts across these network sectors across many developing economies that I have had the honour of working with. So for example, my ordering does *not* mean telecoms regulation (at 5th out of 7) is not arguably more important to developing countries. Rather, it reflects that most of these developing economies are already making relatively decent efforts in their regulation of telecoms vis-à-vis electricity, gas, water & waste water and post. I further confess that the telecoms sub-section is much longer than the others reflecting my bias and longevity working in the telecoms, media and technology sectors (e.g. Nwana, 2014, 2022).

3.5 Regulation vs. Competition in the Electricity Industry: a brief overview

Some 850 million people worldwide (600 million of them in Africa) as of 2023 still do not have access to electricity. The makes regulating the electricity sector across countries across the globe critical. Figure 3.6 earlier shows a graph depiction of Electricity Industry with Nodes A, B, C and D representing Generation Agent, High-Voltage Transmission & Low-Voltage Regional Distribution Agent, Retailing Activities Agent and Multiple Retail Addresses respectively (as Table 3.1 elaborates).

Electricity Industry 'Unbundled' Component	Scope for Competition
Generation	Good
High-Voltage Transmission	Low to Nil
Low-Voltage Regional Distribution	Low to Nil
Retailing	Good

Table 3.5 – Scope for Competition in the Electricity Industry

This industry exhibits all/most of the attributes (and risks) of a network industry with significant potential market failures absent regulation. The scope for competition in the across the key nodes of the electricity industry is summarised in Table 3.5.

Drawing from the previous section's [Section 3.4] excursive narrative of how unbundling generally occurs in order to increase more consumer welfare within network industries, Table 3.5 depicts how the electricity network industry is typically unbundled *in practice*. It shows the components of (i) electricity generation, (ii) high-voltage transmission, (iii) low-voltage regional distribution through Regional Electricity Companies (RECs) and (iv) retailing to households. As shown in Table 3.5, there is typically truly little room for competition with high voltage transmission across the country which would typically remain monopoly segments to be regulated, whilst the generation and retailing components can be liberalised and opened up for new entrants (and therefore competition). Depending on the size and population of the country, it would in most cases only make sense to have one high-voltage transmission company across the country – and possibly too, only one regional distribution firm. However, for bigger countries, it may make sense to have several to many RECs, which are effective monopolies in their respective regions. This is why Table 3.5 still suggests that the scope for competition with regional distribution is low to Nil.

However, it is also worth distinguishing between *existing* infrastructure and *new build* to extend the transmission and/or distribution network. There is potential scope for competition in new build in the form of competition *for the market* - instead of competition *in the market* - such as bidding for a (regulated) licence or franchise for the new build. For instance, bidding could be in the form of the lowest prices to be charged, the so-called Demsetz franchises[136] (Demsetz, 1968). Competition for new build is also relevant to other network industries such as water and wastewater management discussed later.

These all lead to the following Baldwin *et al.* (2012, p. 464)-proposed strategy and model to the economic regulation and liberalisation of the typical electricity network industry, namely:

i.   Commence with the privatisation of the state-owned electricity monopolies;

ii.   Vertical separation – via unbundling – of potentially competitive components as distinct from the persistently monopolistic components (as shown in Table 3.5);

iii. Ensuring non-discriminatory access by retailers to monopolistically, regulated high voltage transmission and regional low voltage distribution components and assets. This is done through access regulation. Transmission and distribution networks are generally subject to price, access and other regulatory controls, typically price caps, rate of return regulation and *regulation of rate structures*[137].

iv.   Restructuring of electricity generation in order to permit competition;

v.   Creation of an independent systems operator in order to manage the transmission network, to schedule generation capacity to meet demand, and to guide transmission infrastructure investments;

vi.   The creation of a wholesale spot electricity markets and exchanges to efficiently balance real-time supply and demand;

vii. Promote and encourage retail new entry and competition where possible, as well as promoting general retail competition and

---

[136] Prof. Harold Demsetz proposed in 1968 that franchise bidding is an alternative and lower cost approach to regulation. He argued that auctioning the rights to a natural monopoly would lead to a similar outcome as regulation, but much cheaper. Franchise bidding has been used in practice often, e.g. in the water sector in France.

[137] As Decker (2023, p. 291) clarifies, price caps and rate of return regulation dictate the overall *level* of allowed revenues that regulated transmission and distribution firms can recoup, there still remains the separate issue of how these revenues are recovered across different customers of their networks. Therefore, the *structure* of high voltage transmission and low voltage distribution network charges are also determined via regulation to address the distributional and efficiency aspects.

consumer protection, where required including with retail price controls.

There are no doubt major challenges in realising this broad model to restructuring an electricity market for much better consumer welfare, but such reforms as above have yielded untold benefits in many countries. For example, introducing regulated upstream wholesale electricity generation markets (see Table 1.1 in Chapter 1) has resulted – in some countries – in major reconfigurations of generation capacity in these countries away from coal and gas towards cleaner forms of energy such as solar sources, hydropower, tidal power, wind power, biomass, geothermal energy and nuclear power. 'Dirty' coal and natural gas were still as of 2019 the dominant inputs to electricity generation at circa 36.7% and 23.5% of all production respectively (Decker, 2023, p. 270/271). This has had the added benefit of decarbonizing the electricity industry too[138].

3.6 Regulation vs. Competition in the Gas Industry: a brief overview

The gas industry exhibits all/most of the attributes (and risks) of a network industry with significant potential market failures absent regulation. Figure 3.6 earlier shows a graph depiction of Gas Industry with Nodes A, B, C and D representing Extraction Agent, National and Distribution Agent, Retailing Activities Agent and Multiple Retail Customers [139] respectively (as Table 3.1 elaborates).

The scope for competition in the across the key nodes of the gas industry is summarised in Table 3.6.

Much of the previous section's narrative discussion on electricity and proposed strategy and model to the economic regulation and liberalisation applies to the gas industry too – and hence is mostly not repeated here.

---

[138] Electricity production till date is a large emitter of greenhouse gasses such as carbon dioxide, sulphur dioxide and nitrogen oxides.

[139] Residential customers, commercial customers, industrial customers and wholesalers.

Gas Industry 'Unbundled' Component	Scope for Competition
Extraction/Production	Good
National Distribution – via High-Pressure National gas pipelines	Low to Nil
Regional Lower-pressure Distribution	Low to Nil
Retailing	Good

Table 3.6 – Scope for Competition in the Gas Industry

Suffice to summarise that the high pressure national and lower-pressure regional distribution components of the unbundling have close to zero chance for introducing competition, and hence should be subject to similar regulations as for the equivalents in the electricity market of the previous section. These components are naturally monopolistic, and hence subject to active price controls via price caps, rate of return regulation, regulation of rate structures and other regulations such as quality of service (QoS) ones. Similarly, to electricity regulation, there are typically two principal competitive components of the gas supply chain as depicted in Table 3.6 namely, the extraction/production and sale of wholesale gas – and the retail sale of gas to end customers. In some jurisdictions, there is vibrant competition amongst extractors/producers, particularly with the discovery and exploitation of more oil or gas fields, or even coal fields since both coal-to-gas and oil-to-gas conversions are feasible. As for the retailing component, some jurisdictions use retail price regulation.

The core and real difference between gas and electricity is that gas is very *storable*. It is storable underground in salt caverns, hard rock caverns, mines, aquifers, depleted oil and gas fields, and even above-ground storage in LNG tanks (Decker, 2023, p. 326). Almost all gas storage facilities/gas fields and processing plants are located far away from urban areas in remote and uninhabited areas and transmitted via high-pressure transmission pipelines. It is also capable of being transported longer distances across national borders and even by sea as LNG. In fact, the storability attribute of gas raises issues not found with electricity, such as the opportunity cost of gas over time. This is because it can be stored today and sold tomorrow at a different price from today's, hence price regulation is also applied to gas storage facility operators in many jurisdictions.

Storage also leads to potentially quite complex trading arrangements for wholesale gas, with wholesale gas spot markets and training hubs.

Natural gas is finite and non-renewable, and therefore it is no surprise that gas prices have displayed a sustained increase over the last two decades driven by, *inter alia,* the evolution of oil prices whilst electricity prices have increased at a slower pace. The largest reserves of natural gas are found in countries/regions like Russia in the lead, the Middle East (Qatar, Iran, Saudi Arabia) and Africa (Nigeria and Algeria). As noted earlier coal and gas are the two biggest inputs for electricity generation. However, it is indeed true that there has recently been discoveries of 'non-conventional gas', i.e., gas trapped between layers of sedimentary shale rocks called *shale gas* – gas trapped in limestone called *tight gas*. The extraction of these gases is called *fracking*, and this process is currently banned in some European countries like Germany, France and Spain – and very controversial in other countries like the UK.

Indeed, gas and electricity are largely *interdependent*, as gas is often used as an input in the production of electricity. The reader can see why – with the similarities across the network graph value chain for both electricity and gas along with this interdependency between the two. As Decker (2023, p.319) surmises

> "The natural gas and electricity industries are often seen as being sufficiently closely related in terms of supply and demand characteristics that regulatory issues can be treated in a similar way. On the supply, both forms of energy typically require transportation along a high pressure (or high voltage) transmission network and lower-pressure (or lower-voltage) distribution network before reaching end customers… On the demand side, the two forms of energy are potentially substitutable for certain types of uses … Finally, it is not uncommon for energy firms to operate in both industries… for retailers to supply both gas and electricity 'dual-fuel' offers to consumers".

Therefore, it makes sense to have the same statutory economic regulator for both utilities, as is the case with Office for Gas and Electricity Markets (Ofgem[140]) in the UK. Most jurisdictions have a single energy regulator.

---

[140] https://www.ofgem.gov.uk/

3.7 Regulation vs. Competition in the Water & Wastewater Industry: a brief overview

The United Nations recognises access to clean, safe and affordable water – as well as to safe-managed sanitation services – as basic human rights.

> "On 28 July 2010, the United Nations General Assembly adopted a historical resolution recognizing "the right to safe and clean drinking water and sanitation as a human right that is essential for the full enjoyment of life and all human rights" (A/RES/64/292). Furthermore, since 2015, the General Assembly and the Human Rights Council have recognized both the right to safe drinking water and the right to sanitation as closely related but distinct human rights" – Source: [141].

The above should be Government policy in all jurisdictions. So, why do billions of people worldwide *not* have these basic human rights? Could the absence and/or failure of good economic regulation of the water and wastewater industry be at the core for the billions without these basic rights?

3.7.1 A brief case for more economic regulation of the Water and Wastewater industry

The brief case here is hardly mine, but the WHO's (World Health Organisation) as the reader is just about to find out. Water and Wastewater regulation are truly crucial to modern economies, but sadly in many jurisdictions in the world – particularly in developing economies – they tend to be managed by Governments or not at all. For example, where water operators are Government-owned and operated, water management and pricing tend to be managed administratively. As for wastewater management, many developing economies (e.g., in Africa, the Caribbean or South East Asia) hardly manage wastewater at all.

---

[141] https://www.ohchr.org/en/water-and-sanitation/about-water-and-sanitation - About water and sanitation | OHCHR

The outcomes are dire as evidenced by the following key facts about Drinking Water and Sanitation from the World Health Organisation (WHO, 2022a, 2022b). Citing directly and extensively[142] from the WHO:

- *"Over 2 billion people live* in water-stressed countries, which is expected to be exacerbated in some regions as result of climate change and population growth.
- Globally, *at least 2 billion people use a drinking water source contaminated with faeces.* Microbial contamination of drinking-water as a result of contamination with faeces poses the greatest risk to drinking-water safety.
- While the most important chemical risks in drinking water arise from arsenic, fluoride or nitrate, emerging contaminants such as pharmaceuticals, pesticides, per- and polyfluoroalkyl substances (PFASs) and microplastics generate public concern.
- Safe and sufficient water facilitates the practice of hygiene, which is a key measure to prevent not only diarrhoeal diseases, but acute respiratory infections and numerous neglected tropical diseases.
- Microbiologically contaminated drinking water can transmit diseases such as diarrhoea, cholera, dysentery, typhoid and polio *and is estimated to cause 485 000 diarrhoeal deaths each year.*
- In 2020, *74% of the global population (5.8 billion people) used a safely managed drinking-water service* – that is, one located on premises, available when needed, and free from contamination" - *the author's emphases*, Source: [143].

As regards sanitation, the WHO (2022b) states (Source: [144]):

- *"In 2020, 54% of the global population (4.2 billion people) used a safely managed sanitation service.*
- *Over 1.7 billion people still do not have basic sanitation services, such as private toilets or latrines.*

---

[142] The author believes it is key for policy makers and regulators in developing economies in particular to read these facts for themselves, and hopefully act urgently on water and wastewater management.

[143] https://www.who.int/news-room/fact-sheets/detail/drinking-water - Drinking-water (who.int)

[144] https://www.who.int/news-room/fact-sheets/detail/sanitation

- Of these, *494 million still defecate in the open, for example in street gutters, behind bushes or into open bodies of water.*
- In 2020, *45% of the household wastewater generated globally was discharged without safe treatment.*
- At least 10% of the world's population is thought to consume food irrigated by wastewater.
- *Poor sanitation reduces human well-being, social and economic development* due to impacts such as anxiety, risk of sexual assault, and lost opportunities for education and work.
- *Poor sanitation is linked to transmission of diarrhoeal diseases such as cholera and dysentery, as well as typhoid, intestinal worm infections and polio.* It exacerbates stunting and contributes to the spread of antimicrobial resistance" *the author's emphases.*

No prizes for guessing the regions of the world where the remaining 26% of the global population without access to "safely managed drinking-water services" – or where the remaining 46% of the global population (4.2 billion people) who do not use "a safely managed sanitation service" - live[145]. Most developing countries do not even have significant wastewater management sub-sectors. Water which people can drink is called *potable* water, as opposed to *non-potable* water that can be used for agricultural and industrial purposes.

To me, these WHO facts speak to more and better economic regulation of the water and wastewater sector, and not more Government or state administrative management – particularly in the countries and regions where these billions - whose rights are being traduced – live. How can water and wastewater services not be better controlled – or regulated – when it affects peoples' basic health and welfare? The reader may be surprised – as I was – that according to UN-Water (2019)[146], the top three demand users for water globally are agriculture (69%), industry including power generation (19%) and households (12%).

State ownership and operation of this sector persists and remain prevalent in most markets partly on the grounds that competition would create great

---

[145] Clue – they are mentioned earlier in this section.

[146] https://unesdoc.unesco.org/ark:/48223/pf0000367276 - The United Nations world water development report 2019: leaving no one behind, facts and figures - UNESCO Digital Library

risks and be bad for the industry – and that the water and waste water sector is the natural monopoly "par excellence" (Littlechild, 1988). The WHO facts presented in this section suggest – at the very least – that the market failures in this sector are not only life-threatening but also perennial and long lasting. This natural monopoly "par excellence" doctrine which seems to have been adopted by many jurisdictions clearly is not working for billions of people living in thousands of locations/regions across the globe. This further suggests that the extremely high levels of vertical integration around the world coupled with them being State-owned monopolies must be scrutinised, particularly in countries experiencing market failures in the water and wastewater industry.

3.7.2 Towards more economic regulation of the Water and Wastewater industry

The water industry exhibits all/most of the attributes (and risks) of a network industry with significant potential market failures absent regulation. Figure 3.9 [network graph] earlier shows a graph depiction of Water & Wastewater Industry with Nodes A, B, C … G representing Water Abstraction Agent, Water Storage & Treatment Agent, National and Distribution Water Agent, Water Retailing Activities Agent, Wastewater Collection/Transportation Activities Agent, Wastewater Treating Activities agent and Waste Disposal Activities agent, respectively (as Table 3.4 elaborates).

The scope for competition in the across the key nodes of the Water and Wastewater industry is summarised in Table 3.7.

Water & Sewage Industry 'Unbundled' Component	Scope for Competition
Water Abstraction	Good
Water Storage & Treatment	Moderate
Water Distribution via national & reticulation[147] piping	Low to Nil

---

[147] Reticulation is the process of installing a network of underground or overhead pipes, typically for the purpose of supplying water or other fluids to a specific area.

Water Retailing	Good
Wastewater Collection & Transportation	Moderate
Wastewater Distribution national & reticulation piping	Low to Nil
Wastewater Treatment	Moderate
Waste Disposal Activities agent	Good

Table 3.7 – Scope for Competition in the Water & Wastewater Industry

Once again, the reader is referred to the narrative 'methodology' discussion on electricity of Section 3.5 which explains where and how competition and regulation is proposed. For the water and wastewater 'unbundled' industry as shown in Table 3.7, following are some more particular details:

- **Water Abstraction**: Water abstraction/extraction typically comes from two sources: from aquifers[148] or from surface water (drawn from reservoirs, rivers and lakes. To abstract from aquifers involves drilling wells into the aquifers and pumping the water out. The scope for competition with water abstraction component is Good because this stage does not have the attributes of a natural monopoly. Water abstraction (or water extraction) is the process of taking water from any source, either temporarily or permanently. Clearly multiple rival firms can be involved in this process from one or multiple sources or there could be competing reservoirs. As with other network utility industries, one way of introducing competition into this abstraction component which has limited prospects of direct infrastructure competition is to allow for *common carriage*. This involves third-party access to the downstream distribution network, and this has been implemented in some jurisdictions in the UK, USA and Australia. However, there are some justifiable concerns about competition in this component that may encourage exploitation of water resources beyond sustainable ecological and environmental levels. There

---

[148] These are underground permeable rocks bearing water.

could also be quality (QoS of the water) issues with multiple competing abstraction providers.

- **Water Storage & Treatment**: Most raw sources of "natural' water abstracted or extracted, even from aquifers, are still contaminated with different compounds and organisms like such as bacteria, viruses and other pollutants. This is the core reason even such abstracted water is treated. To make the water potable, abstracted water needs to be treated, in some cases with disinfectants like chlorine added to the water to kill the bacteria. The scope for competition with water storage and treatment component is Moderate. This is because – even though this component does not have all of the typical attributes of a natural monopoly - the sunk costs here would be much higher than for water abstraction, and Governments would need to licence and vet the set-up of such storage and treatment plants. It would also make sense not to encourage too many entrants into this component market because ineffective competition may accrue. However, some competition in this component would help drive more innovation in treatment methods - potentially leading to potable recycled water as output, instead of effluents that are discharged into rivers or lakes.

- **Water Distribution via national & reticulation piping**: the scope of competition for this component is Low-to-Nil because this component has all the natural attributes of a natural monopoly – thanks to the operation of a vast network of reticulation pipes. This is also partly because, in most of the world, the water sector is generally exempt from unbundling since they largely consists of vertically-integrated monopoly firms controlled by local or State Governments. This said, Australia has implemented unbundling in this component by legally requiring access regulation and pricing controls [on common carriage fees] to realise the unbundling of these pipes by other access seeking competitors. Competition is also low with this component to a large part because this component is expensive business too. In fact, water treatment and distribution accounts to 41% of the total expenditure across the value chain in England and Wales (Decker, 2023, p. 594). These costs are transferred to water customers. In contrast to the transportation of gas and electricity, water is incredibly heavy and hence extremely expensive to transport long distances, and the leakage losses or dealing with broken pipes are very costly. Indeed, Decker notes that two-thirds of the costs associated with the supply of water can be attributed to water distribution (Decker, 2023, p. 598).

- **Water Retailing***:* the scope of competition for this component is Good as this is the final stage of the water supply process to customers' premises. In many jurisdictions, customers pay on a pay-as-you-use basis, but some countries just charge a fixed charge that reflects the value of their properties. Either way, at the retail level, *quality of service* regulation and *price controls* make much sense for this water retailing component from an economic regulation perspective. As regards price controls, most jurisdictions would implement one or both of the two main forms namely, *rate of return regulation* and *price & revenue* caps. Price caps could be set by the RPI-X approach (i.e., retail price index – X). As Decker (2023, p. 291) clarifies, price caps and rate of return regulation dictate the overall level of allowed revenues that regulated water firms can recover. There still remains the separate issue of how these revenues are recovered across different customers of their networks. Where the water operators are State-owned, tariffs for water retailing are set administratively. Regulation of quality (QoS) is obviously critical for a commodity like water, not only for the water product quality itself but also for reducing water losses, control leakages, minimising water interruptions, wastewater quality, sludge disposal, etc. These latter can be measured via performance targets.

- **Wastewater Collection and Transportation of Wastewater***:* the scope of competition for this component is Moderate, largely due to the challenges of transportation. For wastewater collection by its own, the scope for competition is Good. There is little significant wastewater collection activities in many emerging market jurisdictions even though the demand for wastewater services tends to be correlated with the demand for water – as should be the case for modern living. Wastewater (from bathrooms, kitchens, businesses, trade effluents, etc.) is collected in wastewater or *sewerage*[149] systems, and transported through a

---

[149] Sewerage systems refer to the infrastructure which transports sewage via drains, manholes, sanitary/household sewers and storm overflows.

series of pipelines to a treatment plant, or in some cases, to discharge points. Many of the points earlier about water distribution also applied to wastewater distribution, with all the massive sunk costs for the immovable and difficult-to-replicate sewerage infrastructure.

- **Wastewater Treatment:** the scope of competition for this component is Moderate. The treatment involves removals of any solids, or sludge, from the wastewater to levels sufficient for it to be discharged back into the environment. The costs here typically depend to on the relevant standards enforced in the said jurisdiction.

- **Waste Disposal**: the scope of competition for this component is Good. This is the last stage which involves the disposal of the sludge. In some cases, the *sludge* is incinerated, processed further and sold as fertilisers for agricultural businesses or deposited at landfill sites. More recently, sludge is increasingly being used as a source of fuel for biogas in the production of electricity. The residual effluent of this waste disposal process is released into rivers, lakes or into the sea.

As I note above in the context of the electricity industry, competition for new build is also relevant to water and wastewater management. I distinguish between *existing* water & wastewater management infrastructure and i to extend the current networks. So, there is also potential scope for competition in new build in the form of competition for the water and wastewater market - instead of competition *in the current market* - such as bidding for a regulated licence [or a Demsetz (1968) franchise] for the new build, as has happened in France (Meister, 2006).

Overall, it is evident that regulation applies to all activities in the water and wastewater value chain in two ways: firstly, either via State or Government ownership or some form of economic regulation to introduce competition – or second, through some form of control of retail prices and, definitely, via necessary quality of service (QoS) regulation. This noted, most jurisdictions do not have economic regulators for water like the UK does with Ofwat[150]; rather, the regulation of water may be conducted by environmental protection agencies.

3.7.3 Economies of Scale and Scope in Water and Wastewater Industry

The economies of scale and scope in the water and wastewater management process is not as pronounced as in other sectors like gas and electricity. This is partly because this sector can be very fragmented, e.g., Decker (2023, p.599/600) notes that the USA has circa 155,000 public water systems across the country, whilst many European counties[151] have circa 1000 each. This is different wherein the UK's four constituent countries[152] have a combined 13 water and wastewater operators, 9 water-only companies and 6 local water companies between them. It is clear from these findings that that economies of scale and economies of scope arguments may apply to some of the UK operators, and less so with many of the fragmented water sector firms of the USA and European countries.

3.8 Regulation vs. Competition in the Postal Industry: a brief overview

Figure 3.8 earlier shows a graph depiction of the Postal Industry with Nodes A, B, C, D and E , as Table 3.3 elaborates:

- A - Household/Businesses [e.g., Parcels] *Collection* Activities and Delivering letters to centres, e.g., Post Offices agent;
- B - Sorting Activities;
- C - National Trunking Activities;
- D - Regional Trunking Activities; and
- E - Retail Delivery Activities.

---

[150] https://www.ofwat.gov.uk/

[151] Decker cites Austria, the Czech Republic, Denmark, Finland, France, Germany, Greece, Norway, Romania, Spain and Switzerland.

[152] England, Scotland, Wales & Northern Ireland

Postal Industry 'Unbundled' Component	Scope for Competition
Collection	Good
Sorting	Good
National Trunking	Moderate
Regional Trunking	Good
Retail Delivery	Limited-to-Low

Table 3.8 – Scope for Competition in the Postal Industry

The scope for competition in the across the key nodes of the postal industry is summarised in Table 3.8.

The postal industry has been seen as a 'backwater' sector for decades now – but it may be staging a surprising reawakening, thanks to the revolution of e-Commerce and the Digital Economy. There are a couple contrasting attributes about the postal sector worth highlighting across both developed and developing markets. Firstly, in developed countries, mail volumes had been under significant threat due to electronic communications such as email and the many other myriad forms of digital communications. In developing countries, mail volumes never ever made the postal industry a viable industry in the first place, hence the industry's costs in these markets were heavily subsidised by States or Governments. Secondly, in developed markets, *universal service obligations* (USO) were – and still are – fixtures in the sector, imposed upon the monopoly postal providers. Postal USOs enshrine the delivery of any letter from any collection point to any delivery address in a country at a uniform (or standardised) price called the *postalised* prize. Postal USOs were/are just about viable in developed countries, but their imposition on developing countries' sub-scale postal monopolies just rendered them ever less viable businesses. This is because they never had the mail volumes in the first place that were quickly eaten away with digital communications. So, the regulated postal USO has always complicated the introduction of competition into the postal sector.

However, e-Commerce and the evolving Digital Economy are arguably providing an opportunity to reform the postal sectors in both the developing and developed economies. For the 'unbundled' postal industry as shown in Table 3.8, the following are some more particular details on how the postal industry may be liberalised for more competition.

In the European Union, successive postal directives[153] have opened up progressively increased categories of mail to competition. All EU states were required to liberalise their postal markets by end of 2010. The UK was one of the-then leading EU countries to unbundle their postal market and permit competitors to access the retail delivery of former monopoly, the Royal Mail. The EU postal directives stipulate standards for all member states to comply with, including:

- USO: All EU citizens have the right to universal postal service, and to permanent postal service of specified quality at all points of territory at affordable prices for all;

- Products: Postal items of up to 2kg in weight; packets to 10kg; and registered & insured items;

- Access: density of access points (e.g., post boxes) to take into account citizens' needs; Minimum of one collection per working day from each access point; Minimum of one delivery per address per working day (at least 5 days per week);

- Pricing: affordable for all users; prices to be geared to costs; EU States to decide whether uniform tariffs should apply; Providers from USA may conclude individual agreements on prices with customers;

- Quality: EU States to ensure quality of service (QoS) standards that are set for USO; quality standards to be set by National Regulation Authority (NRA); independent performance monitoring at least annually by external body

- All EU member states to liberalise the postal market (by end of 2010).

The stipulations of the EU directives above are clearly meant for developed markets like EU countries with the mail volumes that can sustain such a model. The UK has since left the EU, but Ofcom regulates former monopolist Royal Mail to make a profit of at least 5% - 10% to support the funding of the USO. Royal Mail is required by NRA regulator Ofcom to be *efficient* rather than using price increases to meet its financial targets.

---

[153] 1997/67/EC, 2002/39/EC and 2008/06/EC European Postal Directives - https://single-market-economy.ec.europa.eu/sectors/postal-services/legislation-implementation-and-enforcement_en

Implementing a similar set of mandates in developing countries in South East Asia or Africa would *not* be possible – however, the principles behind each of these standards would apply to developing countries too.

The unbundling of the postal sector can happen as follows.

Postal Collection: the scope for competition with this 'unbundled' postal industry component is Good, subject to sufficient '*headroom*' in the postalised price. Key is the *access price* to the natural monopoly-like Retail Delivery component where competition is Limited-to-Low. Therefore, the postal regulator would set such access prices in a cost-based manner, but in such a way that leaves a specified gap between the standard price of a stamp and the delivery charge. If the gap – or headroom – is big enough, competitors would likely enter into this Postal Collection component, and perhaps even other components like sorting, trunking and retailing. This has been the approach[154] implemented in the UK by postal regulator Ofcom, and its predecessor Postcomm.

Sorting: the scope for competition with this 'unbundled' postal industry component is Good. This is because this component clearly does not have much of all the natural attributes of a natural monopoly.

National & Regional Trunking: the scope for competition with these 'unbundled' postal industry components is Good too. Trunking refers to the transport of post between sorting offices (main or smaller ones), and clearly this is not a natural monopoly-type activity.

Delivery of Letters: the scope for competition in this component is limited if there is already a [former] monopolist firm with economies of scale, and with all the network infrastructure of sorting offices, trunking and the most expensive delivery from local delivery offices. The monopolist would have a network of hundreds (if not thousands) of not-easy-to-replicate postal delivery workers. This is why the *price of access* to this local delivery service of a former or current monopolist is key to opening up the postal sector to competition.

---

[154] Consultation (ofcom.org.uk) - https://www.ofcom.org.uk/__data/assets/pdf_file/0033/97863/Review-of-the-Regulation-of-Royal-Mail.pdf

3.8.1 Postal regulation in developing countries

Though many countries around the world have implemented USOs to ensure that postal services are accessible to all their citizens, regardless of their location or socioeconomic status, it must be noted that not all countries have a defined USO, e.g. Liberia, Niger, Mali or Cameroon – all in Africa. This is partly because home delivery is <u>not</u> a normal standard in many countries, e.g. in the Middle East, the Caribbean, South East Asia or in Africa. For this reason, standards can and must be variable – and not as strict as the standards stipulated by the EU postal directives above. In such markets, delivery is more efficient via PO boxes or to post offices. The USO in such markets is sometimes [or mostly] seen as a burden because of the lack of any significant postal network infrastructure with sufficient economies of scale and scope.

3.8.2 e-Commerce and the Digital Economy promises to upend the Postal Sector

E-commerce and the digital economy promise to provide growing opportunities for postal firms, and hence the postal industry. Consider the following predictions:

- According to Statista[155] - even in mostly developing Africa - revenue in the eCommerce market was projected to reach US$36.15bn in 2023. Revenue is expected to show an annual growth rate (CAGR 2023-2027) of 13.11%, resulting in a projected market volume of US$59.18bn by 2027.
- DHL Express predicted cross-border retail to grow at 25 percent rate between 2015 and 2020[156].

---

[155] e https://www.statista.com/outlook/emo/ecommerce/worldwide?currency=usd - Commerce - Africa | Statista Market Forecast

[156] https://thepaypers.com/ecommerce/dhl-express-predicts-cross-border-retail-to-grow-at-25-percent-rate-between-2015-and-2020--767855 - DHL Express predicts cross-border retail to grow at 25 percent rate between 2015 and 2020 - ThePaypers

However, there are major challenges leading to significant barriers to postal sector growth, particularly in emerging markets, e.g.

- Lack of digital infrastructure
- High internet costs
- Key Infrastructure deficits (e.g. roads and electricity)
- Lack of digital economy platforms, see Nwana (2022) including widespread payment and Identity (ID) verification platforms
- Unreliable postal services.

3.8.3 Summary on Postal Regulation

Postal regulations clearly vary from jurisdiction to jurisdiction, as each country has its own regulator or regulatory body responsible for and governing postal services. Regulations are typically designed to ensure the smooth functioning of postal services, to promote fair competition in unbundled components where possible (see Table 3.8), to protect the interests of consumers and businesses (e.g. though price and quality regulation), and to maintain the integrity and security of the mails and parcels. e-Commerce and the Digital Economy promises to upend the postal sector, but major challenges remain in developing countries.

As mostly covered above, the key regulations in the postal sector include:

Universal Service Obligations (USO*):* Many countries have such regulations . Whether they are functional and working in most developing countries is rather moot.

Postal Service Standards*:* Most postal regulator define and implement service standards. As seen with the postal EU directives, EU postal NRAs have to implement regulations in order to establish service standards for delivery mail/parcels times, their tracking, and other aspects of postal services.

International Mail/Parcel Regulations: In an era of growing cross-border e-ecommerce, some regulations pertain to international mail and parcels, including customs procedures, import/export constraints, and cross-border goods handling requirements. This leads to Government setting tariffs on certain international mails/parcels.

Pricing and Tariffs[157]: as covered earlier, postal regulations could allow for costs-geared pricing 'headroom' to both encourage new entry competition, as well as dictate how postal firms set their prices/tariffs for various postal services. Price and tariffs regulation through price caps and/or rate of return regulations typically apply. Recall, Royal Mail in the UK can only make a profit of circa 5% - 10% (this does not mean a profit cap) to support the funding of the USO, although Royal Mail is still required by NRA regulator Ofcom to be *efficient* - rather than using price increases to meet its financial targets. Government would typically apply tariffs on some products or goods that, for example, are being posted in and out of the country.

Postal Network Access: as seen earlier, access to the local delivery of post is key. Access regulations would allow access of third-party operators to the postal network of the [former] monopoly postal provider, enabling competition in some of the components as shown in Table 3.8.

Competition: the regulation vs. competition dynamic in the postal industry is quite different than for the prior network industries, like electricity, gas and water – which have proven themselves in most countries to be more viable sectors that the postal sector. Table 3.8 shows one view of the likelihood of introducing competition into an unbundled postal sector.

Licensing & Authorization: All postal operators may need to obtain licenses or authorizations from their NRAs in order to operate postal services.

Consumer Protection & Dispute Resolution: Regulations address such issues as complaints managing complaints, disputes, returns, late delivery

---

[157] A price is the amount of money that someone is willing to pay in exchange for a good or service. It represents the value assigned to a product or service in terms of money. A tariff, on the other hand, is a tax or duty imposed by a Government on goods that are imported into or exported out of a country. Tariffs are typically used to protect domestic industries by making imported goods more expensive compared to domestically produced goods. Tariffs are *de facto* taxes.

or lost mail. Regulations may outline processes for resolving disputes between postal firms themselves, customers and other third-party stakeholders.

Security, Privacy and Data Protection: Parcels and mail often contain sensitive information like bank statements, and therefore some postal regulations could include mandates concerning data protection and privacy. Regulations may also pertain to security measures in order to prevent the misuse of postal services for illegal activities.

Finally, a reviewer of this book insightfully pointed out that a different approach could be productive with postal regulation by distinguishing more strongly between *parcels* and *letters*. This is because he rightly highlights the existence of more scope for competition for parcels than for letters. This is certainly the case in developed countries and he argues it would presumably be even more so in developing countries. Recent regulatory developments emphasise this distinction, e.g., Ofcom in the UK which has recently decided that the new price control from April 2024 will cover *only* non-priority ('second class') standard and large letters, excluding all parcels for the first time[158]. I think this is an important trend to highlight in postal regulation.

3.9 Regulation vs. Competition in the Telecoms Industry: a brief overview

The telecommunications industry is a network industry *par excellence.* Unlike the other network industries covered above which largely comprise homogenous networks, the telecoms industry today comprises networks of other heterogenous networks. Therefore, in the telecoms industry today, we see both *intra-modal* competition (i.e., competition amongst operators using the same technology networks such as fixed networks) and *inter-modal* competition (i.e., competition amongst operators using different networks, such as mobile vs. cable vs. fixed vs. satellite networks, etc.).

---

[158] See Ofcom (2024) 'Review of Second Class safeguard caps 2024: Decision on safeguard price caps for Second Class universal services', Statement, 24 January, available at https://www.ofcom.org.uk/consultations-and-statements/category-1/consultation-review-of-second-class-safeguard-caps-2024

The telecoms industry has since been radically transformed over the past three decades particularly with the entry of the Big Tech OTT players [i.e., FANGAM[159], FAAAM[160] or FAANG[161]] with their myriad of OTT services that has defined the Internet Value Chian (IVC) – see Nwana (2022). The entrance of the Big Tech players into the telecommunication industry – thanks to the IVC – has transformed an industry whose business [before the birth of the first iPhone in 2007] was all about transporting voice/PSTN signals into one based today on the transmission of IP-based OTT data traffic (gaming, video streaming, video calls, google searches, etc).

3.9.1 Is telecoms regulation trending towards competition from regulation?

Prima facie, the telecoms industry as a network industry par excellence should – in theory at least - enjoy the classic natural monopoly attributes like of economies of scale, economies of scope, network effects and more. This should lead to a sector wherein *ex-ante* regulation should both dominate and persist forever. However, as already alluded above with the concepts of both intra-modal and inter-modal competition in the telecoms sector, the role of regulation in the old pre-2010 (circa) telecoms sector has reduced markedly in developed countries – with more increasing emphasis on competition. Pre-1990s, European telecoms was dominated by former monopoly fixed-line monopolies like British Telecommunication plc (UK), France Telecom (France), Deutsche Telecom (Germany), etc. Then followed telecoms restructuring policies of the 1980s and 1990s including the privatisation of some of these monopolies as well as the liberalisation and lifting off statutory restrictions on market entry. For example, BT (UK) was privatised by the Margaret Thatcher Government in 1984.

---

[159] Facebook [Meta] , Amazon, Netflix, Google, Apple and Microsoft

[160] Facebook [Meta], Amazon, Alphabet, Apple and Microsoft

[161] Facebook [Meta], Amazon, Apple, Netflix and Google

3.9.1.1 A brief narrative on the European telecoms 'from-regulation-to-competition' story

The entire thesis underpinning European (EU) regulation of the telecoms sector for two decades[162] has been one of transitioning the sector from the stages of monopoly to one of *normal* competition governed by generic/horizontal competition law. The EU has essentially for the past twenty years been corralling all their telecoms NRAs to normalise competition in their telecoms sectors (albeit at their own speeds), but constrained by a uniform telecoms framework necessary for the EU's common and internal market. This happened through the following 4 EU-wide legally-binding directives namely, the Directives of the European Parliament and of the Council of 7th March 2002: 2002/21/EC [163]; 2002/20/EC[164]; 2002/19/EC[165]; 2002/22/EC[166]:

- Directive 2002/19/EC - this Directive established rights and obligations for operators and for undertakings seeking interconnection and/or access to their networks or associated facilities or the *Access Directive.*

- Directive 2002/20/EC - this Directive covered *authorisation* of all electronic communications networks and services whether they are provided to the public or not – the *Authorisation Directive.*

- Directive 2002/21/EC - This Directive established a *harmonised framework for the regulation* of electronic communications services, electronic communications networks, associated facilities and associated services – the *Framework Directive.*

---

[162] Since 2003

[163]
https://eurlex.europa.eu/LexUriServ/LexUriServ.do?uri=OJ:L:2002:108:0033:0050:EN:PDF - 130013006en 33..48 (europa.eu)

[164]
https://eurlex.europa.eu/LexUriServ/LexUriServ.do?uri=OJ:L:2002:108:0021:0032:en:PDF - 130013004en 21..30 (europa.eu)

[165]
https://eurlex.europa.eu/LexUriServ/LexUriServ.do?uri=OJ:L:2002:108:0007:0020:EN:PDF- 130013001en 7..17 (europa.eu)

[166] https://www.legislation.gov.uk/eudr/2002/22/2009-12-19 - Directive 2002/22/EC of the European Parliament and of the Council of 7 March 2002 on universal service and users' rights relating to electronic communications networks and services (Universal Service Directive) (repealed) (legislation.gov.uk)

- Directive 2002/22/EC - This Directive established the *rights of end-users* and the corresponding obligations on undertakings providing publicly available electronic communications networks and services – the *Universal Services Directive.*

I list and details these four now-repealed directives because they (and how they were implemented by the EC and EU NRAs) arguably influenced telecoms regulation across the world the most over the last twenty years, i.e., well beyond the shores of the relatively geographically-small EU. They truly helped shape telecoms regulation across the world, across Africa, Asia, the wider Europe (of course) and the Middle East. However, now, it is important to point out that the [relatively] new 2018 European Electronic Communications Code[167] (EECC) was enacted to bring up to date the regulatory framework governing the European telecoms sector facing the new challenges. The new challenges noted include:

(i)   the emergence of Over the Top (OTT) players to challenge the traditional telecommunications market,

(ii)   the increased demand for connectivity globally requiring increases in High-Capacity Networks (HCN), and

(iii)   the development of next generation mobile connectivity (such as 5G and the emerging 6G).

The code represents a near-complete revision of the entire EU telecoms regulatory framework. So, Directive 2018/1972 [168] not only firmly establishes the EECC, but it also repeals and replaces the Framework Directive, the Authorisation Directive, the Access Directive and the Universal Services Directive. It came into force in December 2018 and Member States had two years to implement its rules. The EECC revamps and updates the following core areas:

- The end-user rights enjoyed by consumers and citizens of electronic communications services in the Union

---

[167] https://digital-strategy.ec.europa.eu/en/policies/eu-electronic-communications-code - Directive 2018/1972 - EU Electronic Communications Code | Shaping Europe's digital future (europa.eu)
[168] *Ibid.*

- The Universal Services regime applicable to electronic communications services in the Union
- The rules governing the assignment and use of radio spectrum
- The regime governing access to infrastructure obligations on operators deemed to have Significant Market Power
- The expansion of scope of the regulatory framework to include new market players, e.g. the OTT players.

The EECC is today - in the EU - the pillar and core piece of legislation to achieve Europe's vaunted Gigabit society, and also to ensure full participation of all EU citizens in the digital economy and society.

The European Commission[169] (EC) has increasingly both been claiming and *acting* that the EU telecoms national sectors are truly being normalised towards competition, and away from heavy regulation – thanks to the repealed directives and the new EECC. The evidence for EU actions (based on claimed normalisation towards competition) follows in the next several sentences.

Back in 2002, the EC prepared a list of regulatory relevant markets [for telecoms] as part of the EU telecoms framework that all NRAs should automatically analyse for the presence of Significant Market Power (SMP). The EC issued a list of 18 such markets in 2003[170] - 7 retail markets and

---

[169] https://european-union.europa.eu/institutions-law-budget/institutions-and-bodies/search-all-eu-institutions-and-bodies/european-commission_en - The European Commission is the EU's politically independent executive arm - European Commission – what it does | European Union (europa.eu)

[170] Retail
1. Access to the public telephone network at a fixed location for residential customers.
2. Access to the public telephone network at a fixed location for non-residential customers.
3. Publicly available local and/or national telephone services provided at a fixed location for residential customers.
4. Publicly available international telephone services provided at a fixed location for residential customers.
5. Publicly available local and/or national telephone services provided at a fixed location for non-residential customers.
6. Publicly available international telephone services provided at a fixed location for non-residential customers.

11 wholesale markets. Mostly, this list included the relevant markets that the EC judged as monopolistic in nature at the time covering principal bottlenecks across then-fixed voice and broadband services, e.g. the monopolistic ownership of the local loop[171] by former monopoly telcos. Four years later in 2007, the EC reduced the number of these relevant markets to be automatically considered from 18 to 7 markets, and by 2014 to just 4[172]. In 2020, the EC further reduced to just 2 markets[173] (EC, 2020) impacting mainly fixed line operators – further confirming the EC's view of lesser and lesser regulation in the telecoms sector. As competition has

---

7.   Minimum set of leased lines

Wholesale
8.   Call origination on the public telephone network provided at a fixed location.
9.   Call termination on individual public telephone networks provided at a fixed location.
10. Transit services in the fixed public telephone network.
11. Wholesale unbundled access (including shared access) to metallic loops and sub-loops for the purpose of providing broadband and voice services.
12. Wholesale broadband access.
13. Wholesale terminating segments of leased lines.
14. Wholesale trunk segments of leased lines.
15. Access and call origination on public mobile telephone networks.
16. Voice call termination on individual mobile networks.
17. The wholesale national market for international roaming on public mobile networks.
18. Broadcasting transmission services, to deliver broadcast content to end users.

[171] The local network that connects homes and business premises to the local telephone exchanges.
[172]

1.   Market 1 - Wholesale call termination on individual public telephone networks provided at a fixed location
2.   Market 2 - Wholesale voice call termination on individual mobile networks
3.   Market 3
     (a) Wholesale local access provided at a fixed location
     (b) Wholesale central access provided at a fixed location for mass-market products
4.   Market 4 - Wholesale high-quality access provided at a fixed location

[173] The two markets are the following: market for wholesale local access (WLA) network provided at a fixed location; and the wholesale dedicated capacity (WDC) market. NRAs can impose remedies on fixed-line operators in these two markets if they find SMP.

taken hold in the telecoms sector in most EU countries, most *ex-ante* retail price regulations have been removed, leaving just fixed line regulation focussed on wholesale products.

Does this mean there will be no sustained *ex-ante* regulation in the telecoms sector going forward – at least in the EU? The answer is probably not-so-fast – such fixed-line wholesale regulations may persist depending on the levels of intra-modal or facilities-based NGN competition and inter-modal competition in every EU jurisdiction. Pertaining to this question, I cite the following very insightful perspective on this question of the ongoing rationale for telecoms regulation – at least in the EU – noting it should be assessed:

> "by comparing the consumer welfare impacts of *imperfect competition* versus *imperfect regulation*. Others argue that there continues to be a rationale for regulatory oversight of the industry given that the concerns about market power persists for NGNs, as do concerns about net neutrality" (Decker, 2023, p. 413) – *the author's emphases.*

This is arguably the limits of regulation in telecoms (or elsewhere), i.e. when imperfect competition may have been judged to outweigh imperfect regulation.

3.9.1.2 A brief narrative on the American 'from-regulation-to-competition' story [telecoms]

The USA took a different approach to telecoms liberalisation and regulation from the EU. The USA is ultimately one exceptionally large telecoms market overseen at the federal level by the Federal Communications Commission (FCC) as federal sector regulator[174], rather than more than two dozen national markets continuously being harmonised and 'normalised' towards competition, as in the EU. In the 1980s, in order to introduce competition into the telecoms market place, the US Government had to deal with the substantial problem of the former behemoth monopoly called AT&T. AT&T had before 1982 consisted of twenty-two AT&T-controlled Bell members. In 1982, following the

---

[174] There also exists State-Owned Utilities Commissions.

settling of the U.S. Department of Justice's antitrust lawsuit against AT&T, the company was [in 1984] broken up and divested into seven (7) Regional Bell Operating Companies (RBOCs[175]) and AT&T itself as a long-distance provider. The RBOCs and AT&T started off still as network industry monopolies with economies of scale, scope and network effects – but in their regional jurisdictions for the RBOCs and across the USA for AT&T. So, later in 1996, the US passed the Telecommunications Act of 1996[176] – with the goals of promoting competition and reducing regulatory barriers in the telecommunications industry. It specifically allowed for more competition in local (i.e., regional baby Bells) and long-distance (AT&T) markets, and it commenced addressing emerging issues related to what we term the 'Internet' today.

The liberalisation and lifting of entry restrictions into the US telecoms sector ensued at pace post this 1996 law, leading to the situation where another group of fixed line [TV] services provider – the Cable Companies (CableCos) – entered into the telecoms sector and competed hard with the incumbent RBOCs in their jurisdictions for both voice and other services. This happened in the 1990s because of the *technology* sector driver (see Chapter 1) which yielded DOCSIS[177]. This standard enabled cable companies providing broadcast services to install telephone switching equipment into their networks. This allowed for offering their customers voice calls in addition to the cable TV services they already provided. Indeed, Comcast and Charter Communications – which both started out as cable TV companies – are today two of the biggest fixed line broadband network providers in the world today.

So, the 1996 law did not only promote competition into local RBOC call markets, it also specifically lifted restrictions on RBOCs themselves from providing inter-state services that was reserved for AT&T alone. The law also meant that the Incumbent Local Exchange Carriers (ILECs)[178] had to offer the new *entrants* Competitive Local Exchange Carriers (CLECs) 'unbundled' network elements and services, and at rate-regulated bases.

---

[175] Also known as Baby-Bells: on January 1, 1984, the seven baby-Bells companies were NYNEX, Pacific Telesis, Ameritech, Bell Atlantic, Southwestern Bell Corporation and BellSouth – created to handle regional voice phone services in the USA.

[176] https://www.congress.gov/104/plaws/publ104/PLAW-104publ104.pdf - PLAW-104publ104.pdf (congress.gov)

[177] Data Over Cable Service Interface Specification

[178] That is the RBOCs themselves and AT&T.

The outcomes of this regulation-to-competition process in the US market is clear to see. Decker (2023, p. 369/70) notes the following:

> "in the USA, there are now over 1300 providers of fixed line residential services, with the five largest providers (including traditional fixed line providers Verizon and AT&T, and the two cable companies Comcast and Charter) accounting for 68 percent of the market... In the USA, there are currently three nationwide wireless providers (AT&T, T-Mobile and Verizon Wireless), as well as three regional providers, and dozens of smaller wireless providers that supply services in a single, often rural, geographic area".

None of the above would have happened in the USA without the careful introduction of *regulation* in order to regulate away the former fixed telecoms monopoly (AT&T), whilst encouraging new entrants into both the regional and national markets through liberalisations (i.e., lifting off former statutory constraints) and promoting competition. The inter-modal as well as intra-modal competition in the USA is evident today in 2024.

3.9.1.3 The EU vs. USA approaches to telecoms regulation

The EU and the USA have clearly taken different approaches to regulating their telecoms sectors over the past two to three decades, driven by their respective legal frameworks. Evidently, the EU's approach has been a both a very *centralising* and harmonising approach with the directives that EU member states transposed into their national laws. For example, in April 2022, the centralising EU referred 10 EU member states[179] to the Court of Justice of the EU (CJEU[180]) "over their failure to fully transpose and communicate to the Commission how national measures transpose the EU Electronic Communications Code"[181] by the deadline of 21 December 2020. In contrast, the USA pursued a more *decentralised* regulatory

---

[179] Spain, Croatia, Latvia, Lithuania, Ireland, Poland, Portugal, Romania, Slovenia and Sweden.

[180] https://european-union.europa.eu/institutions-law-budget/institutions-and-bodies/search-all-eu-institutions-and-bodies/court-justice-european-union-cjeu_en - Court of Justice of the European Union | European Union (europa.eu)

[181] https://ec.europa.eu/commission/presscorner/detail/en/ip_22_1975 - EU Electronic Communications Code (europa.eu)

framework where State-level utility commissions and the FCC both exercise regulatory powers. The EU has emphasised the opening of telecoms markets for competition, by effectively working to create a single European telecommunications market. This has meant facilitating the entry of new players, harmonizing regulations and promoting cross-border competition. The USA has also prioritised competition, notably after the breakup of AT&T in 1984. As mandated by the Telecommunications Act of 1996, the aim has been to promote competition and reduce barriers to entry and encouraging competition in both local and long-distance markets.

Both approaches have delivered significant welfare to their consumers and citizens – this much is evident – demonstrating that there is no 'single bullet' approach to regulation and competition.

3.9.2 Regulation of Telecoms Networks: understanding network *technology* is important to regulation

As has been noted, there are many and differing network *technology* types in the telecoms sector – leading also to much inter-modal competition, as well as intra-modal competition. The technologies cover fixed, cable, wireless, satellite, fixed-wireless access (FWA), Wi-Fi and more – and *understanding both the physical and economic characteristics* of these networks and the services they can provide is key to being able to regulate them properly in order to drive up consumer welfare. The previous section shows how the introduction of the DOCSIS standard in the USA transformed the fortunes of erstwhile cable TV businesses, allowing them - post the USA Telecoms 1996 law - to be able to enter the telecoms voice market. Suddenly, cable providers became fierce competitors to then-traditional voice businesses (RBOCs) – and this new competition provided more choices at lower prices to consumers, driving up consumer welfare.

In Europe, copper networks laid down a century ago for voice signals transmissions - with no knowledge of anything called broadband – were transformed into broadband data transmission networks by a standard call Asymmetric Digital Subscriber Line (ADSL). ADSL is a type of Digital Subscriber Line (DSL) data communications technology that enables faster data transmission over copper telephone lines than a conventional voiceband modem can provide. With ADSL, there is greater bandwidth downstream to the subscriber's premises than upstream – hence asymmetric. If both downstream and upstream bandwidths are the same, it is called SDSL or Symmetric Digital Subscriber Line.

The key point of the above paragraph is not to bamboozle the reader with new terms and acronyms, but rather to show how technology evolution or revolution added more economic value and options [even] to old copper networks. This meant that former monopolies like BT, France Telecom and Deutsche Telecom who all had these copper networks into every home in the UK, France and Germany respectively had to be regulated to allow for competition. They had to be regulated because they had become even more formidable *natural monopolies* who not only provided voice (PSTN) services to their customers, but also could also provide broadband data services too – using a copper network none of their competitors could possibly replicate. Technology provided them these new options and products. In a similar vein to DOCSIS, ADSL and SDSL, other technologies have continued to revolutionise the telecoms sector – most notably the Internet Protocol (IP) which has since swept away the old PSTN-led value chain of the old telecoms industry into a new value chain called the Internet Value Chain (see Nwana, 2022).

The key point here is that to regulate the telecoms industry means to understand and regulate the underlying technologies too, in order to drive up more consumer welfare. If this requires the regulator forcing incumbent operators to provide *regulatory 'unbundling' products* – so be it.

3.9.2.1 Regulating fixed networks towards competition through unbundling the fixed access network

So let us generalise to any fixed network as shown in Figure 3.11. The network could consist of *either* fixed technologies like copper (upgraded with technologies like ADSL), cable (upgraded with technologies like DOCSIS) or hybrid fibre coaxial (HFC) or modern fibre – the specific fixed technology here matter less. The switching[182] technology used here matters less too.

---

[182] Switching refers to the process of making connections between nodes within a network so as to be able to transfer voice signals or data traffic. Circuit switching is used on PSTN network. Packet switching is used on broadband data networks including IP packet switching used.. Lastly, OTT applications like WhatsApp or Skype convert voice, data and

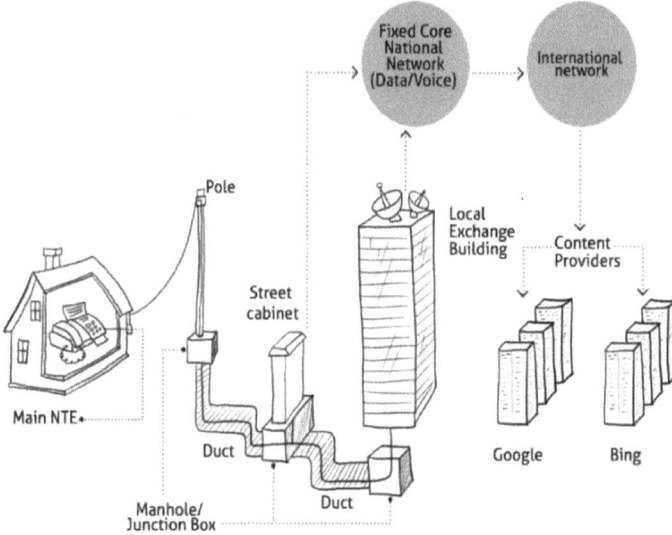

FIXED NETWORK LINK FROM A HOME OR OFFICE
IN AFRICA ACCESSING A GOOGLE SERVER IN
CALIFORNIA OR SOMEONE CALLING CALIFORNIA

Figure 3.11 - Fixed Network Link from a Home or Office in Africa
Accessing a Bing or Google Server[183] in California or Someone Calling
California

Source: Nwana (2014, p.56)

What matters more is that everything in Figure 3.11, from the home/office all the way to the local exchange, is part of the *access network[184]*- with this access network typically be owned and/or controlled by one operator – therefore, a natural network monopoly with natural monopoly bottlenecks with this *local loop* from the local exchange into every home. Market failures could therefore easily ensue in such contexts leading to the need

---

video signals into digital packets which are routed across IP networks like the Internet. This may be referred to as OTT switching.

[183] A server is a computer that holds digital information shared between many users who can connect to it across the Internet or other networks.

[184] So the main network termination element (NTE), the end socket in the home/office, the poles that the fixed telephone and broadband router are plugged into, the ducts, the poles, the masts, the street cabinet, manholes, and junction boxes up to the exchange building are all part of the *access network*.

145

for regulation – the regulatory rationale here is clear: the market failure hypothesis (see Section 2.3.2 1).

There are three broad ways to address such [potential] market failures with fixed line bottlenecks (Decker, 2023, p.373):

(i) **Facilities-based competition:** the first is called facilities-based competition, also called infrastructure competition. In my UK home, there is a copper-based technology network based on Figure 3.11 which was built in (and owned by BT) when the house was built. However, another company also later built a competing and parallel HFC network infrastructure into the home with their own Figure 3.11-like structure of switches, NTEs, cabling, etc. This yielded clear inter-modal competition from the perspective of this single home.

(ii) **'Quasi-facilities'-based competition:** in this case, the new entrant invests in some equipment as well as purchases some 'unbundled' services and elements from the incumbent fixed line operator in order to provide services to the consumer. There is typically only one fixed access network, i.e., there is typically only one pole or duct through which the coaxial, copper, or fibre are threaded going to a single home or office as shown in Figure 3.11. There could be more in places such as with full facilities-based competition above, but typically there is usually just the one. There is typically, as well, only one fixed voice or data line into the house. Considering voice calls alone, this means the company who owns the line to that home has a monopoly on *originating or terminating* all calls on that fixed line, of course. This is because all calls originating and terminating in that premise has to use that fixed access network line. This gives that company that owns that line immense power, which means without regulation, they can charge whatever they like. Regulation takes the form of the national telecoms regulator[185] (or NRA) actually finding that the owner of the line into the home has *market dominance* for the line (and possibly declared as having SMP if they dominate over 40%[186] say of all homes in the country or State), and the NRA

---

[185] Ofcom in the case of the UK or the Nigerian Communications Commission (NCC) in the case of Nigeria. Communications.

[186] In some jurisdictions, the figure could be 50% or even less than 40%, like 33%.

therefore proceeds to *imposing* some *remedies*. And the relevant market of Figure 3.11 is also one of the two remaining markets[187] - the WLA market - that are still subject to EU *ex-ante* regulation if SMP is found. In the UK, BT has SMP nationally in this relevant WLR market, and is therefore required to provide a Wholesale Line Rental (WLR) 'unbundling' product to its competitors.

Figure 3.12 – the EECC/EU Market Review Process

So, regulatory remedies in this case in the EU will typically involve three sorts of controls. First, the regulator - in the case of copper - would force the incumbent monopoly operator to 'unbundle' the local loop – Local Loop Unbundling (LLU) – by providing an LLU product for voice and broadband, in the case of voice a WLR product. In the UK, the LLU remedy for copper broadband/voice was/is called BT Bitstream. This product allowed/allows other companies to use the incumbent's fixed line into the said home as if they owned themselves, thereby allowing operator BskyB to offer broadband services to the customer as if BskyB owned the network[188]. Secondly, the regulator would also be implementing *price controls* or *charge controls* on what the monopoly company can charge other entrant companies (and even itself) for having access to that line using the product like Bitstream. This is the *access charge* or *monthly line rental* costs which the entrant firm pays the incumbent. This charge is usually set on a costs-oriented basis. Thirdly, the regulator also imposes further price controls on how much the company owning that line can charge other companies for terminating calls onto a line that it

---

[187] The two markets are the following: market for wholesale local access (WLA) network provided at a fixed location; and the wholesale dedicated capacity (WDC) market. NRAs can impose remedies on fixed-line operators in these two markets if they find SMP.

[188] The underlying network is still owned by BT.

owns. This is a clear set of regulations to address a bottleneck line in the context of PST voice services.

In summary, as Figure 3.12 depicts, the *ex-ante* market review process in the EU goes through a *market definition* phase (drawing from the prepared list of EECC-prescribed markets), then to a stage of operators being subjected to *assessments for SMP/dominance*, and, if found SMP, to a final stage of *imposing remedies*. This is the process illustrated in this LLU example just described.

(iii) **Resale competition**: with resale competition, a new entrant makes minimal investment in any new equipment unlike the previous two scenarios, and just acts to 'white label' resell the incumbent's services with the key differentiations being in branding and customer service. To resell BT's voice local loop, BT offered the WLR regulatory product to its competitors.

Other similar remedies have been developed in the EU for broadband, NGN and fibre as for the copper-based examples above.

In the USA, much of fixed line regulation relies on price regulation. All ILECs must file tariff schedules with the federal regulator FCC as part of the latter's role in regulating charges for the provision of 'telecommunications services'. These tariffs must be "just and reasonable and may not be unreasonably discriminatory"[189] (FCC, 2017). The former extensive *rate regulation* price controls have since been lightened as facilities-based competition has grown in the USA telecoms sector with fixed line operators. This is as part of the light-tough regulatory framework (FCC, 2018). The regulation of cable (HFC) networks in the USA has typically been less comprehensive than for other fixed line networks largely on the basis that they were typically new telecoms entrants into areas where the RBOCs and AT&T were former fixed monopolies.

---

[189] FCC (2017), Business Data Services in an Internet Protocol Environment et al., https://transition.fcc.gov/Daily_Releases/Daily_Business/2017/db0330/DOC-344162A1.pdf

3.9.2.2 Regulating mobile or wireless networks towards competition

Whereas wired/fixed activities refer to services provided over communications networks which serve *fixed* locations, *wireless* and even *satellite services* can be used whilst on the move. Wireless networks similarly consist of a wireless access network, also called the radio access network (RAN), a fixed core network also connected to other networks (e.g., as in Figure 3.13), the Internet, other operators' networks, international gateways, etc. The real difference between wireless networks and fixed wired networks really resides in the RAN. And the RAN specifically allows a scenario where, instead of an individual being tied to a fixed location, the RAN is able to facilitate *anyone* to access *anything* (i.e., any network service) using a mobile handset/device from *anywhere*, at *any time*.

For this latter reason and others, mobile networks have been regulated differently from fixed line networks. They have also been regulated differently partly because, circa 30+ years ago, they were the new entrants into the telecoms sector to challenge the monopoly of the former State-owned fixed behemoths. The then-expectation was that they would evolve into similar natural monopolies like the fixed operators they challenged. However, with typically more than a couple of mobile network operators (MNOs) in most jurisdictions, this means there is at least some *intra-modal* competition between two or more telecoms operators in most countries[190] – clearly, this was not the case with Fixed line networks. And mobile networks both complement and compete with fixed networks too – providing for added *inter-modal* competition.

This typical scenario in most countries challenges the natural monopoly thesis with regards to mobile or wireless networks because of the implicit existence of facilities-based competition amongst mobile operators, who can set up their own independent RAN and core networks in the country. It is orders of magnitude much less expensive compared to setting up fixed networks to setting up RAN networks who primary resource is radio

---

[190] https://transition.fcc.gov/Daily_Releases/Daily_Business/2017/db0330/DOC-344162A1.pdf - And even some Mobile Virtual Network Operators (MVNOs) in tow too. Sometimes called virtual networks, MVNOs are companies that offer mobile services but do not own or operate their own network. Instead, they use a network run by a mobile operator. For example, giffgaff in the UK is an MVNO – it doesn't have its own network but instead offers its services using O2's mobile network.

spectrum. Talking of spectrum forces a minor diversion into a brief description of mobile network's RAN – which is described because it is the essential differentiator to a fixed line network.

A cellular or mobile network typically has land- and radio-based parts. It consists of the following, as Figure 3.13 illustrates:

- Mobile device (MDs): e.g., mobile phones, smartphones, or other devices, such as cars
- Base station transmitting equipment (BST), specifically a transceiver or a transmitter/receiver for transmitting/receiving radio signals over various radio interfaces technologies called 2G, 2.5G, 3G, 4G and 5G. There are three BSTs shown in the RAN network of Figure 19. We can also ignore the technical details here, but suffice to say 5G can carry more data than 4G, 4G can carry more data than 3G, and 3G can carry more voice and data than 2G, etc. There are also typically thousands of base station sites (BSTs) on a single operator's network across a country.
- A core network: is the central nervous system (or even the brains) of a whole mobile telecommunications network, operating and managing the MDs and radio equipment.
- Public switch telephone network (PSTN), not shown in Figure 3.13 - the land-based part of the network.

RADIO ACCESS NETWORKS

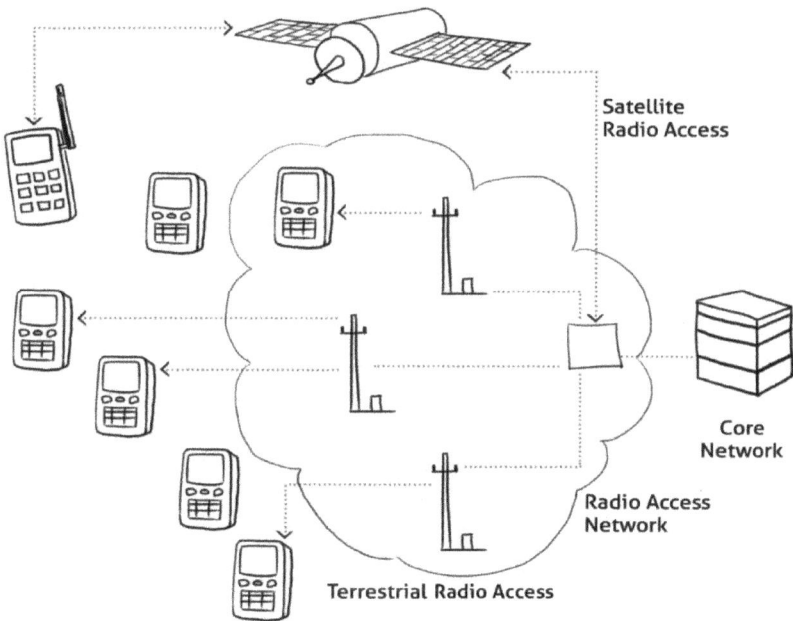

Figure 3.13 - Wireless and Satellite Radio Access Networks
Source: Nwana (2014, p.78)

Following are four key bucket areas that tend to dominate regulation vs. competition activities in the mobile/cellular sector.

Spectrum Regulation: As noted, key to Figure 3.13's RAN depiction are the 2G, 2.5G, 3G, 4G, 5G and soon to coming 6G radios that use up the country's scarce resource of radio frequency spectrum. These all mean that regulating mobile networks has necessarily meant understanding these evolving radio technologies and the benefits they provide to subscribers and even States. *Spectrum regulation* has therefore been key to mobile network regulation because spectrum has rightly been referred to as "the oxygen of the wireless [network] world"[191]. Making the most efficient use of a nation's spectrum resources (see Nwana, 2014, Chapter 4) is a key priority in the telecoms regulation in every jurisdiction.

Indeed, as a type of competition and an important overlap between regulation and competition in telecoms, *spectrum auctions* have been used in most countries to allocate spectrum to mobile operators. Spectrum auctions are also often used to promote downstream competition, and to impose obligations on operators to extend and improve mobile coverage (Myers, 2023). The latter book is an excellent resource on spectrum auctions in the telecoms industry.

The distribution of spectrum helps determine the structure of the mobile industry, and without it there is no possibility of new entry. Without sufficient amounts of it for both coverage and capacity, competition would be impaired for the players with lesser spectrum holdings. This is the reason why the EU's EECC code prioritises the rules governing the assignment and use of radio spectrum, specifically promoting more efficient spectrum management to support 5G rollouts in EU member state to complement concomitant fibre rollouts leading to the EU's Gigabit society.

Infrastructure Sharing Regulation: infrastructure sharing is sometimes used as a competition remedy by regulators to enable and facilitate new entry into the market place. Evidently, if an operator already has hundreds or thousands of BST sites across the country providing it both broad coverage and capacity, a new entrant or a smaller competitor would find it extremely hard to replicate these. For this reasons, some operators may be found by the regulator to have SMP/dominance in sites provision – and the regulator may impose infrastructure sharing remedies on that operator to offer spaces on their BST sites to their competitors. The [potential] market failure rationale here is clear.

Price Regulation: unlike with fixed line networks, mobile networks have not been as subject to strict price controls, particularly direct retail price controls. Retail price controls have been withdrawn in most jurisdictions in preference just light-touch price oversight. This just involves price

---

[191] Julius Genachowski – who is attributed to this quote – was the Chairman of the US FCC from June 2009 to April 2013.

approvals where a regulator must approve a tariff proposed by an operator. Sometimes, only price notifications would do too – where the regulator is simply just notified for information purposes only.

Rather that retail price regulation, *ex-ante* price regulation in the mobile industry has been applied at the wholesale level in many jurisdictions. Such wholesale price controls have been applied to the relevant market of the termination of calls (i.e., *mobile termination charges*) as well as for *roaming*. Wholesale voice call termination on individual mobile networks was (in the EU for decades) – and still largely is many jurisdictions – a relevant candidate market for SMP/dominance assessment of most major mobile network operators. This is evident because of the termination monopoly problem where any network operator who holds your number has the monopoly of terminating all your calls on your mobile phone.

So, in jurisdictions like the EU, the UK and Australia who implement the 'Calling Party Network Pays' (CPNP), wholesale regulation of mobile termination needs to pre-empt the *significant market failure risk* of a terminating operator's power. The terminating operator may not only not choose to terminate the call, but they may also choose to charge excessive prices. If these prices are passed on to consumers, it would reduce consumer welfare – and worse still, the bigger operator may drive a smaller operator out of the market. The same arguments apply to roaming charges [192]. For these reasons, wholesale price regulation of mobile termination and roaming still apply to this day – though the EECC is now of the view that mobile termination and roaming are competitive markets with less need of regulation. The wholesale price controls have taken the form of *price caps* or *rate of return regulation*. The price cap approach is more used whilst rate of return regulation has declined markedly for the mobile industry. The price cap involves the regulator specifying the maximum – or ceiling – of the average increases in prices that an operator can charge for a sustained period of time.

The price cap is typically based on a costs-oriented estimation approach called the Long Run Incremental Cost (LRIC) approach. The thesis behind this is that prices must reflect the costs that would be incurred by a new

---

[192] However, there is an important distinction between termination and roaming. All networks have termination monopolies leading to both large and small networks being regulated for termination. Whereas roaming regulation usually only applies to the largest networks.

efficient operator entrant – only allowing the new efficient entrant to recover its efficient CAPEX and OPEX costs. LRIC also sends a clear signal and nod to new entrants, and hence facilitates promoting more competition. Without LRIC, the industry can be held back inefficiently by old and higher historic CAPEX and OPEX costs which bear no reflection to new today's new and superior equipment costs and efficient labour rates. There is a version of LRIC called LRIC+ which allows for the recovery of fixed and common costs, but increasingly in the EU, a *pure LRIC* approach is employed which does not allow for the recovery of fixed and common costs for call termination. There are other variants of LRIC used elsewhere in the world such as TSLRIC used in Australia or TELRIC used in USA and Japan. In all cases, the broad LRIC principles apply as they are used in setting wholesale price caps.

In other markets like the USA, Canada, Singapore, Hong Kong and others who do not practice the CPNP principle, there has typically *not* been wholesale regulation of termination rates. This is due to the fact that the economics of call termination is fundamentally different for those who do not practice the CPNP principle, and the same termination monopolies do not apply. This latter is because the call recipient pays for the call and also makes the choice of network to belong to. So rather, they [markets like the USA, Canada, Singapore, Hong Kong, etc] have relied on commercially-agreed '*bill and keep*' interconnection agreements amongst MNOs.

Non-Price & Miscellaneous Regulations: As with other sectors, miscellaneous areas like quality of service (QoS) need to be regulated for the benefits of driving up consumer welfare. In general, the following key non-price areas of *regulation* for the benefits of consumers and citizens remain as regards the mobile sector, particularly if *competition* is not working well:

- Quality of Service (QoS) and Quality of Experience (QoE) – telecommunications is an experience which consumers and citizens experience. There would be key demand-side *market failures* if thousands or hundreds of thousands of consumers experience sustained quality of service challenges with mobile network providers. It is egregious to have prepaid consumers experiencing lousy services. The rationale for such non-price competition is clear, but is also difficult to regulate well - a trade-off between imperfect competition and imperfect regulation, as noted above.

- Consumer protection from unfair contracts or not providing consumers better offers available to other consumers remains important. It is frequently the case that there are more recent better tariffs available to attract new consumers that are not available to long-standing consumers.

- Empowering consumers with more consumer information in order for them to be able to make more informed choices. This also follows from the previous bullet.

- Regulating for more consumer switching from one service provider or network to another. It remains key to promote mobile [and also fixed] consumer switching so that consumers realise the benefits of inter-modal and intra-modal competition available to them. Consumer switching typically requires regulatory interventions like that of Mobile Number Portability (MNP), enabling consumers to be able to migrate their mobile service from one provider to another seamlessly and efficiently.

- Regulation for better effective complaints handling – many operators, particularly in developing economies, have terrible complaints managing processes. Such market failures (if widespread) creates significant diminution in consumer welfare, and regulation must enter.

- Regulation for more access, mobile coverage and inclusion is most key. It still is the case that in many developing countries, particularly in LDCs, all citizens are not covered by basic 2G voice signals so that they can originate calls from the most basic of feature phones. There is no coverage where they live. Or even if they are covered, they have no ability to access because of poverty, illiteracy or other demand-side societal failures. Lack of access and being excluded from being able to use public communications not only demonstrates clear demand-side market failures, but also flouts clear public interests rationales in have all connected to basic voice communications.

3.9.2.3 Regulation of Satellite Networks

This book does not major much on the regulation of satellite networks, though they are unquestionably increasingly important to communications in order to facilitate *anyone*[193] to access *anything* (i.e., any network service) using a [mobile/satellite] handset/device from *anywhere*, at *any*

---

[193] Such as providing communications services to people in remote areas.

time. They also come into their element during disasters such as hurricanes, earthquakes, floods and other natural disasters. The reason this area is not expounded upon in this chapter is because satellite regulation mostly happens at the ITU level – it is not an area rife with the regulation vs. competition debate. The inter-modal competitions between mobile vs. satellite or fixed vs. satellite or even satellite vs. Wi-Fi are frankly miniscule, see [Nwana, 2014, p. 84-90] and [Nwana, 2022, p.109-199]. The competition between satellite and the mobile sector arguably happens most over competition for access to scarce radio spectrum resources, with the satellite industry rightly losing out – WRC[194] after WRC – to the mobile industry in their efforts to holding on to satellite spectrum allocations which are typically more efficiently used by mobile and wireless technologies such as 4G, 5G, Wi-Fi and even the emerging 6G.

3.9.2.4 Summary for Telecoms Regulation

The entire section on telecoms commences by stating the observation that the telecommunications industry is a network industry *par excellence*. That unlike the other network industries in this chapter which largely comprise of homogenous networks, the telecoms industry today comprises networks of other heterogenous networks, leading to competition amongst operators using different networks, such as mobile vs. cable vs. fixed vs. satellite networks, etc. There are/were clear economic rationales for regulating the telecommunications sector, not least because it [the former fixed line sector at least] was a natural monopoly:

- the network infrastructure either was (or was seen as) a natural monopoly, in which the benefits of competition were (or were thought to be) outweighed by the costs of duplicating infrastructure;
- i.e. there were extremely high capital and sunk costs in fixed infrastructure, creating barriers to entry (and exit);
- there was no significant diversity of services.

---

[194] World Radio Conference organised by the ITU held every 3 or 4 years to harmonise radiofrequency spectrum rules and regulations involving all member States of the UN.

Telecoms (and other sectors) were also state monopolies that grew from *political* choices:

- they grew out of other state-owned services (e.g., fixed telecoms, rail and postal services);
- Governments have/had preferred to control the means of communication for reasons of national security (internal and external).

So, for economic reasons, telecoms was moved away from monopoly to the diverse intra-modal and inter-modal competition we observe today in many jurisdictions:

- Falling relative costs of infrastructure (especially wireless infrastructure) and of transmission per unit;
- Increasing diversity of services that can be provided over a single network (which raises revenue per line);
- Rising demand (usage/number of users; network externalities);
- New understanding that network and service provision can be separated, yielding both (i) facilities-based competition and (ii) service based competition. Indeed, as I cover earlier, many parts of the telecoms value chain are no longer seen as natural monopolies.

These above proved the Market Failure theory was rife in the telecoms industry.

There were other rationales/theories for regulations too:

- **Power of Ideas Theory**: Political/ideological shifts worldwide from late 1970s onwards shifted towards market solutions.

- **Economic Theory of Regulation:** Competition in telecoms was considered desirable because it tends to generate consumer value through increased investment, greater efficiency, innovation and diversity of service provision and lower prices. Government provision of commercially viable services was all correctly assumed to be inefficient due to monopoly operators, who abused

157

their monopoly power with excessive prices and much fewer subscribers[195]. Recall from the economic theory of Figure 2.1 in Chapter 2 how a monopoly firm would *rationally* choose to produce just quantity Q1 and charge average higher price P1, where Q1 is much less than what is demanded by society at the much higher price, P1. This resulted in a significant departure from economic efficiency (e.g., exclusion of other competitors by dominant firms). However, I acknowledge that with Figure 2.1 in Chapter 2, I am describing the incentive of a profit-maximising firm, whereas Government-owned telecom operators were/are almost certainly *not* restricting supply to increase profit. They were/are just typically inefficiently and/or even incompetently run companies failing to meet demand.

- **Regulatory Capture Theory**: Governments finally also figured out that many of their so-called telecoms regulation from within their SoEs had been thoroughly captured by incumbent fixed operators. This was holding the telecoms sector back.

- **Public Interest Theory:** politicians could no longer explain to their constituents why a neighbouring village or town had more access to telecoms services whilst their own constituencies had so many gaps. Equity issues (such as Universal Service Obligations (USO), specific social pricing for particular social groups, etc.) also weighed in as public interests.

- **Interests Groups Theory**: once Governments started liberalizing telecoms markets, the power of Interests Groups made the entire process virtually unstoppable. International financial institutions made sector restructuring a requirement for funding and wider economic participation. Such *dynamic issues* as incentives to invest, new high-paying jobs and innovation were also pushed via many interest groups stakeholders.

---

[195] Such as due to slow network build-out and sometimes long waiting lists for consumers to get a telephone line.

For these reasons and more, regulation to allow for more competition ensued in the telecoms sector, and technology evolutions/revolutions have all played their part as seen in this section. As seen in this section and chapter so far, there were *structural separations* (i.e., breakups) of monopoly telecoms firms (e.g. the birth of the RBOCs in the USA from AT&T) and/or introduction of competition into 'unbundled' components of the natural monopoly value chain. If the operators were/are still found to have SMP in the components, remedies are imposed on the operators principally including access and charge controls (or pricing regulations). The remedies primarily not only drive for competition into the relevant markets or unbundled components, but also promote non-discrimination requirements on a vertically integrated dominant firm. This section/chapter have shown the vastly beneficial outcomes to regulating the telecoms industry for more competition.

Indeed today, in many telecoms markets or jurisdictions – particularly in developed countries like the EU, UK, Singapore, Hong Kong, Australia and the USA – regulators have the rich-man's-problem challenge of comparing whether the consumer welfare impacts of *imperfect competition* outweighs those from *imperfect regulation* (Decker, 2023, p. 413). In these markets, telecoms regulation is being (or has been) largely 'normalised' towards horizontal Competition Law away from heavy *ex-ante* sector regulation – leaving them with thorny Big Tech OTT vs. Big Telco issues like net neutrality or the market power of NGNs. Sadly, in developing and LDC jurisdictions, the role of *ex-ante* regulation still dominates, largely due to the extremely poor implementation of the regulation vs. competition dynamic in these markets as describe in this section and chapter.

There are other important network industries key to modern living that have not been expounded upon in any of the sections earlier including, notably, the rail network industry and the aviation network industry.

3.10 Regulation vs. Competition in the Rail Network Industry: a brief overview

Railways in all countries already face competition from other 'modes' of transportation like road transport (trucks, cars and busses) as well as from aviation. However, the nature of the competition truly depends on the types of services in question, of which there are two broad types: *passengers services* and *freight services*. Most countries including LDCs direly need railways to provide mass transportation services for passengers as well as for much-needed freight transportation. The demand for rail services continue to increase decade-on-decade in all jurisdictions that already have reasonably good railways services, particularly in the two most populous nations on earth: India and China. Railways are truly invaluable to the economic development of most countries.

Rail infrastructure has traditionally been under Government ownership with a one firm owning and operation the entire vertically integrated structure. This rail systems infrastructure comprises the (i) the railway track lines (ii) railway structures including bridges and tunnels (iii) train signalling for the safe running of trains and for track control (iv) communication systems sub-infrastructure (v) power systems, e.g. electricity to power the trains and (vi) terminal/stations infrastructure located at train stations. The investments required for long term rail infrastructure including the track lines, bridges and tunnels and the costs of maintaining them are humongous. All of these make a single vertically-integrated railway operator a natural monopoly. This is the core rationale for regulation in the railway industry.

Figure 3.14 shows a basic network graph depiction of the Railway Industry with just two nodes: Nodes A and B, which Table 3.9 elaborates on the scope for competition within this 'unbundled' components.

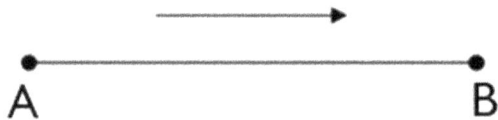

Figure 3.14 – A Basic Graph Model Depiction of Railway Industry

If one is to deviate away from just a single vertically integrated natural monopoly railway operator model, the scope for competition in the Rail industry is typically summarised in Table 3.9.

As seen with Figure 3.14 and Table 3.9, railways present quite different economic regulation challenges compared to the other network graphs of other industries so far. This is because Table 3.9 shows there is *not* that much scope for *unbundling* in the rail industry because it makes much sense to have a single Node A [typically privatised] Operator managing all of the Track, Stations and Signalling whilst Node B represents the Services component - with only a moderate scope for competition.

	Railway Industry 'Unbundled' Component	Scope for Competition
Node A	Track, Stations & Signalling	Low-to-Nil
Node B	Services	Moderate

Table 3.9 – Scope for Competition in the Railway Industry

The train operating services component are not seen to possess the natural characteristics of a natural monopoly as such [typically] private operators themselves would face competition from busses, trucks, cars, scooters, etc. Two options therefore emerge:

(i) **Concession/Franchise Arrangements (for both passenger & freight contracts):** the rail infrastructure (trains, tunnels, bridges, stations and signalling) is separated from train operation, effectively creating long-term *'franchise'* or concession contracts that could be auctioned/beauty-contested and awarded to winning Train Operation Companies (TOC). Such long-term franchises could be awarded to freight of passenger TOCs. Many EU countries use this approach with the terms of passenger TOC contracts going up 15 years, notably the UK, Germany and Sweden.

(ii) **On-Rail Open Access:** another option – a more complicated one – is called the *open access* approach, where third party TOCs bid for 'slots' on certain routes for a specified time. These open access third party TOCs may actually be competing with the franchise long term TOCs simultaneously. This approach improves the more efficient use of the underling rail infrastructure. – and is operating in the EU as well as in Australia.

As seen for all the other network industries, the key methods of regulation include access regulations and price regulation. Railway infrastructure access charges are regulated including *track access charges* and *station access charges*. Similarly, the TOCs are subject to price controls on the fare charges to rail passengers and freight shippers.

The rationale for access price regulation of rail infrastructure operators stem from the economic theory that the costs and industry characteristics of the activities approximate those of a natural monopoly, Rail tracks, tunnels and bridges are most immovable and not easily replicable by alternative facilities-based competition options. The *economies of density* with rail infrastructure is also another clear reason for access price regulation. Economies of density means there are significant cost savings resulting from the spatial proximity of suppliers or providers. Therefore. if there is a high-density population living in wider London in the UK (more than 10 million people), more rail suppliers, infrastructure, and other ancillary railways suppliers would concentrate and agglomerate around London – and therefore costs per passenger/per unit of freight carried are cheaper. As another example, delivering mail and parcels to areas with many mailboxes reduces overall costs and reduces delivery costs. The rationale for end user price regulation is based on the need to protect truly 'captive' end passengers or freight shippers. They have no choice but use the train services. The price regulation usually takes the form of multi-year price caps, typically set on an RPI-X (retail price index minus X) basis.

3.11 Regulation vs. Competition in the Aviation Industry: a brief overview

Air passenger and air freight transportation services have been on the rise for the past decades with more routes being opened up every years to take air passengers to more places more efficiently. In fact, there has been a 100% growth in number of airports in India since 2014, with the number of operational airports in the country doubling from 74 in 2014 to 140 by the close of 2022 according to the respected Economic Times of India[196]. China's certified transport airports have increased (by 2021) to 248 from

---

[196] https://economictimes.indiatimes.com/industry/transportation/airlines-/-aviation/number-of-operational-airports-in-country-rise-to-140-from-74-since-2014-officials/articleshow/96129809.cms?from=mdr - Number of operational airports in country rise to 140 from 74 since 2014: Officials - The Economic Times (indiatimes.com)

less than 150 twenty years ago according to the Civil Aviation Authority of China (CAAC)[197]. These two populous nations are clearly showing that demand for more air passenger travels, and markets like Africa would surely follow over the next twenty years too – as intra-African air passenger transport numbers are currently extremely low.

To start with, it is instructive to state that Aviation regulation is in a class of its own amongst all the network industries for four core reasons (Decker, 2023, p. 547):

i.   In most countries, the aviation industry has always been naturally vertically separated – unlike any of the generic industry structures earlier of Figures 3.2, 3.3 and 3.4. No single Operator ever manages all three of the air-based *airspace*, the land-based *airports* and the flying *airlines*. This means British Airways is an airline operator, but it does not control Heathrow Airport in London, and it certainly does not manage the Heathrow airspace which dozens of other airlines use to fly into London daily.

ii.   There is also a high degree of inter-country or inter-jurisdictional technical and operational coordination based on international conventions, bilateral and multilateral agreements.

iii.   Aviation infrastructure also differs in that there are <u>no</u> extensive physical networks of pipes, wires, rails, etc. as is the case the other network industries covered in this chapter such as telecoms, gas, electricity or water.

iv.   Aviation is also very susceptible to macroeconomic demand and supply shocks like Covid19, oil price shocks, terrorism and other factors that can make the sector quite volatile.

From a regulation perspective, these differences make the aviation sector somewhat unique. In contrast with all the other network industries in this chapter, the aviation value chain already possesses naturally 'unbundled' components. This is because – as explained in the differences above - no single Aviation Operator ever manages all three of the airspace, the airports and the airlines. Figure 3.15 shows a network graph depiction of the Aviation Industry with these three nodes: Nodes A, B and C which Table 3.10 elaborates on.

---

[197] https://www.caac.gov.cn/English/ - P020230227560025233491.pdf (caac.gov.cn)

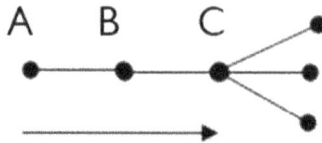

Figure 3.15 – Graph Model Depiction of the Aviation Industry

Network Industry	Node A represents	Node B represents	Node C represents
Aviation	Airspace Navigation Activities	Airport Services	Airline Services

Table 3.10 – Scope for Competition in the Gas Industry

Table 3.11 elaborates on the scope for competition within components.

	Aviation Industry Component	Scope for Competition
Node A	Airspace Navigation Services (ANS)	Low to Nil
Node B	Airport Services	Low to Moderate
Node C	Airline Services	Good

Table 3.11 – Scope for Competition in the Aviation Industry

Let us delve briefly into these three components to justify and elaborate these assessed levels of competition in Table 3.11.

Airspace Navigation Services (ANS): Airspaces can be 'controlled' or 'uncontrolled', with the former mandating all aircraft to follow a specified structured route whilst complying with all air traffic instructions. Airspaces around the world are divided into Flight Information Regions (FIRs). FIR vary in sizes from some covering an entire ocean to even some small geographical countries like the UK having four. A FIR is an

ICAO[198]-specified region of airspace in which flight information services and alerting service are provided. These are the basic levels of air traffic services, providing pertinent and timely information to the safe and efficient conduct of upper *enroute* and lower section flights. They alert the various relevant authorities if an aircraft is in distress. These services are available *to all aircraft through an FIR*, and are provided by one ANSP[199] per controlled airspace sector. Some vast countries like the USA, Australia and Canada have only one ANSP. The last two sentences speak to the monopolistic nature of the air navigation services component – and which is clearly justified on safety grounds – hence Table 3.11 assesses is at 'Low to Nil'. For controlled routes, the scope for competition is clearly zero, whilst for uncontrolled routes, there could theoretically be some low level of competition. Since ANS services are considered a monopoly activity in most markets suggesting clear needs for both *access* and *price* regulations. It would be both absurd and most unsafe for an ANSP not to provide FIR services to an airline for example. Access to airspace – or 'freedoms of the air[200]' – is governed by the 1944 Chicago convention[201] which created a framework for countries to exchange air traffic rights. Article 15[202] of the Chicago Convention on International Civil Aviation stipulates that ANS charges should be costs-based and transparently published and communicated to the ICAO. Therefore, in practice, ANS charges levied to airlines are typically price capped by aviation regulators.

Airport Services: Land-based airports provide a mixture of both aeronautical and non-aeronautical services. The former includes the likes of maintenance and operation of runways, taxiways, allocating airport gates, providing airbridges, providing refuelling services, check-in services, boarding services, etc. The non-aeronautical services include airports leasing their spaces for retail and hospitality services, car park services and so on. In general, competition in the airport services component is judged 'Low to Moderate'. This is Low in most contexts or countries because airlines would typically not have many choices of airports they could choose from to use as part of their routes. Even the most populous African country of Nigeria offers airlines limited [only two]

---

[198] International Civil Aviation Organisation

[199] Air Navigation Service Provider

[200] Freedoms of the Air (icao.int) - https://www.icao.int/pages/freedomsair.aspx

[201] https://www.icao.int/publications/pages/doc7300.aspx - Convention on International Civil Aviation - Doc 7300 (icao.int) -

[202] https://www.icao.int/publications/Documents/7300_cons.pdf - Convention on International Civil Aviation. Ninth Edition - 2006 (icao.int)

international passenger airports in practice namely Lagos and Abuja. Many countries would only provide a choice of one international airport to international airlines. This means some airports may be judged to have *substantial market power*, making them strong candidates for up-front *ex-ante* economic regulation covering access and charge controls. This is the case with London Heathrow and Gatwick airports in the UK. For example, the UK Civil Aviation Authority (CAA) published in a 2023 consultation (CAA, 2023) on the *Economic Regulation of Gatwick Airport Limited* (GAL)[203]. In the introduction of the consultation the CAA writes:

> "Our *economic regulation* of Gatwick Airport Limited (GAL) is based on a set of "commitments" that include, among other things, *a cap on the average level of airport charges*, *a minimum level of investment* and *a system of rebates if GAL misses certain service quality targets*. The commitments framework is intended to be a proportionate and targeted approach to economic regulation, which encourages bilateral contracting and facilitates commercial rather than regulator-led decision making. The current commitments were introduced in 2021 and cover the four-year period to 31 March 2025. They include a cap of *Retail Prices Index (RPI) + 0% on GAL's* published charges and a *minimum investment requirement of £120 million per yea*r, on average, over the six years from 2019/20 to 2024/25"
>
> *– the author's emphases.*

The author's emphases above clearly highlight *ex-ante* regulations that Gatwick airport is subject to due to the fact that it has been assessed as having substantial market power in the UK airports market. The airport is evidently [already] subject to access regulations, price caps controls (i.e., price regulation), quality of service regulation, and even minimum investment requirements. The clear rationale for such economic regulation on Gatwick airport stems from its characteristics being judged or seen as a locational natural monopoly with substantial market power which it can use to the detriment of its users. Natural monopolies tend to have limited incentives to invest leading the UK aviation regulator to nudge Gatwick Airport to 'commit' to minimum investments annually.

---

[203]https://www.caa.co.uk/commercial-industry/airports/economic-regulation/licensing-and-price-control/economic-licensing-of-gatwick-airport/

Airline Services (Air Passenger & Cargo Transport Services): the services provided by the aviation industry fall into two broad categories: air passenger transportation and freight/cargo services. Airports have to be mindful of the type of aircrafts that fly into their airports though the industry is dominated by two namely Boeing and Airbus. This component of aviation is evidently *competitive* given ICAO has allegedly issued more than 5000 unique airline codes to airlines[204]. More authoritatively, a 2019 ICAO report (ICAO, 2019) noted that:

> "Today, 1,303 scheduled airlines operate over 31,717 aircraft, serving 3,759 airports thanks to the support of 170 air navigation services providers"
>
> Source: Foreword of report[205].

Indeed, the state of competition between airlines is a phenomenon of more recent decades following substantial liberalisation and deregulation to remove historical regulation which prevented or limited airline competition. For this reason, fare levels are competitive because they are broadly arrived at through competition. Hence, competition between airlines across different routes has resulted in fares/prices that appear to reflect airlines' underlying costs and/or seasonal consumer demand dynamics. A caveat here is that some routes can have limited competition. Try flying direct from London (UK) to Accra (Ghana) over the last decade (to 2024) – the only carrier of choice is usually British Airways.

This concludes the overviews of regulation vs. competition across several (or many) network industries.

3.12 Chapter Summary

This Chapter has provided an overview of regulatory institutions, and why they are designed the way they are. It has briefly overviewed network industries' market structures in an order explained in Section 3.4.3 – and how these network industries are typically regulated for the benefits of consumers, citizens, passengers, etc. of our countries, drawing both from

---

[204] https://en.wikipedia.org/wiki/Lists_of_airlines# - Lists of airlines - Wikipedia

[205] https://www.icao.int/sustainability/Documents/AVIATION-BENEFITS-2019-web.pdf

a combination of tools from both regulation and competition toolboxes. The chapter has tried to link - as much as possible - the *theories* and hypotheses of Regulation of Chapter 2 to real *practice* across several sectors in the hope that the reader appreciates just how nuanced, complex and misunderstood regulation typically is – and the underlying rationales for regulation in these network industry sectors

For readers who desire a deeper understanding of the subject matters of this chapter, Baldwin *et al.* (2012) and Decker (2023) are two excellent texts to start from.

Chapter 4

Methods of the Practice of Regulation

This chapter provides an overview of the many methods of regulation – several of which have been mentioned in the last chapter (Chapter 3) as it overviewed the various network industry sectors. This is admittedly an exceptionally long chapter, but I chose to retain overviewing the many methods of regulation out there in one chapter.

What are methods of regulation? Well, we have seen in the previous chapter in particular that [economic] regulation of sectors uses statutory interventions to control and/or influence different aspects of these said sectors in order to achieve the regulatory objectives - efficiency, fairness, stability, inclusion and other outcomes Governments may seek. To achieve their statutory goals, regulators employ a combination of many methods of [economic] regulation, with each method targeting different aspects of activities in the sector. For example, as covered in Chapter 3, the regulation method of *price regulation* targets sector pricing activities. *Access regulation* is a method that targets barriers to entry into specific market segments and competitive constraints within sectors access, and/or competitive entry into some components of the sector's value chain. *Quality regulation* targets sector quality of products and services issues including standards, health and safety, and ensuring value for money so that customers are not shortchanged for services they pay for. These methods of regulation apply across most sectors, though the details of their implementation may differ from sector to sector. However, it is important to overview these methods individually even though previous chapters have mentioned many of them.

The methods of regulation overviewed in this chapter include: licensing and certification, access (non-price) regulation, access price regulation, rate of return and price cap/revenue cap [price controls] regulation, SMP and relevant markets regulation, consumer protection regulation, quality and safety regulation, scarce resources & environmental/climate regulation, universal access regulation, enforcement & responsive regulation, risk-based regulation, accounting/functional/structural separation, taxation and subsidies, impact assessments and costs benefits analyses.

It is important to emphasize – as is mentioned in the Preface and previous chapters of this book - that the methods of regulation used vary widely from one country to another. The methods used can also be determined by political considerations (influenced by politicians), the power of current ideas (influenced by activists, propagandists, fearmongers, etc.), public interest (influenced by formal bodies like trade unions, consumer groups, citizen advice bureaus, etc.), and the specific needs of the targeted sector of the economy. We overview these methods following.

4.1 Licensing & Certification

Licensing is a key method of regulation used by – practically - all statutory regulators. All Bills, Acts or Decrees which create regulators in the first place would almost certainly grant regulators licensing powers. However, we briefly overview certification first because though licensing is typically a *legal* requirement for carrying out certain tasks, e.g., performing surgery on fellow humans, certification is a vital indicator of the surgeon's *ability* to carry out such a complex task. This explains why dentists, surgeons and other medical professionals [typically] proudly and transparently display their certifications on the walls their offices.

4.1.1 Certification

Briefly, the Cambridge English Dictionary defines certification as the action or process of providing someone or something with an official document *attesting* to a status or level of achievement. Most certifications expire after a certain period of time and have to be maintained with further education and/or testing. This is because – as explained earlier - certifications expire since they attest to someone being competent to do a job or task, usually by the passing of an examination and/or the completion of a program of study. For example, just as only an attested doctor or physician can treat and prescribe medication to patients, only certified gas or electricity installers would be able to carry out installations in consumer households. In some cases, if the technologies or processes change, these installers *may* need to be certified anew. This may not always be the case - a change in process might not always result in the requirement for new certification. Lawyers do not lose their certificates to practice law because of new legislations, and similarly this applies to plumbers, etc.

However, it is also important to clarify that in the regulatory context, certification might be an attestation by the regulator or standard body or whoever has the role of issuing it, to reassure the third parties – e.g., consumers, customers, partners, etc. about the quality, safety and/or the authenticity of the product, service or relationship - basically a tool for promoting and maintaining trust in the market.

4.1.2 Licensing

Most sectors require up-to-date certified professionals, particularly in the ICT, Electricity, Gas and Finance sectors. Governments rightly require certifications for these professions or industries, ensuring that practitioners and tradesmen meet certain qualifications and adhere to clear ethical and professional standards.

It is worth emphasising the difference between a license and a certificate via a further example. A good example may be how immigrants can possess *certificates* or qualifications in various fields from their countries of origin, but they may *not* be given the *licences* to practice in their host countries where they have arrived as immigrants for a myriad of reasons, e.g. lack of trust in foreign certifications, lack of experience in their newly-arrived countries, etc.

Ofcom

PUBLIC WIRELESS NETWORK LICENCE

This licence document replaces the version of the Licence issued by Ofcom on 18 May 2021, to EE Limited.

Licence no.   0249666

Date of issue: 27 July 2021

Fee payment date: 31 October (annually)

1. The Office of Communications (Ofcom) grants this wireless telegraphy licence ("the Licence") to

    EE Limited
    (Company registration number 02382161)
    ("the Licensee")
    Trident Place
    Mosquito Way
    Hatfield
    Hertfordshire
    AL10 9BW

    to establish, install and use radio transmitting and receiving stations and/or radio apparatus as described in the schedule(s) (hereinafter together called "the Radio Equipment") subject to the terms, set out below.

Licence Term

2. This Licence shall continue in force until revoked by Ofcom or surrendered by the Licensee.

Licence Variation and Revocation

3. Pursuant to schedule 1 paragraph 8 of the Wireless Telegraphy Act 2006 ("the 2006 Act"), Ofcom may not revoke or vary this Licence under schedule 1 paragraph 6 of the 2006 Act save at the request or with the consent of the Licensee except:

    (a) in accordance with clause 6 of this Licence;

    (b) in accordance with schedule 1 paragraph 8(5) of the 2006 Act;

    (c) for reasons related to the management of the radio spectrum, provided that in such case the power to revoke may only be exercised after five years' notice is given in writing and after Ofcom has considered any pertinent factors;

Voice Coverage Obligation

6. The Licensee shall maintain an electronic communications network that is capable of providing mobile voice telecommunications services to an area covering at least 90% of the geographic landmass of the United Kingdom at at least one of the minimum signal strengths set out in Table 1 of this condition. For the avoidance of doubt the Licensee shall be permitted to meet the obligation set out in this condition using any frequencies and technologies available to the Licensee.

Table 1

Technology and Band	Minimum Signal Threshold
GSM 900	-93 dBm
GSM 1800	-93 dBm
UMTS 2100	-103 dBm
LTE 800	-115 dBm

Figure 4.1 – Excerpts of a UK Telecoms Licence - Source:[206]

---

[206] https://www.ofcom.org.uk/__data/assets/pdf_file/0027/82845/Cellular-LICENCE-EE-0249666.pdf - 1800 MHz LICENCE - EE 0249666 (ofcom.org.uk)

It is also important to highlight that licensing is strictly speaking *not* an economic method of regulation[207] like price regulation or access regulation. However, in order to reform any sector of the economy, licensing [new/existing operators] would typically be used by regulators or Governments. What then is a licence?

In brief as I elaborate later, a licence is a legal document which sets outs the rights and obligations prescribed by the regulator to a licensee. On the economic aspect, certifications and licencing are potential barriers to entry that would keep competitors out of the market, and these methods may be pushed forward by incumbents who would particularly use it when they have the powers to capture regulators – c.f. Regulatory Capture Theory in Chapter 3.

Many readers of this chapter may be carrying a driving licence with them in their wallets. That licence, issued by a Government agency typically, grants the driver the *rights* to drive a certain class of roadworthy vehicles on public roads, but these rights also come with certain clearly specified [legal] *obligations*. For example, the legal obligations on any licenced UK driver[208] driving on UK public roads include obligation to meet 'minimum eyesight rules', obligation for the vehicle being driven to be registered with the UK Driver and Vehicle Licensing Agency (DVLA), obligation for the driver having a valid insurance certificate for the vehicle as well as a roadworthiness certificate, etc. The same rights-and-obligations definition applies to licences issued by regulators or regulatory bodies.

Figure 4.1 shows excerpts of an example UK telecoms licence – specifically in this case, a 'public wireless network licence' issued by UK Telecoms and Media regulator, Ofcom[209]. It specifies who the licensee is [EE Limited], the licence number, the date issued, the date when the annual fee payment is due, the address of the licensee, the term of the licence, etc.

---

[207] However, it would fit the definition of economic (vs social regulation) in Chapter 2's Section 2.1.1: "rules that limit who can enter a business (entry controls)" which can be implemented by restricting the number of licences issued.

[208] https://www.gov.uk/legal-obligations-drivers-riders - Legal obligations of drivers and riders - GOV.UK (www.gov.uk) - https://www.gov.uk/legal-obligations-drivers-riders

[209] www.ofcom.org.uk

Later on, in the circa-18 pages long licence (including schedules), there are some obligations including some technically-looking 'voice coverage obligations' shown at the bottom of Figure 4.1. The core licence is only 3 pages long with the remainder of fifteen pages being detailed schedules.

As seen at the bottom of Figure 4.1, the licence obliges that "the Licensee shall maintain an electronic communications network that is capable of providing mobile voice telecommunications services to an area covering at least 90% of the geographic landmass of the United Kingdom" – along with some technical specifications. The schedules to the licence specify how this obligation would be measured and when the obligation should have been fulfilled.

Who is licensed? The answer is that both network and service providers are licensed, or just private networks operators. They could be electricity networks providers, gas services providers or electronics communications networks providers. *Network operators* build and maintain the physical network infrastructure. They hold licences that, at least initially, impose obligations of access, particularly in the case of the monopoly incumbent, in addition to network deployment and coverage obligations and deadlines. The licences would typically also impose mandatory service provisions. *Service providers*—provide services directly to end consumers, whether or not they control the physical network. Through their licences, they may gain rights to resell or rights to network operators' infrastructure, in exchange for certain obligations such as reasonable tariffs/prices, provision of services, etc. *Private networks* may also be licensed, such as those networks by corporate entities for their internal operations.

To summarise what a licence is, the following are the key points of note.

1. **Rights & obligations**: a licence grants rights but also imposes obligations as seen in Figure 4.1. Some of the obligations that regulators include in licences – not shown in this specific licence – include obligations to help it [the regulator] promote competition, protect/promote consumer interests and to ensure investor confidence (e.g., by being able to impose SMP/competition provisions on incumbents without which new investors would not enter the market). However, there is more to a licence.

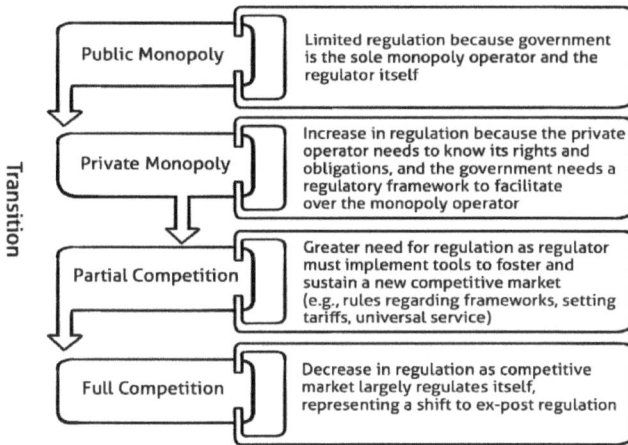

Figure 4.2 - The Need for Regulation (Going from Monopoly to Full Competition)
(Source: significantly adapted from ICT Regulation Toolkit)[210]

2. **Market entry control:** a licence would typically be used to control market entry into a market sector or into a component of a market chain as covered in Chapter 3. For example, when a sector is being transitioned from a public monopoly into full competition as shown in Figure 4.2, licenses may be used in the initial stages of liberalisation to restrict entry, allowing new competitors to develop in a relatively safe environment. Licences also guarantee rights of the licensee. This is because licences boost investor confidence by encouraging more robust deployment of network infrastructure (e.g., gas, electricity, telecoms, water, etc.), while at the same time driving up public and consumer interest/welfare by guaranteeing the provision of, for example, access to emergency services, interconnection with other network operators, driving up quality of service standards, and perhaps even ensuring pricing based on costs.

3. **Provision of access to finite or scarce resources: a licence:** such as that shown in Figure 4.1 – some types of licences grant access to finite resources like radio spectrum, fixed and mobile telephone numbers, IP addresses, and even access to land for the installation of network

---

[210]The ICT Regulation Toolkit, http://www.itu.int/itudoc/gs/promo/bdt/flyer/87876.pdf

175

facilities. Radio spectrum is typically thought of as a 'public good' (e.g., Taylor & Middleton, 2020), though it is strictly speaking a 'common pool resource' (Myers, 2023). Thus, by providing access to it, the Government or regulator also impose obligations – as is the case with the coverage obligations shown in Figure 4.1. Spectrum is a common pool resource rather than a public good because the use of spectrum is rival instead of being non-rival due to interference. Chapter 6 (Section 6.2) of Myers (2023) details a range of licence types such as exclusive, concurrent, sharing, light and licence-exempt.

4. **Generation of Government revenues through licensing and other regulatory fees**: a licence like that shown in Figure 4.1 comes with an obligation to pay annual licence fees to the Government for the operator's right to use a public good. Such fees are typically not an income generation activity always, because they might be limited [only] to covering the cost of providing the licensing service.

5. **Types of Licences:** There are typically three types of licences: individual licences, concession agreements or general authorisations.

    Individual licences such as that shown in Figure 4.1 are typically used to control market entry when they are granted to operators entering newly liberalised markets (through encouraging and promoting competition from the new entrant).

    A Concession agreement[211] is a contract that gives a company or an operator the right to operate a specific business activity within a Government's jurisdiction (or within another company's property), subject to particular terms and conditions. Concession agreements span various sectors and come in many sizes, including oil industry concessions valued in the hundreds of millions of USD dollars, or small hospitality concessions in a shopping mall for a retail space. The concessionaire usually has to pay the party that grants it the concession fees. Concessions are largely viewed as an antiquated approach in some sectors in many jurisdictions (e.g. telecoms), and have been replaced by traditional licences, whilst they are heavily used in other sectors such as mining, oil and gas.

---

[211]   https://www.investopedia.com/terms/c/concessionagreement.asp#   -   Concession Agreement: Definition, What It Is, and How It Works (investopedia.com)

General authorisations are also known as class licences. These are useful when individual licences are not appropriate, e.g., when the regulator wants to encourage as many new entrants as possible. These class licences come with basic rights and obligations, and general regulatory provisions to the class of services authorised. General authorisations have been largely used in the telecoms sector in EU countries since 2003, the effect being that licences are no longer required for providing communications networks or services in the UK and other EU countries by many operators, e.g. MVNOs. In an *open entry* regime, any applicant that meets application criteria is granted entry into the market.

Regulators and Governments can use any or more of these different types of licensing approaches depending on what the needs of the sector are.

4.2 Access (non-Price) Regulation

In Chapter 3 (see Section 3.3.1), we observe three generic industry structures that network industries typically adopt:

- a vertically-integrated monopoly,
- a vertically separated structure with competition in upstream and downstream activities, and
- a vertically separated structure with competition in *some* activities.

Much of Chapter 3 covers how these industry structures (or variants of them) across many sectors can be regulated in order to introduce more competition – and it was observed that one of the several recurring methods of regulation required is *access regulation*, e.g. see Figures 3.3 and 3.4. This is because suppliers at different vertical stages of a supply chain - or at different levels of the generic industry structures above – may require *access* to core and indispensable services or products in order to provide services to their customers. Several of such indispensable products or services are covered in the last chapter, e.g.:

- In the telecommunications sector: telecoms companies [need to] have access to indispensable fixed local area network (local loop) access to customer homes;

- In the gas sector: gas extraction companies [need to] have access to indispensable national high-pressure and low-pressure national/regional gas distribution pipelines;
- In the electricity sector: electricity generation companies [need to] have access to national high voltage transmission and regional low voltage distribution components and assets;
- In the rail sector: train companies [need to] have access to indispensable railway lines or tracks;
- In the postal sector: postal companies having access to the indispensable delivery from local delivery offices to homes and businesses, i.e. to the not-easy-to-replicate last mile postal delivery workers;
- or even horizontal access with companies at the same level, e.g., a small telecoms firm seeking access to *interconnect* to the subscribers of a much larger telecoms firm (c.f. Figure 2.2).

These above are examples of *access seeking* by new entrants to indispensable assets (or *essential facilities*) typically controlled by a monopoly or dominant operator. The challenge is that a vertically-integrated or vertically-separated structures can generate economies of scope and scale, but they may also create and enable discriminatory behaviour with respect to essential facilities controlled by dominant firms. Access regulation typically comes into its element in such contexts in order to regulate the behaviour of dominant and/or monopoly firms to prevent the potential abuse of their significant market power (SMP). It is instructive to make this explicit distinction between (i) the regulator imposing an access requirement - that is, requiring the regulated firm to provide an access product (and sometimes defining key aspects of that access product) which the firm would *not* otherwise provide; and (ii) set setting terms and conditions as discussed below.

As Figures 3.3 and 3.4 (in Chapter 3) show, such [access] regulation typically involves requirements for non-discriminatory *access* to essential facilities, typically in concert with price controls, and oversight of business practices of the dominant firm. Such *non-price* principles and terms of access fall under *Access Regulation*, whilst the principles and terms about *price of access* falls under *Price Regulation* covered in the next section.

Access challenges emerge when the provision of a complete service to end customers requires the combination of two or more essential inputs, one of which is noncompetitive (i.e., a monopoly). Decker (2023, p. 152) provides an excellent summary of the different methods for determining terms of access as follows, starting from commercial negotiations to regulator-prescribed regulations, i.e., progressively from *ex-post* to *ex-ante*.

1. **Commercially negotiated access terms:** access-seeking service providers proceed to negotiate purely commercial access terms and conditions with the access provider – often the dominant and/or monopoly provider. The access seeker has general competition law to fall back onto if the dominant access provider is being unfair and discriminatory, making this an *ex-post* access approach.

2. **Negotiation-arbitration:** the access-seeking provider negotiates access terms and conditions with the dominant access provider, but this approach also has the additional backstop of regulatory arbitration if parties fail to agree terms. This was an approach we adopted at Ofcom when I was a senior telecoms regulator in the UK telecoms sector.

3. **Regulator-established access principles:** the regulator with this approach imposes a clear set of ex-ante framework and principles on specified dominant access providers emphasizing Fair, Reasonable and Non-Discriminatory (FRND-ly) access terms and conditions to access seekers. The regulator may even prescribe price ceilings and price floors, thereby allowing the access provider to abide by the *ex-ante* framework and principles whilst it freely sets its prices towards access seekers.

4. **Regulator-prescribed access terms [regulations]:** in this approach, the regulator assumes full responsibility for prescribing the specific non-price (access) terms and conditions, and even price prescriptions that the dominant access provider can put on their access seekers, i.e. regulations. This is particularly applicable in situations where the dominant access provider is in a conflict-of-interest position where it is both a supplier and a competitor to the access seeker – as is classically the case in a vertically integrated competitive market.

There are of course more details to these four approaches for determining access-seeking terms and conditions, but these overviews suffice for this chapter.

4.3 [Access] Price Regulation

Access price regulation follows seamlessly from non-price (access) regulation because, as explained in the previous section, price regulation would typically accompany non-price access regulation. Access price regulation [to essential facilities] refers to the regulator and/or Government directly regulating the price new entrants need to pay for access to essential facilities in order to prevent unfair pricing, competition and increase choice for consumers. This can also promote investments, better services for consumers, lower prices, and ultimately an increase in consumer welfare. The regulator can implement this by setting price ceilings (maximum prices) and price floors (minimum prices) or both for specific essential goods and services.

Access pricing is a perennial headache of regulators because operators - particularly incumbents seeking to maximise their profits and shareholder value - would typically engage lawyers and consultants in order to challenge the access prices proposed by regulators. It is also an age-old challenge too as is evidenced by the following quote from an excellent 2004 OECD Access Pricing Report (though the following quote pertains to both non-price access and price regulation):

> "As a result of the waves of deregulation of the past two decades, the regulation of the terms and conditions under which competing firms have access to essential inputs provided by rivals has become the single biggest issue facing regulators of public utility industries. This issue is both theoretically complex and inherently controversial. Since the development of competition and the success of liberalisation often depend on the access terms and conditions chosen, there is also a strong public policy interest in getting these terms and conditions "right". At the same time, new entrant firms and incumbents often have a substantial financial

stake in the outcome and therefore a strong interest in negotiating aggressively" – Source OECD[212].

The regulator should just expect such access regulation litigations as a fact of regulatory life. It is important to stick rigidly to well-established *best-practice access price setting principles and frameworks* when seeking to grant access to essential facilities efficiently.

There are two aspects that need to be addressed by the principles and frameworks. First, the *level* at which the access price is set, and secondly, the *structure* of prices. The level is clear as it simply refers to what specific price is set, but the structure is a bit more complex as explained below. The structure of prices is equally as important and critical to effective regulation because it directly has a strong bearing on the incentives of both access seekers and access providers. For example, the structure will determine the difference between the access price and the retail price. Why? The regulator may set both the end-user prices of the incumbent [or set some constraining parameters] as well as setting the access prices themselves. Furthermore, if the structure of end-user prices of the regulated dominant firm is expected to result in an inefficient market outcome (e.g. due to a restriction of competitive forces), the regulator can set a more efficient structure of access prices and rely on competition to force the end-user prices of the incumbent into line with its downstream retail rivals. The structure of the regulated prices will also depend on the need to raise [subsidy] revenues (see later) in excess of that raised through pricing at marginal costs, and the extent to which the operator and/or the regulator can discriminate in its prices. The structure may also be about the relative prices of substitute access products, or prices by time of day, etc.

4.3.1 The Basic Principles of Access Pricing – pricing derived from marginal costs

We note earlier in the previous section that access problems emerge when the provision of a complete service to end customers requires the combination of two or more essential inputs, one of which is

---

[212] https://www.oecd.org/daf/competition/18645197.pdf

noncompetitive (i.e., a monopoly). There are two key main categories of access problems:

- **One-way access problems**: the first category is called "one-way" access - this arises when *access seekers* of a competitive service (likely downstream) need to purchase essential upstream non-competitive service inputs from the *access provider*, but not vice versa, i.e. the access provider does not reciprocate to buy any essential inputs from the access seekers. This is important because, sometimes, there may [or would] be no bargaining power at all from the perspective of the access seekers with respect to the access provider. However, this is not necessarily the case - the access seeker may have a large customer base to drive the required economies of scale and the incumbent may not have access to such customer base. Several access seeking examples are provided in the previous section.

- **Two-way access problems**: the second category is called "two-way" access – and this arises when an access provider supplies some products as essential inputs to other firms, whilst simultaneously purchasing products as essential inputs to its services production from other firms too. Such two-way arrangements are a feature of network industry sectors such as telecommunications, e.g. a fixed network connecting into a mobile network, i.e., fixed-to-mobile access. Evidently (assuming the fixed and mobile networks are operated by different firms), the mobile network operator needs the essential inputs from the fixed network operator in order to provide mobile telecoms services to the latter's [i.e. fixed] end customers – and vice versa. Mobile-to-mobile access, internet-access and payments access (e.g., between banks say) are further examples of two-way access. Such two-way access may be more symmetrical allowing for more commercially negotiated access terms, or very asymmetrical requiring regulatory access intervention.

4.3.1.1 Marginal Costs Pricing Theory – 'First-best' and 'Second-best' pricings

For ether one-way access or two-way access, the same economic principles of efficient access pricing apply – with the most basic principle being that of applying the marginal pricing concept. The reader may or would recall from Chapter 2 that addressing the natural monopoly challenges require regulators to set prices closer to marginal costs (LRMC) – see Figure 2.1. Indeed, Section 2.2.1 provides the basic concepts for price regulation which the reader may want to refer to (again). Recall that practically all network industries are characterised by economies of scale and scope in at least some of their components. Section 2.2.1.2 explains that in the presence such of such economies of scale, density and scope economies, setting all the prices of a firm at marginal cost (thereby achieving *allocative efficiency*[213]) would *not* allow the dominant firm to earn sufficient revenue to cover its total costs. The reader can revisit Figure 2.1 shows how if a private natural monopoly is forced to change production to the socially optimum point - i.e., the point at which price or average revenue (AR) equals marginal cost (LRMC) – then it will make *subnormal profits*, thereby requiring *subsidies*. Governments may choose to fund such subsidies from general tax revenues (i.e., revenues mostly collected from outside the regulated industry), or from specifically taxing on the products/services of firms in the specific sector including the regulated firm.

If such subsidies are not available from the Government, we also observe in Section 2.2.1.1 that the regulator may choose to settle for the private natural monopoly producing a lower quantity of output than the socially optimum allocative efficiency quantity. This would mean that the regulator is accepting or proposing pricing above marginal (allocative efficiency) costs in order for the firm to recoup all its costs, i.e., the subnormal profits costs of Figure 2.1 (and no more).

---

[213] This point of *allocative efficiency* occurs at the optimising of the level of output produced at a price equivalent to the marginal cost of production (See Figure 2.1 in Chapter 2).

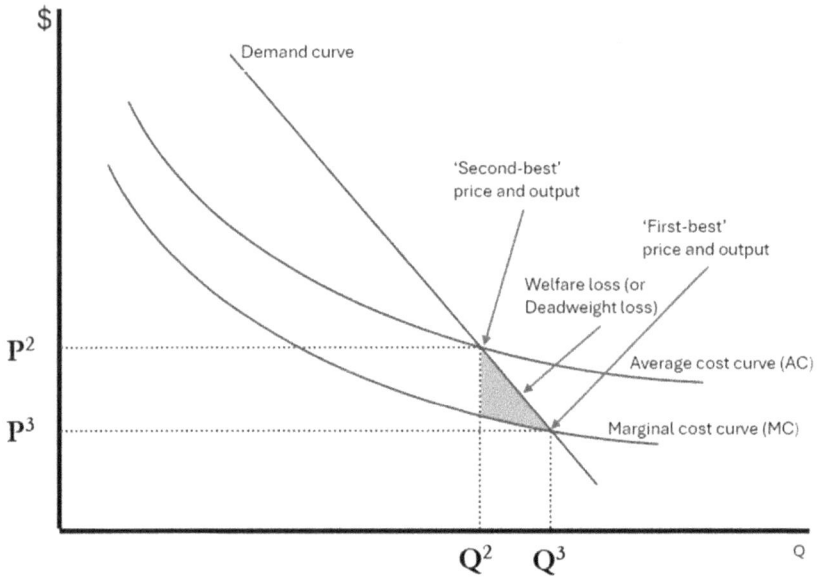

$
P^2
P^3
Q
Q^2 Q^3

Demand curve

'Second-best'
price and output

'First-best'
price and output

Welfare loss (or
Deadweight loss)

Average cost curve (AC)

Marginal cost curve (MC)

Figure 4.3 – Illustrating 'First-best' and 'Second-best' pricing – a
summary version of Chapter 2's Figure 2.1

(Source: Based on and adapted from Decker, 2023, p. 78; reproduced with permission Prof Decker and Publisher)

Figure 4.3 provides an excellent summary of the marginal costs pricing theory that also underpins much determination of access pricing. It clearly depicts – as Figure 2.1 and its narrative is explained in Chapter 2 – that the socially optimum quantity produced and pricing point in order to achieve allocative efficiency happens at Q^3 and P^3 respectively. This is the point at which price or average revenue (AR/Demand curve) equals marginal cost (MC). This is also the point of *allocative efficiency*, i.e., because it optimises the level of output produced at a price equivalent to the marginal cost of production. At this optimum point, society gets the maximum output at the lowest price possible. This point is also called the 'First-best' pricing and output point as shown in Figure 4.3. This core marginal costs theory principle - and 'first-best' and 'second-best' pricings specifically - underpins how access prices are set. However, as we observe earlier in this section (as well as in Chapter 2), this 'first-best' pricing approach would require subsidies to cover the subnormal profits (indeed losses – see Figure 2.1) that would be borne by the incumbent firm if it produces at quantities

Q^3 in Figure 4.3[214]. So, if the Government can raise the revenues from general taxation to cover these losses to the monopoly incumbent, pricing at P^3 for quantity Q^3 would be fine. This is where the principle and theory of the 'first-best' pricing approach can be implemented in practice. Nevertheless, in most developing countries, Government spare cash for subsidies are hard to come by leading them to implement the 'second-best' pricing approach allowing the incumbent firm to supply less than the socially-optimum quantity and at a higher price in order to recover the subnormal losses. The 'second-best' quantity and pricing are Q^2 and P^2 respectively as shown in in Figure 4.3. However, this deviation from not using external cash subsidies leads to an inefficient pricing scenario, as is depicted by the *welfare loss* area of the triangle shown in Figure 4.3.

What is most important to note here is that the marginal costs pricing principle and theory of this section underpins the real-world access pricing approaches overviewed next.

4.3.1.2 Real World Access Pricing Approaches: Ramsey-Boiteux, ECPR, Cost Plus Pricing & Price Caps

Here we look at three main approaches including the Ramsey-Boiteux, ECPR, Cost Plus Pricing and Price Caps. They are all variant approaches that all build on the long-run marginal costs (LRMC) approach of the previous section, not long-run incremental costs (LRIC) [215] as I personally sometimes confuse the two too. As a brief introduction to a couple of these approaches, the Ramsey-Boiteux and the ECPR are occasionally implemented in practice, but more generally provide useful conceptual benchmarks. The objective of Ramsey-Boiteux pricing is the *allocatively* efficient pattern of recovery of fixed and common costs. The objective of ECPR is principally *productive* efficiency, to provide a signal for efficient new entry in competition with the vertically-integrated regulated incumbent firm, i.e., the new entrant will only be profitable at the access price set according to ECPR if it has lower costs than the incumbent for the contested retail product.

---

[214] Figure 4.3 assumes a single product. Where there are multiple products, marginal cost pricing for a subset can sometimes be combined with the recovery of fixed and common costs from other products without the need for a government subsidy (e.g., electricity).

[215] LRMC and LRIC are not identical. The difference is the increment used to assess costs - for LRMC it is a single additional unit, whereas for LRIC it is usually a larger increment of volume (sometimes the entire service volume).

Ramsey-Boiteux 'mark-ups' pricing approach: the use of Ramsey-Boiteux (R-B) pricing arises more clearly in the case of multiple access products, whereas pricing a single access and single retail product includes the additional complication of *margin squeeze* risks and *cream skimming* which are central to the ECPR (see below). Therefore, R-B pricing is arguably more efficient in a multi-product context, and is typically referred to as a second-best policy approach (see Figure 4.3) to what prices a public monopoly should charge for the various products it sells in order to achieve allocative efficiency whilst recovering its fixed and common costs, i.e. maximizing social welfare (the sum of producer and consumer surplus). Therefore, in order to collect subsidy/subnormal profits revenues (as covered above in Figure 4.3) to achieve the second-best policy pricing, it may be appropriate to set prices of one or more substitute or complementary access products above their marginal (LRMC) costs. It is usually efficient with R-B to use various forms of price discrimination [of substitute or complementary access products] by applying mark-ups to the marginal costs of these 'separate' access products.

For example, if different access services produced by the regulated firm are substitutes or complements for one another (e.g., a DSL copper-based broadband service vs. a fibre-based broadband service), the regulator is typically *not* free to set these substitute access prices independently. Such [R-B] pricing aims to minimise the distortion in demand consumption that arises from pricing above marginal costs. In practice, this R-B approach is not much practiced because, in reality, both products would have different demand profiles. In addition, some jurisdictions do not legally allow R-B anyway. Regulators also find it difficult to implement, and the mark-ups could also be slightly arbitrary, and hence R-B tends to generally provide useful conceptual pricing benchmarks.

Efficient Component Pricing Rule (ECPR): the ECPR is fundamentally about the relationship between access and retail prices - not substitute access products as with R-B pricing. In the case of perfect substitutes or close enough (like fibre vs. copper-based broadband discussed above), the relationship between the access price and the end-customer retail price[216] should be dictated by some form of a rule – and one such rule is called the Efficient Component Pricing Rule (ECPR), sometimes referred to as *Retail-Minus*. Though there are several variants of the ECPR rule, the core

---

[216] Or the portion of the retail price finally retained by the rival competitor if the retail price includes a tax.

of this approach is that of a price charged based on the LRMC marginal cost of access (of taking on the new business customer) plus the likely reduction in the regulated firm's profits as a result of losing business to the new entrant. The key assumption here is that it is the new entrant, rather than the regulated dominant firm, who will supply the end customer. Effectively, this is the same as the incumbent's final product price minus the costs the firm would avoid by providing access – this is why it is also called retail-minus. The regulated access provider firm therefore recovers all its common and fixed costs, sunk costs, and even including a return on its capital. The ECPR was developed in the USA in the late 1980s and early 1990s by Professors Baumol [217] and Willig, and therefore is sometimes known as the *Baumol-Willig rule* (Baumol & Sidak, 1994). The ECPR has a strong disadvantage in that it deters new entry, and so tends not to be used too much either.

Cost Plus (Cost-based pricing or LRIC pricing): due to the many limitations and complexities of both the Ramey-Boiteux and ECPR pricing approaches, many regulators opt for a third approach called *Cost Plus*. Once again, this approach involves calculating the long-run marginal cost (LRMC) of providing the access service – *sometimes* on the assumption that the dominant access provider is efficient. This is because Cost Plus regulated access prices may, but do not always, assume efficient costs which depends on the evidence used and the objective. If the cost evidence is the regulated firm's incurred costs, it will typically include inefficiencies. Broadly, incurred costs are more relevant to allocative efficiency, whereas efficient costs are relevant to productive efficiency. All these mean that the cost-plus access price is largely based on direct costs of providing access – sending a much better signal to new entrants. Typically with cost plus, some contribution is added for the access provider's fixed and common costs which can be much broader than overheads, e.g. those arising from economies of scale. However unlike with ECPR, such added costs exclude costs such as any compensation for the regulated firm's lost profits in the downstream retail market due to providing access. Other costs that may be excluded [depending on circumstances] include corporate head offices costs, sales and marketing costs, and directors' remunerations.

In summary, it truly depends on the objective(s) of the regulator. Cost plus access prices can sometimes be set to reflect *incurred,* not efficient costs.

---

[217] The same Professor Baumol whose equations we cover in Chapter 2 (see Section 2.2.1.1).

The latter approach [efficient costs] would lead to low access prices, as the LRMC cost in a network industry structure can be very low compared to bloated incumbent firm costs because of their inefficient and high central corporate costs with too many employees. A *cost-plus* approach can therefore be a very good at attracting new entrants.

4.4 Rate of Return and Price Cap [Price Controls] Regulation

Rate of Return and Price Cap Regulation are also price regulations which are widely used, but differ from access price regulation of the previous section. Indeed, access prices are often regulated using price caps or rate of return regulation. In contrast, as we cover above, access price regulation truly majors on promoting new entry competition into the competitive components of the value chain of natural monopoly sectors as we cover extensively in Chapter 3.

We also cover in the several different industry sectors we overview in Chapter 3 (electricity, post, water & waste management, gas and telecoms) how naturally monopoly firms in these sectors are also typically subject to active *price controls* via rate of return regulation, price caps and regulation of rate structures. As Decker (2023, p. 291) clarifies, price caps and rate of return regulation dictate the overall level of allowed revenues that regulated network and distribution firms can recoup.

Price controls – as we cover plenty in Chapter 3 – strive to balance between the interests of consumers (through protecting them from exploitation by monopoly firms) and the interests of investors (who typically have to sink huge sums of investments into network infrastructures and need returns for their shareholders). If investors perceive that the regulator is only or mostly concerned about the interests of consumers, they will not invest or they will be deterred from investing. On the other hand if the regulator is asleep at the wheels, consumers would get a poor deal through providers exploiting and price-gouging them. We overview two well-known price controls approaches next.

4.4.1 Rate of Return Regulation

Rate of return regulation - until circa twenty-five years ago (i.e., up to 2000) - was arguably the most utilized traditional approach to price setting regulation where the regulator or Government determines a fair price to be charged by a monopoly. It is arguably still the most used form of price regulation in the USA. This 'fair price' is clearly meant to protect customers from being exploited via higher prices due to the monopoly firm's SMP, whilst ensuring the firm covers its costs outlay and earns a fair return for its shareholders.

The *simplified* Rate of Return Regulation basic formula goes as follows (Jamison[218]):

$$R \equiv (E + d + T) + B \bullet r, \textit{broadly} \text{ simplified as}$$
$$R \equiv Opex^{219} + B \bullet r \qquad \qquad \textbf{Equation 4}$$

where:

- R = the total revenue the firm needs to acquire from all the services it provides;
- B = rate base, which is the value of all the firm's invested Capital exPenditure (CaPex) (all capital on the balance sheet less the accumulated depreciation);
- r = the allowed 'fair' rate of return applied to the rate base, i.e., the allowed rate the firm can incur to finance its rate base, including both debt and equity;
- E = the operating expenses (OpEx) associated with supplying those regulatory services, including costs of items such as supplies, labour (but e.g., not those used for construction of networks), and items for resale that are used by the business in a short period of time (i.e., less than one year);

---

[218] Mark A. Jamison (University of Florida), Rate of Return: Regulation, https://bear.warrington.ufl.edu/centers/purc/docs/papers/0528_jamison_rate_of_return.pdf

[219] Jamison defines 'Opex' here as excluding depreciation (which is the usual definition). This simplification suggests that the firm does not receive any revenue for depreciation. Depreciation is the firm recovering the principal of its investment, so excluding it would clearly fail to reward investors adequately. Therefore, this approach excluding depreciation may or is not generally adopted.

- d = annual depreciation expense, which is the annual accounting charge for wear, tear, and obsolescence of capital items such as network infrastructure built; and
- T = all taxes not counted as operating expenses and not directly charged to customer.

Equation 4 is a much simpler formula that the previous three equations of Chapter 2. The rate of return regulation equation essentially states that the firm is allowed to recover all the costs (Revenues) clearly linked to providing all its set of regulated services (i.e., cost items E, d and T) *plus* an allowable 'fair' rate of return on the capital rate base, i.e. B x r. This last (B x r) revenues must be sufficient enough to maintain the firm's investors' appetite and willingness to maintain, replace and even expand the company's asset base. The key requirement is that prices of regulatory services are set to ensure that the total revenues gleaned from the providing the services covers the total costs, plus a fair return on regulated asset base.

As can be seen from the rate of return regulation formula, it is also akin to *Cost Plu*s regulation of the last section because Equation 4 shows a bunch of OpEx costs *added* to revenues obtained from multiplying a bunch of CaPex costs with a rate, r. This is why the broader equation is further simplified to $R \equiv \text{Opex} + B \cdot r$.

		Total
Opex		$250,000,000
'Fair' rate of return	10%	
Rate Base	$500,000,000	
Return on rate base	=10% x $500,000,000	$50,000,000
Total revenue to recover		$300,000,000

Table 4.1 – Illustrating the Application of Rate of Return Formula

Table 4.1 illustrates Equation 4 in simple practice. I hope it simplifies and clarifies even to the reader who may be mathematics-fearing.

There are some clear advantages to this approach. First, it is and it looks reasonably straightforward in theory as per Equation 4 (and Table 4.1), but putting it in practice requires much tricky discretion on the part of the regulator or the Government setting the prices using rate of return regulation. However, it is usually very manageable. Secondly, customers benefit from reasonable prices since all the monopolist firm's operating costs are known or are estimated. This approach provides certainty in revenues for monopoly firms, whilst preventing them from price-gouging customers. Investors will not make huge dividends, but they will benefit from 'fair' and consistent returns.

There are clear disadvantages too. First, the monopolist firm has no true incentive to be efficient because - with a *de facto* cost-plus rate of return approach – it knows it will recover any increasing costs through increasing prices and revenues as Equation 4 shows. Rate of return regulation does not drive an innovative costs-reduction mindset, as the firm will not earn more if costs are reduced – leading to scenarios where customers may still be subjected to higher prices than they would be under free competition. Secondly, this approach can lead to scenarios wherein the regulated firm even accumulates more capital (CaPex) in order to have more annual depreciation expenses, d (see Equation 4)[220], thereby creating a context where they can seek the regulator's permission to raise their rates r (through a *rate case process*[221]), and revenues, R. Economists call this behavioural dilemma the Averch-Johnson effect, after the classic paper by these two authors - Averch & Johnson (1962).

4.4.2 Price Cap & Revenue Cap Regulation

Price capping regulation is today the most widely used form of price regulation across the world including in Europe, Australia, New Zealand, USA and Africa – and across many sectors of economies including telecommunications, water, gas, electricity, rail, bus transportation, and other public utilities and more. Price caps are sometimes referred to as *multi-year rate plans* or *performance-based* regulation.

---

[220] Recall the simplification in Equation 4 excludes depreciation. Capex leads to more depreciation but also to an increase in the rate base on which a return is earned.

[221] This is a process that regulators or Governments would transparently follow to determine whether a firm rate of return (r) - decided tariffs or prices should be adjusted.

Essentially, price cap regulation is a type of economic regulation that sets cap or ceiling limits on the retail, wholesale or basket prices that a firm can charge. It was first applied in a large scale in 1984 in the United Kingdom to British Telecommunications post a recommendation from the influential 1983 Professor Littlechild report (Littlechild, 1983) that we cite from in Chapter 3, Section 3.4. The key characteristic context of a price cap approach is when a firm is able to charge prices that are not linked to their underlying costs for protracted periods of time. Price caps *would* protect consumers from unexpected costs hikes faced by the firm [e.g. price of a kilowatt of electricity or a cubic metre of gas[222]] which the firms want to pass on to consumers - hikes which the firm could have hedged or insured against making it their responsibility.

A price cap is set according to several economic and other factors, such as inflation, a price cap index, expected efficiency savings, and how long the cap will last for before it is reviewed. The basic price cap formula goes as follows:

$$\%\Delta p \leq I - X + K + Q \qquad \textbf{Equation 5}$$

where:

- $\%\Delta p$ = percentage increase in price
- I = is the economy-wide rate of inflation measure, typically the Retail Price Index (RPI)
- X = the offset factor, or a percentage factor set by the regulator
- K = network expansion
- Q = improved quality of service

This formula – if used by the regulator to regulate a firm's prices - constrains a firm over the period of a price control. In essence with price caps, the regulator sets a maximum or ceiling on the increase in prices for the specified set of regulated products or services for a specified period of

---

[222] I acknowledge that these may not be the best examples because there may be a passthrough element in retail energy caps as happened in the UK as a consequence of the Russia-Ukraine crisis.

time, typically between 4 to 6 years. The price increases being constrained via price capping are assumed - to some degree - to be independent of the underlying costs required to provide the regulated products and services. The formula also tries to incentivize network expansion K and quality of service, Q. If we ignore network expansion and quality of service for now, Equation 5 is typically further simplified to

$$\%\Delta p \leq I - X,$$

with the X factor being the "productivity offset". Many regulators would consider network expansion and quality of service as implicit in the productivity offset X factor too. This is because of the *information asymmetry problem* between a regulator and a regulated firm, wherein the latter generally knows more than its regulator about how much it would cost to build a certain level and quality of network improvements or expansion. A key important point (covered later below) is that the price cap is usually set based on a forecast of future efficient costs.

Furthermore, since I is usually taken from the economy wide Consumer Price Index (CPI) measure, then Equation 5 is much simplified as Equation 6 following.

$$\%\Delta p \leq CPI^{223} - X \qquad \qquad \textbf{Equation 6}$$

Interpreting Equation 6 in other words, with price cap regulation, the firm's average price increase is constrained by a price index that generally includes a measure of inflation[224] less a "productivity offset", X, generally reflecting expected changes in the firm's productivity, with network expansion and quality of service implied in the X-factor – as we note earlier.

---

[223] https://www.ons.gov.uk/economy/inflationandpriceindices/methodologies/consumerpriceinflationincludesall3indicescpihcpiandrpiqmi). CPI is currently more common around the world than RPI as an acronym for inflation? The UK historically used RPI, but its regulators have now generally switched to CPI in accordance with the ONS (which states that the RPI index does not meet the required statistical standard).

[224] e.g., the UK's Retail Price Index or the U.S. Gross Domestic Product Implicit Price Deflator

There is a bit more to the X-factor. As Jamison cogently explains:

> "the X-factor should represent the difference between the regulated firm and the average firm in the economy. There are two key differences to consider, namely, the regulated company's ability to *improve productivity*, and *changes in its input costs*. If the regulated company can improve its productivity more than the average firm in the economy, or if the regulated company's input prices increase less than input prices for the average firm, this would imply X > 0. The opposite situations would imply X < 0. If the regulated firm is just like the average firm, this would imply X = 0. For example, consider a situation in which the average firm in the economy improves its productivity by 3 percent per year and its input prices increase 1 percent per year. Further assume that the regulated firm can improve its productivity by 5 percent per year and its input prices actually decrease 2 percent per year. The appropriate X-factor would be X = (5 – 3) – (–2 – 1) = 5" - Source[225].

In the interest of good scholarship, one of the expert economist reviewers of this book critiqued this US-centric derivation of the productivity X-factor thus:

> "Is this really how the productivity factor is set in the USA, through comparing the regulated firm to the average firm in the economy. It sounds odd to me and it is more usual in the UK to estimate the firm's efficient future costs such as through studies on its specific inefficiency, or by comparison to similar benchmark firms in the same country or to firms supplying similar output in other countries. The X factor would then include a catch-up element between incurred costs and the efficient level of costs, as well as the expected year-on-year changes in real costs, e.g. due to technology improvements etc.".

So how does the price cap work in true practice? Typically the regulator groups products and services into price or service baskets and then establishes an (CPI – X) index for each basket called a *price cap index*.

---

[225] https://bear.warrington.ufl.edu/centers/purc/docs/papers/0527_jamison_regulation_pric e_cap.pdf

Establishing price baskets is more efficient because it allows the firm to change prices within the basket as the firm wishes so long as the average percentage change in prices for the services in the basket does not exceed the price cap index for the basket.

The firm will have to seek the permission of the regulator to change any prices in the basket such that the regulator is clear that the overall price cap is being adhered to.

Table 4.2 illustrates how a price cap and a revenue cap will work with a basket of three telecoms services provided by a fixed telecoms provider. It also shows how the price capping provides flexibility for different price changes in the basket, subject to not breaching the price cap. Most price cap regimes base prices on past costs or expected costs and typically last 4 to 6 years.

The key benefits as hopefully observed with the illustration of Table 4.2 is that price caps create incentives to cut costs by fixing prices for several years ahead, and works in the same way for wholesale or retail prices. The choosing of the X-factor is both an art and a science by regulators – and the contentious part of the process is that the regulator makes projections of costs for the regulated firm into the future, and sets a price cap regime yielding overall prices that it expects will cover the firm's costs. How can the regulator possibly know what a firm's future costs should be? One disadvantage is that regulators need to be prepared to be litigated by dominant firms on their projections. Another disadvantage is that setting the price cap regimes are typically protracted because regulators go through multiple rounds of consultations, decisions and inevitable appeals. It can typically take 30 months to decide on a price cap regime from start to finish. This is one of the reasons that once they are set, they usually last 4 to 6 years – they are too painful for the regulator to do often. In the EU, most price controls for telecoms – and therefore price cap regimes in the telecoms sector – have migrated from retail prices to wholesale or network prices.

Price cap: RPI-6.3, i.e. X-factor = 6.3		Revenue Cap: RPI-7.3	
Previous year's RPI: 3			
Therefore, permitted weighted average change in nominal prices under the Price cap: 3 – 6.3 = -3.3 – and for Revenue Cap: 3 – 7.3 = -4.3			
Services in Basket	Previous year's revenues ($millions)	Previous year's revenue proportion	Proposed price change (%)
Rental Service for fixed line into household	500	20% (0.2)	-2
Voice Service	1000	30% (0.3)	-3
Broadband service	800	50% (0.5)	-4
Weighted average price change calculations for price caps regime = (0.2 x -2) + (0.3 x -3) + (0.5 x -4) = (-0.4) + (-0.9) + (-2) = -3.3		Weighted average revenue change calculations for price caps regime = (500 x .98)+(1000 x .97)+(800 x .96) = (490) + (970) + (768) = 2228M 2300M previous year total down to 2228M, means (-4.3%) reduction	
Price cap decision: Price changes are compliant with the Price Cap.			
Revenue cap decision: Price changes are compliant with the Revenue Cap.			

Table 4.2 – Illustrating an implementation of a price cap and a revenue cap regime

[NB: this table deliberately presents both a price cap *and* a revenue cap as alternative representations of the *same* price control]

It is important to note that if the regulated firm improves on its efficiency compared to the X factor based on a forecast (e.g. by deploying new and cheaper technology or reducing OpEx costs), then its profits will go up under the price cap regime. If the firm is less efficient, the profits will go down. The price cap regime may be too generous (i.e., a *lax cap* was set) to the firm resulting in what the regulator deems as excess profits during the price cap regime period. In this case the regulator can implement a one-off adjustment to realign prices more to costs called the '*Po adjustment*'. Alternatively, the regulator will take that into consideration and adjust prices in the next price cap regime period, where it can gradually eliminate the excess profits – this is known as a *glide path*.

As depicted in Table 4.2, Revenue cap regulation is similar to price cap regulation. The regulator similarly establishes an RPI – X index [the revenue cap index] for a basket of services, and allows the firm to change prices within the basket whilst ensuring the percentage change in revenue does not exceed the revenue cap index. Revenue cap regulation is generally more appropriate than price cap regulation when costs do not vary that much with unit sales.

To conclude this section with an example, from the UK telecoms sector, interconnection charges were regulated at incurred (not efficient) fully allocated costs - similar to rate of return regulation - until the mid-1990s when it was then changed to price caps based on LRIC + mark-up.

4.5 SMP/Dominance, Market Analysis Regulation & the SSNIP Test – determining when and how to regulate

Determining *when* and *how* to regulate is the role of SMP/Dominance & Relevant Market Analysis methods of regulations respectively, i.e., determining when to use SMP/Dominance methods whilst determining what it entails a relevant markets analyses. Hence, Figure 4.4 deliberately combines Chapter 3's Figures 3.10 and 3.12 to cover both SMP/Dominance method and the EU/EC market analysis process. At the top in the regulation oval of Figure 4.4, we have Significant Market Power SMP Regulation and Non-SMP Regulation. At the top of the Competition Law oval we have Dominance.

Indeed, the EU pioneered key internationally accepted approaches to competition regulation, particularly in the communications sector. The European framework has four main steps:

1. Market definition using, *inter alia*, the Hypothetical Monopolist Test (HMT);
2. Identification of relevant markets subject to *ex-ante* regulation using the three criteria test (3CT);
3. Market analysis/identification of players with Significant Market Power (SMP) and/or dominance; and
4. Selection and imposition of remedies.

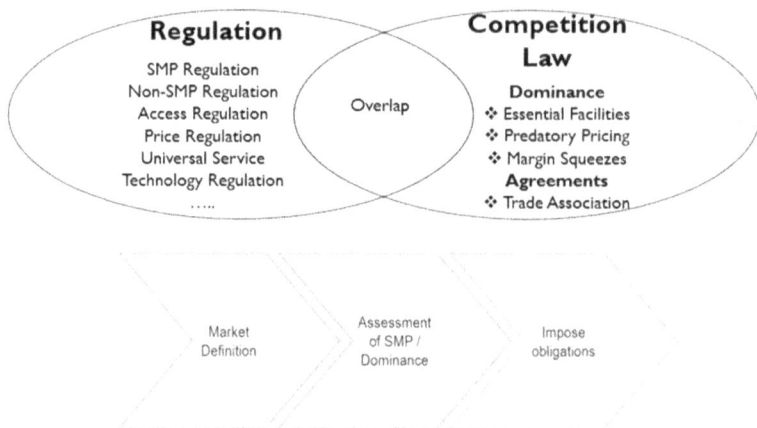

Figure 4.4 – Determining When and How to Regulate

The next four sections tackle the above four steps broadly and sequentially.

4.5.1 Market Definition, the Notion of Relevant Market & the HMT/SSNIP Test

The market definition stage is a critically important first step in competition analysis. Unless and until the market is defined and its boundaries in terms of services and geography are clearly known, it is difficult (though not impossible) to determine where whether any one or more operators have SMP or dominant position. An operator must only be defined as dominant in an explicitly-defined economic market.

A market definition, as Figure 4.4 shows, is the start of a market review process in order to find SMP/dominance – or not. The purpose of a market review is to pre-empt or correct for market failure so that competition *can possibly* replace regulation, where and if appropriate (see again Figure 4.4). Correcting a market failure requires – in the first place - that product and geographic markets are correctly defined so that regulation takes place only in the 'relevant' markets where there is indeed a competition problem.

So, what is a relevant market and why is it needed? The definition of a relevant market is always clearly prescribed in the network sector *law* concerned, in the Competition Law or both of the said jurisdiction. Relevant markets are broadly defined to determine the boundaries within which a competition problem may exist. Recall the boundary components

198

that Chapter 3 delineates for the several network industries that it overviews, seeking opportunities for new entry into some of the components (see Sections 3.5 to 3.10). The notion of relevant market goes beyond these. In [competition] law, a relevant market is a market in which a particular product or service is sold. The relevant market combines the product market and the *geographic market*. For example, the Saudi Telecoms Regulator (CST) has defined and designated circa fifteen relevant markets for their telecoms sector including (source[226]):

- Market 1 - Retail fixed access and local and national fixed call services,
- Market 2 – Retail fixed broadband access services,
- Market 4 - Retail national mobile services,
- Market 5 - Retail international call services,
- Market 13 - Wholesale mobile access and origination services,
- Market 14 - Wholesale mobile termination services,
- Market 15 - Wholesale international voice call services.

The reader can observe from these Saudi relevant telecom markets that they combine the product market and the geographic market, e.g. Market 1 refers to a retail fixed access telecoms product and services across homes and business across the geography of Saudi Arabia. Market 15 refers to wholesale voice services that extend to any geography internationally, i.e. outside the Kingdom of Saudi Arabia (KSA). Therefore, despite the fact that national boundaries and product characteristics are good starting points to define markets, a relevant market clearly consists of a set of products and geographical areas that exercise some competitive constraint on each other. Saudi's telecoms relevant Market 2 above is for 'Retail fixed broadband access services' - it delineates a set of products or services that are considered 'fixed broadband' substitutes by consumers, both in terms of their characteristics and the geographic area where they are offered. The 'fixed broadband' substitutes would typically include copper, fibre or may be even Fixed Wireless Access (FWA)-based products like Wi-Fi. The point of relevant market definition analysis is to identify the boundaries of the market where firms compete, and to assess market power for competition purposes.

---

[226] CITC Final MDDD report - FINAL - 26 10 17 (cst.gov.sa) - https://www.cst.gov.sa/en/reportsandstudies/Reports/Documents/PL-SP-317-E-Market%20Definition%20Designation%20and%20Dominance%20Report.pdf

The test that is commonly used to identify the relevant market is called the Hypothetical Monopolist Test (HMT). The HMT employs the notion of a hypothetical monopolist and asks whether a small but significant (usually assumed to mean a 5-10% increase) non-transient (i.e., at least 1-year's duration) increase in price for the product in question is likely to be profitable for that supplier. The HMT is also called the Small but Significant Non-transitory Increase in Price (or SSNIP) test. Excluding all its esoteric details, the hypothetical test essentially examines if consumers would switch to substitute products in the hypothetical event of small but significant and non-transitory increase in prices (typically between 5-10%) of a particular product or service over a period of say 1 to 2 years. This will depend on the number of customers that move to a substitute service or/and the extent to which alternative suppliers are enticed into the market. If the small but significant non-transient increase in price (or "SSNIP") is profitable, then this will be evidence of the absence of appropriate substitutes, and therefore of the boundaries of a discrete market. If the increase is *not* profitable, the service definition needs to be expanded to include the substitute service(s). I say no more about the HMT/SSNIP test whose details can be seen in this classic OECD (2012) paper[227].

4.5.2 SMP, Dominance & Market Concentration

Recall in Chapter 3, we note that the overlap area in Figure 4.4 represents the ongoing regulation vs. competition dynamic that is ever present with the regulation of network industries - and that it includes the 'dynamic duos' of SMP versus Dominance, i.e., SMP is the Regulation 'equivalent' to Dominance with Competition Law – hence we combine both concepts in this section. Indeed, Dominance and SMP are often used interchangeably.

Dominance is inescapably linked to another economic concept called *market concentration*. As per the online Cambridge dictionary[228], it is a measure of the degree to which a small number of companies control a large part of a market. This is important because such a market concentration measure is usually taken as a proxy for the real intensity of competition. A firm possessing 100% of a market is clearly legally

---

[227] Market Definition (oecd.org) -
https://www.oecd.org/daf/competition/Marketdefinition2012.pdf

[228] https://dictionary.cambridge.org/us/dictionary/english/market-concentration

dominant in most jurisdictions. However, in the case of an oligopoly of few number of companies (e.g. 2 or 3) 'dominating' an entire market segment, the concept of dominance is more contentious legally, e.g., with 2 or 3 retail mobile telephone firms – they may or may not be *jointly* dominant in that relevant market. In such an oligopoly context whether or not they would be *jointly dominant* requires evidence of collusive behaviour between the firms for a finding of joint (or collective) dominance, as is roughly speaking the situation with EU case law.

The main approach to determining dominance is through determining market share thresholds and the strength of competitive constraints. In most jurisdictions, the usual approach is that a firm having a market share persistently in excess of 40% is an indicator of dominance, although dominance assessment is not just mechanical and should include analysing the nature of competition with rivals and the size of barriers to entry.

Another important commonly accepted measure indicator of *market concentration* is that referred to as the Herfindahl–Hirschman Index (HHI). However, HHI is more widely used in merger or oligopoly analysis than in an assessment of single-firm dominance. The HHI is calculated by squaring the market share of each firm in the market and then summing the resulting numbers. For example, for a market consisting of four firms with shares of 30, 30, 20, and 20 percent, the HHI is 2,600 ($30^2 + 30^2 + 20^2 + 20^2 = 2,600$). In contrast, in a market where only two operators share around 50% each, the HHI would be 5,000 ($50^2 + 50^2$).

The HHI indicator takes into account the relative distribution of the sizes of the firms in a market. It approaches zero – never zero - when a market is occupied by a large number of firms of relatively equal size. Imagine 50 firms with 2% market share each, the HHI is 200 (i.e., 2^2 x 50). Imagine 100 firms with 1% market share each, the HHI is 100 (i.e., 1^2 x 100). On the other hand, the HHI reaches its maximum of 10,000 points when a market is controlled by a single firm, i.e. 100% market share or 100^2 which equals 10,000. Therefore, the HHI increases both as the number of firms in the market decreases and as the disparity in size between those firms increases. In major OECD economies, regulatory or competition agencies generally consider markets with HHIs between 1,500 and 2,500 points to be only moderately concentrated. They consider markets with HHI in excess of 2,500 points to be significantly concentrated. In contrast, HHIs are typically greater than 3,000+ in most developing market contexts – as is clearly exemplified by the example above of two operators sharing 50%

of the market each. In many mostly poorly regulated retail mobile markets in South East Asia and Africa, there may be two players with 70% and 30% market shares say leading to an HHI of 5,800. This HHI is this high due to high level of *dominance* of the 70% market share operator. Such dominance levels are usually antithetical to competition, no matter how benevolent the operator may protest to be.

Let us return to the concept of dominance. The concept of SMP/Dominance regulation is a clear recognition that liberalisation and opening up to competition of the network industries like telecoms sector does not [and did not in the past] simply mean the removal of barriers to market entry. Barriers to market entry and unlevel playing fields remain. Therefore as we cover with the theory and hypotheses of regulation in previous chapters, network industries require 'interventionist' regulation (see again Figure 4.4) in order to help level the playing field and assist new entrants to enter and compete in at least some components of the network industry value chain. We explain this using many network industry sectors in Chapter 3. Therefore, SMP/Dominance regulation is the regulatory method and process used by regulators to ultimately impose asymmetric (or one-sided) regulatory obligations upon dominant incumbent players. It is one-sided because it is only imposed on the dominant incumbent network operator. It goes without saying that firms without market power cannot harm competition.

Again, Figure 4.4 depicts the details of the when and how to carry out SMP/Dominance analyses. It is important to note that concepts like SMP and dominance need to be defined explicitly and clearly in the laws that govern the network sectors in any jurisdiction. For example within the EU Communications sector, the EECC code stipulates that a provider will be deemed to have SMP if, either individually, it

> "enjoys a position of economic strength affording it the power to behave to an appreciable extent independently of its competitors, customers and ultimately consumers, *defining the relevant market is of fundamental importance as effective competition can only be assessed against this definition*" - (Source [229] - *the author's emphasis*).

---

[229] Guidelines on market analysis and the assessment of significant market power under the EU regulatory framework for electronic communications networks and services -

Key to the SMP definition above is the notion of a network operator being able to behave independently of its competitors. We leave out the legal complexities of 'joint or collective' dominance. A dominant firm may exercise market power by increasing prices, reducing quality or slowing down on innovation – and regulation must preempt these. Market power is a matter of degree, and it needs to be assessed on a case-by-case basis – through a relevant market definition, assessment of dominance/SMP and finally the imposition of remedies or obligations, as depicted in the lower part of Figure 4.4.

Next, the EECC definition for SMP/Dominance cited above also stipulates that SMP can only be determined, found and asymmetrically imposed on a dominant operator within the context of a *defined relevant market*. Recall that we mention the notion of relevant markets in telecoms in Chapter 3 (without defining it) - noting how the EC issued a list of 18 such relevant markets in 2003 (7 retail markets and 11 wholesale markets), reduced to 7 in 2007, further reduced to 4 in 2014, and even further reduced to just 2 markets in 2020[230] (EC, 2020). Recall we note in Chapter 3 that these reductions stem from the EC's view of lesser and lesser regulation needed in the EU telecoms sector. As competition takes hold in the telecoms sector in most EU countries, most *ex-ante* retail price regulations have been removed, leaving just fixed line regulation focussed on wholesale products. This is the case for the EU – but not necessarily the case in your market where you may still need more defined relevant markets than EU currently has for the telecoms sector, i.e. just two. Compare with the many relevant markets in the telecoms sector in the Kingdom of Saudi Arabia shown later in Tables 4.2 and 4.3.

The typical steps of determining SMP/Dominance and ultimately imposing obligations on a dominant operator follow the steps shown in the bottom of Figure 4.4, i.e. market definition, SMP/dominance assessment and imposing remedies. These three steps are overviewed in the next three subsections, respectively.

2018/C 159/01 - https://eur-lex.europa.eu/legal-content/EN/TXT/PDF/?uri=CELEX:52018XC0507(01)&rid=7

[230] The two markets are the following: market for wholesale local access (WLA) network provided at a fixed location; and the wholesale dedicated capacity (WDC) market. NRAs can impose remedies on fixed-line operators in these two markets if they find SMP.

4.5.3 Dominance Assessment and the Three Criteria Test (3CT)

Once a relevant market is defined, one or more firms may be identified as having Significant Market Power (SMP) in the relevant market. Four steps typically ensue:

(i)   The regulator starts by determining whether regulation is necessary in the relevant markets;

(ii)   An analysis is carried out in each relevant market, to determine whether any (one or more) providers have Significant Market Power (SMP) – this step first yields Candidate Markets;

(iii)   The candidate markets are then subjected to the Three Criteria Test (TCT) covered later to decide whether the relevant market is susceptible to ex-ante regulation.

(iv)   Then remedies (or regulatory obligations) are imposed on those providers identified as having SMP in the said relevant market.

How does one determine that one or more firms have SMP in that relevant market? We cover this earlier in the section on SMP/Dominance. Ultimately, the key question to answer in the case of the EECC is whether the firm under SMP assessment is able to behave independently of its competitors. However, this depends on the definition of dominance in the jurisdiction. For example, in the telecoms sector in the Kingdom of Saudi Arabia (KSA), the 2002 Telecoms Bylaw[231] clearly stipulates that:

- "every service provider that earns 40% or more of the gross revenues in a specific telecommunications market shall be designated a dominant service provider in that market, until and unless [the] CITC[232] specifies otherwise in a Decision; and

- [The] CITC may designate a service provider with more or less than 40% of the gross revenues in a specific telecommunications market as a dominant service provider if, either individually or acting together

---

[231] Under the provisions of Article 40 of the now-repealed 2002 KSA Telecoms Act, the Bylaws were issued by the Ministerial Resolution No. (11), dated 17/05/1423H (corresponding to 27/07/2002). They supplement the also now-repealed KSA 2001 Telecoms Act and include provisions by which the telecommunications sector is regulated.

[232] Regulator CITC has since been rebranded as CST
https://www.cst.gov.sa/en/aboutus/Pages/default.aspx

with others, it enjoys a position of economic strength affording it the power to behave independently of competitors or users".

Therefore, in the KSA, the communications regulator *de facto* has to designate any operator that earns greater than 40% of the revenues in any relevant market as SMP. It may designate another firm with less than 40% of the revenues in that relevant market as SMP if considers that "it enjoys a position of economic strength affording it the power to behave independently of competitors or users". The key message here is to check what your sector law stipulates and defines SMP to mean.

Furthermore, where a network firm has SMP in a specific Relevant Market, it may also be deemed to have SMP in a closely related market. This could be because the links between the two markets are such as to allow the market power held in one market to be leveraged into the other market, thereby strengthening the market power of the firm.

How does one determine whether regulation is necessary in the relevant market, i.e. Step (iii) above? In other words, is *ex-ante* regulation absolutely necessary and justified for the relevant market? The answer as noted above is the Three Criteria Test. In accordance with Article 67(1) of the EECC Code, imposition of ex-ante regulatory obligations may be justified only in markets where the TCT referred to in Article 67 (1) (a), (b), (c) are cumulatively met. Competition law in most jurisdictions sets out the TCT similarly to Article 67 (1) (a) (b) (c)[233] as follows:

    i.   Are there high and non-transitory entry barriers into the relevant market;

    ii.   Does the industry structure tend towards effective competition? and

    iii.   Would competition law alone be sufficient to adequately address the identified market failures in the absence of ex-ante regulation?

---

[233] art 67(1) of the Electronic Communications Code codifies the 'three-criteria' test, which was previously found in the Recommendations on the definition of relevant markets issued by the European Commission - Directive 2018/1972 - EU Electronic Communications Code | Shaping Europe's digital future (europa.eu)

The three criteria test is met if the market meets all of the following criteria: (i) there are high and *non-transitory barriers* to entry, (ii) the market structure is *not* tending towards effective competition and (iii) competition law alone is *insufficient* to adequately address the identified market failures. Where these criteria are met (i.e., the answers to the criteria are Ye, No and No respectively), the application of *ex-ante* regulation would be considered appropriate.

4.5.4 Imposing Remedies

As seen in Figure 4.4, once the relevant market has been defined, and one or more firms are considered to have a dominant position in that relevant market – and the relevant market is susceptible to ex-ante regulation according to the TCT – then the next phase is to decide upon and impose remedies on the firm or firms.

It is important to highlight the contrast between *ex post* competition law and *ex ante* regulation where intervention occurs in advance of behaviour which could be abusive. In competition law, dominance in itself is not *per se* illegal, it is only the abuse of dominance that is an issue. A dominant firm may abuse its dominant position by:

- Exploitative actions: taking advantage of the consumers' – restricting choice, pricing well above costs; or
- Exclusionary actions: by preventing competitors from competing effectively in the market place.

The recommendation of ex-ante remedies to address competition concerns emerging from any dominance assessment findings – including any abuse of dominance - depends on the regulatory statute or law. For example, the KSA Telecoms Bylaw of 2002 (KSA Bylaw, 2001) stipulates the actions or activities of a dominant service provider that constitute an abuse of its dominance or an anti-competitive practice, and prescribes the following powers that the regulator [CST] may take:
  a. "issue a decision requiring one or more persons named in the decision to take one or more of the following actions:
       i. to cease the actions or activities specified in the decision, immediately or at such time prescribed

in the decision, and subject to such conditions prescribed in the decision; and

ii. to make specific changes in actions or activities specified in the decision, as a means of eliminating or reducing the abusive or anti-competitive impact;

b. refer the matter to the violations committee to impose a penalty for violation of the Act pursuant to Article Thirty-eight of the Act and Article Ninety-four (94) of this Bylaw;

c. request that the service provider involved in the abusive actions or activities or anti-competitive practices and the persons affected by such actions, activities or practices meet to attempt to determine remedies to prevent or eliminate the continuation of such actions, activities or practices, and, if necessary resolve any dispute pursuant to Chapter 6 of this Bylaw;

d. require the service provider responsible for the abusive or anti-competitive actions or activities specified in the decision to publish an acknowledgement and apology for such actions, activities or practices in one or more newspapers of wide circulation, in such a form and at such times as the Commission specifies in the decision; and/or

e. require the service provider to provide periodic reports to the Commission to assist in determining whether the actions or activities are continuing and to determine their impact on telecommunications markets, competitors and user".

Table 4.3a shows the 2017 telecoms sector *dominance findings* in each relevant market for retail/wholesale services in the Kingdom of Saudi Arabia.

Table 4.3b shows the *proposed remedies* – consistent with the law - in each of the relevant markets.

We provide this 2017 KSA dominance and relevant markets remedies because they are best practice to many other developing and emerging market countries. The proposed remedies for the dominant players in every relevant market are also reasonably self-explanatory.

Relevant Market	Dominant Service Provider
Retail service markets	
Market 1 - Retail fixed access and local national fixed call services	STC
Market 2 - Retail fixed broadband access service	STC
Market 3 - Retail business data connectivity services at fixed location	STC
Market 4b - Retail national mobile services within Universal Service areas	STC, Mobily, Zain
Market 5b - Retail international call services originating within Universal Service areas	STC, Mobily, Zain
Wholesale service markets	
Market 6 - Wholesale fixed broadband access services	STC
Market 7 - Wholesale physical local fixed access services	STC
Market 8 - Wholesale fixed call origination services	STC
Market 9 - Wholesale fixed call termination services	STC, Atheeb
Market 10 - Wholesale transit services	STC
Market 11 - Wholesale access segment of leased line services and managed network transmission services	STC
Market 12 - Wholesale trunk segment of leased line services and managed network transmission services	STC
Market 13b - Wholesale mobile access and origination services within Universal Service areas	STC, Mobily, Zain
Market 14 - Wholesale mobile termination services	STC, Mobily, Zain
Market 15b - Wholesale international call services originating within Universal Service areas	STC, Mobily, Zain

Table 4.3a – 2017 Telecoms sector dominance findings in retail and wholesale relevant markets in the Kingdom of Saudi Arabia
(Adapted slightly from Source[234])

It is important to note that a new KSA Telecommunications and Information Technology Act enacted by Royal Decree No. M/106 dated 02/11/1443H (equivalent to 1 June 2022) (the Act) was published in the Saudi Official Gazette on 10 June 2022 and took effect on 7 December 2022. The Act repealed the Telecommunications Law enacted by Royal

---

[234] CITC Final MDDD report - FINAL - 26 10 17 (cst.gov.sa) - https://www.cst.gov.sa/en/reportsandstudies/Reports/Documents/PL-SP-317-E-Market%20Definition%20Designation%20and%20Dominance%20Report.pdf

Decree No. M/12 dated 12/03/1422H (4 June 2001) (the Old Law), broadening the scope and focus from telecommunications to include new forms of technology and digital services. The Old Law was the basis for Tables 4.3a and 4.3b.

Market	Dominant Service Provider	Proposed Remedies
Retail service markets		
Market 1 - Retail fixed access and local national fixed call services	STC	• Tariff filling and approval (incl. predation and margin squeeze test) • Cost Studies
Market 2 - Retail fixed broadband access service	STC	• Accounting separation • Replicability test for bundles
Market 3 - Retail business data connectivity services at fixed location	STC	• Tariff filling and approval (incl. predation and margin squeeze test) • Cost Studies • Accounting separation
Market 4b - Retail national mobile services within Universal Service areas	STC, Mobily, Zain	• Tariff approval for any retail prices in Universal Service areas which are not available nationally
Market 5b - Retail international call services originating within Universal Service areas	STC, Mobily, Zain	• Tariff approval for any retail prices in Universal Service areas which are not available nationally
Wholesale service markets		
Market 6 - Wholesale fixed broadband access services	STC	• Requirement to offer service/access on a non-discriminatory basis
Market 7 - Wholesale physical local fixed access services	STC	• Prepare and publish reference offer • Submit access to physical facilities agreements to CITC
Market 8 - Wholesale fixed call origination services	STC	• Cost-based charges • Accounting separation
Market 9 - Wholesale fixed call termination services	STC, Atheeb	• Requirement to offer service/access on a non-discriminatory and reciprocal basis • Submit interconnection agreements to CITC • Cost-based charges • Prepare and publish reference offer (STC only) • Accounting separation (STC only)

Market	Dominant Service Provider	Proposed Remedies
Market 10 - Wholesale transit services	STC	• Requirement to offer service/access on a non-discriminatory basis • Prepare and publish reference offer • Submit access to physical facilities agreements to CITC • Cost-based charges • Accounting separation
Market 11 - Wholesale access segment of leased line services and managed network transmission services	STC	• Requirement to offer service on a non-discriminatory basis • Prepare and publish reference offer • Submit access to physical facilities agreements to CITC • Cost-based charges • Accounting separation
Market 12 - Wholesale trunk segment of leased line services and managed network transmission services	STC	• Requirement to offer service on a non-discriminatory basis • Prepare and publish reference offer • Submit access to physical facilities agreements to CITC • Cost-based charges • Accounting separation • Access to the passive infrastructure
Market 13b - Wholesale mobile access and origination services within Universal Service areas	STC, Mobily, Zain	• Requirement to offer service/access on a non-discriminatory and reciprocal basis • Prepare and publish reference offer (STC only; Mobily and Zain only have to prepare a reference offer if no commercial agreement is reached)
Market 14 - Wholesale mobile termination services	STC, Mobily, Zain	• Requirement to offer service/access on a non-discriminatory and reciprocal basis • Submit interconnection agreements to CITC • Cost-based charges • Prepare and publish reference offer (STC only) • Accounting separation (STC only)
Market 15b - Wholesale international call services originating within Universal Service areas	STC, Mobily, Zain	• Requirement to offer service/access on a non-discriminatory and reciprocal basis • Prepare and publish reference offer (STC only; Mobily and Zain only have to prepare a reference offer if no commercial agreement is reached)

Table 4.3b – 2017 Telecoms sector proposed remedies in each relevant market in the Kingdom of Saudi Arabia *(Adapted slightly from Source[235])*

This concludes the overview of SMP/Dominance Regulation.

4.6 Consumer Protection Regulation

Ultimately – though many people miss this factoid - almost all regulation is for the benefit of consumers and citizens. For example, aviation regulation's most important preoccupation is quite rightly the safety of air passengers. The regulation of the pharmaceutical industry primarily majors on "product efficacy and safety which is critical to patient health" (Towse & Danzon, 2010, p. 548). This must be so. The regulation of financial services markets is largely predicated on the fact that "the last thirty years have seen financial markets become of central importance to long-term *household*[236] savings as Governments withdraw from welfare provision and demand more of financial markets and of households" (Moloney, 2010, p.439). So, Financial regulation majors on households' interests. We could go on. Consumers and households really need protection, not least the disabled, the poor and the vulnerable.

4.6.1 Why Consumer Protection

The iconic Mahatma Gandhi, in 1890, uttered the words in the quote attributed to him, shown in Image 4.1:

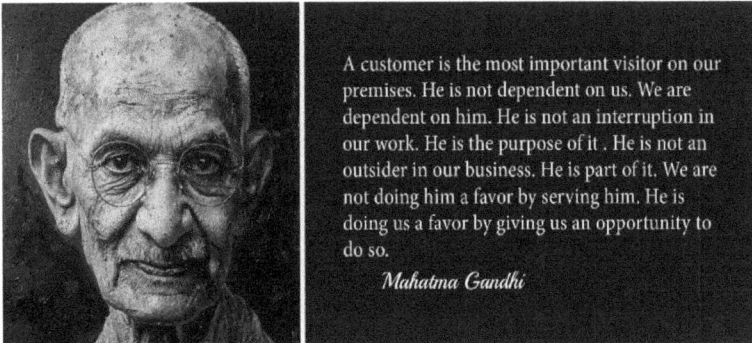

A customer is the most important visitor on our premises. He is not dependent on us. We are dependent on him. He is not an interruption in our work. He is the purpose of it . He is not an outsider in our business. He is part of it. We are not doing him a favor by serving him. He is doing us a favor by giving us an opportunity to do so.

Mahatma Gandhi

Image 4.1 – Mahatma Gandhi Famous Quote on Customers

---

[235] CITC Final MDDD report - FINAL - 26 10 17 (cst.gov.sa) -
https://www.cst.gov.sa/en/reportsandstudies/Reports/Documents/PL-SP-317-E-Market%20Definition%20Designation%20and%20Dominance%20Report.pdf

[236] The author's emphasis.

This is just so apt to use to introduce consumer protection regulation. Note that Ghandi's quote above emphasizes the *singular* consumer. However, a key challenge is that it is very easy for a massive corporate like Google or Microsoft – due to their dominant positions in their markets – to completely ignore or, at best, pay lip service to the individual consumer. Providers do not always have clear incentives to put their customers first for several reasons including profits, sheer inertia on the part of consumers, complex choices, etc. – and these providers typically know they can get away with paying lip service to their consumers too, particularly with lazy or incompetent regulators. Providers also know that consumers could be too lazy to switch to other providers (if they exist at all) to the chagrin of good regulators, and providers exploit this consumer inertia to boost their profits.

Therefore, regulating professionally for the *collective* consumer's public interest is critical – so critical that, as far back as 1962, President John F Kennedy introduced the "Consumer Bill of Rights" emphasizing concepts like "the right to safety", "the right to be informed", "the right to be heard", "the right to be protected against the marketing of products and services that are hazardous to health or to life", "the right to affordable and safe drugs", "the right to have safe appliances in American homes", etc. Indeed, President Kennedy told the US Congress on the 15th March 1962:

> "Consumers, by definition, include us all. They are the largest economic group in the economy, affecting and affected by almost every public and private economic decision. Two-thirds of all spending in the economy is by consumers. But *they are the only important group in the economy who are not effectively organized, whose views are often not heard.*
>
> The federal Government--by nature the highest spokesman for all the people – has a special obligation to be alert to the consumer's needs and to advance the consumer's interests. Ever since legislation was enacted in 1872 to protect the consumer from frauds involving the use of the U.S. mail, *the Congress and Executive Branch have been increasingly aware of their responsibility to make certain that our Nation's economy fairly*

and adequately serves consumers' interests" (Source[237]) - *the author's emphasis.*

President Kennedy's statement is critical. Besides workers, consumers can be the other important group in some economies that is <u>not</u> effectively organized, and whose views are often not heard. His 1962 speech - which he commenced with the two paragraphs I cite above – is a true masterpiece in *consumer protection rationale*. I recommend the reader reads the full text of the President's speech by following the link cited.

Drawing and deriving from the President's speech:

- *Consumers need to be protected from harm*: This includes financial and physical harm, which are at the core of consumer protection challenge. Consumer protection is important across all sectors of the economy. As Taylor (2023) emphasizes, consumer protection is *not* a function of economic regulation and competition; rather, it is about protecting consumers from the wrongdoing of businesses. Increasingly, consumer protection is needed to protect consumers from misleading practices such as using misinformation to sell expensive contracts to vulnerable consumers (electricity, telephone contracts, etc.), lenders and banks' lending to vulnerable consumers who cannot pay at exorbitant interests – i.e., loan sharks, etc. These are activities within regulated industries. Consumers need to be protected from illegal activities, and even "scams", particularly in the telecoms and finance sectors. Consider lonely widows being scammed of all their life savings to fraudsters or vulnerable older people being taken advantage of. However, I note that this 'lonely widow' example is arguably more like criminality in most jurisdictions, and therefore might be outside the scope of regulation. Scammers may not be (or are not usually) registered businesses in a regulated industry. My point here is that consumers need to be protected from – or they need to be alerted of all such likely harms.

- *Formulating consumer policy is key*: To achieve consumer protection, it requires Governments and/or regulators formulating *consumer policy* – this often includes supply-side and demand-side policies. On

---

[237] Special Message to the Congress on Protecting the Consumer Interest. | The American Presidency Project (ucsb.edu)

the supply side, requirements can be introduced (e.g. as license conditions), with expectations for businesses to act in a particular way (e.g. providing clear and sufficient information to consumers – *information remedies*). On the demand-side it typically includes measures to empower consumers to make good choices, informing consumers of their choices as well as providing platforms for consumer feedback (reviews, complaints, etc. – e.g. the Ombudsman, Citizen Advice Bureau, Consumer Organisations, etc.) to tackle the demand-side issues of competition policy. This demand side of competition is crucial because regulators should use this to inform and encourage consumers to make good and discerning choices – in effect, to empower consumers. Empowered consumers are a great antidote to profiteering businesses [238] or fraudsters. If anything, consumers increasingly need to be more empowered as providers increasingly tie them into longer contracts or tempt them into bundle deals [239]. Therefore, consumers' interests are much better enhanced if they are empowered to switch to other providers by them being well informed of alternatives and substitute value-for-money options. Good consumer policy encourages empowered consumers in addition to ensuring that competition policy delivers on multiple providers vigorously competing to win a consumer's business.

- *The Consumer decision-making journey is one of Engage-Assess-Act:* to empower consumers into action is not trivial. First, you need to *engage* them for them to be both aware of and be willing to consider alternatives. Even after the consumer is engaged, he/she must be able to *assess* which product, service or provider best satisfies their needs. For this they need access to trusted and comprehensive information, an understanding of their own likely consumption pattern, and the ability to make comparisons. And after such assessing, the consumer may choose to act, i.e. he/she may decide to start the process of switching to another provider or cancelling a current contract. Good consumer policy should encourage such an engage-assess-act process on the part of the consumer. This mirrors the 3 A's or 4A's framework

---

[238] Consumers can well still be harmed in competitive markets – a business being a monopoly is not always necessary. It is not usually about the median or average consumer. Consumer policy often tends to be about the vulnerable consumer, e.g. the 'lonely widow' I use earlier.

[239] E.g., bundled electricity and gas services being provided by one provider or a consumer getting their TV/Cable, broadband and phone services from a singular provider.

used by the CMA and other UK regulators: Attend, Access, Assess, Act. For a short article on this topic, see Fletcher (2020).

- *Formulating a consumer protection framework is key*: Formulating consumer policy ideally needs a consumer protection framework. Such a framework in general addresses issues such as the role of consumer policy for the specific sector. Such a framework covers and highlights the typical different types of "consumer harm", including financial and physical harm – this can include unreasonable anxiety, mental anguish that consumer may suffer from whilst waiting for services or not being able to get through to their providers. A good consumer protection framework stresses the importance of giving due care to the needs and voices of vulnerable consumers like the disabled, older people or children, and those on low incomes. A good consumer protection framework requires good evidence that is based on demonstrated consumer harm or potential harm, and the causal links to the issues that need remedies. This is invaluable to a well-functioning market.

4.6.2 Who helps Consumers

There are typically several-to-many players involved in consumer protection, i.e. answering the "who" are involved in consumer protection question. These can sometimes be a myriad of players/approaches trying to assist consumers leading to overlapping and/or non-overlapping regulation including:

(i)   **Suppliers (or providers) themselves**: can help, but most suppliers are not benevolent charities. They are profit-maximising companies who are - by definition - conflicted from being good consumer protection advocates. This explains why vibrant competition amongst suppliers is the most optimal way to keep suppliers honest and upright with respect to consumers.

(ii) **Self-regulation**: e.g., we cover in Chapter 3 how some sectors [including the Press] self-regulate for the benefits of both themselves, their customers (i.e. readers, viewers, listeners, browsers, etc.) and broader society.

(iii) **General statutory horizontal regulation**: e.g., by a cross-sector consumer protection regulatory authorities like Nigeria's FCCPC[240];

(iv) **Statutory [vertical] sector regulation**: by regulators with powers and duties to promote competition and protect consumers, e.g. a telecommunications NRA like Ofcom[241];

(v) **Co-regulation with other statutory or consumer bodies:** e.g., how the UK's Advertising Standards Authority (ASA[242]) regulates all advertising across all media alongside telecoms and media regulator Ofcom.

(vi) **Intermediary organisations**: e.g., *price comparison websites* who provide unbiased service information on pricing options for consumers. Such organisations could be regulated statutorily or not. Uswitch[243] is one such intermediary organization. It is a UK-based price comparison service and switching website founded in 2000 which allows consumers to compare prices for a range of energy, personal finance, insurance, and communications services and helps them switch as needed. Every country should have one or more of such consumer-helping organisations. However, it is worth noting that there are also potential concerns with price comparison websites, e.g. cf. the CMA's 2017 market study[244].

(vii) **Consumer advocacy groups**: who represent and campaign for consumers. They also could be statutory role or independent. A good UK example is Which?[245]. This is a UK independent and well-known intermediary organisation that promotes informed consumer choice in the purchase of goods and services. Which? does this through independent testing of products, product and services rankings, pointing out poor products or services, raising

---

[240] https://fccpc.gov.ng/ - Federal Competition & Consumer Protection Commission, Nigeria

[241] www.ifcom.org.uk

[242] https://www.asa.org.uk/

[243] https://www.uswitch.com/

[244] https://www.gov.uk/cma-cases/digital-comparison-tools-market-study

[245] https://www.which.co.uk/ - Which? | Expert testing, reviews and advice - Which?

awareness of consumer rights, and offering consumers and citizens independent advice. I have been a subscriber to Which?'s services for decades.

(viii) **Alternative Dispute Resolution (ADR) Bodies:** many statutory regulations and regulators mandate ADR on sector providers/suppliers. This allows for consumers to have the opportunity to seek out-of-court resolutions to their complaints through the help of an impartial dispute resolution body. The outcomes are binding, and resolving consumer disputes this way is efficient, faster and less costly than going to court. In the UK, there are already several large and well-established ADR schemes in regulated sectors including financial services, energy and telecoms[246]. They typically do this using ombudsmen schemes[247]. An ombudsman is a person who is appointed to look into consumer complaints about companies and other miscellaneous organisations. An ombudsman scheme is independent, free and impartial. Consumers are encouraged to resolve their complaints with the company concerned before they complain to an ombudsman.

(ix) **The Media:** the media in many countries today help provide much-needed checks and controls on [big] suppliers who may be wont to ignore the concerns of the consumers. Most major brands would *not* want to be under the gaze of critical media attention of their products or services as they typically drive down brand value and sales. Millennials [248] and Gen Zs hold brands more accountable on social media too[249].

(x) **Politicians & Government**: politicians are reasonable proxies for consumers who typically can champion consumer concerns and

---

[246] https://www.gov.uk/government/publications/alternative-dispute-resolution-for-consumers/alternative-dispute-resolution-for-consumers - Alternative dispute resolution for consumers - GOV.UK (www.gov.uk)

[247] https://www.ombudsman-services.org/ - Ombudsman Service (ombudsman-services.org)

[248] Also known as Gen Ys

[249] https://www.marketingdive.com/news/study-millennials-hold-brands-more-accountable-on-social-media/503376/ - Study: Millennials hold brands more accountable on social media | Marketing Dive

issues with big suppliers or Government departments directly. They also usually help create consumer protection laws and agencies too. Politicians and Governments also help develop and implement Universal Service Obligation (USO) schemes ensuring that groups such as disabled users, the poor, the blind, the hard-of-hearing, rural dwellers, etc., are not excluded from benefitting from services like communications, health, finance, utilities, posts and more. In general as President Kennedy noted in his 1962 speech cited above "the federal Government--by nature the highest spokesman for all the people--has a special obligation to be alert to the consumer's needs and to advance the consumer's interests". So Governments are – or should be – the ultimate advocates for consumers. They develop Consumer Policy in general.

The list above is not necessarily exhaustive, but pretty comprehensive. A key point here is that consumers typically require and need several to many of these sort of overlapping players in their countries to help them [consumers] with consumer protection and empowerment against big and small suppliers across sectors of the economy.

4.6.3 How does Consumer Protection work in Practice?

This brief section covers the "how" to do good consumer protection, drawing from the what-players and what-methods of the previous section. The "how" of Consumer Protection regulation – as usual – starts with the Law and Regulations. It entails and involves Governments and Regulators enacting laws, regulations and guidelines to protect consumers from unsafe, uninformed, risky, fraudulent, deceptive, unfair business or exploitative practices. This includes regulations related to product and services' safety, quality, pricing, advertising, and fair contractual terms.

Taylor (2023) refers to a "Regulatory journey" for consumer protection. He argues that regulators and consumer protection agencies should be proactive in identifying and remedying consumer harm. He notes that this requires resources and focus, and sometimes collaboration between agencies. Sometimes, conclusive evidence can be difficult to find. Some examples of the "regulatory journey" for detection and remedying consumer harm drawing from the telecoms industry are shown in Table 4.4.

Source of Harm	How do regulators detect harm?	What remedies are there?
Nuisance calls Scam Calls	Compliance Monitoring	Enforcement against nuisance call suppliers Publish scam alerts Block certain robotext messages[250] Consumer Advice
"Bill shock[251]"	Consumer Complaints Advocacy Research Whistleblowers	Consumer Empowerment Improved Transparency Usage caps Elimination of roaming charges Alternative Dispute Resolution (Ombudsman)
Unfair Contract Terms		Enforcement Price Comparison Websites

Table 4.4 – Examples of the "Regulatory Journey" for Detecting and Remedying Consumer Harm in Telecoms (Taylor, 2023)

Table 4.4 depicts the importance of early warning systems to detect sources of harm very early, and providing the right early preventative remedy – e.g. consumer advice, consumer rights information, publishing scam alerts, alternative dispute resolution (ADR), provision of comparative information via price comparison websites, and enforcement options. Such a regulatory journey for consumer protection emphasizes consumer empowerment and consumer protection particular in the contexts of businesses with market power or dominance. Developing the capacity of consumer advocacy groups, co-regulatory groups, consumer advisory councils, self-regulation within the companies, etc. are all key to

[250] For example, in the USA, on March 16, 2023, the FCC in fact adopted its first regulations targeting the growing issue of [robot-generated] scam text messages sent to consumers. See Press Release. https://docs.fcc.gov/public/attachments/DOC-391800A1.pdf - FCC Adopts its First Rules Focused on Scam Texting. March 16, 2023.

[251] Bill shock in telecoms refers to a sudden, unexpected and typically sharp increase in a mobile/cellular consumer's monthly bill that is not caused by the consumer having changed their service contract. It occurs for reasons, including unanticipated roaming or data charges, or unclear or misunderstood advertising.

getting to good outcomes on consumer protection. However, this is not trivial. The devil as usual is in the details.

The Holy Grail outcome is to get consumers to understand and own their individual *Engage-Assess-Act* decision-making journey described earlier. Empowering consumers into action is not trivial as noted before.

To achieve this requires tools for good consumer protection and online protection – as Table 4.4 alludes to - including collecting/measuring key metrics and trends, tools for enforcement, switching processes, quality of services measurements/reporting, commissioning authoritative research, how to conduct good consumer education, and formal and informal approaches to consumer protection.

Consumer protection methods include, not exhaustively, approaches to pre-empt or mitigate consumer harm in the first place, including consumer empowerment, raising awareness of consumer rights and helping consumers protect themselves against harm, effective complaints handling (assuming harm has already been caused), effective and timely enforcement against offenders, targeting regulation at offenders, deregulation efforts at the "good guys" and improving the effectiveness of self- and co-regulation – and the role of the regulator.

4.7 Quality & Safety Regulation

Quality and Safety issues are clearly at the top echelon of reasons – or they must always be – of why Society needs regulators and regulation, not necessarily economic regulation. Take a critical commodity like water - regulation of quality (QoS) is obviously critical for such a key commodity, not only for the water quality itself but also for its safety. In Chapter 3, I make the case for the regulation of water and the wastewater industry by partly citing key facts about Drinking Water and Sanitation from the World Health Organisation (WHO, 2022a, 2022b). This includes facts such as, over 2 billion people live in water-stressed countries, and this is expected to be exacerbated in some regions as result of climate change and population growth. Or that globally, *at least 2 billion people use a drinking water source contaminated with faeces.*

A basic commodity like water is of undrinkable quality and most unsafe for 2 billion of our fellow citizens – how can we *not* act to remedy this with such close connection to the human health and lives of more than a quarter of humanity? And there are other quality of service indicators that are relevant to water and wastewater as covered in Chapter 3 including indicators of reducing water losses, quality of pipe works, water interruption, sewerage system adequacy and more.

Governments - as the ultimate advocates for consumers - develop and establish quality and safety standards for products and services to protect consumer and citizens. This includes regulations concerning food quality and safety, water quality and safety (as noted before), gas safety, roads quality and safety, product labeling, environmental air quality and safety standards, and even workplace quality and safety. Therefore, good Quality and Safety regulation pervades [or should pervade] practically all sectors of the economy.

4.7.1 Regulating Quality Regulation through Standards and Monitored KPIs

There is no substitute to realizing Quality and Safety across sectors of the economy than by clearly researching, defining, establishing, *rigorously* measuring, monitoring and acting on explicitly monitored quality and safety standards and KPIs[252]. The standards and KPIs should relate to *performance and services to consumer*s across a variety of measures – taking into particular consideration complaints from consumers and disputes. This applies to all sectors of the economy without exception, and ideally needs to be mandated in law by the Government[253]. For example, the UK's Competition and Service (Utilities) Act 1992, Chapter 43 describes itself as follows:

> "An Act to make provision *with respect to standards of performance and service to customers* in relation to the telecommunications, gas supply, electricity supply, water supply and sewerage service industries; *to make provision with respect to*

---

[252] Key Performance Indicator

[253] The law is preferable because Consumer Law typically provides protection against harms such as fraud, misrepresentation,, mis-selling and many other consumer harms.

complaints by, and disputes with, customers in those industries; to make provision with respect to the powers of the regulators of those industries and with respect to related matters …; *to make further provision for facilitating effective competition in certain of those industries...*".

Source ²⁵⁴ [The author's emphases].

The Act proceeds to define and specify standards of performance and service to UK customers as summarized in Table 4.5. The preamble cited above emphasizes specifying such standards of performance and service across five core utilities sectors in the UK including telecommunications, gas supply, electricity supply, water supply and sewerage service industries. It is also key to note that the preamble also emphasizes the importance of facilitating effective competition in these industries – because, ultimately, competition is arguably an important economically efficient driver to realizing Quality and Safety regulation[255]. I posit this argument boldly in full cognizance of the fact that some readers may have concerns about competition causing a 'race to the bottom'. In all my years as a regulator, and training regulators, the single most important driver I have perceived for better Quality and Safety regulations has usually been competition. This may be controversial, but I firmly hold this position.

The standards of Performance and Service to Customers shown in Table 4.5 cover broad areas across the five or six sectors covered, but there are more fine details to further define left to the sector regulators. So, the details underneath the broad *quality* prescription in the Act of "standards of performance" in the telecoms, gas supplies or electricity supply industries are left to the respective sector regulators to elaborate in secondary regulations.

---

[254] https://www.legislation.gov.uk/ukpga/1992/43/introduction - Competition and Service (Utilities) Act 1992 (legislation.gov.uk)

[255] I concede the evidence is more anecdotal than firm that the more competitive markets are, the higher the quality and standards

Part I Standards of Performance and Service to Customers	
Telecommunications	**Gas supply**
1. Standards of performance.	11. Standards of performance.
2. Information with respect to levels of performance.	12. Information with respect to levels of performance.
3. Information to be given to customers about overall performance.	13. Information to be given to customers about overall performance.
4. Procedures for dealing with complaints.	14. Procedures for dealing with complaints.
5. Disputes about discrimination etc. in fixing charges.	15. Promotion of efficient use of gas.
6. Billing disputes.	16. Determination of disputes.
7. Deposits.	17. Billing disputes.
8. Disconnections.	18. Preliminary investigation of disputes by Gas Consumers' Council
9. Enforcement of standards of performance, etc.	19. Disconnections.
10. Interpretation.	
Electricity supply	**Water supply**
20. Research concerning views of customers.	26. Research concerning views of customers.
21. Information to be given to customers about overall performance.	27. Information with respect to levels of performance.
22. Procedures for dealing with complaints.	28. Information to be given to customers about overall performance.
23. Billing disputes.	29. Procedures for dealing with complaints.
24. Compliance with standards of overall performance.	
25. Determination of disputes by Director: interim directions.	**Sewerage services**
	30. Research concerning views of customers.
Water supply and sewerage services	31. Information with respect to levels of performance.
34. Determination of disputes by the Director.	32. Information to be given to customers about overall performance.
35. Reference of certain disputes to the Director.	33. Procedures for dealing with complaints.
36. Billing disputes.	

Table 4.5 – Regulating for Quality in UK Utilities (Source: Leinyuy, 2013, compiled from
http://www.legislation.gov.uk/ukpga/1992/43/contents)
(Admittedly, Table 4.5 is repetitive but I preferred to maintain its comprehensiveness on a per sector basis)

The Council of European Energy Regulators (CEER) indicates that

> ".. quality can be measured by the number and duration of power cuts; the power surges or dips which affect our electronic equipment; or the timeliness and efficiency of the customer service provided by electricity companies." – Source[256]:

The benchmarking and analysis of the quality of electricity supply can be focused on three types of quality:

- Continuity of supply

---

[256] http://www.energy-community.org/pls/portal/docs/1522177.PDF

- Voltage quality
- Commercial quality

The CEER report also indicates that

> "*Monitoring* the quality of supply is an essential tool in the overall monitoring of a functioning electricity market, and it is our job to strike a balance between cost efficiency and quality of supply, using a variety of regulatory instruments.[257]"

The detailed Quality Performance indicators across sectors are clearly different and some would include complicated acronyms, formulae and measurements. So, for example, quality performance indicators for mobile/cellular operators would include *inter alia*:

- *2G, 3G, and 4G Call Setup Success Rate (CSSR) per operator:* CSSR is used to describe the percentage or fraction of attempts made while making a call resulting in a successful connection to the dialled number. These are measured through traffic measurement and drive tests. The ideal value of CSSR is 1, which means the network should be capable of accepting 100% of all calls made. These are clear measures of network 2G, 3G and 4G voice quality, respectively.

- *2G, 3G and 4G Call Completion Success Rates (CCSR) per operator*: the call completion success rate refers to the total number of calls that are successfully initiated and connected, compared to the number of calls that fail. Failed calls can occur because of an incorrect phone number, a non-response, or because the customer declines the call.

- *Dropped-Call Rates (DCR) per operator*: the DCR is the percentage or fraction of the telephone calls which, due to technical reasons, were cut off before the communicating persons had finished their conversations and before any one of them had hung up. This fraction or percentage is measured across all calls attempted on the network during a defined period.

- *Network Availability KPIs*: Availability percentages is one of the central KPIs for network reliability. It measures the percentage of

---

[257] *Ibid.*

time that a network is operational and accessible. High availability demonstrates better reliability. Network availability is often calculated using the formula: (Uptime / (Uptime + Downtime)) x 100.

- *Network Reliability KPIs - Mean Time Between Failures (MTBF) & Mean Time to Repair (MTTR) KPIs*: MTBF measures the average time between network failures. A higher MTBF shows better reliability. MTBF also helps predict when the next failure might occur, enabling initiative-taking and pre-emptive maintenance. MTTR measures the average time it takes to repair a network once it has failed. A lower MTTR value shows quicker recovery and better network reliability.

Indeed, there are literally hundreds of such quality performance indicators in the telecoms sector across mobile/cellular, fixed, fibre, satellite, Wi-Fi, Internet, cable and other networks – and covering some of the broad performance areas for telecoms noted in Table 4.5.

Did I warn that there are lots of acronyms related to the KPIs? In addition, the formulae underlying some of these hundreds of indicators too can be even more scary, e.g. see Haryadi[258], but the reader should not be scared away from understanding the broad outlines and leave the esoteric details to the more technically-minded nerds like I used to be.

KPIs along with esoteric equations exist across all sectors of the economy. For example, in the water industry, there are equivalent network reliability KPIs that are typically not observed by the customers. There are KPIs about the cost of burst water pipes: repairs, lost water, disruption to street users, loss of service to consumers and any injury or damage. There are KPIs about the number of houses/properties affected by supply interruptions, percentage of properties affected by low water pressure and percentage of populations affected by hosepipe restrictions. KPIs are used to measure and act on all *quality-concerning* issues across sectors.

---

[258] https://osf.io/preprints/inarxiv/cq8na - 2018_Chapter 1_The Concept of Network Performance and Quality of Service_Sigit Haryadi (1).pdf - Chapter 1 of the Book Titled: "Telecommunication Network Performance and Quality of Service": The Concept of Telecommunication Network Performance and Quality of Service -

The essence of this sub-section is that these quality/performance indicators are monitored and acted upon (i.e. rewarded or penalised) because they act as incentives or mandated regulated requirements [or both] in order to drive up quality. Governments and/or regulators implement these incentives/regulated requirements in different ways including:

Publications
- They publish individual and relative performance of companies.
- They can *name and shame* poor performance thereby linking reputation of companies to brand risk.

Using Third Parties
- As covered under consumer protection regulation, regulators and/or Governments may employ ombudsmen, consumer complaint bodies, and consumer participation in supervisory boards of regulated companies to realise such quality regulation outcomes.

Implement Penalties and Rewards
- Governments or regulators can set limits on certain performance indices.
- This naturally leads to the issuing penalties or rewards based on observed performance.

Creating continuous relationship between price and quality
- Combining quality incentives with price cap regulation is good practice. This can be achieved by specifying dead bands, caps and floors.
- A *dead band* refers to a tolerance range within which quality is allowed to vary. There is a penalty imposed if quality is lower than the target range. Conversely, there is a reward if quality is greater than the target range. Caps and floors define reward and penalty limits.
- For example, in the UK, such a reliability incentive scheme operates for the electricity transmission network The transmission owners are incentivised to maintain a reliable system. Each of the licensees is set a target for reliability, and is rewarded for beating this target and penalised if they under-perform. The target is in the form of a range, and if their performance is within this range (i.e.,

dead band) they are neither penalised nor rewarded. The rewards and penalties are capped for the licensees as a percentage of their total revenue for the year.

4.7.2 Regulating Safety Regulation through Standards and Monitored KPIs

Similarly to KPIs being used to regulate quality in the previous section, there are hundreds of Safety KPIs too implemented across all sectors of the economy. For example, the top five KPIs in the aviation sector cover [259]:

- *Deaths*: ultimately, the primary goal of safety above all else is to avoid any deaths, be they customers, employees or contractors.

- *Processes not followed*: Processes not followed are another important KPI. Such KPIs are used to monitor how many issues arise because employees do not follow prescribed processes. Do you want pre-flight safety checks to be ignored by pilots? Do you want a drunk pilot to fly a plane which was missed by processes to check pilots are fit to get into their cockpits?

- *Bird/wildlife strike*: the aviation industry is rightly paranoid about KPIs covering bird and other wildlife strikes because they can cause significant financial and structural damage to aircrafts. They can only cause significant injury or death to pilots and passengers. Aviation regulators require such strikes to be filed.

- *Bodily injury*: though 'unsafe' aviation service providers may see zero or few deaths, there may be a significant difference in the number of injuries between aviation providers with good safety culture compared to those with bad safety culture. Such injuries cover cuts, punctures, bruises, contusions, fractures, lacerations, etc.

- *Missing information*: *Prima facie*, this probably reads like a strange choice to be a top aviation KPI. However, it measures issues resulting from employees missing critical information including employees not having been trained for a particular process or employees not being apprised of critical safety information.

---

[259] https://aviationsafetyblog.asms-pro.com/blog/top-5-kpis-in-aviation-safety - Top 5 KPIs in Aviation Safety - Free KPI Resources (asms-pro.com)

4.7.3 Quality & Safety Regulation are more Critical in Some Industries than others

Quality & Safety Regulation are most critical in aviation for example. In the early days of 2024, several aviation regulators led by the US's Federal Aviation Administration (FAA) ordered the grounding and "immediate inspections" of 737 Max 9s worldwide. This happened after a part of one these planes fell off during an Alaska Airlines flight on 5th of January 2024[260]. The Alaska Airlines flight from Portland, Oregon to Ontario, California, had reached 16,000ft (4,876m) when it began its emergency descent after a concealed door blew out of the plane carrying 177 passengers and crew causing immediate depressurization. It landed safely back in Portland.

The Federal Aviation Administration immediately grounded all of the types of Boeing 737 Max 9s involved until it was/is "satisfied that they are safe": "The FAA is requiring immediate inspections of certain Boeing 737 MAX 9 planes before they can return to flight"; "safety will continue to drive our decision-making as we assist the NTSB's investigation into Alaska Airlines Flight 1282"; the FAA's first priority is keeping the flying public safe".[261] The FAA's Emergency Airworthiness Directive (EAD) requires operators to inspect affected aircraft before further flight. The required inspections was to last around four to eight hours per aircraft and the EAD will affect approximately 171 airplanes worldwide. It turned out that the FAA's EAD was completely vindicated. Guess what? United Airlines found loose bolts in jet inspections[262]. Alaska Airlines also reported that it has since found "some loose hardware"

---

[260] https://www.bbc.co.uk/news/world-us-canada-67903655 - FAA grounds 171 Boeing planes after mid-air blowout on Alaska Airlines jet - BBC News

[261]https://www.faa.gov/newsroom/updates-boeing-737-9-max-aircraft - FAA Statement on Temporary Grounding of Certain Boeing 737 MAX 9 Aircraft | Federal Aviation Administration

[262] https://www.bbc.co.uk/news/world-us-canada-67919436 - Boeing 737 Max 9: United Airlines finds loose bolts in jet inspections - BBC News

on some Max 9s too[263]. Can the reader envision another industry sector where quality and safety regulations are more critical?

Such quality and safety inspections are evidently indispensable. Key aviation safety KPIs [and more] are truly key and they must be scrupulously monitored and acted upon to maintain safe skies. The reader would agree safe skies are necessary.

4.7.4 Quality & Safety Challenges from Consumers and Citizens

It is important I highlight quality and safety challenges emanating from consumers and citizens too. In almost all of the network industries covered in Chapter 3, operators suffer from interference and damage to their infrastructure often caused by consumers and citizens trying to steal water from pipes, electricity from main cables in the network, etc. - which often results in disasters like flooding, fires, etc. and sadly, even deaths. This behaviour is even common practice in developed markets like the UK, and even much more so in developing countries[264]. This UK[265] example shows guidance that Ofgem published in 2014 relating to suppliers' rights and obligations in the case of gas or electricity theft. In developing and emerging markets, such vandalism of networks are typically criminalised, leading to legal enforcements against such criminality.

---

[263] https://www.reuters.com/business/aerospace-defense/no-data-captured-alaska-airlines-737-cockpit-voice-recorder-ntsb-chair-2024-01-08/ - United, Alaska find loose parts on 737 MAX planes, raising pressure on Boeing | Reuters

[264] https://www.bloomberg.com/news/articles/2024-04-18/nigeria-to-criminalise-fiber-cable-damage-costing-telecoms-billions - Nigeria to Criminalize Fiber Cable Damage Costing Telecoms Billions - Bloomberg

[265] https://www.ofgem.gov.uk/sites/default/files/docs/2014/07/open_letter_-_ppm_in_the_case_of_theft.pdf - Guidance Notes (ofgem.gov.uk)

4.8 Scarce Resources & Environmental Regulation

There are many resources in society that are scarce resources by nature, particularly natural resources. Some examples of scarce natural resources that need careful management for the benefits of consumers and citizens of society include fossil fuels, forests, fresh water, minerals and spectrum airwaves amongst many others.

This section deliberately and mostly makes the case why regulation is important for the range of scarce resources discussed. However, I try and highlight some of the methods of regulation involved in them. For example, there cross-cutting themes such as the use of licensing (c.f., Section 4.1), Quantity Regulation (quotas), National and International dimensions of regulation (e.g., fish stocks, spectrum - both of which are common pool resources), Environmental Regulation, Quality & Safety Regulation, Consumer Protection Regulation, etc.

4.8.1 Fossil Fuels

Fossil Fuels: these are finite and non-renewable resources e.g., natural gas, coal, and oil as they will eventually run out. We cover in Chapter 3 how the largest reserves of natural gas are found in countries/regions like Russia, the Middle East (Qatar, Iran, Saudi Arabia) and Africa (Nigeria and Algeria). Careful and efficient exploitation of fossil fuel oil resources has jettisoned Middle East Economies like UAE, Qatar and Saudi Arabia in particular into the top echelon developing economies of the world[266] to the massive benefits of their citizenry. However, there are cases where such scarce oil and gas resources are arguably *not* being efficiently managed and regulated [to date as of early 2024] to benefit their country's citizens, as in the cases of Nigeria and my native Cameroon. The Nigerian economy has for the last few decades been largely dependent on oil as its main source of liquid revenue, whilst largely failing so far to diversify into other sources of income. For example, "oil and gas accounted for 90 percent of export income in the first quarter of 2022 and 85 percent of Government revenue in Nigeria thereby making the country a *mono-*

---

[266] https://www.investopedia.com/updates/top-developing-countries/ - Top 25 Developed and Developing Countries (investopedia.com)

product economy owing to its dependency on oil and gas"[267]. This makes oil and gas somewhat of a curse too in Nigeria[268] and other developing countries wherein such scarce resources are not being professionally managed and regulated for the benefits of all[269]. As noted in Chapter 3 too, coal and natural gas are the two biggest inputs for electricity generation. These are good reasons for regulating scarce resources properly, not least to emulate the successes a rapidly developing economy and developing Emirate like Saudi Arabia and UAE's Dubai, respectively. Fossil fuels are also major contributors to climate change and other environmental problems including some infamous oil spills damaging the environment[270] – yet another set of reasons why fossil fuels should be [and are] increasingly regulated.

Fossil fuels would typically be subject – depending on the jurisdiction and their priorities/objectives – to regulatory methods including Licensing (For4est), Quantity Regulation (quotas to be exploited as deemed necessary), Environmental Regulation (as fossil fuels contribute to climate change and other environmental problems), Consumer/Citizen Protection Regulation (as polluted environments mitigate against citizen welfare), Quality & Safety Regulation (e.g., oil pollution in the Nigeria Delta region has polluted freshwater water sources), Risks Regulation (e.g., fires), etc.

4.8.2 Forests

Forests & Timber: The Amazon Forest is the world's largest and most well-known tropical rainforest, with the second and third being the Congo Rainforest (in Africa) and the New Guinea Rainforests (Asia), respectively. Under previous President Jair Bolsonaro, deforestation in the Brazilian Amazon surged [271]. The world's rain forests are finite, and such

---

[267]   https://www.thisdaylive.com/index.php/2022/08/31/replacing-oil-as-mainstay-of-nigerian-economy/ - Replacing Oil as Mainstay of Nigerian Economy - THISDAYLIVE

[268] http://news.bbc.co.uk/1/hi/programmes/from_our_own_correspondent/4700588.stm - BBC NEWS | Programmes | From Our Own Correspondent | Nigeria's oil hope and despair

[269]   https://www.bbc.co.uk/news/world-africa-20081268 - Nigeria: 'Oil-gas sector mismanagement costs billions' - BBC News

[270] https://www.bbc.co.uk/news/business-35701607 - Shell being sued in two claims over oil spills in Nigeria - BBC News

[271]https://www.bbc.co.uk/news/science-environment-60333422 - Amazon deforestation: Record high destruction of trees in January - BBC News

deforestation (for timber), illegal logging, and unsustainable forestry practices are leading to the declining of the world's rainforests. The world's rainforests need to be regulated, not only for the precious and largely untouched wild life and ecosystems they inhabit – but also because of their important environmental roles as *carbon sinks*. A forest is considered by most environmental experts to be a carbon sink because it absorbs more carbon (through carbon dioxide or CO_2) from the atmosphere than it releases. Forests absorb CO_2 through photosynthesis when standing or regrowing and the carbon gets tied in forest biomass (i.e., trunks, branches, roots and leaves), in dead organic matter (litter and dead wood) and in soils[272]. The carbon and CO_2 are only released when forests are cleared or degraded. Image 4.2 illustrates this well – and visually makes the case for even growing more young forests.

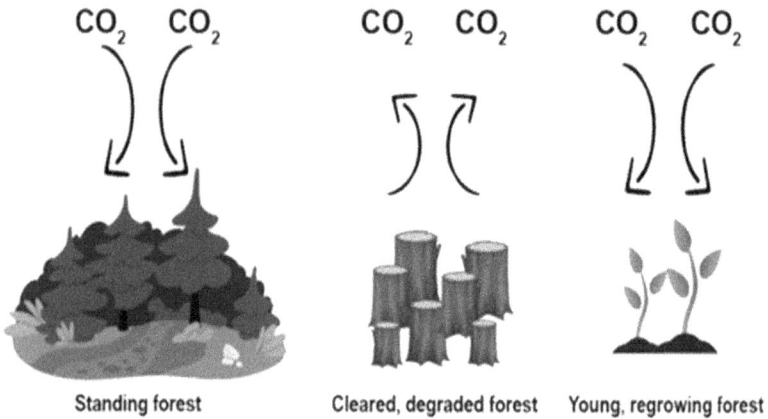

Image 4.2 – Forests as Net Carbon Sinks
(Adapted from this Source: [273] *)*

Forests would typically be subject to regulatory methods including Licensing (i.e., who gets to exploit them most efficiently for society), Quantity Regulation (quotas to be exploited as deemed necessary to ensure sustainability), National and International dimensions of forests regulation [e.g., the Brazilian Amazon, and the Congo Rainforest (Africa) and New Guinea Rainforests (Asia), could arguably be considered a 'world'

---

[272] https://www.wri.org/insights/forests-absorb-twice-much-carbon-they-emit-each-year - Quantifying Carbon Fluxes in the World's Forests | World Resources Institute (wri.org)

[273] https://www.wri.org/insights/forests-absorb-twice-much-carbon-they-emit-each-year - Quantifying Carbon Fluxes in the World's Forests | World Resources Institute (wri.org)

common pool resources], Environmental Regulation (as forests act both as a sources and sinks for carbon as Image 4.2 depicts), Consumer Protection Regulation, Quality & Safety Regulation, etc.

4.8.3 Fresh Water

Fresh water: Water covers 71% of the Earth's surface, but the reader may be surprised to read that only 2.5% of it is freshwater, and most of that is locked up in ice or deep underground. Rivers and lakes hold only a tiny fraction of fresh water – but so much life on Earth depends on it. For the close to 8 billion[274] human beings (as of 2022) that need it for their drinking, farming and industrial uses, this may be a crisis already. The BBC in 2017 asked if the world is running out of fresh water[275]? The world's fresh water is finite and clearly needs careful regulation. This is why water and waste water regulation is ever more needed as covered in Chapter 3's Section 3.7.

Freshwater would typically be subject to regulatory methods including Licensing (i.e., who gets to exploit them most efficiently for society), Quantity Regulation (quotas to be exploited as deemed necessary to ensure sustainability), National and International dimensions of freshwater (e.g., as common pool resources), Environmental Regulation, Consumer Protection Regulation, Quality & Safety Regulation, etc.

4.8.4 Minerals

Minerals: Most minerals tend to be extremely valuable and scarce. Many minerals, such as copper, aluminium, and other rare earth metals such as uranium and coltan, are essential for modern technology and infrastructure. However, they are often difficult to extract and are becoming increasingly scarce. The Congo Rainforest is rich in such minerals including in gold, copper, diamonds, cobalt, uranium, and coltan. Coltan, for example, is a key raw material used to build smartphones, laptops, advanced medical equipment and a range of electronic devices. However, the black metallic

---

[274] https://www.bbc.co.uk/news/av/world-63624651 - How the world got to 8 billion people - and where next - BBC News
[275] https://www.bbc.com/future/article/20170412-is-the-world-running-out-of-fresh-wate

mineral has mostly been found in vast majority quantities in the Democratic Republic of Congo (DRC), a Central African nation. The DRC is also home to about 60% of the world's known cobalt reserves – cobalt is an essential component of lithium-ion batteries used to power electric vehicles. As the demand for cobalt, coltan and their by-products grows annually, the DRC has been mired in increased conflict which has seen 6.6 million Congolese being scattered across the country in camps for internally displaced people so that these so called "conflict minerals" can be mined, plundered and looted[276]. The DRC lost an estimated USD $300bn to corruption during former President Joseph Kabila's 2001 to 2019 reign - enough to lift more than 50 million Congolese people out of poverty[277]. A Swiss Court has formally found that "individuals and entities in the UK, Gibraltar and Switzerland paid almost USD $380m (£280m) in cash bribes to authorities in DRC through an array of shell companies and subsidiaries – and, in this case, the UK's Serious Fraud Office told the Swiss court that it has the evidence to back it"[278]. 50 million poor Congolese could have been taken out of poverty with good leadership and regulation – in just the way Dubai's Sheikh Mohammed Al Maktoum has transformed Dubai[279]. I cannot emphasise enough the key roles of good leadership and regulation in the management of scarce resources.

Minerals would typically be subject to regulatory methods including Licensing (i.e., who gets to exploit them most efficiently for society as they tend to be plundered and looted), Quantity Regulation (quotas to be exploited as deemed necessary), Environmental Regulation (as their exploitation tends to destroy the environment), Consumer Protection Regulation, Quality & Safety Regulation, etc.

---

[276] https://www.theguardian.com/global-development/commentisfree/2021/jul/21/the-uk-has-been-linked-to-congos-conflict-minerals-where-are-the-criminal-charges - The UK has been linked to Congo's 'conflict minerals' – where are the criminal charges? | Vava Tampa | The Guardian

[277] *Ibid.* and https://documents-dds-ny.un.org/doc/UNDOC/GEN/N03/567/36/IMG/N0356736.pdf?OpenElement

[278] *Ibid.*

[279] https://www.bbc.co.uk/news/world-middle-east-51762543 - Sheikh Mohammed Al Maktoum: Who is Dubai's ruler? - BBC News

4.8.5 Electromagnetic Spectrum

Spectrum Airwaves: Electromagnetic Radio Frequency – or spectrum airwaves – is the oxygen of the wireless telecommunications industry. Spectrum is used to deliver so many services to society today. Spectrum is a finite and valuable natural resource, and an essential input for all forms of wireless communication as depicted in Image 4.3.

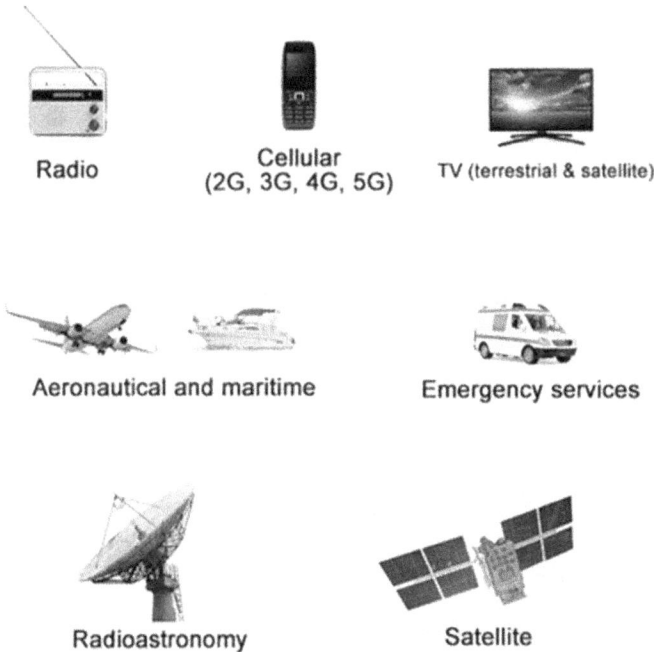

Radio   Cellular (2G, 3G, 4G, 5G)   TV (terrestrial & satellite)

Aeronautical and maritime   Emergency services

Radioastronomy   Satellite

Image 4.3 – Spectrum and a Tiny Subset of its Myriad of Uses
(Adapted from Source: Ofcom UK Spectrum Framework Review Presentation Slides[280])

Spectrum airwaves have to be carefully managed for the benefit of all citizens and consumers in society. In the telecommunications sector, it is undisputedly the most important scarce resource to society that needs to be carefully managed and regulated – so much so that spectrum has to be managed internationally by international law. The International Telecommunication Union (ITU) is the global United Nations-mandated agency responsible for the management of scarce radio-frequency

---

[280] https://www.ofcom.org.uk/__data/assets/pdf_file/0012/34104/sfr_guide.pdf - A Guide to the Spectrum Framework Review (ofcom.org.uk)

spectrum and satellite orbit slots through its Radiocommunication Sector (ITU-R) and its executive arm, the Radiocommunication Bureau (BR)[281].

Where will the world be today without spectrum airwave's use in mobile or cellular communications? "By the end of 2022, over 5.4 billion people globally subscribed to a mobile service, including 4.6 billion people who also used the mobile internet. Mobile technologies and services also generated 5% of global GDP, contributed $5.2 trillion of economic value added, and supported 28 million jobs across the wider mobile ecosystem"[282].

Electromagnetic spectrum is typically be subject to regulatory methods including Licensing (i.e., who gets to exploit them most efficiently for society, not least since the externality of interference needs to be controlled), Access (non-price) Regulation (in order to maximise the most users and uses of spectrum as Image 4.3 depicts), Access (price) Regulation including spectrum auctions (Myers, 2023), Quantity Regulation (quotas to achieve competition objectives), Environmental Regulation (the exploitation of spectrum through installations of radio equipment at radio sites raises environmental/societal concerns including NIMBY-ism [283]), Consumer Protection Regulation, Quality, Safety & Risks Regulation (e.g., very high frequencies like X-rays and gamma rays are incredibly dangerous), etc.

4.8.6 Fish Stocks

Even the world's fish stocks need to be controlled or regulated as they are scarce. Fish stock resources are not unlimited and overfishing can impact stocks reproductive capacity. Overfishing refers to a situation when fish are caught faster than their stocks can be replenished, leading to an overall depletion of fish populations that may result in their collapse. According to the World Bank, almost 90% of global marine fish stocks are fully

---

[281]   https://www.itu.int/en/mediacentre/backgrounders/Pages/itu-r-managing-the-radio-frequency-spectrum-for-the-world.aspx# - ITU-R: Managing the radio-frequency spectrum for the world

[282]   https://www.gsma.com/spectrum/resources/power-of-mobile-spectrum/ - GSMA | Mobile and the Power of Spectrum - Spectrum

[283] Not in My Back Yard (NIMBY) protests.

exploited or overfished[284]. This cannot be good. Such overfishing pose threats to the marine and sea ecosystems, also affecting millions of people worldwide who greatly rely on fishing to make a living.

Without some regulation over who fishes *what* and *where*, some fish stocks may or would collapse or stop being economical to catch. This is why EU member states have defined a common fisheries policy in order to manage fish stock resources ensuring that these can be fished sustainably whilst providing healthy food at reasonable prices Hence, the EU specifies and sets annual catch limits for most commercial fish stocks – also called total allowable catches (TACs). Each TAC is shared among the EU member states through national quotas. Individual member states are responsible for ensuring that their quotas are not overfished. The EU also clearly maps out exclusive economic zones (EEZ) of the EU's member states – areas which each EU country holds rights to exploit marine resources in their zone[285].

Fish stocks are typically be subject to regulatory methods including Licensing (i.e., who gets to exploit them most efficiently for society), Access (non-price) Regulation (in order to maximise the most users, large and small), Access (price) Regulation, Quantity Regulation (quotas to as in quotas for sustainability), Environmental Regulation (the exploitation of fish stocks sometimes damages the environment), Consumer Protection Regulation (e.g., ensuring fish stocks and not suffering from pollution), etc.

4.8.6 Environmental (& Climate) Regulation

Broadly and briefly, as has been gleaned from this section – environmental regulations are aimed at protecting the environment, and often involve setting limits on pollution emissions, regulating waste disposal, and promoting sustainable practices, e.g., across our seas, forests, the air we breathe (Clean Air laws), and much more. Such regulations impose limits or put responsibilities on individuals, corporations, and other entities for

---

[284] Data | The World Bank - https://datatopics.worldbank.org/sdgatlas/archive/2017/SDG-14-life-below-water.html

[285] https://www.consilium.europa.eu/en/policies/eu-fish-stocks/ - Management of the EU's fish stocks - Consilium (europa.eu)

the purpose of preventing environmental damage or enhancing degraded environments.

Environmental regulation is sadly very paltry in many emerging market countries in Asia, Middle East and Africa who can do with much less polluted cities. The 2023 twenty-five (25) most polluted cities[286] include cities in Saudi Arabia, Pakistan, Bangladesh, India, Iraq, South Africa, Nepal, Bahrain, Kuwait, Iran, China, Uganda and Mali – with Indian cities dominating in the twenty five. Many cities in Africa too just do not take pride in the environment with disposed rubbish piled up on streets attracting mosquitoes and rodents, and much of the greenery in the cities being replaced with shanty towns and slums. These (and more) are basic environmental challenges that environmental regulators should address in emerging market countries.

Environmental and climate change concerns have been the subject of many international meetings [287] and several key international *regulatory* agreements. This is because climate change transcends national borders. Greenhouse pollution anywhere impacts people everywhere. Addressing this global challenge necessitates coordinated efforts at the international level. Here are some key international agreements that regulate climate change:

- Montreal Protocol (1987)[288]: Concerns about the depletion of the ozone layer led to the Montreal Protocol uniting all the then-197 member states of the United Nations. It regulated/regulates nearly 100 chemicals known as ozone-depleting substances. It remains the only UN treaty ratified by every member state. This protocol demonstrates that urgent environmental action (at least on ozone restoration) could yield global results.

---

[286] https://smartairfilters.com/en/blog/top-cities-worst-air-pollution/ - 25 Most Polluted Cities in the World (2023 Rankings) – Smart Air (smartairfilters.com)

[287] https://www.climaterealityproject.org/blog/global-climate-agreements-through-years - Global Climate Agreements Through the Years | The Climate Reality Project

[288] https://www.unep.org/ozonaction/who-we-are/about-montreal-protocol - About Montreal Protocol (unep.org)

- Earth Summit (1992)[289]: the 1992 Rio de Janeiro United Nations Conference on Environment and Development (also known as the Earth Summit) yielded the United Nations Framework Convention on Climate Change (UNFCCC). Later by year end that year, 158 member states had signed the UNFCCC, setting in train the annual Conferences of the Parties (COP) Meetings.

- Kyoto Protocol (1997)[290]: COP-3 yielded the first global treaty regulating (by reducing) global warming greenhouse gas emissions/pollution. The major industrialized nations agreed to cumulatively cut their greenhouse gas pollution to 5% below 1990 levels within 10–15 years. Controversially, India and China were not considered industrialized nations under the Kyoto protocol and were therefore exempt from its regulations. The Kyoto Protocol was adopted on the 11th of December 1997, but it only entered into force on 16th February 2005. There are currently 192 Parties to the Kyoto Protocol[291].

In summary, international agreements play a crucial role in regulating transborder issues like climate change. Such agreements provide a framework for collaboration, commitment and action on a global scale.

4.8.7 Summary on Scarce Resources & Environmental Regulation

It is not the goal of this sub-section to delve into the details of how to manage and regulate these incredibly important scarce resources to society - such details are the subject of books, conferences and agencies in their own rights covering them. Rather, it is to point out that scarce resources to society usually also need to be carefully [economically] regulated too. Many developing economies in Africa, Caribbean and South East Asia miss this basic reality – and are surprised that a significant percentage of their citizens do *not* have access to basic fresh water and electricity, their rainforests are being decimated and their minerals are being plundered by

---

[289] https://www.un.org/en/conferences/environment/rio1992 - United Nations Conference on Environment and Development, Rio de Janeiro, Brazil, 3-14 June 1992 | United Nations

[290] https://unfccc.int/kyoto_protocol - What is the Kyoto Protocol? | UNFCCC

[291] *Ibid.*

extremely corrupt politicians and others, including unscrupulous foreign powers who know better.

Scarce resources – like the very oxygen we all breathe – need regulating for the benefits of all, and not just the few. Our environment clearly needs better regulation or controls, particularly in emerging markets.

4.9 Universal Service Regulation

This is one of the methods of regulation that I am most passionate about. Why? This is because there exists so many basic services to modern society that escapes significant percentages of the populations of many developing countries like the one I hail from. How can commodities like basic drinking water, phone communications, waste management, electricity, basic bank accounts, basic literacy, basic health services, etc., *not* be available to billions of the 8 billion of humanity that live today? Sadly, this is the reality – and regulators and Governments the world over must always seek to extend such basic services to *all* their citizenry. This is frankly easier said than done in practice due to so many [high] barriers – but this should never stop us trying. For this reason, many countries have developed and continue to develop Universal Service Obligations (USO) across several basic services. Whether they are functional and working in most developing countries is frankly rather moot.

4.9.1 What is Universal Service?

It is important to start with a few definitions and objectives that underpin this term "universal service". As Figure 4.5 hopefully clarifies, Universal Service is any service that the Government expects to be a*vailable, affordable* and *accessible* throughout the population. Therefore, universal service has two key aspects to it. First, it means the service must be made available to all $\underline{X}^{292}$, perhaps within a given area or of the entire population. Second it should be made available at a uniform and affordable price. There are cons as well as the pros to uniform prices. Sometimes affordability can be better and more efficiently achieved through targeting than blanket uniform prices (which may subsidise many people for whom

---

[292] Examples of "X" are given later.

full-cost prices would be affordable). There are examples of targeted tariffs and products to promote affordability in telecoms and energy, for example.

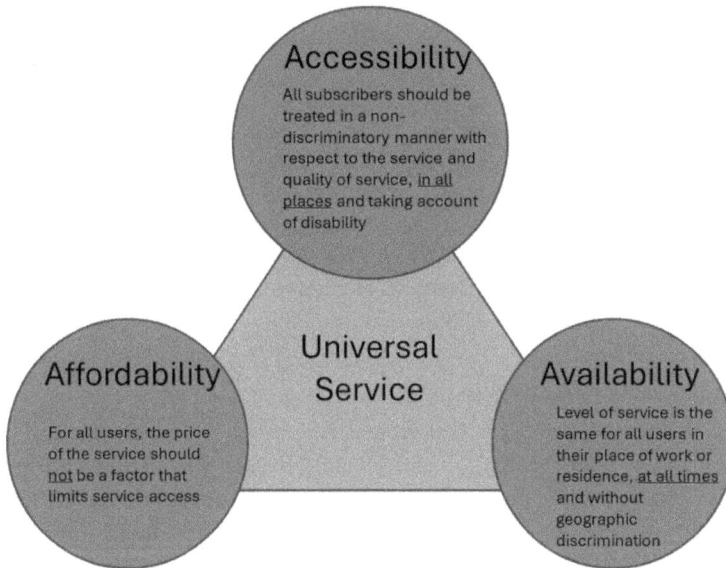

Figure 4.5 – What is Universal Service? *(Source: Dr Charles Jenne[293])*

This definition – in addition to Figure 4.5 - begs some important questions that need clarifying:

- What is "service"? Well, it could refer to any service deemed or designated by the Government as "essential" or central for daily modern living to most of its population. Therefore, it could mean literacy, basic health, basic voice telephony, radio broadcasting, schools, Internet, public transport, e-Government, etc. It really depends on the Government's designation of key services central to the economic, political and social life of its citizens, e.g. it may designate radio broadcasts to all because Government wants to be able to achieve the education and conveying of information to all of its citizens for them to be able to make informed choices on who to vote for.

---

[293] Dr Charles Jenne is a close collaborator and colleague of the author at Cenerva Ltd.

- What is "availability"? This refers to the *who* and/or *where* the designated service would be provided by the relevant suppliers – given the reality that suppliers do not typically supply their services to everyone in society, and to every location where they live. In other words, 'universal' availability or supply is typically unachievable for most services. Why should this be so? There are typically supply-side market failures and inhibitive costs at play including:
  - Poor roads to take services to certain parts of the country.
  - Poor economics to provide services to certain parts of the country: why would a waste management company build a sewage system in a rural part of a poor country like Malawi in Africa or Papua New Guinea (PNG) in South East Asia when it will never make a return on that infrastructure investment?
  - Not enough technical knowledge or skilled personnel: in many parts of rural, poor Africa – it is difficult to recruit and retain proficient teachers and medical staff to go stay and teach in schools and hospitals in these rural areas. This leads to minimum or no availability of school and health services in these rural areas.

- What is "access" in the Accessibility of Figure 4.5? Access to what? The access is to the designated "essential" services of course. However, a service being available in a certain area does not necessarily mean it is accessible to all of a country's citizens. Why? Chiefly, it may be because the services are not *affordable* to all who live under the service's area. Private education is available in most countries [in the urban areas and even in some rural areas], but it is completely unaffordable to large swathes of the population. Ditto for private health, subscription TV services, etc. Therefore, there are demand-side market failures that militate against accessibility.

- What is "affordability"? Well in most cases, Governments want to see uniform and affordable prices for these essential services. Can you imagine if the prices of a 2nd class postage stamp varied according to whether you live in the urban city or rural village? How absurd would it be if it is cheaper for the city-folk than for the rural dwellers due to the better demand-supply economics in urban vs. rural areas? Hence, Governments and regulators typically mandate unform prices for postage stamps across the entire country. What happens if the uniform prices are unaffordable to the median and/or average (mean) citizen in terms of them on the poor-to-rich continuum in society? This question is rhetorical because the postal services would not be used even where it is available. The point here is that affordability is "relative" to the country and even to specific small regions or areas in the country. Therefore, in many cases, the desire to maintain "affordability" – not just uniform prices – leads to prices of particular designated services often being pegged below costs. The uniformity in prices itself remains a problem because it means servicing customers in high-cost areas (e.g. rural areas) may or would typically be loss making.

- What is "universal"? Earlier I note that universal service means the service must be made available to all X, perhaps within a given area or of the entire population – in addition to being made available at a uniform and affordable price. However, I did not specify what X refers to. The reason is because X would typically represent different descriptors depending on the designated essential services and the countries concerned. X (qualifying "universal") may be referring to the following descriptors depending on the services designated:
    o "Community": the notion of universal for a service like post offices services may be delimited to refer to a defined community, e.g. every district "community" must be endowed with at least one post office.
    o "Location-based" or "Specified geographical area-based": the notion of universal for a service like mobile/cellular is strictly speaking location-based (or specified geographical area-based) because telecom regulators know the exact locations of telecoms transmitting base station equipment, and therefore they can predict [with good technical accuracy] the coverage area of the mobile/cellular service, and hence the availability at specific geographical areas.
    o "Homes": the notion of universal of certain services like human wastewater management (covering toilet waste) would typically be delimited to cover homes.

243

o "Streets": the notion of universal for a service like home waste collection services would typically be delimited to all streets on which homes are situated.

o "Offices": the notion of universal of a business broadband and Internet service may be delimited to target offices and some selected home offices too.

o "Entire country": some services like satellite broadcast services can cover the entire country.

The key message here is that the word "universal" itself is typically service and/or geography-specific and more. This explains why the USA historically limited some level of affordable access *only* to fixed telephone service in the telecoms sector – and not much more. This means the regulator (the FCC) expected a fixed telephone to be available within a certain radius (in miles) of every single US home. The word "universal" is very relative indeed.

- Where does funding come from? As ever, funding is one of these important questions. Universal service usually involves the provision of some services or provision in some areas which is loss-making. These losses are ultimately paid by citizens or consumers, e.g. citizens if the Government provides a direct subsidy funded through general taxation, or consumers through cross-subsidy from profitable to loss-making services.

4.9.2 Why Universal Service? SDGs & Regulation

I believe this question is already comprehensively answered above. However, this section would introduce the United Nation's "universal" notion of Sustainable Development Goals (or SDGs) to supplement.

What are SDGs? In 2015, all United Nations Member States committed to strive for peace and prosperity for all people on earth and to protect the planet, now and into the future. These promises were made in the form of the Sustainable Development Goals (SDGs). The SDGs are a collection of 17 global goals adopted by all United Nations Member States designed to be a "blueprint to achieve a better and more sustainable future for all".

Specifically,

> "The Sustainable Development Goals are the blueprint to achieve a better and more sustainable future for all. They address the global challenges we face, including those related to poverty, inequality, climate change, environmental degradation, peace and justice. The 17 Goals are all interconnected, and in order to leave no one behind, it is important that we achieve them all by 2030"[294].

The 17 Sustainable Goals are as follows:
- Goal 1: No Poverty
- Goal 2: Zero Hunger
- Goal 3: Good Health and Well-being
- Goal 4: Quality Education
- Goal 5: Gender Equality
- Goal 6: Clean Water and Sanitation
- Goal 7: Affordable and Clean Energy
- Goal 8: Decent Work and Economic Growth
- Goal 9: Industry, Innovation and Infrastructure
- Goal 10: Reduced Inequality
- Goal 11: Sustainable Cities and Communities
- Goal 12: Responsible Consumption and Production
- Goal 13: Climate Action
- Goal 14: Life Below Water
- Goal 15: Life on Land
- Goal 16: Peace and Justice Strong Institutions
- Goal 17: Partnerships to achieve the Goals

Good luck to the United Nations on most developing countries meeting these goals by the target year of 2030! I perceive close to zero chance of most poor South East Asian and African countries realizing these goals by 2045 – yet alone 2030.

---

[294] https://www.un.org/sustainabledevelopment/sustainable-development-goals/ - Take Action for the Sustainable Development Goals - United Nations Sustainable Development

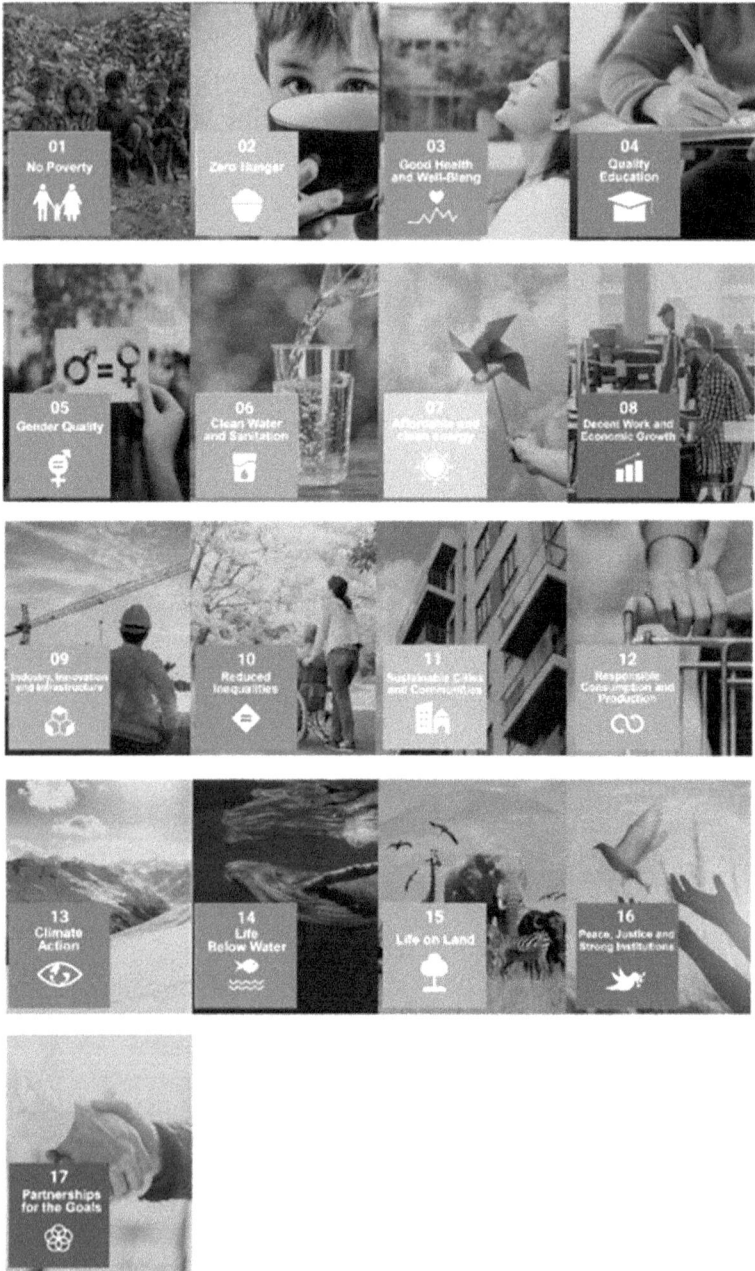

Image 44 – The United Nations 17 SDGs – Adapted from Source[295].

However from the perspective of Universal Service regulation, these goals represent clear "universal service" objectives and goals that countries should be striving to achieve. Consider Goals 1 to 3 of 'No Poverty', 'Zero Hunger' and 'Good Health and Well-being' respectively. These are "services" that these all countries have committed to make "universal" in their countries by 2030. So the SDGs are an urgent call for action by all countries - developed and developing - in a global partnership to realise them.

The key message here is that the SDGs provide yet another level of *why* Universal Service regulation is not only appropriate – but timely – across a whole host of basic services. Countries would need to use policy and *regulation* in order to implement these SDGs.

4.9.3 Universal Service Obligations and Examples

It is important to note that a Universal Service definition for a *designated* service should provide a baseline level of service necessary to everyone. Enhanced services and quality premiums should not be part of the Universal Service Offer (USO). Most countries therefore would need to designate USOs for the services they deem as "essential" – and regulators and policy makers would have to find ways to implement them whilst defining and interpreting what "universal" may mean for every service context.

Some example USOs drawn from the telecoms industry across the world are captured in Table 4.6 – showing the great variations across countries. Even some developing countries like Pakistan are brave enough to include broadband Internet access as part of its USO – which is very challenging for a country like Pakistan. Perhaps this was driven by the SDGs that were ratified in 2015.

Country	Universal Service Obligation (USO) Policy
Hong Kong (Source: OFCA website[296])	The USO specifies that basic services should be made reasonably available to all persons in Hong Kong, at service charges capped by the published tariffs. *The USO mainly covers basic fixed voice telephony services and public payphones.* Broadband or mobile services are not covered under the USO, and the coverage of such services is mainly a commercial decision.
Ireland (2016/21 ComReg Decision[297])	We may designate an undertaking, or undertakings, to satisfy any reasonable request to provide, at a fixed location, a connection to the public communications network ("PCN") and a publicly available telephone service over the network connection that allows for originating and receiving of national and international calls. *The connection must be capable of supporting voice, facsimile and data communications at data rates that are sufficient to permit functional internet access ("FIA").* In this Decision, we refer to this collectively as access at a fixed location ("AFL USO").
Pakistan (Ministry of Information Technology, Telecoms Policy 2015)	The Services falling under scope of USF include the following: • Telephone services to local, national, mobile, toll free, premium rate and international numbers… • Access to emergency services (as under voice licenses). • *Broadband Internet access.* • E-mail, fax and other related services. • Telecentres, including the equipment, buildings and other capex and opex associated with the Telecentre itself. • Broadband Internet access to support multiple terminals at telecentres at speeds consistent with the size of the concurrent user base
UAE (TRA Policy Document, 2017)	Access to the same minimum set of services at the same price, regardless of location – "all consumers in permanent dwellings should have access to services which are *capable of delivering basic voice, TV services, and high-speed data packages of at least 10mbps*".
UK (2020[298])	From March 2020, consumer has right to request *broadband speed of at least at least* 10mbps (with monthly price capped at nationally regulated tariff) provided the cost of provision does not exceed £3,400 (although consumer can pay the excess).

Table 4.6 – Universal Service Obligation Examples in Telecoms[299]

---

[296] https://www.ofca.gov.hk/en - OFCA Hong Kong

[297] https://www.comreg.ie/media/2021/11/RTC-AFL-USO_R-NON-CONFIDENTIAL-5.11.21.pdf - RTC-AFL-USO_R-NON-CONFIDENTIAL-5.11.21.pdf (comreg.ie)

[298] https://commonslibrary.parliament.uk/research-briefings/cbp-8146/ - The Universal Service Obligation (USO) for Broadband - House of Commons Library (parliament.uk)

[299] With thanks to Dr Charles Jenne for this compilation of telecoms USOs.

USOs do not also remain stagnant over time as they are reviewed [and added to] as technologies and the economics of service provisions improve to benefit consumers and citizens more. For example, some countries have extended their *voice-only* telecoms universal obligations to include broadband/internet provisions:

- Finland - Broadband Internet was introduced and included in the Finnish telecoms USOs for the first time in 2010 with speeds specified at only 1Mbps in 2010, which was later doubled to 2Mbps in 2015[300], and quintupled to 10Mbps in 2021. Finland became the first country in the world to make broadband a legal right for every citizen in 2010[301].

- Spain – the 2011 Law on Sustainable Economy included Internet access of 1Mbps into the USO for the first time (Source - OECD[302]).

- Malta – in June 2011, the Maltese regulator mandated universal access to "functional internet access" as a universal service at 4Mbps. This has since been increased to 30Mbps download and 1.5Mbps upload in 2021[303].

- Switzerland – a broadband connection providing minimum download and upload speeds of 600/100 Kbps is part of the scope of universal service obligations (Source - OECD[304]).

---

[300] https://omdia.tech.informa.com/om031670/finland-country-regulation-overview--2023 - Finland: Country Regulation Overview – 2023 Omdia (informa.com)

[301] https://www.bbc.co.uk/news/10461048 - Finland makes broadband a 'legal right' - BBC News & https://www.loc.gov/item/global-legal-monitor/2010-07-06/finland-legal-right-to-broadband-for-all-citizens/ - Finland: Legal Right to Broadband for All Citizens | Library of Congress (loc.gov)

[302] https://www.oecd-ilibrary.org/science-and-technology/universal-service-policies-in-the-context-of-national-broadband-plans_5k94gz19flq4-en - 5k94gz19flq4-en.pdf (oecd-ilibrary.org)

[303] Availability of Broadband Internet Access Service - Universal Service (mca.org.mt) - https://www.mca.org.mt/sites/default/files/Availability%20of%20Broadband%20as%20a%20Universal%20Service%20-%20Decision%20Notice%20-%2022%20Oct%202021.pdf

[304] https://www.oecd-ilibrary.org/science-and-technology/universal-service-policies-in-the-context-of-national-broadband-plans_5k94gz19flq4-en - 5k94gz19flq4-en.pdf (oecd-ilibrary.org)

- Turkey – Minimum upwards and downwards broadband speeds of 256 Kbps and 512 Kbps are included as part of the scope of universal service obligations (Source - OECD[305]).
- The 2018 European Electronic Communications Communications (EECC) Code[306] embraces universal service broadband as a USO across the EU.
- Etc.

4.9.4 How to Drive the Realisation of Universal Services – the World Bank "Gaps Model"

It is one thing setting and specifying the terms and conditions of the USO. It is totally another to make them happen in practice and for them to be enjoyed by all citizens in a country. As an example, many – if not most – countries mandate USOs to ensure the adequate, universal and reasonably priced provision of postal [if not voice/broadband telecommunications] services in all regions of the country. Well, in many African countries, the postal services USO is close to unachievable, yet alone any telecoms ones. This is because of major [macroeconomic] barriers covered earlier like poverty in particular in developing economies, but also poor leadership, poor and lazy regulators and policy makers, poor roads and more.

The question here then is what happens beyond securing the USO? How is it made to come about in practice? The answer is not straightforward because it depends on the service concerned (e.g., hospitals, primary education, postal, telecoms, etc.), the dynamics of the sector concerned, whether it is a service entirely provided by the public sector (i.e., the Government), the private sector or some combination of both – and more factors including the realities of the challenging macroeconomic and other barriers. The reality in most countries is that the USO service would need to be provided by some combination of both the private and public sectors. This brings the role of a good competent regulator ever more to the fore. This is because the Government would have to start by clarifying the parties involved in the governance of the USO service concerned.

---

[305] *Ibid.*

[306] https://digital-strategy.ec.europa.eu/en/policies/eu-electronic-communications-code - Directive 2018/1972 - EU Electronic Communications Code | Shaping Europe's digital future (europa.eu)

4.9.4.1 Implementing a USO – a brief Postal Example

For example, in the case of a postal USO [wherein all citizens access postal services at all parts of country at affordable prices], there are typically three clear parties involved in the Governance, namely:

- *The Government itself*: it defines the postal policy including specifying the USO, defines and specifies the roles of regulator and typically a designated postal operator. It also establishes the laws and statutes to support the policy, i.e., the legal foundation usually in some primary legislation (unless the USO is funded directly by Government).

- *The Regulator*: the regulator is typically responsible for regulating the postal industry, ensuring the USO is delivered efficiently. The regulator defines how USO is to be funded, setting quality standards, licensing the designated postal USO operator and possibly other postal operators, e.g. couriers, e-commerce players, etc.

- *The Designated USO Postal Operator*: this operator is typically responsible for meeting the terms of its licence, delivering the USO and meeting Quality of Service (QoS) standards. This designated operator is obliged to provide services to the T&Cs specified and carry any commercial losses as necessary – which are hopefully covered by Government subsidies. This is a case of a Universal Service Obligation (USO) *with* compensation, but there are other services where the scheme involves a Universal Service Obligation (USO) *without* compensation from the Government – particularly if the Private Sector and/or a Universal Service Fund (USF) would suffice. This is so that loss-making services have to be subsidised from profitable services, meaning that consumers buying the profitable services subsidise those benefiting from the loss-making services. Compensation covers the net cost to the USO operator of providing services.

For example, Postcomm was established as the UK's postal regulator in 2000 with a primary duty to ensure the provision of a universal postal service. Postcomm was empowered to licence a universal service provider – called Royal Mail. Postcomm was also empowered to promote effective competition between postal operators (in interests of consumers) and that all operators are/were to be licensed. The UK postal market was eventually fully liberalised in 2006. Ofcom[307] (UK) has since (in 2010) taken on the role of regulating the postal sector in the UK since traditional letter mail has been in deep decline due to substitution by digital media alternatives. E-commerce is also a significant growth area being exploited by many postal authorities.

For more details on the postal sector, the reader may consult the Universal Postal Union's (UPU) 2019 Postal Reform Guide[308]. In it (see Article 17 of the Guide), the UPU specifies its recommended USO Postal standards that UPU member countries should abide by including:

- Priority & non priority items to 2kg.
- Letters, postcards, printed papers & packets to 2kg.
- Items for the blind, up to 7 kilograms.
- Special bags containing newspapers, periodicals, books and similar printed documentation for the same addressee at the same address called "M bags", up to 30 kilograms.
- Postal parcels to 20kg: UPU member countries are recommended to ensure that their designated operators accept, handle, convey and deliver parcel-post items up to 20 kilograms.

Such "harmonized" standards also help with uniformity across countries too as international mails are posted.

Regarding the funding options for the compensation for a postal/telecoms USO, they typically include:

- Direct government funding: the advantage of direct funding here is that there is no need for regulator to try to calculate net cost of compensation. However, how long will the Government be on the hook of funding the subsidy? Would it be a single one-off whole of life payment or periodic payments? What are the post-subsidy obligations, e.g. open access to the USO designated operator's

---

[307] www.ofcom.org.uk

[308] https://www.upu.int/UPU/media/upu/files/postalSolutions/developmentCooperation/GuideReformPostalEn.pdf - GuideReformPostalEn.pdf (upu.int)

network to other players? These are still tricky issues to define and implement that may still require a competent sector regulator.

- Universal Service charges: typically, a levy set as a % of revenue to all postal operators – which will get passed on to the generality of consumers. The challenge here is the need to have a number of credible providers to generate effective competition who can be levied in the first place. This approach distributes burden proportionally amongst all sector players and customers, and the amount required should be a small percentage ($< 3\%$) of revenue. However, this may also deter new entrants and this can be overcome by setting a revenue floor before payments become due.

- Reduction in payments: for taxes or other national scarce resources that the USO designated operators may be using, e.g., mobile spectrum that is used to deliver more widespread coverage if postal operator also happens to be a telecoms operator.

- Self-funding: by other postal service providers if costs are modest and, if they can be "persuaded" to do so. Again, this assumes having a number of credible providers to generate effective competition.

4.9.4.2 Implementing Universal Service – the World Bank "Gaps Model"

I am a big fan of the "Gaps" model (Navas-Sabater *et al.*, 2002) that was pioneered by the World Bank in the context of driving access to telecommunications services for all. I am such a fan of this model because I believe the concepts underpinning this classic model applies to other sectors too. It also implicitly depicts how both the private and public sectors can "cooperate" and "coordinate" to deliver a universal service for all. The model is depicted in Figure 4.6.

The 'theory' underpinning the model is that there is a wide array of mechanisms available for telecommunications decision makers to increase access to telecommunications services – necessitating the need of a general analytical framework model. Therefore Navas-Sabater *et al.* (2002) proposed this classic framework of Figure 4.6 called the Gaps Analysis model. In essence, the model divides underserved areas into two different segments or "gaps": the *Market Efficiency Gap* and the *Access Gap*. I believe this model translates to other sectors too. So, let us cover the key tenets of this Market Gap and Access Gap Model:

253

- **The Axes:** The Y-axis is the *supply-side* axis starting from the lowest costs access supply areas [that commercial players would cover first] to the highest cost access areas [typically rural or least densely populated areas that are more expensive and likely uncommercial to supply]. The X-axis is the demand-side of consumers, citizens and households ranging from the high-income households [or richer citizens who would take up the services first without any hesitation] to lower-income households [or poor citizens who would struggle to pay for any services].

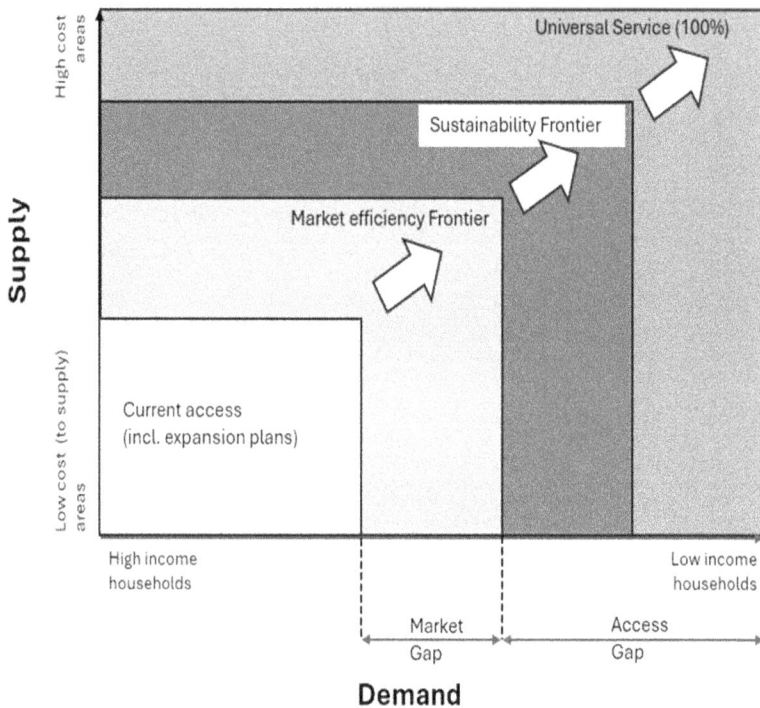

Figure 4.6 – The World Bank Market Gap and Access Gap Model

Sources: Based on and adapted from Navas-Sabater et al. (2002) & Muente-Kunigami & Navas-Sabater (2010)

- **The Current Access (including expansion plans)**: this represents the households (or citizens) demand with high-enough incomes to pay and who are currently supplied by services. This area also includes any expansion planned services.

- **The Market Gap & the Market Efficiency Frontier**: The market gap refers to that difference between the level of demand penetration that can be reached under current plans (including expansion plans) and that [typically] *private-sector* led level that the market could achieve by means of an ideal competition law-driven, regulatory and legal environment (the reader may want to revisit Figure 2.3 in Chapter 2 and Figure 4.4 earlier in this chapter). This gap could be eliminated with adequate changes in current regulations (in addition to new competitive measures taken by the regulator as Figure 4.4 suggests) – and therefore this gap should *not* require public transfers. In other words, the application of the optimal set of competition law-driven vs. regulatory instruments for the market sector would close the market gap to the *market efficiency frontier*.

- **The Access Gap:** alternatively, the access gap depicts that portion of the market that even under the optimal legal, competition law-driven and regulatory environment would *not* be reached by market players due to their high costs and/or low-income levels. Public subsidies are usually considered in order to go beyond the coverage of the market efficiency frontier into the access gap.

- **The Sustainability Frontier & the Universal Service Frontier**: The Access Gap can itself be split into two different zones as seen in Figure 4.6: the first that takes us to the *Sustainability Frontier* and the second and takes us to the *Universal Service Frontier* (ideally 100% though it would be realistically less for many services in most countries). The sustainability frontier divides two different types of projects: first, those projects requiring only a one-off subsidy to 'kick start' operations and thereafter the areas support themselves on an ongoing basis; second, those projects that would require ongoing subsidies in perpetuity. From an economic regulatory perspective, this is a most important distinction. It is clearly efficient to discern projects that that are expected to recover their operational costs and remain profitable from a singular "jump start" public financing compared to those that will always require public subsidies.

- **The Boundaries of the Market and Access Gap Models vary by country and by service**: It is important to note explicitly - what may be obvious - that all boundaries under this framework are not static. Rather, they depend on many factors including all the sector drivers of Chapter 1 such as technology, macroeconomy, industry, consumer behaviour, innovation of new services/applications, and others. The current access, market efficiency frontier, sustainability frontier and universal service frontier boundaries for a mobile 2G service in a country may be 70%, 80%, 90% and 100%, respectively. However, the boundaries for electricity services in the same country may be 30%, 50%, 60% and 80%, respectively. Note that these latter boundary numbers are much less than the former, and note that a universal service boundary of no more than 80% is proposed for electricity - suggesting that the Government may have [had] to concede that a 100% electricity service in that country is unachievable for the near future. This sort of reality speaks to a continuous review of universal access targets, policies and mechanisms, and the need to adapt them.

I contend that this 2002-proposed World Bank Market Gap and Access Gap model is still most relevant to good economic regulation of most services across most sectors. It forces good regulators to do their utmost to estimate the boundaries for the various services, and use them as evidence – amongst other key considerations like the outputs of relevant market reviews. This way good regulators and/or Governments can:

- Optimise competition law and regulation in order to reach the market efficiency frontier for the service;
- Investigate and implement concrete policies, along with the right choice of projects (and geographical areas) that only require one-off subsidies to 'kick start' operations to reach the sustainability frontier;
- Clearly discern the projects and areas that would always require subsidies in perpetuity.

Hopefully, the reader can see the power of this model shown in Figure 4.6 in the implementation – not only of USO schemes in particular – but also in using good economic regulation to ascertain the boundaries of where regulatory interventions in terms of one-off or perpetual public subsidies are required.

4.10 Enforcement & Responsive Regulation

There is a famous quote rightly or wrongly attributed to the late, brilliant management theorist, Professor Peter Drucker[309] which reads: "what gets measured gets managed". With regulation I propose we can take this one step further: "what gets bothered to be regulated with an explicit set of rules must be enforced". This is certainly true of regulation – particularly, in order to influence and optimize regulatory successes by achieving more of the specified regulatory objectives. *Enforcement* of regulations is key in this regard. Why bother to specify and set regulations and not enforce them? Can you imagine the chaos that ensues on the roads if traffic light rules and regulations [of red, amber and green] are just considered to be optional rules and mostly ignored by motorists? Traffic light rules are enforced by police or by cameras in many developed countries leading to much order on the roads. The opposite is true in many developing countries leading to disorder. Therefore, good enforcement leads to 'behaviour modification' on the part of drivers, promoting both *deterrence* and *compliance* to the rules. Indeed, it is key to distinguish between 'means' (deterrence) and 'ends' (compliance) - deterrence is a way to incentivise behaviour modification and achieve compliance.

The same is true for [economic] regulation of sectors: quality *Enforcement Regulation* would generally promote behaviour modifications towards deterrence and compliance to the rules.

4.10.1 Responsive Regulation – a persuasion-led enforcement approach

This section also introduces the Ayres & Braithwaite's (1992) notion of *Responsive Regulation*. Their influential book goes beyond enforcement regulation being all about deterrence and compliance by arguing that enforcement of regulations can be "a fruitful combination of persuasion and sanctions", p. 25. To support their tenet generally, the authors argue persuasively that enforcement regulation of businesses in the United States by the US Government is often ineffective despite being more adversarial in tone than in other countries. Their book draws on both empirical studies of enforcement regulation from across the globe world as well as from

---

[309] https://en.wikiquote.org/wiki/Peter_Drucker - Peter Drucker - Wikiquote

modern game theory to illustrate innovative solutions to this adversarial enforcement problem.

Figure 4.7 – The Enforcement Pyramid
(Source: Ayres & Braithwaite, 1992)

A central tenet to their notion of responsive regulation is therefore that compliance is more likely to be realized by market players if the regulator operates the explicit enforcement pyramid as depicted in Figure 4.7. The pyramid shows a range of enforcement sanctions commencing with 'persuasion' at the base of the pyramid, then on to a 'warning letter', then on to 'civil penalty', then on to 'criminal penalty', through 'licence suspension' and finally 'licence revocation'.

Ayres & Braithwaite argue that enforcement regulation should always start at the base of the pyramid – i.e., with persuasion, which is non-penal, and ratchet up with more punitive/penal responses if the securing of compliance fails with lower-pyramid efforts. The enforcement pyramid is aimed at a singular regulated firm.

As an ex-regulator, I think this enforcement pyramid approach can be appropriate and regulators should consider adopting this approach on a case-by-case basis. From my experience, this step-by-step escalation would not be appropriate in many cases wherein the risks of "playing this nice" to some well-funded market players who are abusing their dominance may lead to weaker players exiting the market whilst this escalation process ensues. In other words, the higher the severity of the risk of not enforcing against the infringing player – it would be proportionate and right to escalate to the instruments higher up the pyramid though mindful of prejudicing the relationship between regulator and regulated firm. Sometimes too, such a proportionate escalation enables a de-escalation in which the regulator achieves its objectives whilst the regulated firm moves into compliance in a timelier manner than would otherwise happen escalating step-by-step up the pyramid.

There is more to the responsive regulation method that is more theoretical than practical in my view, and that goes beyond the purpose of this chapter. For example, their enforcement *strategies* pyramid starting with self-regulation at the base escalating up to 'command' regulation with non-discretionary punishment at the top. However, I wanted to highlight both the practical benefits and risks of the basic enforcement pyramid of Figure 4.7. I have personally used it in my consultancy with clients on a case-by-case basis. For readers who desire a deeper understanding on responsive regulation, Ayres & Braithwaite (1992) is good, recommended reading.

4.10.2 Quality of Enforcement tracks Quality of Regulation

It is a sad truism that I see many regulators in developing countries who carry out *only* sporadic or – at best – selective enforcements of their regulations and rules. This sends terrible signals all round:

- To other market players who see rules being flouted and decide they can break them too (or even that they think they will lose out commercially if they follow the rules when their competitors flout them);
- To investors who would quickly decide that the regulator is neither a referee nor an enforcer – and therefore not a good market to invest in; to potential new entrants who would decide not to enter the market at all;
- Lack of enforcement also further weakens the weaker market players because it appears okay for the stronger players to abuse their dominance over the weaker players; and even consumers and citizens would also choose not to trust the regulator.

There is a strong correlation in most sectors between the quality of enforcement and the quality of regulation – and Governments and regulators should realise this. Enforcement is both an art and a science. There is an art to setting rules and regulations that are easy to enforce,

259

which is less costly for the regulator – whilst discouraging creative compliance. There is the science of devising complicated rules with complex equations whilst using the heavy stick of enforcement to punish infringers and maximise compliance levels – which are both painful and expensive. There are clear trade-offs here whilst maintaining accountability, due process and costs – a core reason why Ayres and Braithwaite (1992) proposed the concept of responsive regulation noted above.

4.10.3 The DREAM Framework to Enforcement Regulation

I note at the start of this section on Enforcement & Responsive Regulation that good enforcement leads to 'behaviour modification' on the part of drivers, promoting both deterrence and compliance to the rules. Baldwin *et al*.(2012), chapter 11, propose a helpful, broader regulatory framework consisting of five key tasks as shown in Table 4.7.

1	**D**etecting	The gaining of information on undesirable and non-compliant behaviour.
2	**R**esponding	The developing of policies, rules, and tools to deal with the problems discovered.
3	**E**nforcing	The application of policies, rules and tools on the ground.
4	**A**ssessing	The measuring of success or failure in enforcement activities.
5	**M**odifying	Adjusting tools and strategies in order to improve compliance and address problematic behaviour.

Table 4.7 – The DREAM Framework of Enforcement Regulation
Source: Baldwin *et al.* (2012), p.227

The DREAM (Detecting, Responding, Enforcing, Assessing, and Modifying) Framework seeks to address real-world enforcement challenges making it a practical framework for regulators to consider. As Table 4.7 shows, it starts with *Detecting* - the identification of non-compliant and undesirable behaviour; then on to *Responding* – the development of policies, rules, and tools to deal with the problems

260

discovered; then on to *Enforcing* - the application of policies, rules, and tools on the ground; then *Assessing* - measurement of success or failure in enforcement activities; and lastly *Modifying* – or the adjustment of tools and strategies in order to improve compliance and address problematic behaviours. The framework also examines issues arising from regulation of errant firms, including the sanctions that can be used to influence such firms, the extent of corporate criminal fault, and the difficulties of proving liability. Next, I cover some key practical highlights of the DREAM tasks.

- **Detection:** It is important to uncover non-compliant and undesirable behaviours given the key to the DREAM approach is deterrence and compliance. The practical challenge is there is usually much information asymmetry between the regulator and the regulated firm in addition to limited enforcement resources. Worse still, the regulated firms know these too. Therefore, whistleblowers or hotlines to report such behaviours may help. More importantly and practically, regulators would need to draw from their regulatory objectives and rules to develop clear conceptions of the errant behaviours they want to enforce against. This is more practical and efficient to know what you are looking for. Even when some errant behaviours are suspected, it may be non-trivial to prove non-compliance. Therefore, the *level* of non-compliance is also important to gather along with "off-the-screen" activities that can be gleaned from whistleblowers or hotlines. Regulators need to define what would constitute compliance with the rules and regulations and what would constitute non-compliance too.

- **Responding:** the developing of policies, rules, and tools to deal with the problems discovered follows on from the Detection phase. In developing rules, I usually note to my clients another rule! Do not develop any rules that you cannot enforce against with a good degree of success. The rules do not only have to be legally watertight, but they also have to be:
  - *precisely-worded* – so as to discourage creative compliance;
  - *specific in their coverage* - as in what is undesirable and who is responsible;
  - *inclusive* – under-inclusive rules are notoriously bad to enforce. If the regulator develops rules that do not include certain hazard situations or predicted unwanted behaviours, then the rule would miss some key concerns making compliance unlikely;

- o *clear* - on which enforcement strategies apply when and why;
- o *capable of being enforced* - with the range of strategies in the enforcement pyramid of Figure 4.7 (and even more including advice, education and promotion).

- **Enforcement**: regulators seek compliance with laws and regulations, as well as deterrence. This is clear – but I will certainly advocate for compliance to be preferred over deterrence, though both are usually needed. It is important to unpack two distinctions, especially in the meaning of the word 'compliance' here: (i) means vs ends; and (ii) formal vs informal methods. I use the word 'compliance' here in this paragraph to describe the ends, not the means[310]. As Ayres & Braithwaite's (1992) enforcement pyramid of responsive regulation recommends, compliance enforcement need not necessarily be penal and formal – but could start with the informal of persuasion, education, advice and negotiation. Formal prosecution to achieve compliance is frequently too big a stick to use early. The compliance approach is further preferred to the deterrence approach because it allows for valuable information exchange between regulator and the regulated firm, and it educates the latter to think constructively about modes of compliance. Deterrence - on the other hand – comes down hard on errant behaviours severely so that the regulated firm would think twice about infringing any other laws or regulations. The deterrence may be a large fine – but the regulator should also be mindful that this could end up in protracted proceedings in the courts or in other tribunals.

- **Assessment**: It is important to assess how well the current enforcement system is working, or else how does the regulator know what to improve? There are practical challenges though. First, if non-compliance behaviours are "off-the-screen", the regulator is none the wiser to improve, unless there is some form of whistleblowing or hotline tipping. Secondly, the legal and policy bases must be truly clear. Thirdly, it is much easier to measure and count enforcement inputs or decisions carried out by the regulator but more difficult to

---

[310] Sometimes, the word 'compliance' is being used to refer both to the desirable ends and also to one specific set of means, e.g., persuasion, education, advice and negotiation (instead of penalties and deterrence).

measure the outcomes, as there may be a 'lag effect' in the order of years. Fourthly, due to the latter reason, assessing 'effectiveness' of enforcement actions is hard in the short to medium term whilst the regulator waits for long term outcomes. Either way, such assessments are still key irrespective of these challenges.

- **Modification**: this last and fifth stage seeks to adjust the tools, policies and strategies in order to improve compliance and minimise problematic behaviours. It is an essential task, particularly given the challenges to get much value out of the Assessment stage in the short-to-medium term.

Baldwin *et al.* (2012), p.227-258 provides more details on the DREAM enforcement framework.

4.11 Risk-Based Regulation

Risk-based Regulation is arguably *not* a full-blown method of regulation like many of the previous ten that precede it in this chapter. It is more about prioritizing of regulatory actions according to an assessment of the risks that market players present to the regulator in achieving its objectives. In a sense, it is similar to Meta-regulation described in Seciton 3.1.5. Recall from this section that Baldwin et al. (2012, p.147) note that the term 'meta-regulation' refers to "processes in which the regulatory authority oversees a control or risk management system, rather than conducts regulation directly – it '*steers rather than rows*'". So, Risk Regulation concerns the primary 'control' duties of regulation that are conducted within the risk management systems of industry firms and other regulated entities.

4.11.1 Example Context of the Need for Risk-Based Regulation

To provide some context, recall I note in Chapter 2 how - following the global financial crisis of 2008 - Governments found themselves forced to lay down new rules to further safeguard the stability of financial systems, to further regulate banks and financial institutions, and to further protect investors. I also note that according to Investopedia[311], the 2008 Financial Crisis sent the world into a great recession with 8.8 million jobs lost, unemployment spiking by 10% by October 2009, 8 million home foreclosures, USD 19.2 Trillion household wealth wiped out and much more. This was no trivial regulatory failure.

Arguably, the real culprit here lay in the absence of a clear *Risks-Based assessment* of the risks that specific market players presented to sector regulators after all the excessive deregulation in the Banking and Finance Sectors of the 1980s/90s. The reader may recall that in the USA, the emergence of losses in sub-prime loans in 2007 triggered the crisis and exposed other risky loans and over-inflated asset prices like houses or properties. With the mounting of loan losses and the collapse of Lehman Brothers[312] on September 15, 2008, a huge market panic broke out in the inter-bank loan market with banks refusing to lend to one another. The contagion into Europe and elsewhere was swift. Simultaneously in the UK, on the 14th September 2007, the British bank Northern Rock that had expanded aggressively [by turning to international money markets to fund its rapid growth] was revealed to be in a severe financial liquidity crisis. This eventually led to the first UK bank run for over 140 years[313]. Banks in the USA, UK, Europe, etc. started collapsing and Governments had to intervene with huge bailouts to protect consumers' savings.

What is worse in the context of the UK is that the 2008 Financial crisis still happened after the risk-based regulation approach had been

> "institutionally endorsed most emphatically in 2005 when the Hampton Review recommended that all UK regulators should operate a risk-based system" - Baldwin *et al.* (2012), p.281

This raises key questions about the efficacy and effectiveness of risk-based regulation in the UK between 2005 and 2008, and frankly, whether it is any better today in the 2020s. What risks-based regulation analyses of these major banking players existed? It is hardly the case that some of these

---

[311] https://www.investopedia.com/news/10-years-later-lessons-financial-crisis/ - Over 10 Years Later, Lessons From the Financial Crisis (investopedia.com)

[312] A Wall Street investment bank

[313] https://express.adobe.com/page/DAlRb7HdWiHqA/ - The financial crisis - 10 years on (adobe.com) -

risks to excessive deregulation of the financial and banking sector were not predicted – they were! and many of the risks were known to regulators and Governments[314].

4.11.2 Challenges with Risk-Based Regulation

With the previous context spelling out the need for risk-based regulation, the reader may think there is a clear method to risk-based regulation. There arguably is not. Risk-based regulation starts with the regulator clearly identifying its objectives and the risks that regulated entities present to achieving those objectives – the sorts of risks the Lehman Brothers, Northern Rock, Goldman Sachs and other major financial players presented to the regulation of the financial and banking sectors pre- the 2008 crisis. However, it turns out that there are many challenges with the practical implementation of risk-based regulation:

- What sort of system should be developed for assessing such risks and scoring them for these major market players?
- What categories of risks, e.g. 'inherent' risks to do with intrinsic risks to firms like then-Lehman Brothers; or their 'management and control risks' pertaining to the organisation's internal controls (clearly - with the benefit of hindsight - there were major management and control risks), etc.
- Should the risks scoring be quantitative or qualitative or both? Would a High, Medium and Low risks system suffice?
- How are resources allocated to the risks?
- Which risks will the regulator *not* prioritise and why?
- If regulators pay most attention to particular firms, will others 'fly under the radar' and present future systemic risks?
- How is the quality and character of the management of the firm and their risk controls truly assessed?
- Would two firms with similar high-risk scores have different information to work with, and therefore comply differently? This is an implementation challenge.

---

[314] https://www.investopedia.com/articles/economics/09/investment-bubble.asp - Components of the 2008 Bubble (investopedia.com)

- The role of the political contexts in which risk-based regulation is operating?

I highlight all these questions to emphasise the fact that there is not much standards about risk-based regulation to provide concrete steps and recommendations to follow. For this reason, I sought to seek a best practice risk-based regulation example.

4.11.3 Mitigating Covid 19: an OECD 'Best-Practice' Example of Risk-Based Regulation

In 2021, the OECD published a Regulatory Policy Outlook chapter titled: *Risk-based regulation: Making sure that rules are science-based, targeted, effective and efficient*[315]. In the chapter, the OECD argues strongly that the Covid-19 pandemic demonstrated how essential risk-based regulation is, and that "recovering from the crisis – and preparing for future crises – requires a correct understanding of risk mechanisms".

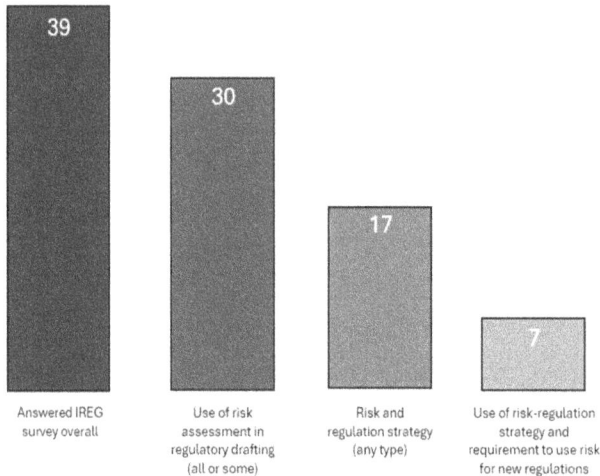

Note: Data are based on 38 OECD members and the European Union

Figure 4.8 – Varying Use of Risk and Regulatory Tools for Covid-19 Risk-Based Regulation *(Source: OECD Report* [316])

---

[315] https://www.oecd.org/gov/regulatory-policy/chapter-six-risk-based-regulation.pdf - chapter-six-risk-based-regulation.pdf (oecd.org)

[316] *Ibid.*

The OECD's context in this case was Covid-19 risk-based regulation prevention, specifically: "the relative risk levels of different issues (e.g. for Covid-19 prevention: hygiene of surfaces vs. distance between people vs. ventilation, with   evidence showing that the former is vastly less important than the latter), facilities, businesses, etc. need to be assessed so that rules address the most risky aspects, and regulators direct resources to the right places"[317].

Risk of Transmission √ Low ⚠ Medium X High		Low occupancy			High occupancy		
		Outdoors and well ventilated	Indoors and well ventilated	Poorly ventilated	Outdoors and well ventilated	Indoors and well ventilated	Poorly ventilated
Wearing face coverings, contact for short time	Silent	√	√	√	√	√	⚠
	Speaking	√	√	√	√	√	⚠
	Shouting, singing	√	√	⚠	⚠	⚠	X
Wearing face coverings, contact for prolonged time	Silent	√	√	⚠	√	⚠	X
	Speaking	√	√ *	⚠	⚠ *	⚠	X
	Shouting, singing	⚠	⚠	X	⚠	X	X
No face coverings, contact for short time	Silent	√	√	⚠	⚠	⚠	X
	Speaking	√	⚠	⚠	⚠	X	X
	Shouting, singing	⚠	⚠	X	X	X	X
No face coverings, contact for prolonged time	Silent	√	⚠	X	⚠	X	X
	Speaking	⚠	⚠	X	X	X	X
	Shouting, singing	⚠	X	X	X	X	X

* Borderline case that is highly dependent on quantitative definitions of distancing, number of individuals, and time of exposure

Source: Jones, N R et al (2020), Two metres or one: what is the evidence for physical distancing in Covid-19.

Figure 4.9 – OECD Science-Based Covid-19 Matrix (that can clearly be used to generate the rules in this Covid-19 context)
Source: based on and adapted from OECD Report[318]

The OECD carried out a significant survey on 38 OECD members and the EU itself on their application and use of risk and regulatory tools for

---

[317] *Ibid.*

[318] https://www.oecd.org/gov/regulatory-policy/chapter-six-risk-based-regulation.pdf - chapter-six-risk-based-regulation.pdf (oecd.org)

Covid-19 risk-based regulation. Interestingly, the OECD concluded that even though the majority of OECD countries performed risk assessments for some type of rules, most countries took different and unsystematic approaches to basing regulations on risk. This is clearly shown in Figure 4.8 showing only seven of 39 OECD countries using 'risk-regulation strategy and requirement to use risk for new regulations'. This sort of picture painted by Figure 4.8 accords with my earlier-listed many questions and challenges about risk-based regulation of the prior section.

Therefore, OECD went on proposed the following "science-based matrix of Covid-19 transmission risk shown could form the basis for effective, risk-based regulation" – which the OECD claims has rarely be used by regulators.

The risks of transmission are captured as Low, Medium or High at the top of Figure 4.9 – with clear ratings across Low Occupancy and High Occupancy scenarios. The Covid-19 matrix of risk-based regulation of Figure 4.9 showed areas where burdensome rules with little positive impact on health and safety was generated in some OECD member states.

In effect, Figure 4.9 provides a simplified 'best practice' approach ro risks assessment based on risk-based regulation for this Covid-19 risk-based regulation context as defined earlier in this section.

4.11.4 Key Lessons from OECD on Risk-Based Regulation

The key takeaway from the OECD example on the design and delivery of regulation in a risk-focused and risk-proportional way is that risk-based regulation is an essential approach to improving efficiency, strengthening effectiveness, and reducing administrative burden on stakeholders – in this case citizens. Specifically, the OECD argues that the "Covid-19 crisis has shown the obstacles that regulation can pose to crisis response when it is not proportionate to risk, or when trade-offs between different risks are not adequately foreseen. It also has shown the importance of allowing and managing regulatory flexibility in emergency situations, and to leverage new technologies"[319].

---

[319] *Ibid.*

The OECD summarises some key lessons[320] that I surmise below:

(i) **Detecting risks requires a clearer definition**: "Risk" should be understood as the combination of the likelihood of harm of any kind, and the potential magnitude and severity of the harm.

(ii) **Risk-based regulation should be outcomes-focused**: Critically, risk-based regulation is about focusing on outcomes rather than specific rules and process as the main goal of regulation.

(iii) **Lack of harmonization on risk-based regulatory approaches is a barrier**: the adoption of risk-based regulatory approaches, unharmonized and unequally spread across countries and regulatory functions. They are also often limited to phases of the regulatory policy cycle and sectors. This was confirmed by data collected from the pilot questions in the iREG survey shown in Figure 4.8.

(iv) **Risk-based regulation would help prioritise of regulatory efforts**: as shown with Figure 4.9, risk-assessment can and would serve to prioritise regulatory efforts and tailor the choice and design of regulatory instruments. This can happen within and across regulatory domains. It goes beyond understanding the level of risk to characterising each risk in order to design the adequate regulatory response.

(v) **A data-driven approach to risk prioritization is key**: the OECD argues that as a first and useful step, risk prioritisation can be done sector-by-sector and/or by type of activity. However, data should be collected and when such data for risk analysis and prioritisation are available, a more differentiated, data-driven approach to risk assessment and targeting is then essential. Risk should be assessed in an objective and data-driven way. The OECD notes that significant advances have been made in recent years including through the use of Artificial Intelligence and Machine Learning to improve data analysis, and many jurisdictions and services have introduced new risk-based tools and practices, including in the Covid-19 context.

(vi) **"Non-risk-based" regulation is overrated**: it is important to get past the obstacles to risk-based regulation. There are obstacles to the uptake of risk-based regulation including inertia and resistance in institutions with a "risk-averse" culture, public pressure, the

---

[320] *Ibid.*

lack of necessary tools and resources, path dependency, etc. The OECD argues that a number of these stem from misconceptions about risk-based regulation, as well as an over-estimation of how effective "non-risk-based" regulation actually is.

Drawing from the sixth and last lesson above, it is evident that "non-risk-based" regulatory approaches did not pre-empt the 2018 financial crisis. This is arguably good enough reason to consider risk-based regulation in most sectors of the economy.

4.12 Evidenced-Based Regulation

Evidence-based regulation is both underrated and underused by many developing market regulators I see. As part of a consultancy engagement with the Smart Africa[321] 2023 Training programme, I commented that making decisions on regulation without key supporting evidence is like driving down the road at night in a car without headlights[322]. I mean it seriously because of the amount of so-called regulating and regulations I observe across poorer South East Asian, Caribbean and African regulators without much local context evidence and data to underpin them.

As I argue in Chapter 1, how can optimal regulations and rules be defined for a sector in a country *without*:

- A good understanding with much evidential data of the macroeconomy of that country? Issues like inflation, debt, interest rates, etc.

- A good understanding and evidence on technology changes?

- A good understanding and evidential data on what local consumers are demanding from the sector? E.g. African telco consumers demand mobile money solutions, not demanded by EU's telco consumers.

- A good understanding and evidential data on the supply-side boundaries and gaps for key services in the economy as shown in the market and access gaps model of Figure 4.6.

---

[321] https://smartafrica.org/ - Smart Africa – Connect – Innovate – Transform
[322] https://www.linkedin.com/feed/update/urn:li:activity:7026224091179184130/ - (29) Post | Feed | LinkedIn

- A good understanding of the relevant markets, market concentrations, and clear market data to be able to determine SMP/Dominance in these relevant markets? It is important for any remedies to be supported defined data and robust evidence.
- Etc.
- There are also risks of unintended consequences that need to be analysed and pre-empted too.

The reader should just have another glance of all the methods of regulation described in this chapter so far. They all require much data and evidence collection.

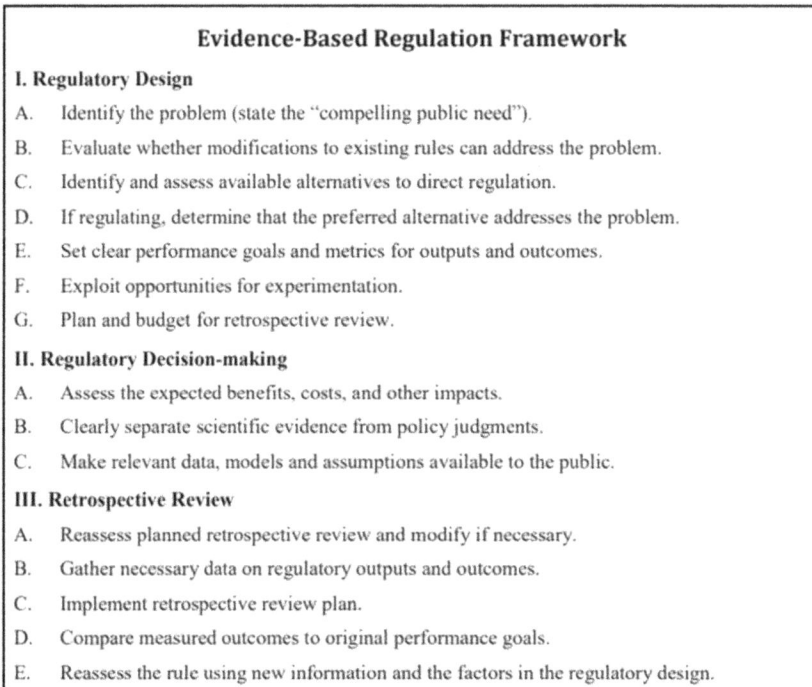

Evidence-Based Regulation Framework

I. Regulatory Design

A.   Identify the problem (state the "compelling public need").

B.   Evaluate whether modifications to existing rules can address the problem.

C.   Identify and assess available alternatives to direct regulation.

D.   If regulating, determine that the preferred alternative addresses the problem.

E.   Set clear performance goals and metrics for outputs and outcomes.

F.   Exploit opportunities for experimentation.

G.   Plan and budget for retrospective review.

II. Regulatory Decision-making

A.   Assess the expected benefits, costs, and other impacts.

B.   Clearly separate scientific evidence from policy judgments.

C.   Make relevant data, models and assumptions available to the public.

III. Retrospective Review

A.   Reassess planned retrospective review and modify if necessary.

B.   Gather necessary data on regulatory outputs and outcomes.

C.   Implement retrospective review plan.

D.   Compare measured outcomes to original performance goals.

E.   Reassess the rule using new information and the factors in the regulatory design.

Figure 4.10 – An Evidence-Based Regulatory Framework (Source[323])

As Peacock *et al.* (2018) rightly argue, evidence-based regulation and recommendations need to be tailored to the context of regulatory agencies.

---

[323] https://regulatorystudies.columbian.gwu.edu/proposed-framework-evidence-based-regulation - A Proposed Framework for Evidence-Based Regulation | Regulatory Studies Center | Trachtenberg School of Public Policy & Public Administration | Columbian College of Arts & Sciences | The George Washington University (gwu.edu)

They therefore propose the use of an Evidence-Based Regulation (EBR) framework shown in Figure 4.10. I believe the proposed EBR is quite self-explanatory and provides a useful checklists framework to consider.

The EBR process plans for, then collects, and then uses evidence throughout the life of a regulation to predict, evaluate, and improve outcomes. This must be right. The authors of this framework proceed to listing and discussing the main barriers that regulatory agencies face in implementing an EBR approach, namely:

(i) agency non-compliance with regulatory requirements: most regulatory laws and statutes demand regulatory decision making to be evidence based;

(ii) inadequate funding for evaluation of the outcomes of regulation; and

(iii) the complex nature of using data to build evidence.

I would add to the above list 'inexperience' on the part of many regulators and, sadly, incompetence and untrained staff too. I add no more on evidence-based regulation because I think every single other page of this book emphasise this in one way or the other.

4.13 Standards & Principles-Based Regulation

I reflected on including the discussion on standards in this section and amalgamating with Section 4.7 (on Quality & Safety Regulation) which also refers to standards. Both this section and Section 4.7 emphasise safety and quality. However, I find in emerging markets that Standards and Principles are either misunderstood or underrated. I also hold this firm view that statutory Quality and Safety Regulators should exist in developing and emerging markets countries too, and I would like to advocate more for such meta-regulators (see Section 3.1.5) – rather than typical sectoral regulators like for telecoms and electricity - to ensure that Health and Safety Standards are stringently defined and adhered to. I return to this at the end of this section. I firmed up my view too on having this separate section when I read Baldwin *et al.'s.* (2012) chapter on

Standards and Principles-Based Regulation[324]. In addition, many sectors of our economy world would truly be confusing and 'uncontrolled' without standards.

Good regulation will be nigh impossible in most sectors without standards or principles, and their enforcement. We can exemplify this by covering a brief standards context. On 6 February 2023, two major earthquakes - measuring 7.8 and 7.5 on the magnitude scale - flattened buildings of all kinds and killed thousands of people across southern Turkey and northern Syria[325]. According to Wikipedia[326], the confirmed death toll stood at 59,259 (50,783 in Turkey and 8,476 in Syria)[327]. In the following weeks there were over 10,000 aftershocks, causing destruction over an area roughly the size of Germany, and there was over US$100 billion in assessed damages[328] and 1.5 million people were left homeless. These numbers are truly mind-boggling as Robert Ferrell notes[329].

However, if modern construction standards and techniques required for building in an earthquake-prone zone were adopted, new buildings would have likely withstood the quakes of this magnitude. Particularly, given that in 2018, 120 experts coordinated to revise Turkey's building code, emphasizing the need for adopting earthquake resilience[330] in the way the buildings are constructed. The 2018 revised earthquake code was a comprehensive update to a prior 2007 one. The reality – as we now know – is that these requirements were only updated 'on paper'. The fact that even some of the newest apartment blocks crumbled to dust sparked a massive outcry in Turkey about building standards and led to urgent questions about building safety standards and their enforcement in Turkey.

---

[324] Chapter 14, Baldwin *et al.* (2012).

[325] https://www.bbc.co.uk/news/64568826 - Turkey earthquake: Why did so many buildings collapse? - BBC News

[326] 15th February 2024

[327] https://en.wikipedia.org/wiki/2023_Turkey%E2%80%93Syria_earthquakes -2023 Turkey–Syria earthquakes - Wikipedia, 15th February 2024.

[328] https://www1.wsrb.com/blog/turkey-building-codes-and-the-importance-of-regulation - Turkey, Building Codes, and the Importance of Regulation (wsrb.com)

[329] *Ibid.*

[330] https://www.preventionweb.net/news/turkey-new-building-code-earthquake-resilience - Turkey: New building code for earthquake resilience | PreventionWeb

In an article titled 'Turkey's lax policing of building codes known before quake', the reputable AP News reported:

> "This is a disaster caused by *shoddy construction*, not by an earthquake"[331] [*the author's emphasis*].

The bottom line therefore is that the lack of effective regulation exacerbated the negative impacts of the 2023 earthquakes in Turkey, causing more people to lose their homes and their lives. As Robert Ferrell contrasts:

> "In contrast, the Japanese methods of earthquake code regulation have mitigated the potential costs. In the last decade, throughout 13 different earthquake events, only 100 deaths have been reported. The Japanese code, and the enforcement therein, have provided a workable example for other countries around the world, including the United States"[332].

There was another set of earthquakes[333] on the 1st of January 2024 hitting central Japan - more than 30 earthquakes, ranging in magnitude from 3.6 to 7.6. It killed a minimum of 161[334], not the thousands in the case of Turkey.

I revert to why I chose *not* to cover the above earthquake scenarios as part of the Quality and Safety Regulation section above. The issues with the Turkish [earthquake] buildings collapsing are both a *Quality* issue and a *Safety* issue that can be regulated using Quality and Safety Regulations (QoS). I reiterate that I find in emerging and developing markets that *Standards and Principles* are misunderstood or underrated. However, I have observed that Q&S regulation in developing countries of the Caribbean and Africa is left to statutory sectoral regulators. Such

---

[331] https://apnews.com/article/politics-2023-turkey-syria-earthquake-government-istanbul-fbd6af578a6056569879b5ef6c55d322 - Turkey's lax policing of building codes known before quake | AP News

[332] https://www.preventionweb.net/news/turkey-new-building-code-earthquake-resilience - Turkey: New building code for earthquake resilience | PreventionWeb

[333] Japan earthquake: Eerie search for bodies near epicentre - BBC News

[334] https://www.bbc.co.uk/news/world-asia-67872944 - Japan earthquake death toll rises to 161 - BBC News

regulators tend to be more focused on regulating monopolies, and their risk of abusing their dominance through poor quality and safety conditions using sector specific regulations. For example, I have observed non-earthquake-related building collapses across such markets – thanks to no real health and safety standards, building codes or their rigorous enforcement in the construction of buildings. Hence, I unapologetically have used this section to focus on advocacy for the existence of distinct Quality and Safety Regulators like the UK's Health & Safety Executive (HSE[335]). As a separate regulatory authority in the UK, the HSE regulates for workplace health and safety, and they are "dedicated to protecting people and places, and helping everyone lead safer and healthier lives"[336]. Therefore, their duties cut across almost all sectors, and they ensure that Health and Safety Standards are adhered to.

The Turkey earthquake example – particularly when contrasted to Japan's building codes and their enforcement – clearly highlights the importance of standards regulation [and their enforcement].

4.13.1 Standards-Based Regulation

What are standards? The Collins English Dictionary provides several definitions for the word 'standard'[337] that are apposite for this section:

- "A standard is a level of quality or achievement, especially a level that is thought to be acceptable".
- "A standard is something that you use in order to judge the quality of something else".
- "Standards are moral principles which affect people's attitudes and behaviour" – e.g., ethical standards.
- "You use standard to describe things which are usual and normal".

---

[335] https://www.hse.gov.uk/ - HSE: Information about health and safety at work

[336] https://www.hse.gov.uk/aboutus/our-mission-and-priorities.htm - Our mission and priorities (hse.gov.uk)

[337] https://www.collinsdictionary.com/dictionary/english/standard - STANDARD definition and meaning | Collins English Dictionary (collinsdictionary.com)

Therefore standards vary across definitions and dimensions. As Baldwin *et al.* (2012) note[338]:

- Standards may look to cover behaviour at the *prevention* stage, e.g. Health & Safety standards to prevent injuries in the workplace and elsewhere.
- Standards may focus on the *act* that leads to a harmful outcome, e.g., standards on the use equipment (e.g., scaffolding equipment set up and use, driving heavy machinery, etc.).
- Standards may focus on the *harmful result* itself, e.g., when required to impose sanctions.

These lead to four broad categories of standards in most sectors:

- **Specification (or Design) Standards**: these standards focus on prevention by regulating or controlling processes that give rise to dangerous situations, e.g. with industrial activities such as covering manufacturing processes. These tend to be intrusive design standards which regulated firms would have to comply with, and the regulator typically has to lead the way technically. These sort of standards tend to be moderately costly to implement and comply with.

- **Performance (or Output) Standards**: such standards demand a specified level of delivery at the *act* stage, e.g., an emission standard in the pollution field. Such standards are technologically less restrictive than design standards - allowing firms more room for designing for better performance. Enforcement costs would be higher than with design standards because it is more difficult to check against a less-prescribed specification. The regulator would have to first understand the details of the firm's designs to deliver the outputs and check if they are compliant with both the spirit and letter of the design standards.

- **Target (or Outcome) Standards**: such standards bypass the challenges of linking standards to regulatory goals by stating the outcomes or goals directly. So, such standards do *not* prescribe

---

[338] page 296

particular types of processes or levels of risks; rather, it mandates the avoidance of certain harmful outcomes, e.g. in the pollution field, it is unacceptable after any emissions of pollutants into the water if it would result in the water no longer having the capacity to support fish. Therefore, firms are left with more latitude on how best to achieve the regulatory targets. The regulator would need to develop some design standards, collect data, analyse and report – in order to be able to monitor compliance.

- **Ethical (or Human Behaviour) Standards**: we all know that despite the best laid-down specification, performance or target standards – unethical human behaviours would thwart them all. Unethical medical professionals in developing countries sometimes 'prey' financially on the poor patients who are in very vulnerable situations.

Regulatory standard settings in all these contexts above would typically involve lengthy consultations between the regulator and regulated firms, even in situations where there are professional bodies-defined standards. Regulating properly in any sector needs standards and their enforcement.

4.13.2 Types of Standards (Technical and Others)

Technical standards are invaluable to safety, quality, and also interoperability. Standards abound in most sectors:

- Wi-Fi Standards (Telecoms): what will we do in our age without Wi-Fi? Practically all electronic devices nowadays including fridges, televisions, play stations, printers, etc. all have Wi-Fi in them.
- GSM (2G, 3G, 4G and 5G) Standards (Telecoms): with these standards, we are all able to take our phones abroad to other countries and continents, and they work like they do in our home countries.

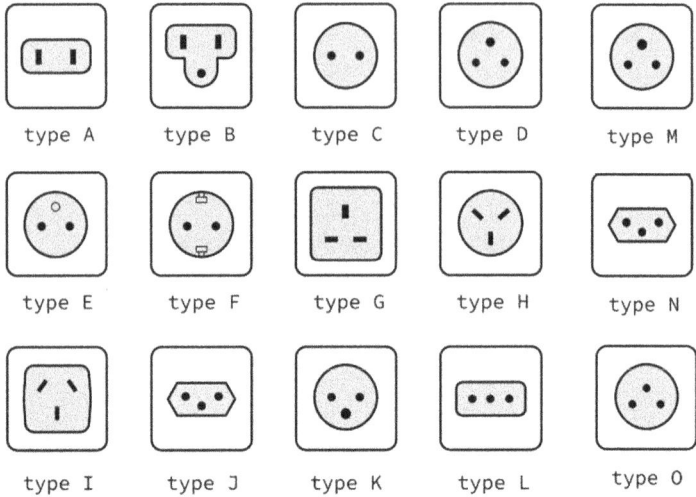

Figure 4.11 – Global Plug Socket Types

(Significantly adapted from Source[339])

- Plug & Socket standards (Electrical): There are 14 different types of plug socket in use around the world. They are categorised from A to N as shown in Figure 4.11 – all based on different standards.

- Medical Equipment standards (Health): there are hundreds standards for medical equipment and devices to ensure the highest levels of safety, performance, and reliability - ranging from surgical instruments to diagnostic tools.

- Rail Systems standards (Transport): there are dozens of comprehensive standards for rail systems in order to prioritize safety, performance, and interoperability.

- Freight Container standards (Transport): there are many standards for freight containers that aim to ensure durability, security, and interoperability, facilitating smooth and reliable global trade.

- Safety Standards (Health & Safety): there are hundreds of standards covering: Safety for gas burners and gas-burning appliances; child safety; safety of lifts/elevators; safety of

---

[339] https://x.com/nixintel/status/1266343128166010880 - nixintel - nixintel@bsky.social on X: "There are 14 different types of plug socket in use around the world. They are categorised from A to N: https://t.co/DfabdJW26J" / X (twitter.com)

machinery; safety of toys; etc. - to help reduce accidents in the workplace and at homes.

- Energy Management standards (Energy): there are standards for energy management systems, energy saving systems and more - to help cut energy consumption.

- Food Hygiene standards (Food): these cover cleaning, cooking, chilling and cross-contamination to help prevent food from being contaminated. There are Food Standards Agencies[340] across the globe.

- Agriculture and Farming standards (Agriculture): there are standards covering the farming industry, help farming operations use efficient and sustainable practices from farm to eating.

- Quality Management standards (Quality): to help drive up quality efficiency and reduce product failures.

- Ethical standards (Ethics): all professions require professionals who act according to the highest ethics.

- Standards of Conduct (SoC): such standards specify requirements on how to treat consumers fairly. For example, Ofgem's (UK) SoC Guidance[341] are enforceable overarching rules that ensure that Ofgem's licensees treat each domestic and Non-domestic customer fairly. The guide is relevant for all suppliers of Domestic and Non-Domestic Customers.

- Etc.

The point of the above brief list of categories of [mostly technical] standards is to make the point that all sectors abound with necessary standards and guidelines which greatly facilitate regulation in these sectors. There are literally hundreds of thousands of standards and guidelines from hundreds of standard bodies worldwide. There are national and international standards. Just the International Standards Organisation (ISO[342]) alone, established in 1947 to promote global standardisation, has more than 24,000 standards and a membership of 166 countries.

---

[340] https://en.wikipedia.org/wiki/Food_Standards_Agency - Food Standards Agency - Wikipedia 10th February 2024.

[341] https://www.ofgem.gov.uk/sites/default/files/docs/2019/02/licence_guide_standards_of _conduct_0.pdf

[342] https://www.iso.org/home.html - ISO - International Organization for Standardization

These technical standards of this section should be contrasted with the Health & Safety Standards that underlie the Turkey and Japan earthquakes. Most of such technical standards actually may have no risk (of life) issues associated with them at all, and may just offer alternative safe ways of doing the same thing across countries.

4.13.3 Principles-Based Regulation

Practically all regulators also require regulated firms to act to further certain defined principles, or Principles-Based Regulation (PBR). With PBR, the regulators use principles to specify regulatory objectives and values sought, leaving the regulated firms to devise their own systems for implementing the principles. Principles can be incorporated into regulatory norms (i.e., the regulations or rules) or they may apply during on-the-ground implementation. The regulated firms are not instructed – command-and-control style – leaving it up to the firms to devise methods for controlling risks. PBR is therefore consistent with the delegation of controls from the regulator to regulated firms – much akin to meta-regulation[343] described in Chapter 3. Regulators do not spend time on compliance with any precise rules; rather, they focus on how regulated firms devise systems that implement the principles.

There is much trust in the competence and responsibility of the regulated firms here – which sometimes are sadly misplaced. For example, PBR has been much likened to its sister Risk-Based Regulation[344] described in a prior section which helped contribute to the 2008/9 Financial Crisis. 'Light touch' PBR regulation has somewhat fallen out of favour with regulators since the Financial Crisis. They are expected to supplement any PBR in the sector with firmer rules, regulations and enforcement.

Baldwin *et al.* (2012), p.297-311 provides more 'colour' on the Standards and Principles-Based Regulation.

---

[343] My view is that Principles-Based Regulation (PBR) is not as synonymous with meta-regulation. This is because Risk-Based Regulation is - as I explain at the start of this entire Section 4.13. PBR is arguably an example of, and narrower category than meta-regulation.

[344] See previous footnote to understand my use of the word 'sister' here.

4.14 Accounting, Functional & Structural Separation

In Chapter 3, I note that there were structural separations (i.e., breakups) of monopoly telecoms firms (e.g. the birth of the RBOCs in the USA from AT&T) and/or introduction of competition into 'unbundled' components of the natural monopoly value chain. Structural separation is the most aggressive method of regulating some monopoly bottleneck assets.

In general, separation of the bottleneck assets from the rest of a vertically integrated firm is an important *ex-ante* method to regulate bottleneck resources. There are three broad degrees of separation: accounting, functional and structural.

- **Accounting Separation:** accounting separation refers to the use of financial records to keep distinct different lines of business within a single entity. Under the EECC code, accounting separation is one of the SMP conditions that may be imposed by an NRA as a result of a market review. It is the least intrusive form of separation, requiring that greater transparency in accounts is implemented in order to disclose the real costs involved in the production of regulated bottleneck resources and avoid cross-subsidisation and margin squeezes. This remedy is also key to enabling cost-oriented pricing.

- **Functional Separation:** functional separation typically requires the creation of separate business units within vertically-integrated operators. Crucially, it does not change ownership of bottleneck resources. The key elements of functional separation include:
  o the transfer of employees functions, employees themselves, and information (systems) and other assets to a separate business unit;
  o a requirement to make available the same products on the same terms to all customers;
  o separation of functions and information, and suitable governance arrangements.

Such changes would be needed to the existing regulatory framework by introducing an additional available remedy to reinforce existing non-discrimination remedies. It must be clear, however, that before imposing a functional separation remedy, the NRA must carefully evaluate the particular costs and benefits of the measure.

- **Structural Separation:** this implies – as with the creation of the RBOCs in the USA from AT&T - that the vertically integrated operator is forced by regulation to separate the bottleneck assets away from the rest of the company. Unlike with what happened with the RBOCS, the independent unit may still be owned by the incumbent company, be sold to a third party or even be nationalized.

4.15 Taxation and Subsidies

To be clear, taxes and subsidies are *not* included here as a method of regulation. Rather, I include them because taxes and subsidies are instruments that Governments use to influence economic behaviours in many sectors of the economy. In particular, subsidies can support industries that provide public goods or have strategic importance. However, their [taxes and subsidies] use sometimes completely undermines the regulatory goals and objectives that some sector regulators are striving to realise.

Governments have to strike a balance between generating revenue from taxation and guarding against the negative impact and risks of taxation on the *take-up* of services. Similarly, excessive subsidies over a long period of time stunt the growth of the sector – no matter how good the regulator and regulations in the sector might be.

We cover in this paper [Stork, Nwana et al., 2020] how ICT and OTT taxes have been having significant negative impacts across the ICT sectors of many emerging market countries – much to the chagrin of ICT sector regulators who see their works undermined. This is a core reason why Governments should ensure any taxes and subsidies implemented are to be preceded by Regulatory Impact Assessments and Cost Benefits Analyses, including across sectors of the economy.

4.16 Impact Assessments (IAs) & Cost-Benefit Analyses (CBAs)

Impact Assessments (IAs), Regulatory Impact Assessments (RIA) and Cost-Benefit Analyses (CBA) are very critical tools required in evaluating policy, regulatory and even tax proposals, regimes, or rules – in order to pre-empt any possible negative externalities.

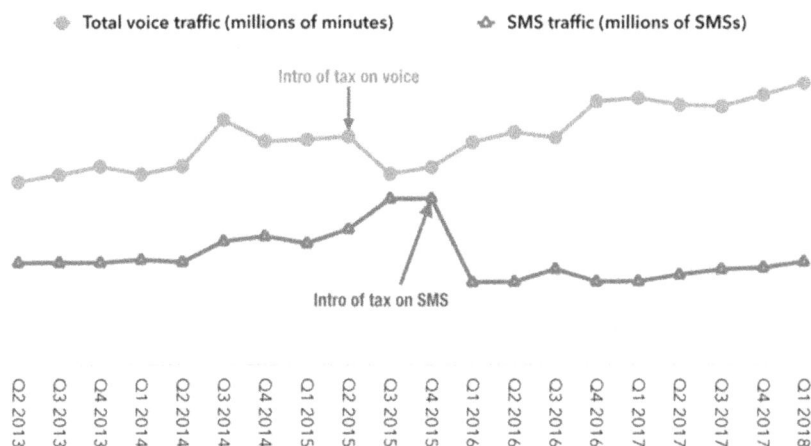

Figure 4.12 – Negative Impact of Taxes on Voices and SMS in Guinea
[Sources: Esselaar and Stork (2018); Stork, Nwana et al., 2020]

I cannot possibly recount to the reader the numerous times over the last decade that I have seen policies and regulations implemented across emerging market countries which end up going very badly wrong – yet with some prior IA, RIA and/or CBA – the negative consequences could have been averted or minimized.

Consider the negative impacts of taxes example illustrated in Figure 4.12 from the West African country of Guinea. It gives an example of – first - a drop in voice traffic after the introduction of an excise duty on voice in Guinea in Q2 2015. This drop could have been predicted with an Impact Assessment along with a CBA. The Guinean Treasury received less tax revenues overall as a result of the introduction of the voice excise duty due to drop in the usage of mobile/cellular voice communications in Guinea. Arguably due to this drop in tax revenues coming in, the Minister introduced another [second] excise duty on SMS in Guinea in Q4 2015, i.e., 2 quarters later after the negative impact of the first tax on voice. Well predictably, there was another even more significant drop in the use of SMS traffic. Though it started to grow again after the big drop, three years later, it never reached the volume prior to the introduction of the tax. The second tax effectively killed SMS traffic in Guinea, presumably in favour of Internet Protocol options like WhatsApp. These two tax moves failed miserably leading to less Treasury receipts, but even worse, it led to the reduction of voice and SMS communications in the country with even worse second-order effects. The obvious question here is could these negative impacts have been predicted? My clear answer is an unambiguous Yes – through an IA and a CBA. A good Impact Assessment and Cost-Benefit Analysis of these policies would have warned the Minister of almost-certain negative impacts. In fact, the Minister was afforded an opportunity after the 'failure' of the first voice tax in Q2 2015 to conduct just such an IA before the 2nd SMS tax was introduced two quarters later.

4.16.1 Definitions & Purposes of IAs, RIAs and CBAs

An Impact Assessment (IA) therefore is a formal process used to measure the effectiveness, relevance, and sustainability of a set of proposed actions, interventions or policies by a body such as a Government ministry, regulatory agency or even a corporate organisation. The IA considers the implications and impacts that the [proposed] action or intervention [will have] or has had on groups of consumers, citizens, specific groups like women or children, businesses, and/or the environment. "Ultimately, impact assessment seeks to establish a relationship between an organization's inputs, outputs, and outcomes"[345]. Impact assessments are used – or should be used - in a wide range of contexts, from major policy decisions to specific programmatic projects across public sector, private sector and even Non-Governmental Organisations (NGOs).

The purpose of an IA is well summarized by the International Association for Impact Assessment (IAIA[346]) into four distinct goals (Source: [347]):

---

[345] https://www.sureimpact.com/post/impact-assessment-guide - What Is Impact Assessment? A Complete Introduction (sureimpact.com)

[346] https://www.iaia.org/news-details.php?ID=30 - What is impact assessment? (iaia.org)

[347]https://www.sureimpact.com/post/impact-assessment-guide# - What Is Impact Assessment? A Complete Introduction (sureimpact.com)

- To understand the possible consequences of a proposed policy, action, change, or intervention and plan ahead to respond to any positive and negative impacts.

- To encourage accountability to stakeholders, including consumers, citizens, shareholders, employees, donors, partners, customers, and other likely beneficiaries or losers from the policy.

- To identify necessary procedures and methods for future policy, planning, and project cycles.

- To make environmentally, socially, and economically sustainable decisions for organizational growth and development.

Figure 4.12 illustrates why such IAs are a must in most situations. IAs have increasing gained importance in recent years too because they are core tools within the 'better regulation' programmes of the UK, EU, OECD and other jurisdictions. Baldwin *et al.* (2012, p. 311) note that the 'better' (as opposed to less) regulation movement can be traced back to the UK's Prime Minister Tony Blair Government in 1997 which led to the establishment of a Better Regulation Executive by 2006 within the Cabinet Office, with the goals of reducing regulations and promoting a better regulatory agenda in Europe[348].

An RIA is defined at the OECD level as "a systemic approach to critically assessing the positive and negative effects of proposed and existing regulations and non-regulatory alternatives" [349]. A Regulatory Impact Assessment (RIA) is in many ways very similar to an IA though regulatory led, i.e., it concerns some [potential] regulatory action or intervention. In essence, they are the same with an RIA being a transparent way of comparing the different regulatory policy proposals, regimes, or rules whilst paying attention to an analysis of anticipated costs. RIAs also systemically and formally assess the positive and negative impacts of existing and/or proposed regulations and non-regulatory options.

---

[348] Better regulation is currently as of 2024 a policy of the EC to ensure evidence-based and transparent EU law-making based on the stakeholder views of those that may be affected. Better regulation follows eight principles: proportionality, accountability, consistency, transparency, targeted, collaboration, and support.
https://commission.europa.eu/law/law-making-process/planning-and-proposing-law/better-regulation_en

[349] https://www.oecd.org/regreform/regulatory-policy/ria.htm# - Regulatory impact assessment - OECD

A Cost-Benefit analysis (CBA) is a crucial tool in carrying out Regulatory Impact Assessments (RIAs) in order to evaluate the efficiency and effectiveness of regulatory actions and interventions. It is a formal approach that helps regulators, policymakers and Government agencies and Governments themselves to compare the costs and benefits of a proposed regulations or policies. The process involves estimating the costs of the regulation and comparing it to the expected benefits that will be derived from it. Let me digress to be more precise about the relationship between CBA and RIA:

> "CBAs are often considered to involve *quantification* of effects whereas RIAs include *qualitatively* assessed effects as well as those which are quantified. It is worth emphasising upfront that it is desirable to quantify effects where this can reasonably be achieved, but that qualitative effects can also be important because some impacts are not amenable to reliable quantification"[350].

In Myers (2023, pp99-102), he discusses the strengths and limitations of impact assessments using the change of use of the 700 MHz band as a practical example.

Typically for a regulator for example, the RIA must set out the costs and benefits analysis (CBA) of the proposals for business, the NGO sector and for the public sector. The costs to business do not include wider costs to the economy or consumers, although these may be included if so desired. When the RIA is completed, it should ideally be signed by the CEO or another senior Board members of the regulator. This is to declare that they are satisfied that the benefits of the proposal outweigh the costs.

RIAs are recommended as central regulatory improvement tools by the reputable OECD[351]. However, I have come across many cases across emerging markets where IAs, RIAS and CBAs are not conducted. The frequent 'excuses' include:

---

[350] Prof Geoffrey Myers, Personal communications as part of his review of this book.

[351] https://www.oecd.org/regreform/regulatory-policy/ria.htm# - Regulatory impact assessment - OECD

- The urgency of the [proposed] policy or regulatory action or intervention makes it impractical or inappropriate to conduct one. This is a pitiful excuse as Figure 4.12 demonstrates.

- They are *not* required to conduct one by law. In some cases, I have found this to be true, whilst in other countries like South Africa, they were just wrong. Amongst emerging economies and developing countries, there have been many examples of attempts to introduce RIAs as a systematic assessment of the impacts of proposed new legislation or regulation[352], e.g. in South Africa, the RIA approach was approved by Cabinet as far back as February 2007 with guidelines available since 2012[353].

- Governments and Regulators neither have the time, competence internally and data to conduct regulatory analyses - nor the financial resources to pay external consultants to carry them out. This is more believable but frankly unacceptable. Regulatory actions and interventions impact real people daily.

- It is hard to estimates costs and benefits along with all the different probabilities of certain outcomes accruing including valuation of different risks. This is true – but this is also the job of good regulators and policy makers who employ smart economists to assist with these. It is important to add that *not* all effects can sensibly be quantified, but they can still be systematically analysed and contribute to illuminating the regulatory choices.

IAs, RIAs and CBAs are truly needed with most important regulatory, policy and tax interventions.

---

[352] Microsoft Word - RIA_GSR14.docx (itu.int) – according to this 2014 ITU Report, RIAs have (at least) been attempted to be introduced in the following emerging economies: including in Brazil, Chile, Colombia, Costa Rica and Ecuador in Latin America;, Cambodia, Laos PDR, Malaysia, Mongolia, Philippines and Vietnam in Asia; Botswana, Egypt, Uganda, Nigeria, Tanzania and South Africa in Africa - https://www.itu.int/en/ITU-D/Conferences/GSR/Documents/GSR2014/Discussion%20papers%20and%20presentatio ns%20-%20GSR14/Session%207%20GSR14%20-%20Discussion%20paper%20-%20RI A.pdf

[353] See Guidelines for the implementation of the Regulatory Impact Analysis (RIA) process in South Africa's Western Cape Government, available online at the following website: https://www.westerncape.gov.za/assets/departments/premier/office_premier/regulatory_i mpact_assessment_brochure_2019.pdf

4.16.2 RIAs, CBAs & Governments

RIAs and CBAs should all be second nature to Governments and Regulators. Governments are interested in improving the delivery of public services and ensuring that public funds are spent (Leinyuy, 2013):

- on activities that provide greatest benefits to society.
- in the most efficient way whilst achieving allocative and productive efficiency and mitigating risk of failures like Figure 4.12 above.

So Governments (in particular) should require:

- Appraising policy proposals before significant funds are committed, including decisions at appraisal stage affecting the lifecycle of policies, programmes and projects.
- Evaluating past and present policy activities/initiatives essential to avoiding past mistakes and learning from experience.
- Indeed, there is clear need for thorough, long-term and analytically robust approach to both appraisal and evaluation – and RIAs and CBAs are good tools to realizing such robust approaches.

Indeed in the UK[354], the UK's Green Book[355] - guidance issued by His Majesty's Treasury of the UK Government on how to appraise policies, programmes and projects – prescribes the following:

- "All new policies, programmes and projects, whether revenue, capital or regulatory, should be subject to comprehensive but proportionate assessment, wherever it is practicable, so as best to promote the public interest."
- "... no policy, programme or project is adopted without first having the answer to the following questions: Are there better ways to achieve this objective? Are there better uses for these resources?"

---

[354] The UK holds itself as a world leader in carrying out IAs, RIAs and appraisals for regulatory, policy and law-making.

[355] https://www.gov.uk/government/publications/the-green-book-appraisal-and-evaluation-in-central-government/the-green-book-2020 - The Green Book (2022) - GOV.UK (www.gov.uk)

The Green Book presents techniques and issues that should be considered when conducting assessments, and guidance to promote efficient policy development and resource allocation across Government. It also notes that "emphasis on the need to take account of the wider social costs and benefits of proposals, and the need to ensure the proper use of public resources". UK Departments or Regulatory agencies are responsible for ensuring that their own manuals or guidelines are consistent with the principles contained in the Green Book.

I believe that such a similar Green Book approach to assessments should be used across all Governments across the globe.

4.16.3 An Example RIA

This example I present following aims at convincing you the reader why I consider it to be best practice, and I try and establishing upfront what key themes it demonstrates The example systematically assesses costs and benefits of different policy options *relative to the status quo;* it shows that not all effects have to be quantified, because in this example the costs are quantified but the benefits are not quantified. It shows that even combining quantified and unquantified effects is still very helpful to inform the judgment required by decision makers. For example, this example provides an estimate of how large the unquantified benefits would need to be to justify going ahead so that they can decide whether that scale of benefits is reasonable or plausible.

The example best-practice RIA template from the UK Government is shown in Figure 4.13. Figure 4.14 shows a completed signed IA for a new proposed secondary legislation titled: *Mandating climate-related financial disclosures by publicly quoted companies, large private companies and Limited Liability Partnerships (LLPs).* It clearly shows negative social value and business impacts at circa £-1,144 m over the period. This Figure 4.14 RIA (Mandated Option 2a) accompanied the consultations carried out for this secondary legislation and assessed several regulatory policy options:

- Option 0 - Do Nothing
- Option 1 - Voluntary Disclosure, and
- Option 2 - Mandatory disclosure.

The consultation preferred mandatory Option 2 which spelt out four sub-options: 2a, 2b, 2c and 2d: Only the preferred Option 2a is mentioned below whilst the others assessed are also available at the following website[356].

- Option 2a: Mandatory disclosure covering the following: Relevant Public Interest Entities (PIEs), including Premium and Standard listed companies with over 500 employees, UK registered companies with securities admitted to AiM[357] with more than 500 employees, LLPs covered by the "500 test" and UK registered companies which are not included in the categories above and are covered by the "500 test".

It is clear that the Government realises the impact of this legislation as costly to business to comply with but has proceeded anyway, but limited the applicability of the regulation (i.e. secondary law) to just Public Interest Entities as Option 2a describes.

---

[356] https://assets.publishing.service.gov.uk/media/605a201d8fa8f545d23f8a25/impact-assessment.pdf - Impact Assessment (publishing.service.gov.uk)

[357] AIM | London Stock Exchange - https://www.londonstockexchange.com/raise-finance/equity/aim

Title: IA No:	**Impact Assessment (IA)**		
RPC Reference No: Lead department or agency: Other departments or agencies:	Date: 01/01/2020		
	Stage: Development/Options		
	Source of intervention: Domestic		
	Type of measure: Primary legislation		
	Contact for enquiries:		

Summary: Intervention and Options	**RPC Opinion:** RPC Opinion Status

Cost of Preferred (or more likely) Option (in 2019 prices)			
Total Net Present Social Value £m	**Business Net Present Value** £m	**Net cost to business per year** £m	**Business Impact Target Status** Qualifying provision

What is the problem under consideration? Why is government action or intervention necessary?
- What is the issue being addressed?
- What are the current or future harms that is being tackled?
- Why is government best placed to resolve the issue?

Maximum of 7 lines

What are the policy objectives of the action or intervention and the intended effects?
- What are the intended outcomes of intervention?
- [optional] Can these be described in a specific, measurable, achievable, realistic and time-limited (SMART), or similar, way?
- What are the desired effects – what will change as a result of intervention?
- What will the indicators of success be?

Maximum of 7 lines

What policy options have been considered, including any alternatives to regulation? Please justify preferred option (further details in Evidence Base)
- Include a description of the "do nothing" option and non-regulatory options

Maximum of 10 lines

Will the policy be reviewed? It will/will not be reviewed. If applicable, set review date: Month/Year			
Is this measure likely to impact on international trade and investment?	Yes / No		
Are any of these organisations in scope?	Micro Yes/No	Small Yes/No	Medium Yes/No	Large Yes/No
What is the CO$_2$ equivalent change in greenhouse gas emissions? (Million tonnes CO$_2$ equivalent)	Traded:	Non-traded:	

I have read the Impact Assessment and I am satisfied that, given the available evidence, it represents a reasonable view of the likely costs, benefits and impact of the leading options.

Signed by the responsible SELECT SIGNATORY _____ Date. _____

Figure 4.13 - RIA Template for the Government of the United Kingdom
(Source: [358])

---

[358]https://www.gov.uk/government/publications/impact-assessment-template-for-government-policies - Impact assessment and options assessment templates - GOV.UK (www.gov.uk)

Summary: Analysis & Evidence   Policy Option 2a (Preferred Option)

Description: *Mandatory disclosure covering the following. Relevant Public Interest Entities (PIEs), including Premium and Standard listed companies with over 500 employees, UK registered companies with securities admitted to AIM with more than 500 employees, LLPs covered by the "500 test" and UK registered companies which are not included in the categories above and are covered by the "500 test".*

FULL ECONOMIC ASSESSMENT

Price Base Year 2019	PV Base Year 2020	Time Period Years	Net Benefit (Present Value (PV)) (£m)		
			Low: n/a	High: n/a	Best Estimate: -1144.5

COSTS (£m)	Total Transition (Constant Price)	Years	Average Annual (excl. Transition) (Constant Price)	Total Cost (Present Value)
Low				
High		1		
Best Estimate	18.4		130.4	1144.5

Description and scale of key monetised costs by 'main affected groups'
Monetised costs include the additional reporting costs to 1,700 companies that fall within scope of the incoming requirements. This includes the cost of disclosing their governance strategy, risk management and calculating and disclosing the metrics and targets used to assess and manage climate related risks. One-off monetised costs include the cost to government of producing guidance and the cost of familiarisation, which we expect to occur in the first year of implementation and apply to all in scope.

Other key non-monetised costs by 'main affected groups'
Monetised costs not included within this Impact Assessment include the cost to the regulator for the monitoring and enforcement of incoming requirements.

BENEFITS (£m)	Total Transition (Constant Price)	Years	Average Annual (excl. Transition) (Constant Price)	Total Benefit (Present Value)
Low	0		0	0
High	0		0	0
Best Estimate	0		0	0

Description and scale of key monetised benefits by 'main affected groups'
Benefits have not been monetised given the difficulty of estimating the change in the allocation of capital.

Other key non-monetised benefits by 'main affected groups'
We expect this option to lead companies to develop a stronger understanding of the climate-related risks they face and therefore be better equipped to develop a strategy to effectively monitor and manage those risks and take advantage of opportunities. Proper disclosure of climate-related risks, in line with TCFD recommendations, will better inform investors how companies are likely to be impacted by climate change; supporting a more efficient allocation of capital and more orderly transition, through improved information and shifting investment flows in line with climate risks. The benefits of managing climate-related risks is likely to be substantial e.g The Bank of England estimates that loan exposures to fossil fuel producers, energy utilities and emission intensive sectors are equivalent to around 70% of the largest UK banks' regulatory capital.

Key assumptions/sensitivities/risks	Discount rate	3.5

- The number of entities in scope is expected to remain broadly stable over the appraisal period of 10 years.
- The average cost to each company that falls in scope is assumed to be equal, albeit we recognise that the cost to each company will vary depending on their business model, the complexity of their corporate structure, starting level of expertise internally, etc.
- A key uncertainty is the extent to which the costs estimated within this IA are likely to be additional. It is likely that some of the companies in scope of this option are already complying with TCFD recommendations to some degree or have pre-existing risk management and governance processes that can be adapted to TCFD. However, given the lack of evidence, we have assumed that none of the companies in scope are complying with recommendations set out under TCFD.

BUSINESS ASSESSMENT (Option 4a)

Direct impact on business (Equivalent Annual) £m:			Score for Business Impact Target (qualifying provisions only) £m: 664.7
Costs: 132.9	Benefits: 0	Net: 132.9	

Figure 4.14 – A Completed RIA Template for a Secondary Legislation Proposal in the UK (Source: [359])

---

[359] https://assets.publishing.service.gov.uk/media/605a201d8fa8f545d23f8a25/impact-assessment.pdf - Impact Assessment (publishing.service.gov.uk)

4.16.4 An Example CBA: the UK DTT Example

To illustrate a CBA, I draw from Nwana (2014) where I present a real example of the final costs and benefits that were *predicted in 2004* for the UK Digital Terrestrial Television (DTT) project which concluded in 2012 which switched off analogue TV in the UK. It predicted an estimated £2.3 billion NPV benefits of full digital switchover (Starks, 2004)—the following text is verbatim from the 2004 report:

- it improves spectrum efficiency—and, more specifically, that it will enable the 20-25% without digital terrestrial coverage to have this option (likely to be of special appeal to those not wishing to subscribe to pay TV)
- it will enhance reception in areas of existing coverage
- it will enable the broadcasters to make savings on their transmission costs and, in particular, avoid the need for whole-scale reinvestment in the present analogue transmitters during the period 2010-2015
- 14 frequency channels can be freed for re-use, whether for new broadcasting purposes or, subject to international agreement, more flexibly
- there will also be scope for additional new broadcasting services within the spectrum retained for digital terrestrial television (e.g. on one or two further multiplexes and/or for local television).

However, full switchover also carries some compulsory costs in that:

- those who do not want digital television at all, but do want their familiar services, will be required to acquire it
- those who are content to have it for one TV set only will be required to adapt all the TV sets which they wish to continue using after analogue switch-off
- those who wish to be able to record a different channel from the one to which their TV receiver is tuned, will need to replace their VCR—and re-plugging will be required in many other VCR households (Starks, 2004).

The final NPV analysis from the business case is shown in Figure 4.15.

Benefits	£m
Consumer benefit in current non-DTT areas	2725
Consumer benefit from additional services in retailed spectrum	659
Consumer benefit from re-use of released spectrum	1011
Imputed consumer benefit of compulsory migration	657
Broadcaster benefit from savings on analogue transmission	1233
Total benefits	**6285**
Costs	
Compulsory consumer investment in reception	3195
Broadcaster investment in digital infrastructure	619
Marketing & practical support costs (excluding any targeted assistance)	163
Total costs	**3977**
Total NPV	**2308**

Figure 4.15 — The UK 2004 DTT Costs-Benefits and NPV Analysis

With such a significant positive NPV of the cost benefit analysis, naturally the ministers at the time approved and gave the go-ahead for the project. I observe at this junction that the benefits turned out to have been understated. Indeed, the sale of 800 MHz/2.6GHz bands generated auction receipts of £2.34 billion, which I led, but this was in 2013!

In summary, the CBA analysis was important because

- it enabled ministers to decide *how and when* to proceed with the Digital Switchover of Television (DSO) in the UK;
- it helped prepare for the proceeding project and programme to effect DTT switchover; and
- the business case and NPV was also be used to attract international or national investment to finance the project.

All in all, it is highly recommended that such projects have clearly identified costs benefit analyses and business cases. For more on RIAs, I recommend this OECD website[360] as an excellent repository on RIAs. Another very good alternative is FasterCapital's[361].

This method of IAs and CBAs concludes on this chapter on methods of regulation I chose to cover in this book. I argue that the methods of regulation covered in this chapter and book are very comprehensive of the methods used by regulators worldwide.

4.17 Chapter Summary

This chapter has overviewed many methods of regulation in this admittedly exceptionally long chapter. It draws from numerous sources, but my hope is that it has gone some way to demystify the *who, what, where, when to use, how to use* and, most importantly, *why* of all these methods of regulation.

---

[360] https://www.oecd.org/regreform/regulatory-policy/ria.htm - Regulatory impact assessment - OECD

[361] https://fastercapital.com/content/Regulatory-Impact-Assessment--Evaluating-Regulations-with-CBA.html#Understanding-Cost-Benefit-Analysis-CBA-in-RIA - Regulatory Impact Assessment: Evaluating Regulations with CBA - FasterCapital

Chapter 5

Demystifying Economic Regulation – A 101 Practitioner's Guide

This chapter draws from all the previous chapters in order to describe one *perspective*[362] of both the art and science of day-to-day regulation done within regulatory agencies.

5.1 Introducing two simplistic 'Formulae' for Good and Practical Regulation

In many of my introductory lectures on how day-to-day economic regulation works, I start with the following two 'simplistic' formulae:

Practical Regulation = Law + Economics + Technology/Engineering [Networks] + Key Supporting Evidence Base + Good Practice Principles (consistent, predictable and rational) + Soft Power + Much Commonsense [+ Hard Power, e.g., Fines, Sanctions, Penalties]   **Formula I**

Good Regulation = Addressing Market Failures + Checking Market Power of Dominant Firms + Application of best practice methods of regulation to do the formers **Formula II**

Where <u>Market Failure</u> [363]= Some combination of these characteristics of the market: High Prices, Low Quality, Low Coverage, Low Innovation, Low Choice for Consumers, No New Entry/Entrants, Existence of Monopolies, etc.

---

[362] Mine – the author's.

[363] More sophisticated definitions of market failure are provided in Chapters 2, 3 and later on this this chapter.

Where <u>Dominant Firm</u> = Every service provider that earns 40% or more of the gross revenues in a specific relevant market shall be considered a dominant service provider in that market.

Where <u>Best Practice Methods of Regulation</u> = All the methods of regulation covered in Chapter 4

Another rewrite version of Formula 1[364] on Practical Regulation follows:

Practical Regulation = **Technical** (Law, Economics, Technology/Engineering [Networks], Evidence Base) + **Principles** (Fairness, Balance, Best Practice, and Commonsense - consistent, predictable and rational) + **Implementation** (Soft Power, and Hard Power - fines, sanctions, penalties – Enforcement process)

- the **TPI Formula**

I also like this *TPI Formula* version because

Economic regulation particularly involves addressing Market Failures which means **Technical** analyses to gather evidence to demonstrate market power of the dominant firms, applying **Principles** and best practice, and eventually putting in place an **Implementation** process that could include enforcement action if necessary – as shown in Formula 1.

For the rest of the chapter, though, I proceed with Formula I, but the reader who prefers the TPI version of the formula is welcomed to adopt it.

5.1.1 The Anatomy of this Chapter on the Demystification of Economic Regulation

I provide the anatomy of how I attempt to demystify practical day-to-day economic regulation in this chapter. Table 5.1 provides the logic of the demystification.

---

[364] Courtesy of a reviewer of this book, Dr Jibirila Leinyuy.

Demystifying Logic	Section
Introducing two simplistic 'Formulae' for Good and Practical Regulation	Section 5.1
Indicating when regulation is and is **not** necessary	Section 5.1
The basic level demystification of Day-to-Day practical Regulation can be articulated using **Formula I**	Section 5.2
The next level of demystification of Day-to-Day practical Regulation can be articulated using **Formula II** - a basic top-level methodology of regulation	Section 5.3
Using Formulae I and II requires the demystification of why **Law** and **Economics** are vital to Good and Practical day-to-day Regulation[365]	Section 5.4
It is key to demystify the fact that Good practical day-to-day regulation is both an **art** and a **science – that need to be balanced.** More practice makes it better.	Section 5.5
Drawing from Chapters 1, 2, 3 and 4, there is a deeper and more complex structure to Day-to-Day practical Regulation – but even this can be demystified too using an **Inputs-Output diagram model**.	Section 5.6
Therefore as noted in the Preface of this book, it can be concluded that good and practical regulation is both **complex and nuanced** - but it can and should be demystified.	Section 5.7

Table 5.1 – The Anatomy of the Demystification Logic of Good Practical Regulation of this Chapter

---

[365] Most of the 2000+ trainees on regulation we [Cenerva/ICC-UK] have had the honour of interacting with have noted in post training questionnaires and face-to-face to their trainers they do not get to be trained on the legal and economic bases of regulation.

5.1.2 An Analytical Framework on When to Regulate

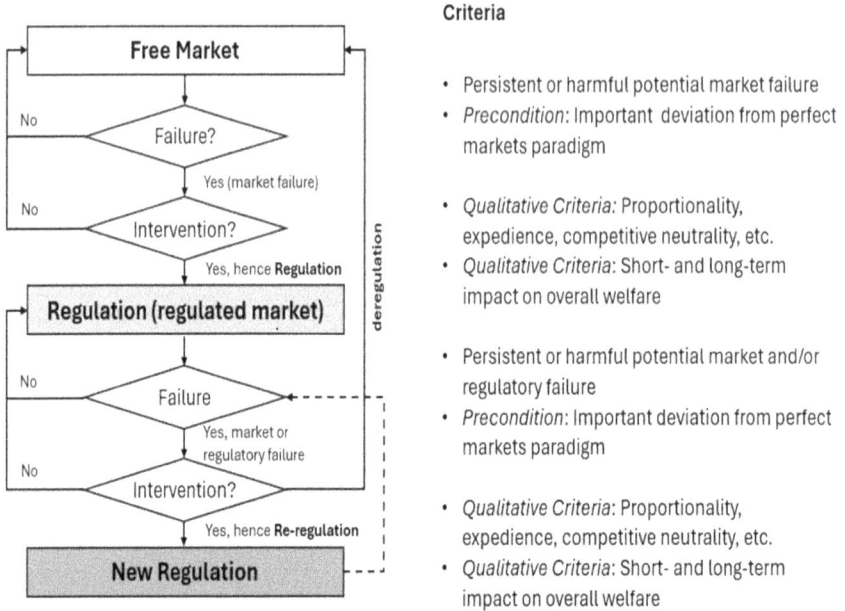

Figure 5.1 – Illustration of a General Framework of *When* and *When Not* to Regulate

(Original Source of Diagram: Jaag & Trinkner, 2009[366] *- with some updates by the Author; nevertheless, updated diagram printed with written permission of the original authors, Jaag & Trinkner)*

It should *not* be axiomatic that regulation is always statutorily necessary. There are many parts of our economies which are not subject to statutory sector regulation. Therefore, it is important to start a chapter like this with a clear articulation of when regulation is not necessary, and when it is. For this, I draw on a classic Swiss Economics paper (Jaag & Trinkner, 2009, 2011) titled *A General Framework for Regulation and Liberalization in Network Industries*.

Figure 5.1 from the Jaag & Trinkner (2009) classic paper illustrates the basic theoretical framework of when to regulate (and when not to regulate). As the authors expertly explain, the framework begins from a free market

---

[366] https://www.swiss-economics.ch/RePEc/files/0016JaagTrinkner.pdf -
0016JaagTrinkner.pdf (swiss-economics.ch)

300

primacy assumption. The online Investopedia defines a *free market* as follows:

> "The free market is an economic system based on supply and demand *with little or no government control*. It is a summary description of all voluntary exchanges that take place in a given economic environment. Free markets are characterized by a spontaneous and decentralized order of arrangements through which individuals make economic decisions."[367]

We see many free markets in our economies. In developing economies in Africa whose economies are dominated by the non-industrialised agriculture sector, look out for free markets in peasant agriculture - where there are hundreds of small-scale farmers/retailers selling identical products[368] to the market, and thousands of buyers buying them daily for their daily/weekly foods. In developed markets in Europe and the USA, look out for free markets with farmers markets, cars, digital gadgets and grocery stores. These markets tend to function properly, providing small scale farmers/retailers – in the case of developing economies mentioned earlier - with the right incentives to enter markets, set prices driven by demand and supply[369], and the [small-scale] farmers produce at a socially-optimal level[370]. There is practically no Government control in such free markets. Of course, these markets sometime fail in the countries in Africa that suffer from drought or macroeconomic shocks and wars – leading to *market failure*.

---

[367] https://www.investopedia.com/terms/f/freemarket.asp - Free Market Definition & Impact on the Economy (investopedia.com)

[368] Potatoes, tomatoes, plantains, bananas, maize, carrots and other vegetables, etc.

[369] For example, if it is not the season for tomatoes, the supply diminishes and prices rise if demand exceeds supply.

[370] Thanks to feedback from one of the reviewers of this book, I need to nuance this. Small scale farmers in Africa, for example, hardly produce at an efficient level. Their average output is smaller – low productivity, some of it due to failure to adopt technology that can enhance their productivity, there is also lack of coordination of production which results in over supply of some products and undersupply of others – hence the need for cooperatives as in China and in some Asian countries – but in Sub-Saharan Africa specifically, cooperatives have failed so badly due to lack of accountability or potentially lack of regulation. There is also information failure in such markets and all these leads to greater poverty.

What Figure 5.1 brilliantly illustrates is that, if there is no market failure – or no such potential market failure – there may be no need to intervene, as shown at the top of the Figure. However, if markets are not free and fail persistently, Governments may choose to intervene through regulation as shown towards the bottom half of the Figure. Sometimes the regulations imposed by Government to address the initial market failure do not yield the social and/or political outcomes desired by Government, e.g., affordable groceries, housing or affordable schooling leading to the Government re-regulating. On the right side of Figure 5.1, I retain Jaag & Trinkner (2009) summaries of the key criteria that should be considered when assessing the need for regulatory remedies. I believe they are self-explanatory.

There are always a number of obstacles to markets functioning well in that sense leading to market failures. The rest of the chapter assumes that regulation is necessary because of market failures due to several possible reasons or hypotheses – hence my introducing two simplistic 'Formulae' for (i) Practical and (ii)Good Regulation, the second of which explicitly mentions addressing market failures.

5.2 Demystifying Practical Regulation using Formula I

In order to "demystify" regulation – as I have *ambitiously* set out in this chapter – I have chosen to start with some simple "formulae" to take out most of the complexity, and then 're-add' progressively regulation's 'complexity and nuance' that I describe in the Preface of this book.

Good (economic) and practical regulation is both an *art* and a *science*. I use these two simplistic formulae, to start the process of describing the art and science of regulating.

5.2.1 Explaining the Simple Regulation Formula I

As a reminder from the first page of this chapter, Formula I stipulates that Practical Regulation = Law + Economics + Technology/Engineering [Networks] + Key Supporting Evidence Base + Good Practice Principles (consistent, predictable and rational) + Soft Power + Much Commonsense [+ Hard Power, e.g., Fines, Sanctions, Penalties].

The following is what we try and convey to our trainees on regulation:

- **Law:** Regulation starts with the law. Regulation is rooted in an absolute legal basis (Nwana, 2014[371]). Without a legal framework, regulators themselves would not exist. The legislature of the country (e.g., Parliament or Senate) crafts laws and statutes, including those that establish public bodies like regulatory agencies. Sometimes, the regulator emanates from one piece of statute or legislation, such as the Nigerian Communications Act of 2003 which founded and established NCC as the independent regulator in Nigeria.[372] In some other countries, the regulator's legal basis is founded in statutory duties contained in several pieces of legislation. Ofcom's (United Kingdom) legal basis derives from at least ten[373] pieces of legislation. Enforcements cannot happen without using laws – albeit regulatory instruments or recourse to civil or criminal law and courts. So, all decisions inside a regulatory agency are guided by laws and lawyers.

- **+ Economics:** Network[374] Regulation is also mostly rooted on an economic basis, or – put another way - many (if not most) regulatory agencies are *economic* regulators. This means that they use (or are supposed to use) economic theories (cf. Chapter 2) in their regulating, because such economic theories, *inter alia*, explain how scarce resources are allocated in society. Furthermore, regulators and Good economic regulation employs economic methods of regulation covered in Chapter 4. Therefore by economic regulation, I refer to both direct [Government] legislation and statutory regulation of prices and entry into specific industries or markets. So, most regulators employ economists who

---

[371] Chapter 11.

[372] Nigerian Communications Act, http://www.ncc.gov.ng

[373] Communications Act (2003), Wireless Telegraphy Act (2006), Broadcasting Acts (1990, 1996), Competition Act (1998), Enterprise Act (2002), Postal Services Act (2000, 2011), and the Digital Economy Act (2010; 2017). www.ofcom.org.uk

[374] As I explain in the Preface, "Network regulation" more generally, is so much broader. There is a range of regulators who are not economic regulators e.g., technical regulators, medical regulators, ethical regulators, etc.

use economic theories and methods to address market failure and market power challenges in the sector.

- + **Technology/Engineering [Networks]:** as covered in Chapter 1, industry (supply side) and technology are two critical drivers of any sector of the economy. For example, newer and more fuel-efficient airplanes provide better experience to air passengers, longer routes, more destinations than older airplanes. However, certain routes – like with the network industries characteristics of Chapter 3 – become monopoly routes for certain carriers. Try flying *direct* from London (UK) to Accra (Ghana) over the last decade (to 2024) – the only carrier of choice is usually British Airways. Worse for many customers, you can only fly direct to Accra (Ghana) from the UK from London's Heathrow airport making the latter a natural monopoly. My point is new technologies and engineering are enabling cheaper services but also creating *natural monopoly* facilities or networks bottlenecks in practically all network sectors covered in Chapter 3, e.g. a single company controlling the singular fixed telecoms line into your home, the unique gas pipe into your home, or the electricity or cable lines into your home are all monopoly [engineering] bottlenecks. As covered in Chapter 3, the approach then for achieving effective competition with such network industries often involves breaking down the value chain – or unbundling - into separate distinct components, and posing the questions of each of the components: which components are potentially competitive and which remain monopolistic. The [engineering] components that still remain monopoly bottlenecks are subject to mandatory *regulation*, where the owners of these monopoly assets are forced by regulation to open up access [via access regulation] to their competitors and regulated input costs to their *competition*.

The day-to-day regulation of network industries (as observed in Chapter 3) needs collaboration between economists and technical experts who have sufficient knowledge and experience to understand specific network technologies and their engineering in order to ensure effective competition.

- + **Key Supporting Evidence Base** as covered in Chapter 4, making decisions on regulation without key supporting evidence is like driving down the road at night in a car without headlights.

304

- **+ Good Practice Principles (consistent, predictable and rational):** as I cover in Nwana (2014, Chapter 11), the esteemed UK regulator Ofcom has built up significant credibility and international reputation by religiously abiding by and living by the seven "regulatory principles" shown in Figure 5.2. It appears to me that these principles would apply to most TMT regulators too, anywhere. The principles and the regulator's daily actions must be consistent (fair across market players), predictable and rational – and I will also add proportionate.

Otherwise if the regulator treats two similar breaches across two different licensees differently, this will not only send a poor signal to market players about the regulator's fairness, objectivity and predictability, it may also end up in the regulator tied up in needless litigations.

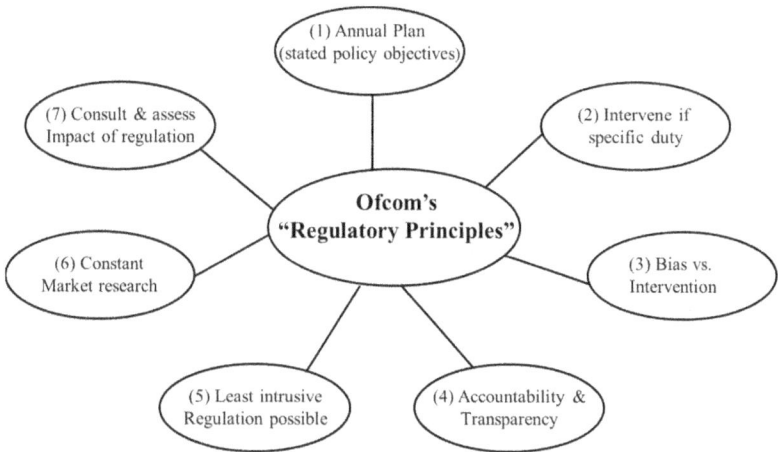

Figure 5.2 —How Ofcom Regulates: The Seven Ofcom Regulatory Principles

- **+ Soft Power (the use of the Information Remedy):** as a regulator, I experienced first-hand the importance of Soft Power. Soft power in regulation entails getting licence holders and other market players to want the outcomes the regulator wants through voluntary cooperation, rather than coercing them with legal instruments. Soft power contrasts with "hard power" which uses coercion, fines, sanctions and payments. As shown in Figure 4.7

in Chapter 4 [on Enforcement regulation], Ayres & Braithwaite (1992) argue that enforcement regulation should always start at the base of the pyramid – i.e., with persuasion and warnings which are non-penal, before ever ratcheting up with more punitive/penal responses if the securing of compliance fails with lower-pyramid efforts. I always found as a regulator that using 'hard powers' such as criminal sanctions, licence suspension or licence revocations usually meant the regulator had failed to take opportunities to get market players to want the outcomes that the regulator wants. For example, we regularly produced analyses and reports showing trends in customer complaints and other industry issues and presented the evidence to licensees[375] in order to influence their behaviour and actions towards improving the quality of service, consumer experience, etc. Usually, such interactions 'did the trick' because the licensees would typically respond to such 'soft power' Information Remedy approaches and tend more towards the wants of the regulator – without any need for threatening 'hard power'. The use of hard power – in my view – demonstrates some prior failure(s) on the part of the regulator.

I recommend such a *soft power* practical approach with compliance monitoring functions of regulators. This approach could be followed in the first instance to influence operators behaviour, to mitigate the risks of any serious breach of the licence conditions and to encourage compliance with the Standards of Conduct (SoC). If compliance issues are identified, they may be dealt with informally in the first place with the operators taking commitment to make the required changes to ensure the desired outcome.

However, the use of soft power could also extend to delivering further value to consumers and citizens beyond just realising compliance to existing regulations. This link[376] shows a good example of the use of soft power in this regard – it shows the use of Soft Power to both ensure compliance and aligning the objectives of the Regulator and the Operator. This specific

---

[375] These could include trends in customer complaints about the licensee, QoS KPI measures trends, coverage 'not-spots' in their coverage, network failures, etc.

[376]https://www.ofgem.gov.uk/sites/default/files/docs/2017/12/licence_lite_derogation_de cision_-_greater_london_authority_20_12_2017_002.pdf

decision was published by Ofgem (UK) to grant the Greater London Authority (GLA) the licence to start supplying electricity in competition to the big energy suppliers. The Derogation[377] is essentially a soft power *exemption* from enforcement from the regulator Ofgem (UK) when the latter is satisfied that the benefits of non-compliance to deliver a unique value to consumers and citizens are greater than the cost of compliance. The derogation guidance[378] provides further details.

- **+ [Hard Power e.g., Fines, Sanctions, Penalties]:** I use square brackets here because it is usually so much preferable not to get to using hard power in the first place. However and sadly, there are occasions where the actions of the licensee are so egregiously a breach of the regulations that the regulator is left with no other option but to exercise hard power options.

This formula (i.e. Formula I) is clearly simplistic, but I argue that it is quite practical to day-to-day regulation within a regulator. This is because it reminds the regulator employee that most – if not all – issues they [would] deal with daily starts with the law and legal statutes. Next, economics thinking reminds the employee that regulators are set up to maximise the benefits to consumers and citizens. Then technology should always be top of mind too because it is one of the key industry drivers in most sectors. The regulator should ensure that the staff always use reliable and up-to-date evidence in decision making whilst employing well-tried regulatory principles. A good regulator should always try and have a bias towards 'soft power' before engaging 'hard power'.

---

[377] Cambridge English Dictionary defines derogation as "the act of officially stating that a law or rule no longer needs to be obeyed".

[378] https://www.ofgem.gov.uk/sites/default/files/docs/2015/06/guidance_for_derogation_r equests_from_domestic_retail_market_review_licence_conditions_version_2_0.pdf - guidance_for_derogation_requests_from_domestic_retail_market_review_licence_conditi ons_version_2_0.pdf (ofgem.gov.uk)

5.2.1.1 Beware of "Silos" inside Regulators: an Important Commentary on Formula 1 (TPI Formula)

One of the expert reviewers of this book commented on Formula 1 (TPI Formula) thus:

> "Something missing by having separate bullet points on *law, economics* and *technology* is that in addition to regulators requiring each of these types of expertise, good regulators combine them effectively into an *integrated analysis. If each skill group operates in its own separate silo, it is a problem*[379]" My emphases.

I cannot emphasise enough how salutary and important this commentary warning is. I have no intention to write the separate bullets on all the elements on Formula I's details above for them to be considered as 'separate' in practical and good day-to-day regulation. I thereby am *not* encouraging 'silos' of such disparate expert sets of expertise inside regulators as they address day-to-day regulatory tasks – far from it. As the reviewer points out, *integrated analyses* combining the skillsets and expertise of lawyers, economists, technologists and others is a bedrock of the best network and economic regulators like [380]Ofcom (UK) which I was truly honoured to have worked at. I hope the rest of this chapter also disavows the reader of silos within regulators who do not conduct integrated analyses. Myers (2023, pp 62-63) expertly analyses some of the challenges in coordinating between skill groups.

5.2.2 Illustrating the Use of Formula I in an Asian Telecoms Regulator

In the example, we have anonymised both the country and the licensees' details (renamed MobileOp1 and Mobile Op2).

It concerned a licensee (MobileOp1) holding valuable scarce spectrum rights for years in the high-demand radio frequency spectrum bands, yet

---

[379] Prof Geoffrey Myers, personal communications as a reviewer of this book.

[380] www.ofcom.org.uk

they have allegedly not been honouring the obligations that go with these radio frequency spectrum rights by building mobile networks that consumers use. The Regulator was considering enforcement actions (see Section 4.10 in Chapter 4) against the licensee if they establish that the licensee was in breach of its licence conditions.

The case was more prescient because a new credible international mobile entrant brand (MobileOp2) who had entered the market and would like to have these scarce high-demand spectrum bands be reassigned from MobileOp1 to MobileOp2. I particularly helped assist the said-regulator with this case amongst dozens of other cases.

I advised on an *'integrated analysis'* memo to the board with a clear objective to address how the regulator should proceed *legally, efficiently* and *proportionately* on the reassignment of MobileOp1's high-demand spectrums to a [potential] higher value user (MobileOp2) in the country. The words 'legal', 'efficient' and 'proportionate' are especially important words inside a regulator – or they should be. So, the memo establishes the "facts of the case" and propose a way forward to realise this objective, consistent with both Communications Act and the Radio Spectrum Regulations[381] of the country. In other words, as emphasised in Formula I, the resolution to this case starts from the Law.

Figure 5.3 shows the actual Table of Contents (ToC) of the *brief* 12-page report on this case that I worked with the internal regulator team to go to the board. Board members are terribly busy people and therefore such brief reports are preferred to gain Board approvals before the regulator proceeds to public consultations and/or discussions with licensees.

---

[381] i.e., the supreme Sector law and the secondary relevant regulations (derived from the law)

Figure 5.3 – Table of Contents of an Actual Board Brief to a Regulator
(Using Formula I)

The Table of Contents (ToC) of Figure 5.3 demonstrates the application of
Formula I as explained next: Law + Economics + Technology/Engineering
[Networks] + Key Supporting Evidence Base + Good Practice Principles
(consistent, predictable and rational) + Soft Power + Much Commonsense
[+ Hard Power, e.g., Fines, Sanctions, Penalties].

- **Law**: The entire memo production process started from the law as
  per Formula I, i.e. from analysing the legal stipulations of the
  Communications Act and both (i) the Radio Frequency Spectrum
  and (ii) the Licensing regulations of the country relevant to the
  case. This was summarised in Section 2.2 as shown in the ToC of
  Figure 5.3.

- **Key Supporting Evidence Base**: The "Facts of the Case" of
  Section 2.1 starts with the evidential information, i.e. what radio
  frequency licences that MobileOp1 currently holds and what such
  frequency licences can be used for in 2023, as opposed to in 2010
  when the licences were issued. This is important because
  technology moves fast in the telecoms industry. The facts also

310

spelt out licence numbers, start dates and expiry dates of the licences. Other analyses reported on the percentage of total radio frequency held by MobileOp1 compared with other mobile operators in the country. So, this section constituted some of the 'Key Supporting Evidence Base' of Formula I.

- **Technology/Engineering**: Section 2.3 on a 'Techno-Economic Analysis' is an interesting one; it concerned Technology/Engineering aspect of Formula I. The interesting bit concerned the fact that the Communications Act and Regulations of the country mandate for the "efficient use of spectrum". A good regulator would interpret this mandate both economically and technically, amongst other interpretations, i.e. using economics and technology. Why technology? The reader may ask. The basic answer is that radio frequency spectrum is all about Physics – and hence technology. However and more specifically in this case, the technologies using the spectrum bands that were licensed in 2010 had moved on significantly by 2023. This effectively resulted in those radio frequency licences being much more valuable in 2023 because they could be used to provide more telecoms services, i.e. 2G/4G voice, broadband LTE and Internet services in 2023 in contrast to just 2G voice-only services in 2010. It is clearly an important consideration if MobileOp1 is not putting into good use an asset that has even greater technical 'value', let alone the economic value.

- **Good Practice Principles:** Section 2.5 of the memo also researched and covered, *inter alia*, other precedents on what the Regulator had done on cases of licensees allegedly breaching the obligations of the licences. In this case, there were no clear precedents. However, it was important to research this in order to meet the 'Good Practice Principles (consistent, predictable, rational, proportionate, etc.)' of Formula I. A good regulator must be consistent with relevant prior precedent cases in addition to abiding by these best-practice regulatory principles. This latter sentence is truly key. The regulator should be aware of prior precedents, and regulator consistency is an important consideration[382].

---

[382] Importantly, I am *not* stating that it must in all cases follow precedent. Of course, it should follow precedent where it is legally binding and where the current case has no features to distinguish it from the precedent. But it is more common for the precedent to reflect a prior exercise of regulatory judgement, which means that the regulator *should and must* ask itself whether the prior judgement is still appropriate. Circumstances may have

- **Soft and Hard Power**: Section 3 of the ToC (Figure 5.3) shows several options including 'hard' (revoking licence) and 'soft' (regulator-brokered) options. Formula I notes the use of soft and hard power.

The core Board memo concluded with the following Options shown in the Options table of Table 5.2.

	= favourable evaluation		= cautious evaluation		= unfavourable evaluation

	OPTION	COMMENT	EVALUATION
Options Analyses			
Option 1	**Do Nothing**	Untenable	✖
Option 2	**Regulator suspends or revokes MobileOp1's spectrum licences**	The objective of this memo covers how <Regulator> proceeds *efficiently, legally* and *proportionately* on the likely reassignment of MobileOp1's high-demand spectrums to a higher value user in the <Country> would likely not be met. However, it may be worth pursuing if Option 4 fails or is deemed not legal.	⚠
Option 3	**Regulator varies MobileOp1's spectrum licences**	Like Option 1, worth pursuing if Option 4 fails or is deemed not legal. Option 3 does not appear as clear in terms of +ve outcomes as Option 2	⚠ ⇨ towards ✖
Option 4	**Regulator brokers a MobileOp1-MobileOp2 spectrum reassignment "deal"**	Appears the most optimal approach of all these analyses	◯

Table 5.2 – Options Summary Analysis of a Formula I Application

moved on, so that blindly following precedent may by now have become the wrong course of action, or events may have shown that the prior judgement was flawed. However, before departing from precedent the regulator should explicitly consider whether the benefits outweigh take the risk of adverse effects caused by departing from regulatory consistency

Clearly, the Board memo explored four options, and clearly recommended the fourth option as shown in Table 5.2. The Board agreed and therefore a 'soft' Regulator-brokered Option 4 approach was followed in this case – with a clear backup to revert to a 'hard' Option 2, if the recommended option failed. There is always a 'Do Nothing' option, i.e. Option 1. However, in this case, the memo deemed this 'untenable' and the Board agreed with this assessment.

I hope the elaborations above (aided by Figure 5.3 and Table 5.2) on the use of Formula I in real life demonstrate how the 'simplistic' Formula I can be especially useful in addressing many cases and issues that regulators face day-to-day. I hope the reader would also agree that much of it is 'Much Commonsense' too as Formula I contends. I also hope the reader notes the "integrated analysis" of legal, economic and technical expertise ethos built into the memo.

5.3 Demystifying Good economic regulation using Formula II

Let us take this up a notch (in complexity) with **Formula II** presented at the beginning of this chapter, i.e., Good economic regulation = Addressing Market Failures + Checking Market Power of Dominant Firms + Application of best practice methods of regulation to realise the formers.

5.3.1 Explaining the Good economic regulation Formula II – a basic top-level methodology of regulation

It is still a 'simple' formula, but not as simple as Formula I. This is because Formula II introduces more complicated notions like 'market failures', 'market power', 'dominant' firms and 'best practice methods of regulation' (cf. Chapter 4). At the beginning of this chapter, I provide some simple definitions of these notions for the purposes of this chapter – though previous chapters in this book have covered these concepts in some considerable detail too.

With **Formula II**, the following is what we try and convey to the trainees we are always honoured to interact with

(i) **'Addressing' market failures:** statutory regulators are established to pre-empt markets failures and to protect the interest of consumers and citizens – otherwise, what is their purpose? Efficient markets should not exhibit characteristics such as High Prices, Low Quality, Low Coverage, Low Innovation, Low Choice for Consumers, No New Entry/Entrants, Existence of Monopolies, etc. These are bad outcomes which often suggest markets are failing – if not failed. However, as we see in Chapter 4 in some detail (see Section 4.5), there is no such thing as a generic sector market. Regulators have to deal with this defined notions of 'relevant markets' – which are defined based on economic criteria. So, I note to trainees as I do in Chapter 3 and especially Chapter 4, that the relevant markets would need to be defined, establish players with market power in the relevant markets, dominant firms in these relevant markets designated and remedies imposed on them if there is evidence of abuse of dominance. The remedies typically use several of the methods of regulation detailed in Chapter 4. However as seen in Chapters 3 and 4, to stop markets from failing, regulators do many things beyond imposing remedies on dominant players. For examples, they licence new players to drive up competition; they regulate prices; they regulate access to bottleneck assets; they regulate for consumer protection; they regulate scarce resources like spectrum and forests, etc. These broadly describe how 'addressing' market failures work.

(ii) **'Checking' market power of dominant firms:** what I try and convey here is the following. First, it is utmost that markets do not fail under the watch of any good regulator as covered earlier. So much of the 'addressing market failures' is pre-emptive. The regulator wants to help 'set up' the sector market in such a way that market failures do *not* arise in the first place. Second (with a big 'But'), the reality is that there will always exist dominant firms in most market sectors whose market power needs to be 'checked' and controlled. Third, I emphasise as regulatory lawyers and economists[383] do that a firm being dominant does not equate to that firm abusing its dominance. It is quite possible to have

---

[383] I am neither a lawyer nor an economist as the reader should know by now. Arguably, this is more the view of lawyers than of economists who tend to expect firms to maximise their profits, which in turn typically means abusing their market power (behaviour which is privately profitable but socially undesirable).

'benign' dominant firms who play fair to all their competitors; I do not personally tend to see them. So if the law defines that every service provider that earns 40% or more of the gross revenues in a specific relevant market shall be considered a dominant service provider in that market, then that service provider must be checked by a good regulator to ensure it is not abusing its dominant position. Such 'checking' is easier said than done. The best regulators in the world assign scores of expensive human resources to check the market power of dominant firms. When I was at the telecoms and media regulator, Ofcom (UK), a significant percentage of Ofcom's resources[384] were dedicated to checking (i.e. controlling) BT Plc – the incumbent and dominant fixed telecoms operator at the time. Such Ofcom regulation was key because it enabled so many other new entrants to enter and compete with BT Plc on fixed voice and broadband across the UK, even though they were using BT's monopoly bottleneck assets which had been unbundled, as I explain in Chapters 3 and 4.

(iii) **Application of best practice methods of regulation to realise the former two goals:** here I convey the obvious point that to realise these objectives of 'addressing market failures' and 'checking the market power of dominant firms' requires the application of many of the best practice methods of regulation detailed in Chapter 4.

This elaboration of Formula II is deliberately 'simplistic', but it essentially describes what many statutory sector regulators do from a *big picture perspective.* I use this formula too because it is a good place to start in order to begin "peeling the onion" into more complex subjects. Formula II asks the regulator to anticipate how the markets it is responsible for could fail – and what the regulator could do about it. This would 'force' the regulator into thinking about defining the *relevant markets* for the sector, identifying the players with market power, dominant players and the rest. It requires the regulator to pre-empt any potential failures in these defined relevant markets and take pre-emptive measures through licensing new players, access regulation and more. Whilst at these, Formula II also requires the 'checking' of the designated dominant players – or frankly all players

---

[384] I estimate that in that specific and arguably unique period it was circa 15% of Ofcom's if not more.

with 'significant' market power – however 'significant' is defined. Lastly, Formula II requires the regulator to be aware of and define which methods of regulation (see Chapter 4) apply in their local market context to realise the prior two parts of the Formula.

These may all be obvious to the better regulators in the world, but I have seen so many regulators not being able to understand and articulate these concepts of Formula II – yet alone being able to implement them. It is no surprise such regulators are failing their consumers and citizens with abounding [relevant] market failures in these markets. You do not believe me? As I note in the Preface of this book and elsewhere, the reader can overview most developing economies and I venture they would see many market failures in electricity, water and waste water, postal, aviation and several other network industries covered in Chapter 3 – yet there are sector regulators for these sectors in these countries. This is at the core of why I bothered to write a chapter of this nature, and this entire book.

Indeed, I contend that Formula II provides the tenets of a basic top-level methodology of [economic] regulation in general. A lot of what I cover in Chapters 3 and 4 – and indeed Chapter 2 - concerns 'peeling the onions' to reveal more complexity that lies beyond this top-level 'formula'. This is the subject of a later section (Section 5.4).

5.3.2 Illustrating the use of Formula II using the Regulation of Bottlenecks

I do not go through similar detailed illustration here like I do with Formula I in the last section because I would like to refer the reader to (re)read Section 4.5 of Chapter 4 on SMP/Dominance, Market Analysis Regulation and the SSNIP Test. Further to this, all the regulation vs. competition network sector case studies of Chapter 3[385] describe particularly good illustrations of the use of Formula II – as they strive to address market failures in network industries or check the market power of dominant operators by using methods and remedies of regulation.

---

[385] Covering network sectors including electricity, gas, water & wastewater, postal, telecoms, rail and aviation.

One key theme that emerges from all the network industries case studies of Chapter 3 is the recurring challenge of the regulation of bottlenecks which are extremely difficult to replicate. Rail tracks cannot be replicated easily, neither can the network infrastructure for retail gas (pipes), electricity (cables) and fixed fibre lines into households. In many countries, bottleneck assets remain state-owned or state-controlled to date, e.g., airports, train stations, roads, bridges and tunnels, train tracks, electricity grids, last mile infrastructures in telecommunications as observed in Chapter 3, etc. To introduce competition and generate the benefits of markets to consumers, it is absolutely crucial in liberalised sectors or markets that new entrant players (competitors) get timely access to such bottleneck facilities at reasonable terms and conditions, with access prices that prevent the abuse of market power by the incumbent owners of such bottleneck assets. Whilst some sector-specific access regulation might be seen as a massive intervention into the bottleneck owner's property rights, "the goal of any regulation of a stable monopolistic bottleneck is to enable non-discriminatory access to these bottlenecks at reasonable conditions while minimizing the infringement of property rights on the bottleneck resource" (Jaag & Trinkner, 2009, 2011).

	ex post		ex ante
Competition law	X		
– Price regulation in case of market power	(X)		
– Access based on non-discrimination	X		
– (Merger control)			X
Sector specific regulation	X	or	X
– Price regulation	X	or	X
– Access regulation	X	or	X
– Accounting / functional / structural Separation			X
– Ownership Regulation			X

Table 5.3 – Typical Methods or Remedies of Regulation used to Regulate Bottlenecks in Network Industries

(Original Source of Diagram: Jaag & Trinkner, 2009[386] - with some updates by the Author; nevertheless, updated diagram printed with written permission of the original authors, Jaag & Trinkner)

---

[386]   https://www.swiss-economics.ch/RePEc/files/0016JaagTrinkner.pdf   -
0016JaagTrinkner.pdf (swiss-economics.ch)

Recall Formula II strives to *Address Market Failures*, Check Market Power of Dominant Firms and *Application of best practice methods of regulation to realise the formers*. Distilling from the network industries case studies of Chapter 3, the reader will discern that the clear *market failure* hypothesis is that of non-replicable Natural Monopoly bottlenecks. The methods of regulation or remedies that are repeatedly used across the network industries case studies of Chapter 3 to address these market failures are typically (i) Access (non-price) Regulation (ii) Price Regulation (iii) Accounting Separation (iv) Functional or Structural Separation or (v) other Ownership Regulation. These are beautifully illustrated in Table 5.3.

Since the goal of any bottleneck regulation is to enable non-discriminatory access to these bottlenecks at reasonable conditions while minimizing the infringement of property rights of the incumbent, Table 5.3 provides an overview. The top segment of Table 5.3 illustrates the truism that regulation of such bottleneck assts starts with the law – in most jurisdictions, Competition Law statutes. Horizontal competition law may be able to address the market failures *ex-post*, but as Chapter 3's network industries shows, sector-specific regulation and regulators are typically necessary to implement the methods and remedies of regulation at the bottom of Table 5.3.

For completeness, recall Chapter 3 notes that there are three broad ways to address such bottleneck market failures with fixed line bottlenecks (Decker, 2023, p.373): *Facilities-based competition* or infrastructure competition; *'Quasi-facilities'-based competition*: in this case, the new entrant invests in some equipment as well as purchases some 'unbundled' services and elements from the incumbent fixed line; and *Resale competition*: with resale competition, a new entrant makes minimal investment in any new equipment unlike the previous two scenarios, and just acts to 'white label' resell the incumbent's services with the key differentiations being in branding and customer service.

Many of the trainees we/I have had the honour of interacting with, have told us – in feedback questionnaires and more – that they have found these two 'simplistic' formulae of regulation (Formulae I and II) especially useful in their day-to-day art and science of regulating.

5.4 Demystifying the Legal & Economic Bases of Regulation

Demystifying regulation requires the demystification of Sector Laws and Regulatory Economics. Even using Formulae I and II also requires the demystification of why Law and Economics are vital to Good Practical day-to-day Regulation. In Formula I, I just asserted that Good Regulation = Law + Economics + more. I take a moment in this section to elaborate a bit more on the legal and economic bases because I think it is important that all regulators seek to understand beyond what I cover earlier in this chapter. Even the technical/engineering staff of regulators should appreciate the vitality of the law and economics to Good economic regulation. In our trainings, we try and urge – and demystify – the reading of Sector Laws and Regulation. Most regulatory staff have never read any of them – this is terrible. They should.

5.4.1 The Legal Basis of Regulation

I have already noted earlier that regulation is rooted in an absolute legal basis, and that without a legal framework, regulators would not exist. Hence, the legislature of the country (e.g., Parliament or Senate) crafts laws and statutes, including those that establish public bodies like regulatory agencies. However, what should a lay non-legal expert working within a regulator understand from such Sector Laws? What are the key precepts to look out for? They should look out for the following four precepts as they read these sector laws: Duties, Powers, Functions and Factors. I cover these next, drawing insight from Nwana (2014) and using examples from the UK telecoms sector.

A regulator's legal powers typically come in the form of duties, powers, functions, and factors. Below is a list of commonsense-type distinctions and exemplars of these legal terms. I confess to being no lawyer whatsoever, though I am privileged to have worked with some of the brightest ones in the United Kingdom and elsewhere.

- **Duties:** Most regulators would have a duty to further the interest of citizens and consumers. The duty would specifically be something like to "protect the interest of citizens in all matters communications," whilst citizens would refer to "all members of the public in the said country." Duties tend to use words like "ensure" or "required to secure", which translate to verbs like "must" or "shall," as in the regulator "must do X" or the "shall do Y." Another two typical duties of most converged telecoms, media and technology (TMT) regulators are "ensuring the optimal use of electromagnetic spectrum" or "ensuring a wide range of TV and radio services of high quality and wide appeal." The reader can clearly note or derive from these example duties that when telecoms and media regulators strive towards widespread availability/access and affordability of TMT services including voice, data, mobile Internet, TV, radio, fixed Internet, and other media— it is because these are duties they must carry out baked in sector laws, legislation and statutes. The regulator interprets these duties, powers and more and regulates to make them happen. You can now further attest why Good economic regulation is so vital for every sector. So when the reader reads a Sector Law and comes across such action language/verbs like "to ensure", "to protect", "must", "shall", etc. – these are Duties that the regulator must carry out.

Figure 5.4 for an example real law from the Eastern Caribbean in which I note the duties led by 'to ensure'. The reader should look closely at Figure 5.4 to see other duties: "to promote", "to encourage", "to establish" and more.

- **Powers:** Simplistically, regulators can *only* do what they have been given the powers in Law to do. So, they can have duties above, but if they do not have the powers to achieve them, then the regulator would be toothless. Powers are instruments regulators "may" choose to use; they do not necessarily have to use them all the time. A regulator's powers and functions are set out in statutes. For example, for a regulator to achieve being an evidenced-based decision-making body, it typically needs information-gathering powers written into legislation which enables it to formally request confidential information from private and public companies. For the regulator to carry out a competition assessment, the regulator would need access to such company-confidential information. Similarly, a regulator needs dispute resolution powers to be able to arbitrate industry disputes or enforcement powers to enforce their regulations and rules. So when the reader reads a Sector Law and comes across words such as "the regulator may" – that is a Power. In some Sector Laws, the powers are spelt out clearly in a section of the Statute, e.g. 'Powers of the Commission' as shown in Figure 5.5.

3. OBJECTS OF THIS ACT

(1) The principal object of this Act is to give effect to the purposes of the Treaty and to regulate an electronic communications service and an electronic communications network in [Name of ECTEL Contracting State].

(2) Without limiting the generality of subsection (1) the objects of this Act include—

(a) to ensure that policies in relation to the management of electronic communications are in harmony with the recommendations of ECTEL;

(b) to ensure that the public interest and national security are preserved;

(c) to ensure consumer protection and the meeting of the needs of all users, including disabled users, the elderly or users with social needs, in terms of access to an electronic communications service and facility;

(d) to ensure the compliance by licensees for the protection of personal data, for secrecy of correspondence and with the principle of net neutrality;

(e) to ensure the absence of discrimination for traffic routing and access to an electronic communications service;

(f) to ensure the ability of retail customers to access and disseminate information and access applications and an electronic communications service of their choice;

(g) to ensure the application of appropriate standards in the operation of an electronic communications network and electronic communications service;

(h) to ensure the overall development of electronic communications in the interest of the sustainable development of [Name of ECTEL Contracting State];

(i) to promote and maintain fair and efficient market conduct and sustainable competition between licensees;

(j) to encourage, promote, facilitate and otherwise assist in the development of investment, innovation and competitiveness in electronic communications in [Name of ECTEL Contracting State];

(k) to establish a licensing system that is responsive to the changes in electronic communications;

(l) to ensure the provision of electronic communications at rates consistent with efficient electronic communications service;

(m) to allow for the exercise of regulatory functions in respect of the determination and approval of prices, tariffs and charges for the provision of electronic communication;

(n) to ensure the effective and efficient use of spectrum; and

(o) to ensure the possibility of using all types of technologies and all types of electronic communications services in the frequency bands available to these services, subject to technical feasibility.

Figure 5.4 – A Brief Excerpt of the ECTEL Eastern Caribbean Communications Act[387]

("Duties start with phrases like "to ensure", "to establish", "to promote", etc.)"

---

[387]https://www.ectel.int/wp-content/uploads/2020/09/Electronic-Communications-Bill-200703-1.pdf

12. **POWERS OF THE COMMISSION**

(1)   The Commission may do all things necessary or convenient to be done for or in connection with the performance of its functions.

(2)   Without limiting the generality of subsection (1), the Commission may —

    (a)   acquire information relevant to the performance of its functions including whether or not a person is in breach of this Act, the Regulations, a licence, frequency authorisation or a direction given by the Commission;

    (b)   require payment of fees and recover outstanding fees;

    (c)   institute legal proceedings including legal proceedings against a licensee or frequency authorisation holder for the purposes of compliance with this Act;

    (d)   hold public consultations pertaining to its functions;

    (e)   issue directions in writing to a licensee or frequency authorisation holder to direct the licensee or frequency authorisation holder to take such measures or cease such activities as may be necessary for the purpose of ensuring compliance with this Act;

    (f)   on the recommendation of ECTEL and by publication in the Official Gazette, issue codes of practice relating to an electronic communications service or an electronic communications network and —

        (i)   make the codes of practice available for public scrutiny at the office of the Commission during business hours or on the websites operated by ECTEL and the Commission, or
        (ii)   reproduce the codes of practice at the request of any member of the public on payment of the prescribed fee;

11

Figure 5.5 – A Brief Excerpt of the ECTEL Eastern Caribbean Communications Act[388]

("Powers user verb phrases like "may acquire", "may issue", "may hold", etc.)

- **Functions:** Any act establishing a new regulator is replete with many functions too, and as noted earlier, many functions are also derived from supranational entities like the African Union or the European Union. Typically functions in TMT regulators would include:

---

[388]https://www.ectel.int/wp-content/uploads/2020/09/Electronic-Communications-Bill-200703-1.pdf

- the granting and licensing of radio and TV licenses as well as licensing of digital services—without which digital switchover of TV will not be possible;
- functions to promote competition;
- functions to manage the use of spectrum;
- functions to encourage innovation and investment;
- functions to draw up codes of practice for "rights-of-way" access;
- functions to protect consumers;
- functions to regulate TV and radio; and
- functions over the state broadcaster, etc.

You can surmise that, simplistically, functions combine powers and duties. Many sector laws spell out explicitly the functions.

- **Factors:** Factors refer to important issues and language like the regulator "must have regard to." Factors also include language like "taking into account" the "interests of consumers" or "different needs and interests of users of electromagnetic spectrum." They could also cover

  - protecting vulnerable children;
  - having regards to the needs of the disabled, elderly, and those on low income;
  - having regard to ethnic communities and rural and urban areas;
  - having regard to persons living in different regions of the country; and
  - having regard to diversity and equality.

Duties, functions, powers, and factors are clearly germane to regulators, and are absolutely essential to achieving the goals of good regulating without what looks like a simple factor of "having regard to rural and urban areas," the regulator may have no basis to interpret its remit and regulate for rural broadband too – because it would likely not be *economically* viable to push operators to go beyond the market efficiency frontier (cf. Section 4.9 in Chapter 4 and see Figure 4.6). However, because this is a duty and/or relevant *factor* in the Sector Law, regulators can issue regulations or provide obligations in the licences they issue in order for operators to roll out networks well beyond what they deem economically viable – but without bankrupting the operators too.

Here is an example of the application of a factor by Ofgem (the UK's gas and electricity markets regulator) in a 2018 written decision:

> "*Having regard to* our principal objective of protecting the interests of energy consumers and other relevant statutory duties, and based on the information submitted by the Licensee, *we consider that granting a time-limited derogation to allow the Licensee to proceed with its proposed scheme does not undermine the objectives of our retail market policies.* We have committed to encouraging and providing suppliers with flexibility to deliver better outcomes for consumers. This includes supporting initiatives that may increase consumer engagement and regular prompts for consumers to engage and switch away from poor value or inappropriate contracts. The Competition and Markets Authority (CMA) recommended in its priority list of measures, *that we consider initiatives aimed at promoting engagement in the domestic retail energy market*" (Source: [389] - *my emphases*).

The decision above not only demonstrates Ofgem *having regard to* its principal duty of protecting the interests of the UK's energy consumers, but how this 'having regard to' factor has led Ofgem to grant a time-limited derogation, i.e., officially informing the licensee that it does not need to comply with a rule that needs to be obeyed. In addition, Ofgem is also clearly 'having regard' to the CMA's recommendation too.

Now that the non-legal reader has perused Figures 5.4 and 5.5 – and they do 'not bite' - I urge the reader now to pick up their Sector Laws, download them from the website, etc. Read it and you will come across these four key precepts. This brief section may just help demystify Sector Laws for the reader – and get more regulator staff to actually read their Sector Laws and Regulations.

Another exercise I recommend now is for the Board of the regulator to request and sign off on a complete table of all their duties and factors in particular. Every time I have successfully got a Board to do this in developing markets, they are usually surprised on how much of their duties they hardly know anything about – yet alone having realised them. They

---

[389] https://www.ofgem.gov.uk/sites/default/files/docs/2019/05/derogation_decision_and_d irections_to_british_gas_-_end_svt_03_04_2018_us.pdf

get away with it mostly because there hardly exists any proper oversight of statutory regulators in emerging markets of South East Asia, Africa, the Caribbean and Latin America.

5.4.2 The Economic Bases of Regulation

I cover some of economic bases this in some depth in Chapter 2 but not all, so it is worth summarising next for completeness – and just in case the reader reads this chapter before reading Chapter 2. It introduces some new – but important concepts – like 'consumer surplus,' 'producer surplus' and 'broader social value'.

As I note before, the primary role of most decent regulators is to further (or maximise) the interests of their consumers and citizens in relation to matters related to the sector, e.g. in Communication matters, Electricity matters, Water matters, etc. Regulators also try and protect consumers in the face of markets that do not work effectively for them. This role - and as I note several times earlier in this chapter/book which few emerging markets regulators tend to realise it - is broadly informed by economic theories. Indeed, most network industry regulators (see Chapter 3), whether they realise it or not, are *economic* regulators. They use (or are expected to use) economic analysis based on economic theories in their regulating. They are expected to understand and explain how the economic value or benefits (called "economic rents" by economists) are shared between consumers (consumer groups), and producers (the industry and its supply chain). In addition to economic benefits/rents which consumers and producers enjoy, the protection of the interests of citizens in all network industries is also grounded in public interest goals (or factors as we saw earlier), such as diversity and equality.

5.4.2.1 Introducing Demand-Supply Economic Curves

Well, some basic economic concepts will clarify and demystify why regulators are really economic regulators and explain why the use of economics actually help maximise the interests of consumers. Are you wondering what on earth could this mean? Let us revert to some basic economics by (re)introducing demand-supply curves. Some readers who have already read Chapter 2 would have come across demand and supply economic curves like the simplified one shown in Figure 5.6. It still bears repeating in this "Demystifying Economic Regulation" chapter – as long as I simplify the explanations some more, which is what I try to do next.

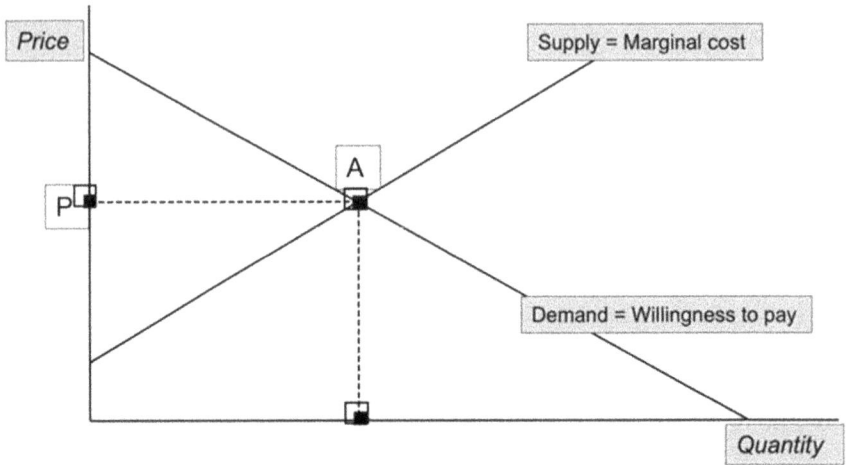

Figure 5.6 - Demand and Supply Curves/Graphs

Figure 5.6 shows a market equilibrium price, P. This simple figure depicts how markets allocate scarce resources. And these are markets with decentralised agents pursuing their own self-interests. Let us explain some more. Imagine a scenario of production of mobile phones. (The same principle applies to other products too.)

The *demand curve* slopes downwards from top-left to bottom-right. So the "demand" curve is equivalent to a "willingness to pay" curve: the higher the price of the phone, the less consumers are willing to pay, and hence the quantity demanded is less; the lower the price, the more consumers are willing to pay, leading to a larger quantity demanded.

The *supply curve*, on the other hand, slopes upwards from bottom-left to top-right. This is because as the price of the phone increases, suppliers are incentivised to enter the market in order to supply more phones. The supply curve is equivalent to the "marginal cost" curve. Suppliers will continue to supply more phones into the market as long as the marginal costs of the new units are less than the prevailing price. So if the marginal cost is $50 and the price is $70, suppliers will continue manufacturing phones because it is profitable for them to do so.

5.4.2.2 Introducing Consumer Surplus & Producer Surplus

You will note I made some minor amendments to Figure 5.6, yielding Figure 5.7 with some unfamiliar terms: consumer surplus and producer surplus. What do these concepts mean?

Well, let us start with some more basic economic concepts to clarify and demystify why regulators are economic regulators and explain why economic concepts or theories actually help. The equilibrium position is defined by means of the equilibrium price. We are at the *equilibrium price*, when at this price the quantity of phones that buyers are willing and able to buy is equal to the quantity of phones that sellers are willing and able to sell—that is, the price at which demand equals supply. You should visualise supply (or *marginal cost curve*) is the sum total of all the supply curves of all the phone suppliers, and the demand curve is the sum total of all the demand curves for the various phones in that price range. The equilibrium price is also an average price point.

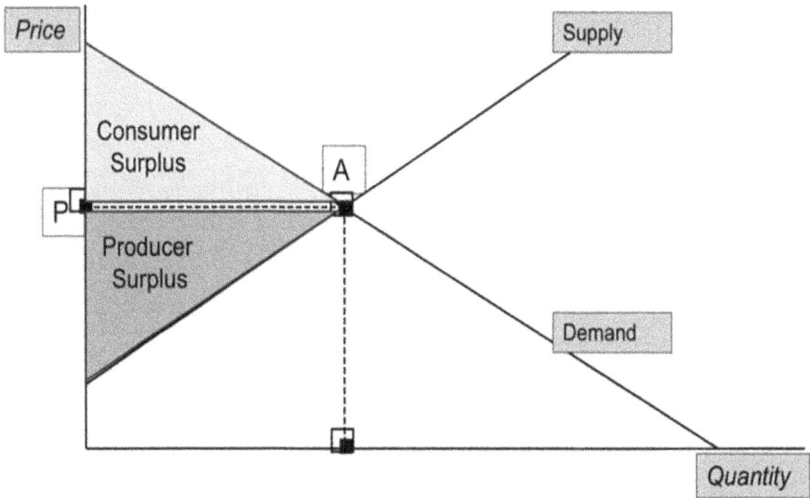

Figure 5.7 - Producer and Consumer Surplus and Economic Regulation

There are some people who would pay a lot more than this equilibrium price. Let us imagine there are ten buyers of these phones and the equilibrium price is $100. Let us suppose that a good 30 percent (i.e., three people) value the phone at more than $100 and would be prepared to pay more. The rest are only prepared to pay $100 maximum. So Customer A may be prepared to pay $150 (i.e., s/he is enjoying a surplus of $50). Customers B and C are prepared to pay $130 and $120, respectively, yielding further surplus of $50 between the two of them. Overall, there will be a consumer surplus of $100 from all ten customers.

The sum total of what customers are prepared to pay above the equilibrium price is called the *consumer surplus*, and it is shown by the top triangle in Figure 5.7 (also labelled consumer surplus). Clearly, the more customers and citizens feel they are getting value from a product or service, the greater the value of the consumer surplus would be. The *producer surplus* (i.e., the lower triangle in Figure 5.7 – labelled producer surplus) is also clearly the surplus above the marginal cost (i.e., supply) line. This is the sum total of the positive differences that customers pay above costs. In other words, this triangle represents the *profits* to the supplying firms.

5.4.2.3 Introducing Consumer/Producer Surplus & Good Economic Regulation

Let us return to what all these demand and supply curves have to do with good economic regulation. We have described, albeit briefly, consumer surplus and producer surplus above. However, what is their relevance to independent and economic regulation? The answer briefly follows. Only a flavour is provided here. There is much more to the following in the relevant economic textbooks cited in Chapter 2.

It begins with how an independent regulator chooses to interpret its duties. Take one typical duty, that of promoting '*optimal*' use of spectrum. The regulator would independently [390] interpret this duty as promoting "efficient use of spectrum," and "efficient use" can be further interpreted as "maximising benefits to society from using spectrum, including broader social value." [391] Economic regulation dictates that maximising benefits to society from using spectrum equates to maximising total surplus (TS), i.e.,

---

[390] The statutes do not stipulate how this duty should be interpreted by the regulator.

[391] Source: Ofcom UK's interpretation of its key spectrum duty: "To secure the optimal use of the spectrum, having regard to the different needs and interests of all users" – Ensuring optimal value from spectrum (publishing.service.gov.uk) - https://assets.publishing.service.gov.uk/media/63fcc234e90e0740d6029a5e/Frontier_Eco nomics_-_Ensuring_optimal_value_from_spectrum_-_2023_Publication_v2.pdf

the consumer surplus (CS) and the producer surplus (PS). This makes sense because if customers all feel they are getting a good deal maximising CS, and producers are maximising their profits (PS), then society benefits optimally because both consumers and producers are happy.

This is how economic concepts are used to regulate, yielding economic regulation. Profits are arguably easier to measure. However, measuring CS is complex but not impossible to estimate. I note that profits are only arguably "easier" to measure because in many contexts they are harder to measure, especially for multiproduct firms in network industries. For example, there are difficult questions about the cost of capital, how costs should be allocated between products, differences between accounting measures and economic profitability, etc. However, it is the case that profits are easier to measure than consumer surplus. For a practical example, there have been studies estimating the total surplus derived from the use of spectrum in the UK, including estimates of both consumer surplus and producer surplus[392].

Therefore, to achieve optimal societal benefits (of some radio frequency spectrum, say – but the following equally applies to other scarce resources like minerals, forests or freshwater, cf. Section 4.8 in Chapter 4):

- An efficient allocation which maximises the sum of consumer and producer surplus needs to happen. So the radio frequency spectrum goes to player(s) who would maximise their profits (PS)[393] as well as maximise consumers' surplus (CS).
- A free and competitive market would exist wherein purchasers who value the goods or services the highest (i.e., with the highest willingness to pay) get the goods. That is, the purchaser who values my old car that I am selling on eBay the most should get the car. Similarly, in our attempt to mimic the free market, e.g. of cars, the

---

[392] https://www.gov.uk/government/publications/impact-of-radio-spectrum-on-the-uk-economy-and-factors-influencing-future-spectrum-demand

[393] As a reviewer of this book astutely picked out, there is an important caveat here – market power. In the existence of market power, there is welfare loss. More profit is earned by a monopolist than if the market were competitive. So, when profit from exploiting market power is involved, we do not want to see profits maximised. The reason is the deadweight loss - the welfare loss arising from market power which reduces the total surplus earned (deadweight loss is the potential total surplus which is lost because it accrues neither to producers nor to consumers). Revisit Chapter 2's analysis on deadweight loss.

purchasers who value the radio frequency spectrum[394] the most should get the spectrum. Similarly, sellers with the lowest costs produce the goods. Again, there is an important caveat here. Since spectrum is an input, we want the spectrum to be allocated to producers who generate the most surplus in the downstream (retail) market. Economists assure us that there is a broad correlation between the operator's valuation and downstream surplus. However, there is also a significant risk of divergence, such as one operator hoovering up so much of the spectrum that it has market power in the downstream market. This is why most spectrum auctions include competition safeguards such as spectrum caps. Myers (2023, p. 117) covers this very point explicitly: "in other words, auction measures for downstream competition and for coverage extension seek to align auction efficiency with output efficiency, so that the auction winners will then deliver the greatest social and public value."

Another key important economic concept to regulation is the concept of efficiency, including allocative efficiency, productive efficiency, and dynamic efficiency.

Good economic regulation attempts to satisfy the three efficiency conditions of allocative, productive, and dynamic efficiency.

- **Allocative efficiency:** This is a static concept, and it relates to the optimal use of scarce resources, maximising the sum of consumer surplus and producer surplus. It requires that if a consumer is willing to pay an amount for a good that exceeds what it would cost society to provide her with this good, then that customer gets the good. Put another way, if she *would* pay twenty dollars for a good, and it would cost fifteen dollars to provide it to her, then she should get it. In even more plain English and relating it to regulation more, if the good is in fixed supply and cannot be

---

[394] I acknowledge – hence my use of the word 'mimic' - that using spectrum to illustrate free and competitive markets is rather bit tricky because spectrum allocation is not really done using the free market mechanism – we employ auctions to mimic the competitive market but sometimes limiting the amount of spectrum a single supplier may get might be considered – and we also have defragmentation issues which can result from uncontrolled allocation which is just based on highest bidder principle.

expanded (e.g., the spectrum[395]), it should go to the person or firm who *values it the most*, as this clearly signals that they are more likely to make the best use of it for society, i.e., they are more likely to drive up consumer and producer surplus (CS + PS in Figure 5.7), or total surplus, with its use.

- **Productive efficiency:** This is also another static concept implying there is no waste in the supplying firm's productive process. This typically implies there is no (or little) technical waste, costs are minimised, and there is also no waste due to mismanagement. Take radio frequency spectrum again. 4G is more productively efficient than 3G, which is more efficient than 2G. This is because for the same amount of radio spectrum, a firm is able to get more capacity and throughput (measured in Mbps) from 4G than for 3G, say. It is akin to the spectrum being "less wasted" with better technologies, or, more accurately, the recent technologies get more out of the same spectrum. Costs minimisation and lack of waste due to mismanagement clearly would drive *down* prices and drive up profits for the firm. In plain English, productive efficiency suggests the firm with the best technology who drives down costs and has the best management team should also be preferred to get the scarce resource/good (e.g., spectrum licences, forests licences, mineral licences). They are more likely to drive up consumer and producer surplus the most. Society should prefer such firms over other less productive ones.

- **Dynamic efficiency**: Dynamic efficiency is different from the above two (allocative and productive efficiency). Dynamic efficiency is achieved when resources move over time to their highest value uses. This means it involves the transition from one type of efficient use to another higher type of efficient use of the resource. Dynamic efficiency is at the heart of liberalisation and technology neutrality, the concept that regulators license spectrum but do not prescribe what technology the spectrum should be used for within limits. When spectrum is liberalised for a class of technologies (e.g., 2G, 3G, and 4G), it allows for dynamic efficiency because the firm who has the license for that spectrum may use it more efficiently over time by migrating its use to more

---

[395] See earlier footnote on spectrum assignments not being a free and competitive market – but one that tries to mimic the latter.

331

efficient technologies. You have just read my articulation of dynamic efficiency. However, I acknowledge that this is one view - and that there is another view that dynamic efficiency is not so different.

Nevertheless, these three efficiencies are important to economic regulation. They are at the heart of decisions made by regulators to allocate scarce resources. They (including the concepts of consumer and producer surplus) clearly show the importance of market-based thinking (and economics) in the allocation of scarce resources and why regulators of such scarce resources are economic regulators. Hopefully, you have now obtained a taste of the science of economic regulation. A flavour of the art follows next.

Let us now link some economic concepts we have met before like market failure, market power and dominance, etc. to these three efficiencies. They may give you even more economic bragging rights (there are some serious regulatory implications behind them, hence why they are included):

- **Market failure**: Drawing from the above three efficiencies, market failure occurs where markets cannot achieve a fully-efficient allocation. In other words, if the scarce resources (e.g., some spectrum bands, forest rights, mineral rights, etc.) go to the wrong hands, which does not maximise consumer and producer surplus, this is not optimal for society.

- **Market power/dominance/anticompetitive behaviour**: again, this refers to the ability of a firm to maintain uncontested supernormal economic profits in the long term. This is clearly related to the concept of dominance in economic competition policy, i.e., the "ability of firms to behave to some extent independently of competitors, customers, and, ultimately, consumers." This is not good. As I cover earlier, dominance sometimes can be benevolent and benign. In itself, dominance is not a problem *per se*, but the abuse of a dominant position clearly is! And it is one type of market failure noted in Chapter 2 - If a dominant player starts displaying anticompetitive behaviour, the regulator must intervene, full stop.

- **Regulatory intervention**: Intervention by regulators is easier said than done as we see in Chapters 3 and 4. Most of the time, regulators try to intervene when firms are already so dominant and big with an army of lawyers and much more financial firepower. This is truly nontrivial for the regulator. A regulator would have to carry out a market review and make a determination and then move on to deciding what remedies it needs to put in place to correct the market failure in question. There are two key points to add here:

    o As a counterpart to market failure, regulatory failure occurs where regulatory intervention fails to achieve a fully-efficient allocation – for instance, see the examples of regulatory failures in Section 2.5.
    o As explained in Section 3.9, the regulator's choice is usually between imperfect competition and imperfect regulation.

Any regulatory interventions must take strong cognizance of these two points too – that have been detailed in earlier chapters.

5.4.2.4 Broader Social Value (BSV) and Economic Regulation

This concept of broader social value has not been mentioned so far in this volume. So, what exactly does it mean?

It relates to total economic value framework, which I had the privilege of being exposed to at regulator Ofcom. It is briefly explained in the following.

As covered earlier, the statutory duties of a best-in-class communications regulator like UK's Ofcom require it to take account of the interests of both consumers and citizens. Believe me when I assert that this is easier said than done. How does the regulator prove that in arriving at regulatory policy choices it has taken into account citizen and consumer interests? In achieving the evaluation of policies and economic regulatory questions, Ofcom then needs to be able to demonstrate that the interests of consumers and citizens have been taken into account.

One of the ways in which Ofcom has addressed this problem is to define a "Total Value Framework," as shown in Figure 5.8. The framework identifies the disparate and different types of economic value which may arise from the production and consumption of goods and services, and it shows how all of these amalgamate to yield the "total value to society," i.e., the sum of the consumer and citizen values.

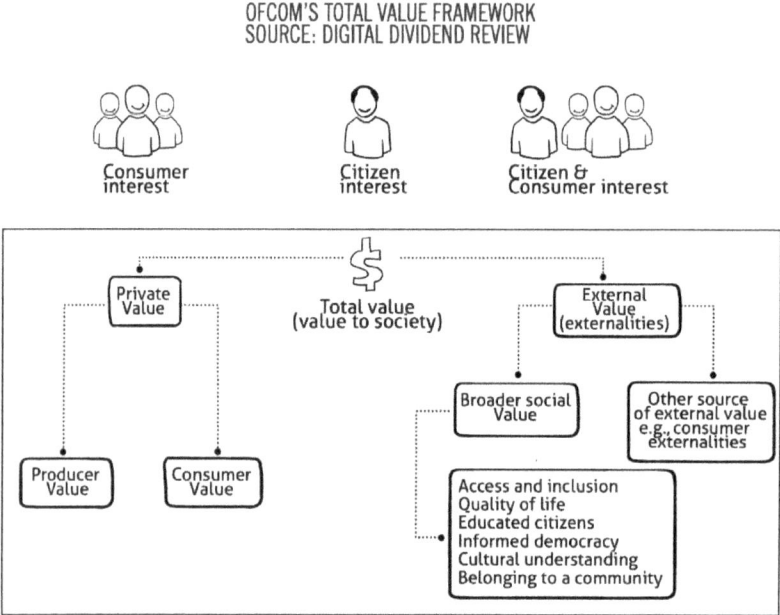

OFCOM'S TOTAL VALUE FRAMEWORK
SOURCE: DIGITAL DIVIDEND REVIEW

Consumer interest

Citizen interest

Citizen & Consumer interest

Private Value

Total value (value to society)

External Value (externalities)

Broader social Value

Other source of external value e.g., consumer externalities

Producer Value

Consumer Value

Access and inclusion
Quality of life
Educated citizens
Informed democracy
Cultural understanding
Belonging to a community

Figure 5.8—Ofcom's (UK) Total Value Framework

(Source: adapted from Digital Dividend Review[396])

As can be seen in the framework, total value to society (TVS) accrues from the sum of private value and external value. Private value is what we have covered above and consists of producer value or producer surplus + consumer value/surplus, i.e., PS + CS. The external value is similarly the sum of broader social value and other sources of external value. Broader social value (BSV) refers to the interests of citizens (not consumers) that may be met by the production or consumption of goods or services.

---

[396] Ofcom's total value framework is set out at Figure 4 (p28) in Ofcom (2007) 'Digital Dividend Review: A statement on our approach to awarding the digital dividend', https://www.ofcom.org.uk/__data/assets/pdf_file/0018/33615/statement.pdf

However, these people do derive value from such services as *citizens*. It could be an educational health programme or a national football match that one subscriber only is paying for on his/her TV set, i.e., there is a sole consumer, but a dozen other nonpayers watch. There is value to this *access* and how these dozen people feel *included* in seeing their national team play and them feeling like a community of nationals. There is value in these dozen people improving the quality of their lives via watching the educational health programme. There is much value in having educated citizens if they all watch factual and news programming, as well as having an informed democracy. These all contribute to BSV, and this example hopefully goes a long way to explaining why BSV for broadcasting is important.

However, private value may be confusing in some contexts with BSV. For example, viewing advertising-funded TV broadcasting without paying for it is private value, i.e. consumer surplus from the viewer's benefit/willingness to pay exceeds the price paid (i.e., zero financial price to the viewer in this example). So, broader social value includes things like the community inclusion that I outline in the last paragraph. To summarise on BSV, Myers (2023, p.57) also uses Ofcom's total value framework and he proceeds to describe broader social value (BSV) as "aspects of public value which are especially important, like informed democracy and belonging to a community, when developing policies in areas such as public service broadcasting or universal mobile coverage".

Other sources of external value could be positive or negative. Such externalities refer to positive or negative value which accrues when the production or consumption of a good or service impacts those *not* producing or consuming that good or service. For example, an industrial plant may be manufacturing much-needed detergents but pollutes the air for miles and emits effluent (sewage) which make citizens living in the area feel sick. They have to go to the hospital to get treatment. Overall, even though there is good private value created here (i.e., PS + CS), there is also a negative value in the costs of such externalities.

Using such a total value framework, regulatory policies can then be assessed in terms of how well they might maximise total value to society or just private value.

5.5 Practical Regulation is both Art and Science

It is key to demystify the fact that Good practical day-to-day regulation is both an art and a science – that needs to be balanced. More practice makes it better. I already note earlier at least a couple of times in this chapter that good day-to-day practical regulating is both an art and a science. However, what exactly do I mean noting this?

> " "Art" means something intuitive, imprecise, and subjective, a skill cultivated through practice and imagination. "Science" means something researched, measured, and objective, a hard statistic backed by federal funding and white coats"[397].

I like the above art vs. science distinction from the Yale Scientific magazine. Good day-to-day regulation is an art. I hope it is clear from my application of my simplistic Formula I to the Asian telecom case of Section 5.2 that there is an 'art' to what we/I did. Producing the formula (Formula I) – indeed both Formulae of Section 5.1 – are clear works of "art" on my part. It is because – as per the definition of art vs. science above – Formulae I and II are somethings intuitive, imprecise, and subjective, but they have been cultivated through practice and some science. The application of the formula to the telecoms scenario is a further art – because it is imprecise and subjective in places. Relevant market definitions (cf. Chapter 4, Section 4.5) are equally works of art because they are imprecise and subjective too – and the same applies to the application of most of the methods of regulation of Chapter 4.

However, there is clear science to aspects of regulation – aspects that are researched, measurable, objective and repeatable. Many regulatory KPIs used for enforcement regulation are objectively measurable. Market shares or market concentration are objectively measurable. However, market power and market dominance assessments usually involve judgement.

So, good (economic) regulation is a "balancing act." Drawing from my first-hand experience at Ofcom (United Kingdom), the objective of Good economic regulation is to secure good regulatory outcomes for consumers

---

[397] https://www.yalescientific.org/2013/02/the-art-and-science-of/ - The Art and Science Of… – Yale Scientific Magazine

and citizens. A good regulator like Ofcom abides by all the seven key principles noted earlier (see Figure 5.2) in concert with good economic regulation precepts whilst balancing, i.e., weighing up, sometimes truly conflicting duties.

Not all the duties that regulators get asked to perform are internally consistent. For example, the duty to maximise broadband Internet availability comes up squarely against a duty to protect children/minors from the certain tasteless content which dominates the content online. Therefore, part of the *art* of Good economic regulation lies in this balancing and in how the regulator marshals its arguments to optimally achieve its good outcomes whilst minimizing the unwanted ones. Figure 5.9 summarises pictorially just how Ofcom balances this art.

THE "BALANCING ACT" OF REGULATION --- WEIGHING UP CONFLICTING DUTIES, FUNCTIONS, AND FACTORS

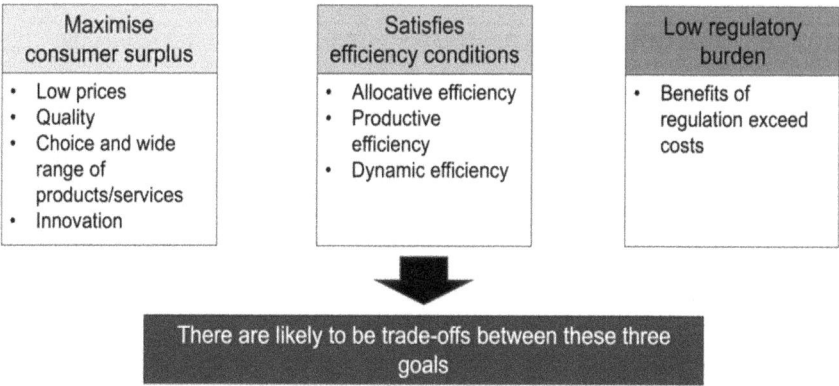

Maximise consumer surplus	Satisfies efficiency conditions	Low regulatory burden
• Low prices • Quality • Choice and wide range of products/services • Innovation	• Allocative efficiency • Productive efficiency • Dynamic efficiency	• Benefits of regulation exceed costs

There are likely to be trade-offs between these three goals

Figure 5.9 —The "Balancing Act" of Regulation—Weighing Up Conflicting Duties, Functions, and Factors (Source: Ofcom UK)

It depicts the use of the economic regulatory concepts discussed so far and how the *art* of world-class regulation also derives from (i) balancing the maximisation of consumer surplus (because regulators are there to look after consumer and citizen interests) (ii) whilst satisfying the above triumvirate of efficiency conditions [allocative, productive and dynamic] and (iii) minimising regulatory burden. It is genuinely easier said than done. This balancing happens in concert with abiding by all the regulatory principles above (see Figure 5.2), and the result is usually significant outcomes for consumers and citizens. It is clearly easier summarised here than done. Much expertise and experience is needed to execute this expertly – this is the art of regulation at play yet again. As I also note in Chapter 2, (Section 2.5.1), deciding on the 'right' theories/hypotheses to use requires much judgment which carries risks – it is yet again an *art* that comes with experience.

5.6 The More Complex Anatomy of Good and Practical Regulation

Drawing from Chapters 1, 2, 3 and 4, there is a deeper and more complex structure to Day-to-day practical Regulation – but even this can be demystified too using an Inputs-Output diagram model. This is shown in the more complex Input-Output model of Figure 5.10.

5.6.1 Explaining the more Complex Input-Output Model of Regulation

Figure 5.10 depicts a more detailed anatomy of the 'Art & Science' of the Regulation process. Starting at the top from left to right, it shows two columns of inputs and one column of outputs on the extreme right. I take each of the Input and Output columns in turn, and describe the importance of why each of these inputs/outputs are key to the regulatory process.

5.6.1.1 Inputs to Day-to-day Regulation (Figure 5.10)

The Inputs are derived and drawn from the chapters of this book (including this one) as shown clearly in Figure 5.10.

1. **The Inputs of Laws (cf. Chapter 5)**: as I cover earlier in this chapter – twice at least already – regulation starts with the law or laws, be they international, regional or national. Laws are the most important inputs into the regulation process of every sector. Some sectors like aviation and telecoms really rely on international laws from ICAO and the ITU respectively, more than others. Just sticking with aviation as an example to illustrate the importance of the Input of International Laws,

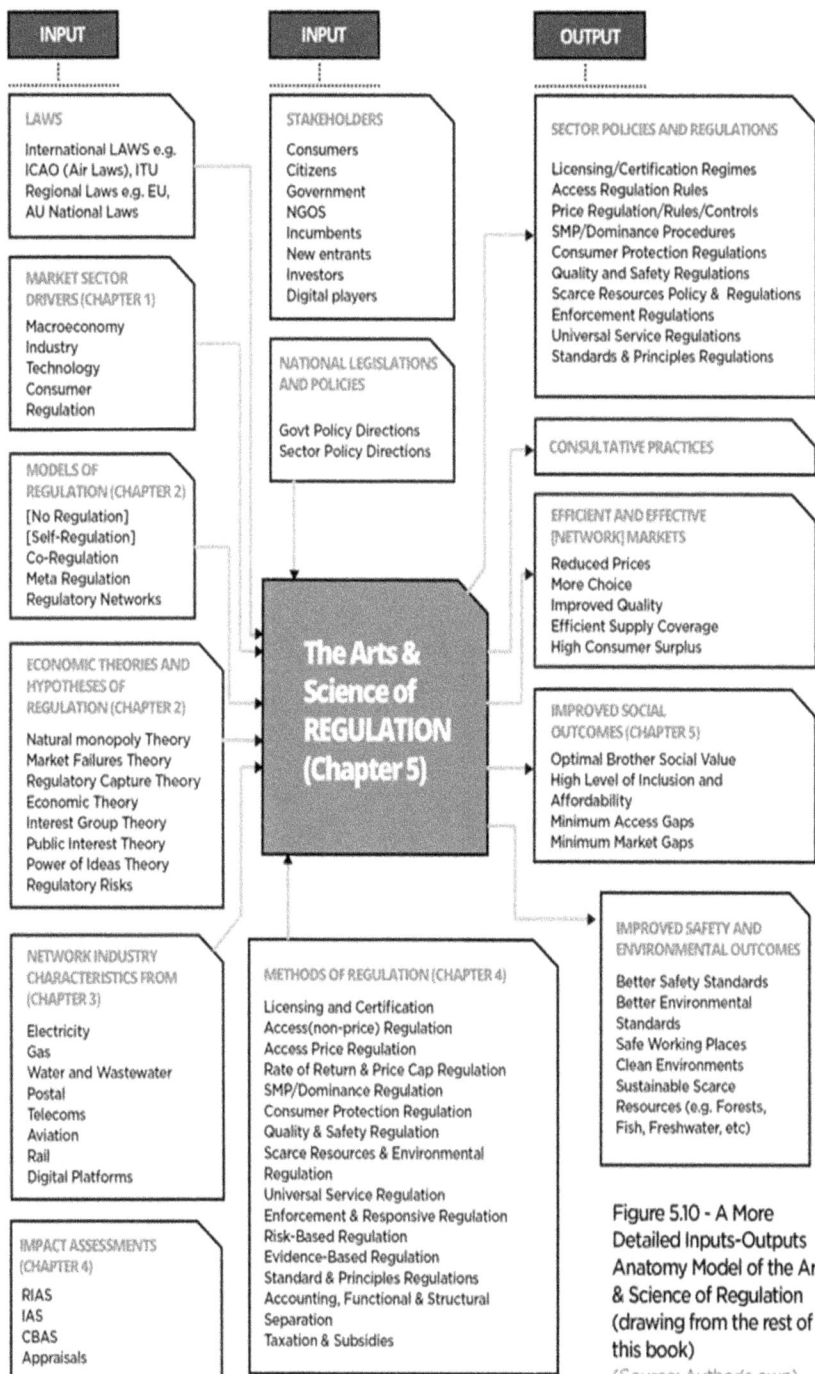

INPUT

INPUT

OUTPUT

LAWS

International LAWS e.g. ICAO (Air Laws), ITU Regional Laws e.g. EU, AU National Laws

MARKET SECTOR DRIVERS (CHAPTER 1)

Macroeconomy
Industry
Technology
Consumer
Regulation

MODELS OF REGULATION (CHAPTER 2)

[No Regulation]
[Self-Regulation]
Co-Regulation
Meta Regulation
Regulatory Networks

ECONOMIC THEORIES AND HYPOTHESES OF REGULATION (CHAPTER 2)

Natural monopoly Theory
Market Failures Theory
Regulatory Capture Theory
Economic Theory
Interest Group Theory
Public Interest Theory
Power of Ideas Theory
Regulatory Risks

NETWORK INDUSTRY CHARACTERISTICS FROM (CHAPTER 3)

Electricity
Gas
Water and Wastewater
Postal
Telecoms
Aviation
Rail
Digital Platforms

IMPACT ASSESSMENTS (CHAPTER 4)

RIAS
IAS
CBAS
Appraisals

STAKEHOLDERS

Consumers
Citizens
Government
NGOS
Incumbents
New entrants
Investors
Digital players

NATIONAL LEGISLATIONS AND POLICIES

Govt Policy Directions
Sector Policy Directions

The Arts & Science of REGULATION (Chapter 5)

METHODS OF REGULATION (CHAPTER 4)

Licensing and Certification
Access(non-price) Regulation
Access Price Regulation
Rate of Return & Price Cap Regulation
SMP/Dominance Regulation
Consumer Protection Regulation
Quality & Safety Regulation
Scarce Resources & Environmental Regulation
Universal Service Regulation
Enforcement & Responsive Regulation
Risk-Based Regulation
Evidence-Based Regulation
Standard & Principles Regulations
Accounting, Functional & Structural Separation
Taxation & Subsidies

SECTOR POLICIES AND REGULATIONS

Licensing/Certification Regimes
Access Regulation Rules
Price Regulation/Rules/Controls
SMP/Dominance Procedures
Consumer Protection Regulations
Quality and Safety Regulations
Scarce Resources Policy & Regulations
Enforcement Regulations
Universal Service Regulations
Standards & Principles Regulations

CONSULTATIVE PRACTICES

EFFICIENT AND EFFECTIVE [NETWORK] MARKETS

Reduced Prices
More Choice
Improved Quality
Efficient Supply Coverage
High Consumer Surplus

IMPROVED SOCIAL OUTCOMES (CHAPTER 5)

Optimal Brother Social Value
High Level of Inclusion and Affordability
Minimum Access Gaps
Minimum Market Gaps

IMPROVED SAFETY AND ENVIRONMENTAL OUTCOMES

Better Safety Standards
Better Environmental Standards
Safe Working Places
Clean Environments
Sustainable Scarce Resources (e.g. Forests, Fish, Freshwater, etc)

Figure 5.10 - A More Detailed Inputs-Outputs Anatomy Model of the Art & Science of Regulation (drawing from the rest of this book)

(Source: Author's own)

Chapter 3 explains that airspaces are 'controlled' or 'uncontrolled', with the former mandating all aircraft to follow a specified structured route whilst complying with all air traffic instructions.

It also covers that airspaces around the world are divided into Flight Information Regions (FIRs). FIRs vary in size from some covering an entire ocean to even some small geographical countries like the UK having four. A FIR is an ICAO[398]-specified region of airspace in which flight information services and alerting service are provided to all aircraft through an FIR, and are provided by one ANSP[399] per controlled airspace sector. Such services are vital to national and international aviation safety and can only happen because ICAO has established and operates a body of rules and regulations called Civil Aviation Law or Air Law. The International Civil Aviation Organization (ICAO) - is a specialist United Nations agency set up to define international safety, environmental and operating standards for civil aviation. The primary goal of Air Law is to enhance the efficiency and safety of international flights and ensure the orderly development of civil aviation worldwide[400], and some key aspects of Air Law include (as described in this site):

- Aircraft Classification: Air Law defines various types and categories of aircraft based on their design, weight, and purpose. Different regulations may apply to different classes of aircraft.

- Personnel Licensing Regulations: Air Law regulations cover the licensing and certifications required of pilots, cabin crew members, air traffic controllers, and other aviation staff – setting standards for their training, experience and medical fitness.

- Airspace: Air Law outlines the division of airspace into controlled and uncontrolled FIRs, each with different specific rules, regulations and restrictions. They include regulations for controlled airspace, restricted airspace, and special-use airspace.

- Flight Rules: Air Law establishes the rules, amongst others, which regulate flight operations, such as the key procedures for take-off, landing, and enroute flight.

---

[398] International Civil Aviation Organisation

[399] Air Navigation Service Provider

[400] https://flight-courses.com - Civil Aviation Law (ICAO) | Aviation theory and examination (flight-courses.com)

- Safety Regulations: Safety is a critical concern in civil aviation, and Air Law establishes rules and regulations to ensure the safe operation of aircrafts, including their maintenance, inspections and emergency procedures.

- Air Traffic Management: Air Law covers the organization and management of air traffic, including air traffic control procedures, separation of aircraft standards, and communication rules.

- International Agreements and Treaties: Air Law includes provisions for international agreements and treaties that facilitate cooperation between countries in areas like air traffic rights, airworthiness standards, and accident investigation.

Without Air Law covering subjects as listed above, where would the aviation industry be? Chaos would reign as I hope the reader agrees. The international and national aviation sectors completely rely on International Air Law – in addition to other regional and national laws – as essential inputs to the regulation of the sector. In the same way, the telecommunications sector rely on International Telecommunications Laws and Regulations established and operated by the ITU[401]. Like ICAO, the International Telecommunication Union (ITU) is the United Nations specialized agency for information and communication technologies – ICTs[402].

2. **The Inputs of Models of Regulation (from Chapter 3):** revisit Figure 5.10 - as Chapter 3 overviews, there are six broad approaches (or models) to regulation as shown in Figure 3.1 of Chapter 3 including No Regulation, Self-Regulation, Co-regulation, Statutory Regulation, Meta-Regulation and Regulatory Networks. These models refer to the various different approaches or layers of regulatory control used by Governments, Industries, and other Organisations to 'control' various aspects of societal behaviour, standards, compliance and enforcement. The chapter notes that each of these models has its strengths and limitations, and their effectiveness depends on the context in which they are

---

[401] https://www.itu.int/ITU-T/itr/ - International Telecommunication Regulations (ITRs) (itu.int)

[402] It is worth mentioning the politics of international standard bodies like the ITU and ICAO – Developed countries like the UK are always seeking to influence the standards to ensure that they align with UK's interests and that none of the standards is against their interests.

applied. It is the responsibility of Government and/or established regulators to consider the context that requires regulation carefully, and decide which of the model(s) of regulation is/are most optimal for the sector. Governments would do so by striking the right balance between Government/Regulator intervention, industry responsibility, and societal interests. Therefore, to regulate a sector needs clear decisions on the model of regulation needed for that sector and why. It should not be taken for granted that it is obvious how every sector in every country is regulated because it is typically done in a certain way in other developed countries for example. As covered in Chapter 3, there is currently a co-regulation model employed in the UK in the regulation of advertising across all media. The Advertising Standards Authority (ASA [403]) is the country's specialist independent regulator of advertising across all media. Co-regulation sees the ASA given responsibility on a day-to-day basis for regulating the content of broadcast (TV and radio) ads under contract from statutory media regulator Ofcom[404]. This works for the UK but would/may not be the right choice to regulate the same sector in other countries. Hence it is key to ensure that a particular form of regulation is right for your country before adopting it from other countries.

3. **The Inputs of Economic Theories & Hypotheses (from Chapter 2):** these are key economic thinking and insights that act as inputs into the regulatory process - revisit Figure 5.10. As Chapter 2 explains, no sector is regulated without some explicit or implicit rationale(s), and theories of change or hypotheses for regulating the sector. It is important to understand the causal relationship between the actions taken by the regulator and the expected or intended outcomes. It is important to mitigate the risks of regulatory failure and the potential unexpected or unintended consequences. Can you imagine the risks and failures if the international/national aviation industry [of the former input of Laws] was not regulated by Air Laws and Regulations? It is frankly unfathomable. In Chapter 2, theories of regulation are noted as referring to understanding and analysing *who, what, why, when* and *which* ways (i.e., *how*) Governments and/or other regulatory agencies [that Governments set up] intervene in various

---

[403] https://www.asa.org.uk/ - Home - ASA | CAP

[404] www.ofcom.org.uk

342

sectors of the economy – in order to achieve certain publicly desired outcomes, particularly in instances where the market would fail to deliver these outcomes. Such theories of regulation are sets of propositions or hypotheses about the rationales for regulating that sector in the first place, which players and actors contribute to that need for regulating and typical patterns of interaction between regulatory actors. Economic theories and hypotheses are needed inputs in order to design and evaluate regulations. As Figure 5.10 depicts – typical of network industries (see Chapter 3) – such theories/hypotheses include natural monopoly theory, market failure theory, regulatory capture theory, economic theory, interest group theory, public interest theory, power of ideas theory and regulatory risks/failures. These are covered in detail in Chapter 2. In practice, there are typically two or more of these theories at play underpinning the regulation of all network industry sectors as are covered in Chapter 3. For example in the railway industry, at least three theories would underpin the regulation of this sector in many countries: a vertically-integrated railway sector with a single operator makes for a *natural monopoly* (theory 1) with a high risk of regulatory capture (theory 2) – and yet there is a significant public interest (theory 3) rationale to regulate rail to reduce pollution, increase mass transportation and drive more efficient economies. There are – or should be – similar clear theories [explicit or otherwise] that underpin the regulation of every sector of the economy. No such theories suggest that regulation may be premature or not necessary.

4. **The Inputs of Network Characteristics (from Chapter 3):** revisit Figure 5.10. Chapter 3 overviews – in much detail using basic network theory - key network industry market structures and their distinctive characteristics leading to the different approaches to their statutory regulation. This is partly because much statutory regulation involves network industries, which in turn means we must understand their characteristics and challenges. As noted in Section 3.1 of the chapter – statutory regulation is the most traditional and direct model of regulatory governance which allows Governments to regulate critical areas of our economies such telecoms, water, energy, rail, financial markets, health, public safety, environmental protection, and competition regulation. The distinctive characteristics of these [network] industries (e.g. Figures 3.2, 3.3, 3.4, etc.), in many cases, naturally drive the necessary theories of regulation needed to regulate them.

5. **The Inputs of Methods of Regulation (from Chapter 4):** where would regulation be without its myriad of methods of regulation detailed in Chapter 4? A rhetorical question indeed – but these methods of regulation are essential tools in the practice of regulation across all sectors. Revisit Figure 5. For example, with the first Input [on Laws], I note Personnel Licensing Air Law regulations that cover the licensing and certifications required of pilots, cabin crew members, air traffic controllers, and other aviation staff – setting standards for their training, experience and medical fitness. Aviation – like other sectors – clearly use the Licensing and Certification method of regulation.

6. **The Inputs of Understanding Market Sector Drivers (from Chapter 1):** the five main drivers of every sector shown of Figure 1.1 of Chapter 1 and elaborated on in detail in the chapter. Revisit Figure 5.10. To regulate a sector properly truly requires the evidence from these drivers (and more) for the local context market. It should be clear at this juncture that the rest of the four drivers of every sector apart from regulation itself (i.e., the macroeconomy of the country, technological changes happening internationally/locally, local consumers' behaviours and needs, and industry changes) all provide the background context 'environment' in which Good economic regulation is *practiced* daily by regulators using sound theories and methods of regulation. I note in Chapter 1 how I have observed in many emerging market countries where regulations and rules are being promulgated almost devoid of any considerations of these other drivers. The best in class regulators in the world would never do this. Any consultations produced and published by a regulator must research and take into account all these drivers before making the proposals in any consultation document. For example, it would be nonsensical to make proposals on increases in tariffs which bear no relationship to the level of inflation [rates] in the local market – or make regulatory proposals on mobile financial services without a deep understanding and analysis of these market drivers. Ministers, senior policy makers and senior regulators who do not have a good understanding of these drivers in their markets would certainly be short-changing their consumers and citizens with the proposals, policies and regulations they make. This calls for in-depth market research and consumer trends analyses carried out by the regulator in addition to market sector and analyses of markets that the regulator regulates.

7. **The Inputs from Stakeholders:** revisit Figure 5.10. Drafting good legislations, rules and regulations require consultations with stakeholders. Regulators would also have to consult on how they intend to implement the legislation and rules via general consultations and later on secondary draft laws and regulations, e.g. draft statutory instruments (SIs). These all emerge from evidence-based consultations, including detailed economic and technical analyses which are transparent, auditable, and defensible. These all take time and effort on the part of a regulator because the inputs from various stakeholder classes need to be considered and taken seriously. Stakeholder classes whose inputs are vital to Good economic regulation include consumers, citizens, Government (itself), NGOs, Incumbents, New Entrants, Investors, digital players and more.

8. **The Inputs of Impact Assessments (from Chapter 4):** as Chapter 4 notes, Impact Assessments (IAs), Regulatory Impact Assessments (RIA) and Cost-Benefit Analyses (CBAs) are extremely critical tools required in evaluating policy, regulatory measures and even tax proposals, regimes, or rules – in order to pre-empt any of their possible negative externalities. I note in the chapter how I cannot recount to the reader the numerous times over the last decade that I have seen policies and regulations implemented across emerging market countries which end up going very horribly wrong – yet with some prior IA, RIA and/or CBA – the negative consequences could have been averted or minimized. See the debacle of Figure 4.12. These are real important inputs into any good best-practice regulatory process.

I emphasise that impact assessments and evaluations are part of the *accountability* process too. In the UK, the Government has created the ETF[405] (Evaluation Task Force) which oversees the evaluations across Government (sitting under His Majesty's Treasury), and also the RPC[406] (Regulatory Policy Committee) which clears IAs and gives them RAG Ratings. These are accountability tools for democratic societies. A dictator who is

---

[405] https://www.gov.uk/government/organisations/evaluation-task-force - Evaluation Task Force - GOV.UK (www.gov.uk)

[406] https://www.gov.uk/government/organisations/regulatory-policy-committee - Regulatory Policy Committee - GOV.UK (www.gov.uk)

accountable to no one does not need to demonstrate that the benefits of such interventions outweigh the costs (CBA).

9. **The Inputs of National Policies and Policy Directions:** Revisit Figure 5.10. National Government sector policies and policy position/directions are usually key inputs into regulation too. To illustrate this more fully, my team and I was recently (April 2024) involved with a national regulatory authority (NRA) who wishes to review Postal Regulation in its entirety in their country. We requested for Government policies and positions on issues including:

   - Would the Postal Market be fully or just partially liberalized, supporting more competition from digital media companies as well as more traditional competition?

   - How the postal infrastructure in the country is seen going forward: would it be part of critical national infrastructure and communication infrastructure as the Digital Economy looms large?

   - Would Post Offices be seen as a major advantage beyond post, e.g. supporting other Government services and social cohesion like health, insurance, Internet, etc.?

   - Would delivery be assisted via district-level PO boxes or through post offices themselves or both?

   - Would the Government adopt Universal Postal Union (UPU) – USO Standards?

   - Would USO be necessary for any designated national postal player? Not all countries have a defined USO for post e.g. Liberia.

   - Are all users to access postal services at all parts of country at affordable prices – or just some parts of the country will do?

   Such policy directions and more – which most/all sectors of the economy have - are very key inputs into the regulation process.

10. **Other Miscellaneous Inputs (e.g., competent regulatory staff):** there are other Inputs into the regulatory process that are not covered in Figure 5.10 including the existence of competent regulatory staff to conduct the regulating, regular trainings of the staff and others.

5.6.1.2 Outputs of Day-to-day Regulation

Revisit Figure 5.10. I am careful to use the word 'outputs' in this section, as well as the word 'outcomes.' There is a key difference between the two. The Centre for Public Impact highlights the difference that *outputs* are the immediate, easily measurable effects of a policy, whereas *outcomes* are the ultimate changes that a policy will yield[407]. Enhancing outputs does not always necessarily lead to improved outcomes. They provide an excellent example that increasing the number of police officers on the streets may prove successful in terms of outputs, but it would *not* necessarily lead to the desired outcome of reducing crime[408].

The outputs categories for day-to-day regulation include the following as shown in Figure 5.10.

1. **The Outputs on Sector Policies & Regulations:** many firm regulatory sector policies and many equally firm regulations and rules are clear outputs of regulatory art and science processes. They typically include:
    *   Licensing and Certification Regimes and Frameworks
    *   Access Regulations and Rules
    *   Price Regulation Rules and Price Controls
    *   SMP/Dominance Procedures, Rules and Dominance Determinations
    *   Consumer Protection Regulations
    *   Sector Quality and Safety Regulations, Rules, Measurement KPIs and how they will be measured
    *   Scarce Resources Policy & Regulations, e.g. Spectrum Policies and Regulations, Mining Rights Policy, etc.
    *   Enforcement Regulations
    *   Universal Service Policies & Regulations Standard, Universal Service Funds established, USO Determinations

---

[407] https://www.centreforpublicimpact.org/insights/outcomes-and-outputs-public-sector - Fundamentals Unpacked: outcomes and outputs in the public sector | Centre For Public Impact (CPI)

[408] *Ibid.*

- Many other Regulations and Standards [Technical & others], e.g. pollution standards.

2. **The Outputs of Consultative Practices:** revisit Figure 5.10. Good network regulators may/would publish several detailed consultations annually on areas such as those in the list above under the outputs on sector policies and regulations. Many a time, there are consultation and (re)consultations on the same subject – particularly complicated areas such as auctions for radio frequency spectrum licences.

3. **The Outputs of Effective and Efficient Markets:** see Figure 5.10. Statutory regulators – as per Formula II – are set up to pre-empt markets from failing in the first place and/or checking the market power of dominant players in the market. These efforts would – if successful – lead to effective and efficient markets. Such markets would demonstrate Reduced Prices, More Choice, Improved Quality, Efficient Supply Coverage, High Consumer Surplus and more.

4. **The Outputs of Improved Social Outcomes:** see Figure 5.10. As covered in Chapters 2/4, the effective and efficient market outcomes would typically not deliver optimal social outcomes too. The 'second-best' Policy Pricing (shown in Figure 4.3) regulation of average cost pricing described in Chapter 2 leads to a welfare improvement and a reduction in the deadweight loss compared to an unregulated monopoly. In other words, the deadweight loss depicted in Figure 2.1/Figure 4.3 is a measure of the welfare loss caused by an unregulated monopoly which is removed by regulation. This is an example of what a socially-conscious regulator may choose to do. Other improved social outcomes include optimal BSV, High levels of Inclusion & Affordability, Minimum Access Gaps and Minimum Market Gaps. These latter issues are covered under the method of Universal Service Regulation in Section 4.9 and earlier in this chapter.

5. **The Outputs of Improved Safety and Environmental Outcomes:** see Figure 5.10. Good economic regulation would not only result in the outputs of Sector Policies & Regulations, but hopefully in improved safety and environmental outcomes. Such outcomes include Better Safety Standard, Better Environmental Standard, Safe Working Place, Clean Environmental, Sustainable Scarce Resources (e.g. Forests, Fish, Fresh Water, etc.)

The above outputs categories are not exhaustive, but well-representative of the broad outputs (and later outcomes) of Good economic regulation.

5.7 Illustrations of the Use of the Detailed Anatomy Model

The more detailed Anatomy Inputs-Outputs Model of the Art & Science of Regulation of Figure 5.10 can be used – or navigated – in numerous ways during the process of day-to-day regulation.

For example, Figure 5.11 depicts how it can be used to realise new Output Regulations, e.g. New Access Regulations/Rules or Consumer Protection Regulations.

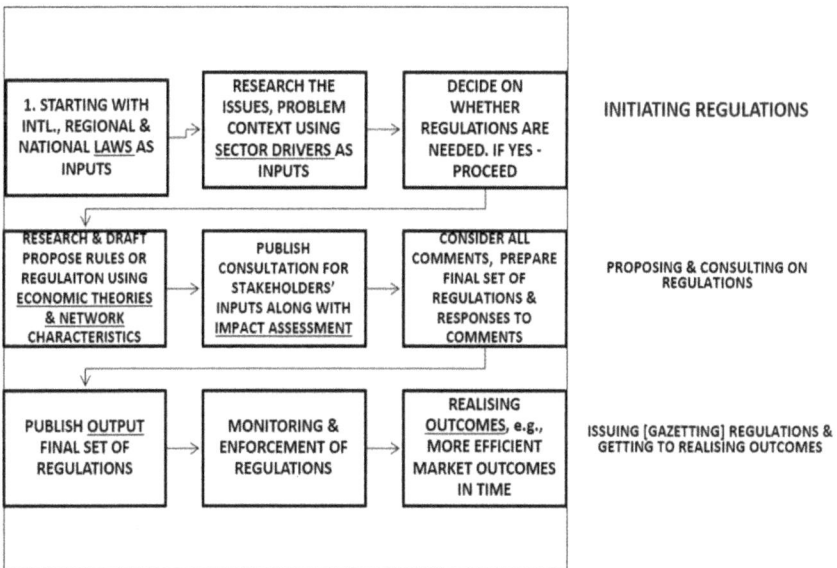

Figure 5.11 – Navigating the more Detailed Anatomy of the Art & Science of Regulation (c.f. Figure 5.10) to Realise New Output Regulations, e.g. New Access Regulations/Rules or Consumer Protection Regulations

It depicts three core phases:

- **Initiating the Regulations**: this starts with the Laws, moving on to researching the problem context/issues (including regulatory failures and risks), market sector drivers' evidence and using these to decide whether regulations are needed or not.

- **Proposing and Consulting on Draft Regulations**: the econominc theories and hypotheses rationale for regulating as well as sector network characteristics would be thoroughly researched. That would inform the draft regulations that would be published for consultation with stakeholders. All comments are considered, finalised set of regulations drafted as well as the responses to the comments from stakeholders.

- **Regulations are Issued, Monitored & Enforced**: this regulations may come into force through gazetting in some countries or through the publication of an 'Statement' from the consultation. Beyond this point, the regulations are monitored and enforcement – and hopefully they would enable improved outcomes for consumers and/or citizens.

Figure 5.12 shows another scenario illustration of the use of the detailed Figures 5.10/5.11 models in shaping the conduct of an SMP/Dominance determination market reviews detailed in Chapter 4. Once again, it suggests it must start from the prevailing laws and regulations in force whilst taking into consideration the economic theories and hypotheses (cf. Chapter 2), and industry characteristics (cf. Chapter 3) of the sector being reviewed. The relevant markets would be identified and defined using the SSNIP/HMT test and the 3CT test as described in Chapter 4. The markets are analysed, and if market power is established, one or more operators may/would be designated as dominant operators and the proportionate remedies imposed on them. If no market power is found, obligations (if any exist) may be removed from a previously designated dominant operator(s) – as Figure 5.12 depicts.

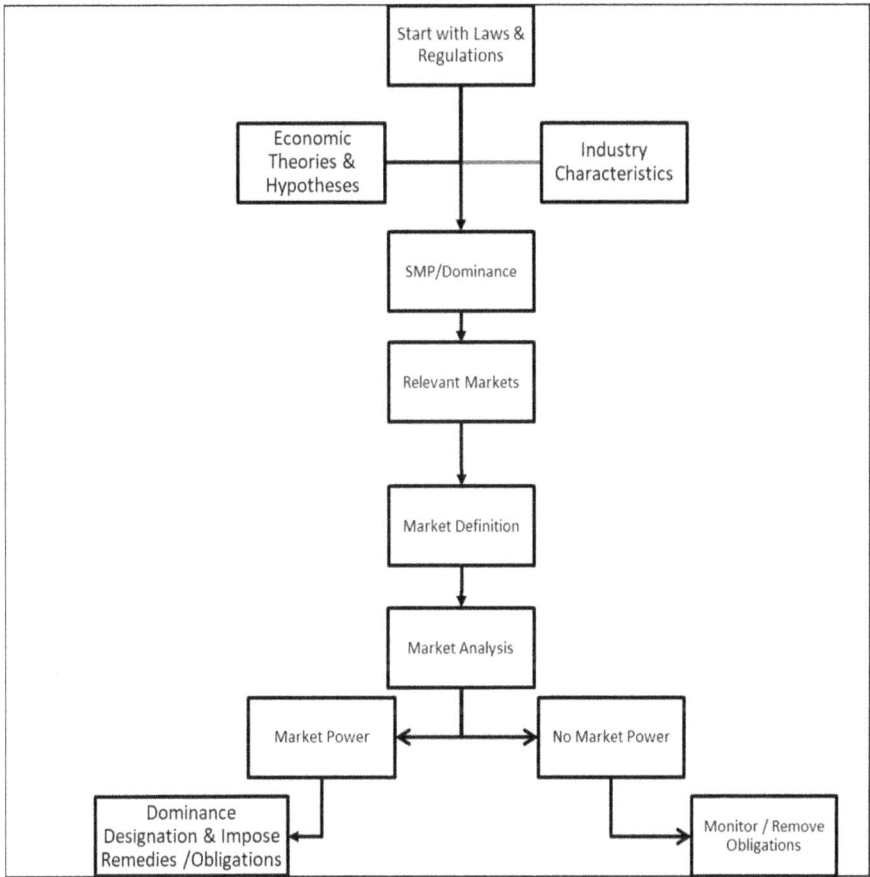

Figure 5.12 – SMP/Dominance Process using the more Detailed
Anatomy of the Art & Science of Regulation (c.f. Figure 5.10)

These examples illustrated in Figures 5.11 and 5.12 are simpler scenarios,
as the reader would appreciate in the next example illustrated in Figure
5.13.

Figure 5.13 illustrates the *general* use of the detailed anatomy of regulation
model of Figure 5.10 to Network Industries (as covered in the case studies
in Chapter 3). I would like to first acknowledge the brilliance of the
original version of this diagram from the Jaag & Trinkner (2009) classic
paper. I have made some minor updates from the original but 75% of what
Figure 5.13 still mirrors the original. The figure may at first sight look
complex, but Jaag & Trinkner's (2009) graphical depiction is sheer genius,

and is a clear illustration of the navigation and use of Figure 10's anatomy of regulation model to network industries.

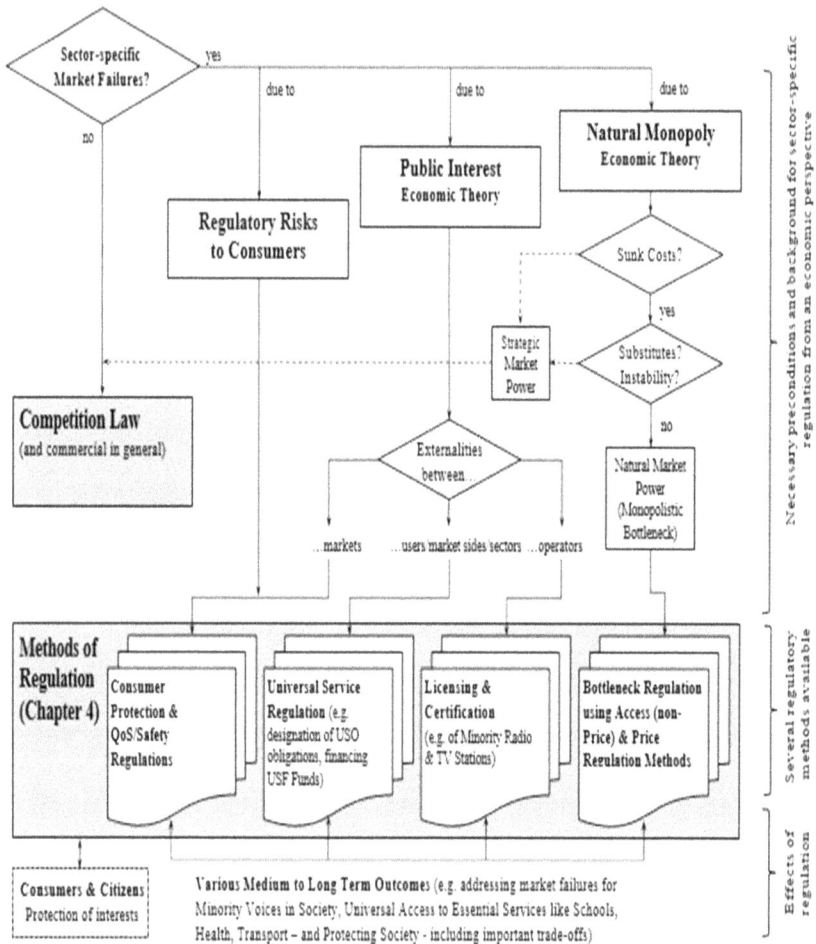

Figure 5.13 – A more general use of the Application of the detailed Anatomy Model of Regulation (i.e., Figure 5.10) to Network Industries
(Original Source of Diagram: Jaag & Trinkner, 2009[409] - with some updates by the Author; updated diagram printed with written permission of the original authors, Jaag & Trinkner)

---

[409] https://www.swiss-economics.ch/RePEc/files/0016JaagTrinkner.pdf

Let me highlight the following key essentials of Figure 5.13.

i.   **Starting from Formula II, navigate the Figure 10 detailed anatomy model of regulation to research the economic theories/hypotheses causes of the sector-specific market failures**: as Formula II stipulates, good [sector-specific] regulation addresses (or pre-empts *ex-ante*) market failures and checks the power of dominant players using the methods and remedies of regulation covered in Chapter 4. This is why the top of Figure 5.13 illustrates that if there are no sector-specific market failures observed, then the sector can default to horizontal competition law.

ii.   **In Case Persistent or Harmful Potential Market Failures, research the likely hypotheses theories of Harm**: in this case – and as the anatomy of regulation model of Figure 5.10 suggests – the regulator will research and evolve hypotheses of the likely reasons for the failures, of which there are usually several. In the case that I illustrate in Figure 5.13, there are possibly three theories/hypotheses including (i) Natural Monopoly (ii) Public Interest and (iii) Regulatory Risks to Consumers.

a.   The Natural Monopoly hypothesis when researched leads to a typical challenge of bottleneck regulation due the incumbents' irreplicable and Sunk monopoly assets. And as we see in the several case studies in Chapter 3, the classic methods of regulation of Chapter 4 applied include Access (non-price) regulation, Price Regulation and other methods such as Separation (Accounting, Finance & Structural) as shown in Table 5.3 earlier

b.   The Public Interest Theory when researched – as Figure 5.13 suggests - may confirm market failures and other negative externalities towards certain sections of society such as children, rural areas of the country not being covered with essential services, affordability challenges with the poor, market failures with minority groups such as sizeable immigrants populations, etc. Methods of regulation like Licensing & Certification may be employed to address some of such market failures, e.g. licensing minority radio/TV stations to give them voices in society, revising TV/Radio licence obligations if children are suffering negative externalities of being exposed to age-inappropriate content, Universal Service Regulations and USO designations to address rural vs. urban market failures and more.

c.   The Regulatory Risks to Consumers Theory when researched leads to the possible application of Consumer Protection, Quality of Service and Safety Regulations.

Therefore, the schematic of Figure 5.13 further and graphically demystifies (and simplifies) the art and science of regulation, as well as demonstrates a more complex use of the Inputs-Outputs model of Figure 5.10.

iii.   **There could be more hypotheses of sector-specific market failures than shown in Figure 5.13**: one of the beauties of the Jaag & Trinkner (2009)'s figure is that there could be more than three theories of harm than those shown. This figure shows how the Law (Competition laws and regulations), economic theories and Methods of Regulations come together in the process of regulation.

iv.   **The Bottom of Figure 5.13 illustrates Outcomes**: as covered in Section 5.6, 'outcomes' lag 'outputs'. The figure notes some of the expected outcomes in the medium to long term.

This brings us to the end of the illustrations of the demystifications and simplifications of the art and science of regulation in this chapter.

5.8 Regulation is indeed Complex and Nuanced, but it can be Demystified

In the Preface of this book, I opine that regulation is indeed both complex and nuanced. The 'complex' part should be clear as this entire book proves. The 'nuance' part means there are differences or distinctions in the meaning of regulation and how it is implemented, not least because it is both an art and a science – and there is much balancing involved as Section 5.5 explains. There are therefore many 'shades' to Good economic regulation, different refinements, subtleties than I cover in this chapter and book. The 'culture' of regulation of your country almost certainly adds other nuances to the nature and style of regulation in your local context.

So, it is indeed the case that Regulation is complex and nuanced, but it is capable of being demystified and simplified, as I hope this chapter in particular – and the rest of the book in general - demonstrate. I hope my dissection of the 'whole' of Good economic regulation into its many constituent parts across this book – and building them back together in this chapter, helps with the demystification. Even in regulation contexts which are genuinely more complicated, graphical representations of the market failures as shown in Figure 5.13 helps demystify and simplify the complexity.

5.9 Chapter Summary

This is an intensely *personal* chapter which gives the entire book its name. 'Personal' because I draw from all the wisdom and knowledge of the previous chapters in order to describe <u>my</u> perspective of both the art and science of day-to-day regulation done within regulatory agencies. Economic Regulation truly needs to be demystified – and this chapter has provided my perspective on this important task. Other practitioner economic regulators may want to write up and publish theirs too.

Chapter 6

The Future of Regulation: Challenges of Digital Platforms and Increasing Digitalisation

This chapter provides an overview of the challenges to the regulation of Digital Platforms as well as the challenges that come with increasing digitalisation of our economies. Digital platforms includes the likes of Google's ultra-dominant search engine platform and other platforms including and beyond FANGAM[410]. Additionally, this chapter discusses the challenges to regulating current network sectors with all the increasing digitalization happening with them. It also revisits the increasing roles of the different models of regulation (of Chapter 3) with increasing digitalization across our economies. Penultimately, it briefly overviews regulatory approaches to the increasing employment of Artificial Intelligence (AI) and Machine Learning technologies across our economies. Finally, it briefly overviews the issues involved in the emerging regulation of Cloud Computing, i.e. cloud computing regulation.

6.1 An Example Challenge of Regulating a [Mega] Digital Platform: Google and Alphabet v EC

Perhaps it is easier to introduce the challenges of regulating the mega digital platforms with a real example of the sort of *harms* that need regulating, and how difficult it is proving to regulate them. I draw this example from Nwana (2022), specifically from a section in the book where I ask the question: "Are the Gatekeeping companies to the Internet already too big to Regulate?" – page 132-138? 'Gatekeeping' – as the reader will find out later in this chapter – has a specific meaning. I am afraid that I concede that the answer to this question is largely Yes. In the section of the 2022 book, I recount the *Google and Alphabet vs. European*

---

[410] Facebook [Meta], Amazon, Netflix, Google [Alphabet], Apple & Microsoft

Commission case[411] (Moreno-Belloso, 2021) as follows (what I want the reader to get from the following narrative story is a flavour of some of the challenges in the day-to-day regulation of mega digital platforms).

In 2017, Google was fined a whopping €2.42bn by the EC for abusing its dominance in Online shopping. It was found to have done so by having consistently promoted its own shopping comparison service at the top of its own search results as shown in Figure 6.1.

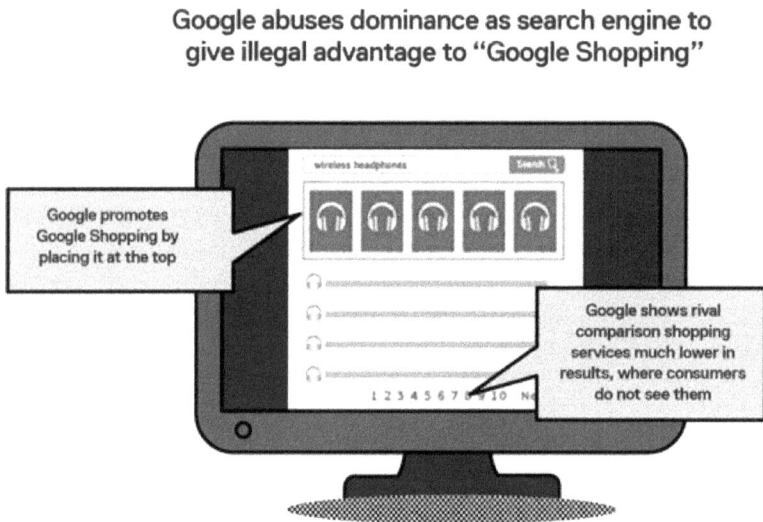

Figure 6.1 – Illustration of how Google abused its dominant position in Google Search to give advantage to Google Shopping
Source (Nwana, 2022, p. 133 – adapted from [412])

This broke EU antitrust or competition rules. Commissioner Vestager requested Google remedied this breach within 90 days or further penalties would be imposed of up to 5% of average daily worldwide turnover of Alphabet, Google's parent company. She noted:

---

[411] https://papers.ssrn.com/sol3/papers.cfm?abstract_id=3965639 - Google v Commission (Google Shopping): A Case Summary by Natalia Moreno Belloso :: SSRN - this is an excellent 6-page summary of a 140-page legal judgement.

[412] https://www.datafeedwatch.com/blog/everything-you-need-to-know-about-google-shopping-css - Google Shopping €2.42 Billion Fine - Right or Wrong? (datafeedwatch.com)

"Google has produced many innovative products and services that have literally revolutionised our lives. That's a good thing. But Google's strategy for its comparison-shopping service wasn't just about attracting customers by making its product better than those of its rivals. Instead, Google abused its market dominance as a search engine by promoting its own comparison-shopping service in its search results, and demoting those of competitors.

What Google has done is illegal under EU antitrust rules. It denied other companies the chance to compete on the merits and to innovate. And most importantly, it denied European consumers a genuine choice of services and the full benefits of innovation"[413].

Well, what do you think happened after such a clear EC finding? Some argue not much has changed and that the market has even deteriorated further, whilst most of the "abused" companies (i.e., the numerous comparison websites that entered the market) have exited the market[414]. Some argue Google has played the European regulatory system[415], stalling with the array of expensive lawyers it hired – and even worse, that Google may have engaged in propagating fake comparison sites to give the impression that the market is more competitive. Others have argued that the EC case was very weak.

However, wait for it, 3 years later in 2020 (after the fine), Google started its appeal against the shopping fine of 2017[416], arguing that the case had neither legal nor economic merit. It argued that the EC excluded key players such as Amazon out of its antitrust or competition analyses, thereby dragging another big West Coast (of USA) giant into the case.

In a statement to the BBC, Google said:

---

[413] https://ec.europa.eu/commission/presscorner/detail/en/IP_17_1784 - Antitrust: Commission fines Google €2.42 billion (europa.eu)

[414] https://www.theparliamentmagazine.eu/news/article/time-to-bring-google-shopping-case-to-a-close - Time to bring Google Shopping case to a close (theparliamentmagazine.eu)

[415] https://competition-cases.ec.europa.eu/cases/AT.39740 - Competition Policy (europa.eu) – see the process and investigations dating back to 2010 on this site on just this case

[416] https://www.bbc.co.uk/news/technology-51462397 - Google starts appeal against £2bn shopping fine - BBC News

"We're appealing [against] the European Commission's 2017 Google Shopping decision because it is wrong on the *law, the facts, and the economics.* Shopping ads have always helped people find the products they are looking for quickly and easily, and helped merchants to reach potential customers...we look forward to making our case in court and demonstrating that we have improved quality and increased choice for consumers"[417]. *The author's emphases.*

Well, here is what I think. These big digital platforms giants can drag cases out whilst some of those that brought the antitrust (competition) complaints against them just fall by the wayside. As the BBC article notes, *"one of the lead complainants in this Google Shopping [Foundem] case filed its complaint about Google as far back as 2009! Google was finally fined in 2017".* Google starts appealing the fine in 2020.

I live in Europe, and it is factual that the numerous comparison web sites that emerged after 2010 have literally all disappeared. However, it is also factually true that Google innovated and innovates their Google Shopping service much better than the imitation comparison sites that came up, and so they arguably fell away because consumers 'voted' with their clicks for a better comparison service in Google Shopping. Nevertheless, we do not know how many truly innovative and potentially competitive comparison websites fell away too because their marketing budgets dried out as they tried to get themselves from page 4 (see Figure 6.1) to the first page on Google search. So, I think the Google Shopping argument of – 'hey look over there too, consumers compare using Amazon' - is just convenient. Pointing to yet another American Internet behemoth when the major harm is the thousands of EU comparison websites who did not stand a chance is a convenient diversion.

In the meantime, Google has changed the shopping box to show both its own ads and the ads of other shopping comparison services who can bid for these advertising slots. Google's slots are of course assured.

As an addendum to this case, this record €2.42bn Google antitrust fine was upheld by Europe's second-highest court who dismissed Google's challenge to the fine. "The General Court largely dismisses Google's action against the decision of the Commission finding that Google abused its dominant position by favouring its own comparison-shopping service

---

[417] *Ibid.*

over competing comparison-shopping services," the Court said in a press release in November 2021[418].

When I wrote about this above back in 2022, I noted that "Google is likely to appeal to the higher EU Court of Justice (CJEU). The saga continues after an already seven-year investigation" (Nwana, 2022, p.136).

Well – guess what? They did! Google's appeal against that judgment is currently pending before the Court of Justice (C-48/22 P), as can be seen on the EC's web page[419]. On this page, the reader will find that this appeal is still live as of January 2024, with the latest Opinion [at the time of writing] being delivered on 11th January 2024[420].

What I really want you the reader to take away from this excursion into the Google (Search) Shopping case is threefold:

(i) how difficult it is for even some of the best-resourced antitrust agencies in the world (the EC) to check and control the Internet giants or mega Digital platforms like Google/Alphabet.

(ii) how long it takes and what happens to the "abused" firms in that time. As a summary, starting from a 2009 Foundem antitrust complaint, leading to a 2017 whopping €2.42bn fine, an appeal by Google 3 years later in 2020, a decision by the General Court in November 2021, followed by a final appeal by Google to the CJEU – and the saga is still going on as I write in early 2024!

(iii) how nuanced some of the arguments are. For example, see more on this Kluwer Competition Law Blog[421].

---

[418] https://curia.europa.eu/jcms/upload/docs/application/pdf/2021-11/cp210197en.pdf - The General Court largely dismisses Google's action against the decision of the Commission finding that Google abused its dominant position by favouring its own comparison shopping service over competing comparison shopping services (europa.eu)

[419] https://curia.europa.eu/juris/documents.jsf?num=C-48/22 - CURIA - List of results (europa.eu)

[420] https://curia.europa.eu/juris/document/document.jsf;jsessionid=D3CB279665B8382CE5CB52807B72E232?text=&docid=281162&pageIndex=0&doclang=en&mode=req&dir=&occ=first&part=1&cid=2678169 - CURIA - Documents (europa.eu)

[421] https://competitionlawblog.kluwercompetitionlaw.com/2021/11/15/google-shopping-the-general-court-takes-its-position/ - Google Shopping: The General Court takes its position - Kluwer Competition Law Blog

For a book of this nature on the theory, methods and practice of regulation, it is important the reader is introduced to the challenges of regulating the mega-digital platforms by example of real-world challenges as covered in this Google and Alphabet vs. EC Google Shopping Case in this section. Nwana (2022) overviews many other cases involving these mega digital platforms.

6.2 What are Digital Platforms and their Characteristics?

It is important to be clear on what constitutes Digital Platforms and what they are not. The seminal OECD (2019) report/book defines online [digital] platforms as:

> "digital services that that *facilitate interactions between two or more distinct but independent sets of users (whether firms or individuals)* who interact through the service via the Internet. This definition excludes businesses such as direct business-to-consumer (B2C), e-commerce and ad-free content streaming, as those serve only one set of consumers. It does, however, include businesses such as third-party B2C e-commerce and ad-supported content streaming, because those services involve *two separate sets of users*" – the author's emphasis.

Therefore, these ICT [digital] platforms facilitate *interactions* between *two or more independent groups* of platform users. Indeed, the analogue (non-digital) world can boast of platforms too, like shopping malls/centres where third-party mall owners seek to match two independent groups of platform users: in this case, mall owners match shops to customers. Stock exchanges are platforms because buyers of shares are matched with sellers. Even village markets are platforms too because sellers of fresh produce get matched and transact with buyers who need the fresh vegetables and more. Newspapers and magazine publishers are platforms who attract distinct [sets] of readers and advertisers. University research parks platforms attract distinct new company start-ups and matches them with investors, and in some cases university academics with expertise to support the R&D of the start-ups.

However, there are more to digital platforms than their analogue equivalents, hence, the question of what are the characteristics of Digital

Platforms? The OECD (2019) paper notes the following key economic characteristics of Digital Platforms, beyond the fact that they facilitate interactions between two or more distinct groups of platform users.

i. **Positive *direct* network effects (same-side network effects)**: a digital platform benefits from direct network effects when its value to its users increases as more online users use it. These network effects is also called "same side", as the value of users on one side of the market increases as other users join that side of the market. Social media and Instant Messaging (IM) platforms enjoy similar same-side network effects because the utility of the platform increases as the user base on the same side increases. For example, you are more inclined to join Facebook if most of your family members are already on it, increasing the utility to both you and the rest of your family. However, not all digital platforms have positive direct network effects. Dating platforms for example would typically have negative direct effects because you may choose *not* to join the platform at all if you realise some relatives or exes are already members on it. You may not want them to know your personal life business. Although alongside any such negative effects, there are also positive network effects on dating apps because an app is more attractive to a new user if it includes a larger number of potential dating partners.

ii. **Positive *indirect* network effects [422] (two-side or multi-side network effects)**: in addition to "same side" network effects above, digital platforms typically also benefit from "cross-side" network effects too, wherein the value or utility to users on one side of the market increases as the number of users on the other side of the market increases. So, positive indirect network effects occur when a distinct group of platform users (e.g., third-party sellers on a B2C platform) benefit as more users from another distinct group join the platform (e.g., buyers who use the platform). This is because multi-sided platforms or markets connect two or

---

[422] Indirect network effect, not direct, arises from the interaction between different sides of the market - the value of the platform to one side (app buyers) is increased by the number of users on the other side (app developers/sellers).

more independent segments/groups, and use intermediation or matchmaking. Mobile operating systems stores like iOS and Android are digital marketplaces that bring together app developers who list their apps on these marketplaces, and app buyers who buy and download the apps. The value of the market to buyers increase as more apps are listed on the marketplace, i.e., the buyers' value depends on the interaction with the other side of the market, the number of app providers. Groups/segments include (i) the billions of consumers that actively use platforms like Facebook or Google (ii) the advertisers who flock to be matched with the consumers they seek (iii) suppliers of goods and services who are attracted to such platforms, (iv) media content creators, etc. The emergence of these different "sides" just reinforces the concentration of these digital platforms.

iii.   **Cross-subsidisation**: this characteristic builds on the former one, i.e., benefitting from the multi-sided nature of some digital markets. More specifically, digital platforms subsidise the growing of the user base on one side of the platform. For example, it makes much rational business sense for search engines or social media sites like Facebook/TikTok to make access to their platforms free to users. They also deploy their marketing budgets in growing the number of users joining their platforms – not because they would make profitable revenues from these Facebook/TikTok users – but because they know they would benefit from advertising revenues on the *other side* of the digital platform. So, one side offers 'free' services, cross-subsidised by advertising revenues from the other side.

iv.   **Scale without mass**: this characteristic is classically unique of digital platforms. "Scale without mass" was famously coined in the title of the Brynjolfsson *et al.* (2008) paper. 'Mass' – in this context - refers to a firms' physical presence in the location of the user or the customer's market. This scale without mass phenomenon refers to the possibility to grow exponentially, quickly and extensively – but inexpensively – in comparison to scaling up physical goods businesses. This is due to the "extremely low and still dwindling unit costs for processing, storing, replicating and transmitting data" (OECD, 2019). This leads to platforms like Google growing to serving billions of people without much tangible increase in CapEx and OpEx costs. Scale without mass is also tax-problematic because the attribution of profits is/was both based on physical characteristics, and was used to align profits (and taxation) with value creation[423]. No longer!

v.   **Potential global reach**: this is unarguable. According to the respected Statista, as of October 2023, more than 3 Billion users log onto to the Facebook platform every month, 2.491 Billion (YouTube), 2 Billion (WhatsApp) and 2 Billion (Instagram)[424].

vi. **Panoramic scope**: this refers to another phenomenon where some digital platform companies benefit from economies of scope due to two or more services that they provide on the platform, or across platforms. This is more typically referred to as an ecosystem effect. Consider the panoramic scope allegation across two Google/Alphabet services of the previous section - that Google abused its market dominance as a *search engine* by promoting its own *comparison-shopping service* (Google Shopping) in its search results, and demoting those of competitors (see Figure 6.1). Google's economies of scope derives from its extensive data collection activities on users' behaviour across its platforms 'constellation' of Google Search, YouTube, Google Maps, Google Shopping, Google News and Google Gmail (see Figure 6.2 later). Facebook also experiences panoramic economies of scope by allowing Instagram to use Facebook's advertising infrastructure and ecosystem.

vii. **Generation and use of 'Big data'**: this is unarguable too. Non-digital businesses do generate and exploit user data, but not on the incredible scale of digital platforms. The sheer volume, variety and velocity of the data being stored and analysed is simply mindboggling. Big data is real, and *big data technologies* describe a new generation of technologies and architectures, designed to economically extract value from very large volumes of a wide

---

423

https://www.researchgate.net/publication/343154097_Scale_without_Mass_Permanent_E stablishments_in_the_Digital_Economy - "Scale without mass is problematic because the current definition of nexus under Article 5 of the 2017 OECD Model Tax Convention and the attribution of profits under Articles 7 and 9 are both based on physical characteristics used to align profits (and taxation) with value creation" – Source:

424 https://www.semrush.com/blog/most-popular-social-media-platforms/ - 28 Top Social Media Platforms Worldwide (semrush.com)

variety of data, by enabling high-velocity capture, discovery, and/or analysis[425]. This only happens on digital platforms. It is highly creative the way digital platforms make use of data, which differs depending on the business model. Consider the case of advertising-funded platforms like *Google and Facebook/Meta which use data to build up a personalised profile of individuals in order to charge higher prices to advertisers for targeted advertising to them*. Netflix obtains less value from personalised data, but it uses data on individuals' viewing patterns to improve the quality of the platform's recommendations, and to inform the choice of new content to invest in.

viii.   **Disruptive innovation**: the most successful digital platforms are the most disruptive, i.e., they drastically alter markets leading to new ones – and they are not incremental. Just consider how e-shopping has drastically altered shopping habits with platforms like Amazon and eBay. Also in January 2007, Apple Founder - the Late Steve Jobs - changed the ICT world with the first iPhone. Steve Jobs debuted the iPhone as follows:

> "Well, today we're introducing three revolutionary products of this class. The first one is a *widescreen iPod with touch controls*. The second is *a revolutionary mobile phone.* And the third is a *breakthrough Internet communications device.* So, three things: a widescreen iPod with touch controls; a revolutionary mobile phone; and a breakthrough Internet communications device. An iPod, a phone, and an Internet communicator. An iPod, a phone… are you getting it? These are not three separate devices, this is one device, and we are calling it iPhone. Today, Apple is going to reinvent the phone, and here it is".
>
> Transcript of Steve Jobs iPhone 2007 Presentation[426]

As they say, the rest is history. The iPhone drastically disrupted the ICT industry and all the old PSTN value chains (see Nwana, 2022, p.120-122).

---

[425] https://journalofbigdata.springeropen.com/articles/10.1186/s40537-016-0059-y

[426] https://singjupost.com/steve-jobs-iphone-2007-presentation-full-transcript/ - Steve Jobs iPhone 2007 Presentation (Full Transcript) – The Singju Post

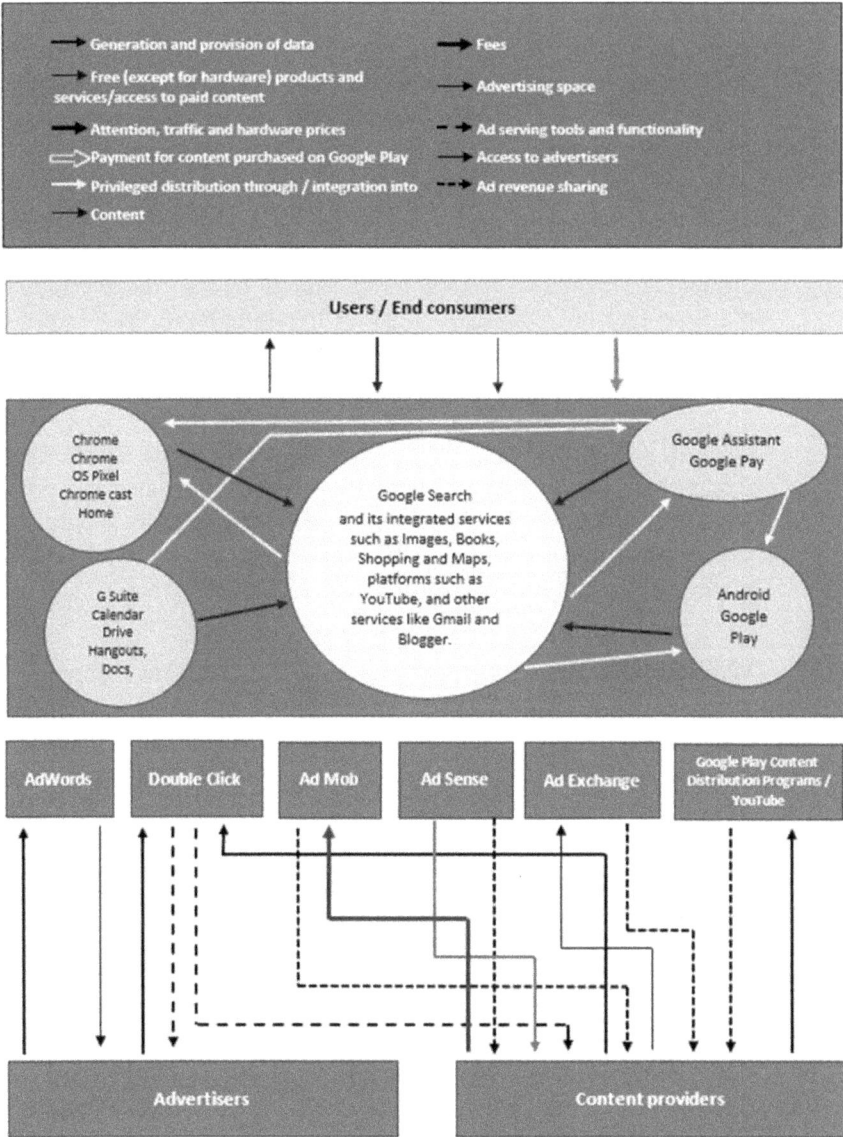

Figure 6.2 – The Google Ecosystem

(Adapted from Source [427])

[427] https://read.oecd-ilibrary.org/science-and-technology/an-introduction-to-online-platforms-and-their-role-in-the-digital-transformation_53e5f593-en#page159 - An Introduction to Online Platforms and Their Role in the Digital Transformation | READ online (oecd-ilibrary.org), p. 159.

ix.   **Switching Costs (& Lock ins) & Default Bias**: this is unarguable also. The barriers to switching from some mega digital platforms are just humongous - just think about the last time you used Bing instead of Google, or how difficult it is to switch from Google Android to Apple iOS and vice versa! Users tend to be locked-in into such digital platforms. It is non-trivial to transfer a personalised account profile from Facebook (with all the photos, videos, posts, product information, and profiled data) to another digital platform like TikTok. The data is tied to the particular platform and its ecosystem. Look at the complexity of Google's ecosystem of illustrated in Figure 6.2. It is truly one to behold. However in the interest of scholarship, it is important I note that though there are these switching costs involved, they are often due more to *behavioural effects* than physical difficulties. It is straightforward to install and use search apps provided by competitors to Google such as Bing. But very few people do so, in part due to *default bias*, e.g. this was a finding in the UK CMA's market study on Online platforms and digital advertising[428].

x.   **Winner-take-all or winner-take-most or 'Tipping' markets**: when one combines, *inter alia*, positive network effects, economies of scale, scope and the generation and use of big data – some digital platforms exhibit winner-take-all or winner-take-most tendencies. As OECD (2019) highlights, it took just 4.5 years after launch for Facebook to achieve 100 million users, compared to 16 years for the world to get to 100 million mobile phones, and 75 years to reach 100 million fixed/wired phones. With more than 3 Billion logging onto the Facebook every month, 2.491 Billion onto YouTube, 2 Billion onto WhatsApp and 2 Billion onto Instagram[429] - these platforms have 'won' until further revolutions happen. This winner-take-all/winner-take-most phenomenon is also called *tipping markets*. This is arguably best illustrated by looking at the market shares and how much larger are say Google's market share in Search, Android in Mobile OS and Amazon's in e-commerce compared to their rivals – see Figure 6.5 which clearly illustrates the former two for Brazil.

---

[428]https://www.gov.uk/cma-cases/online-platforms-and-digital-advertising-market-study.

[429] https://www.semrush.com/blog/most-popular-social-media-platforms/ - 28 Top Social Media Platforms Worldwide (semrush.com)

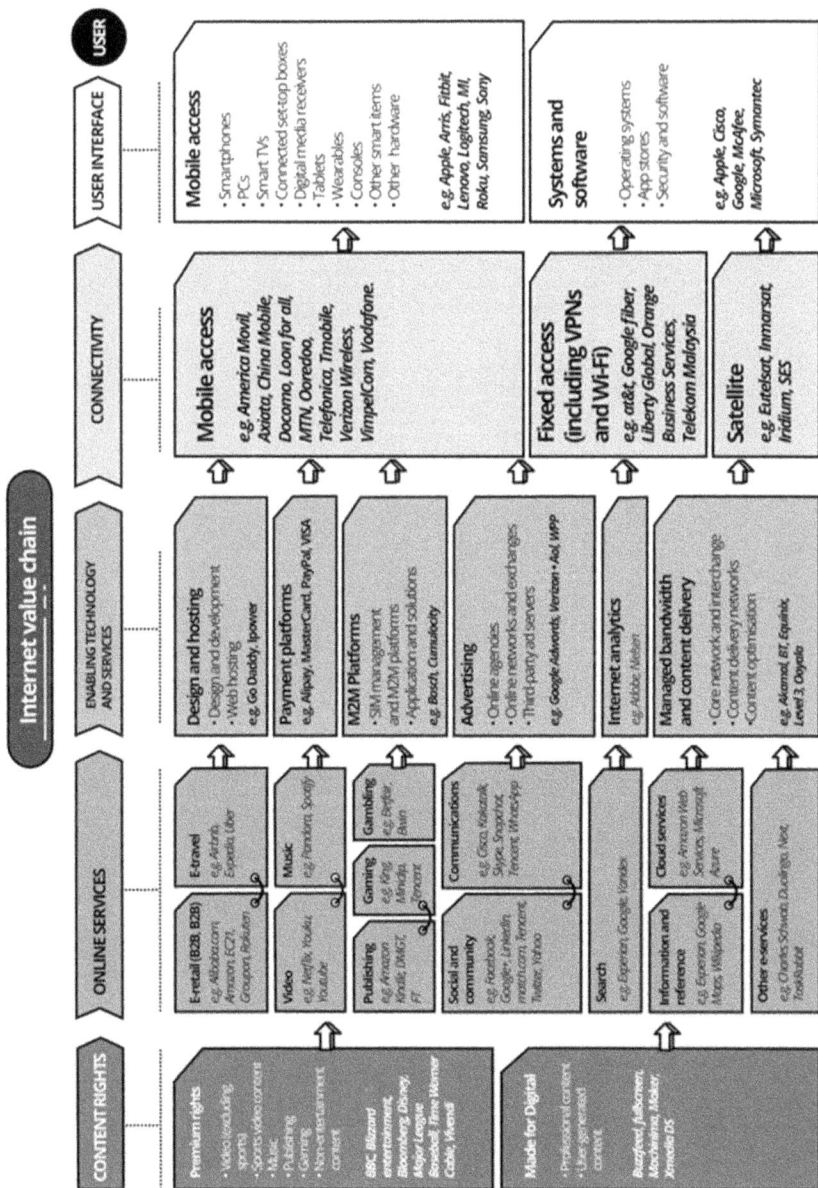

Figure 6.3a—The GSMA/A.T. Kearney 2016 Internet Value Chain
(Source: Adapted from [430])
(Reproduced with permission of the GSMA)

---

[430] https://www.gsma.com/solutions-and-impact/connectivity-for-good/public-policy/wp-content/uploads/2016/05/GSMA_The-internet-Value-Chain_WEB.pdf

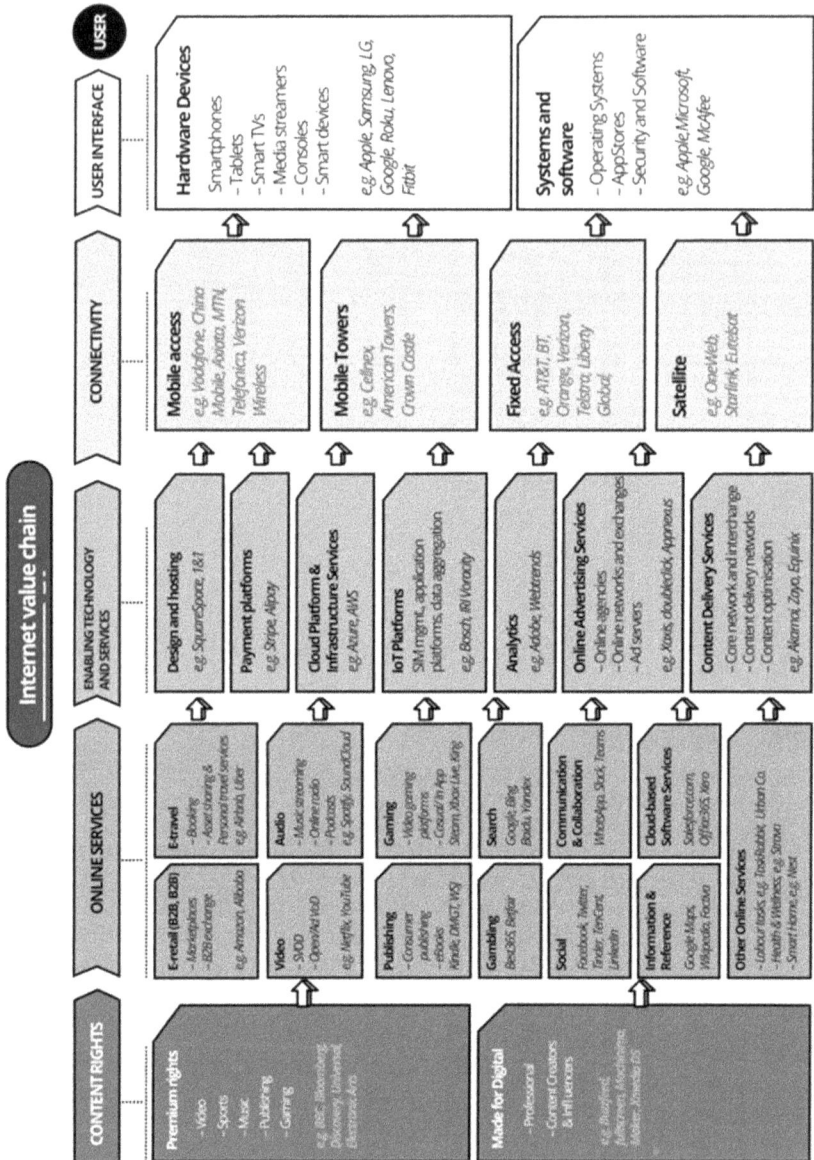

Internet value chain

CONTENT RIGHTS

Premium rights
- Video
- Sports
- Music
- Publishing
- Gaming

e.g. BBC, Bloomberg, Discovery, Universal, Electronic Arts

Made for Digital
- Professional
- Content Creators & Influencers

e.g. Buzzfeed, Johnson & Murphy, Miller, Xhosetta BS

ONLINE SERVICES

E-retail (B2B, B2B)
- Marketplaces
- B2B exchange

e.g. Amazon, Alibaba

Video
- SVOD
- OpenVoD

e.g. Netflix, YouTube

E-travel
- Booking
- Asset sharing & Personal travel services

e.g. Airbnb, Uber

Audio
- Music streaming
- Online radio
- Podcasts

e.g. Spotify, SoundCloud

Publishing
- Consumer publishing
- eBooks

Kindle, DMGT, WSJ

Gaming
- Video gaming platforms
- Casual/in-app

Steam, Xbox Live, King

Gambling
Bet365, Betfair

Search
Google, Bing
Baidu, Yandex

Social
Facebook, Twitter,
Tinder, TenCent
LinkedIn

Communication & Collaboration
WhatsApp, Slack, Teams

Information & Reference
Google Maps,
Wikipedia, Factiva

Cloud-based Software Services
Salesforce.com,
Office365, Xero

Other Online Services
- Labour tasks e.g. TaskRabbit, Urban Co.
- Health & Wellness e.g. Simon
- Smart Home e.g. Nest

ENABLING TECHNOLOGY AND SERVICES

Design and hosting
e.g. SquareSpace, 1&1

Payment platforms
e.g. Stripe, Alipay

Cloud Platform & Infrastructure Services
e.g. Azure, AWS

IoT Platforms
SIM mgmt., application platforms, data aggregation
e.g. Bosch, RTI Veronity

Analytics
e.g. Adobe, Webtrends

Online Advertising Services
- Online agencies
- Online networks and exchanges
- Ad servers
e.g. Xandr, doubleclick, Appnexus

Content Delivery Services
- Core network and interchange
- Content delivery networks
- Content optimisation
e.g. Akamai, Zayo, Equinix

CONNECTIVITY

Mobile access
e.g. Vodafone, China Mobile, Axiata, MTN, Telefonica, Verizon Wireless

Mobile Towers
e.g. Cellnex, American Towers, Crown Castle

Fixed Access
e.g. AT&T, BT, Orange, Verizon, Telstra, Liberty Global

Satellite
e.g. OneWeb, Starlink, Eutelsat

USER INTERFACE

Hardware Devices
- Smartphones
- Tablets
- Smart TVs
- Media streamers
- Consoles
- Smart devices
e.g. Apple, Samsung, LG, Google, Roku, Lenovo, Fitbit

Systems and software
- Operating Systems
- AppStores
- Security and Software
e.g. Apple, Microsoft, Google, McAfee

USER

Figure 6.3b - The GSMA/A.T. Kearney 2022 Internet Value Chain
(Source: [431]) - (Reproduced with permission of the GSMA)

---

[431] https://www.gsma.com/solutions-and-impact/connectivity-for-good/public-policy/wp-content/uploads/2022/05/Internet-Value-Chain-2022-1.pdf - Internet-Value-Chain-2022-1.pdf (gsma.com)

Once again, the Google ecosystem shown in Figure 6.2 arguably shows how the winner-take-all or winner-take-most 'natural monopoly' emanates with such a complex value-driven ecosystem. It is understood that these characteristics present challenges to the regulation of digital platforms, well beyond those of network industries covered in Chapter 3. I use 'natural monopoly' in inverted commas in order to make the point that traditional natural monopolies, as per Chapter 2, arise from the *cost side/supply side* economies of scale, whereas winner-takes-most in digital markets is driven as much by the *demand side* such as network effects.

6.3 Examples of Digital Platforms

The last two sections (6.1 & 6.2) have mentioned some key digital platforms such as Google Search, YouTube, Facebook and Instagram. It is arguably best to illustrate comprehensively the variety of digital platforms today by drawing from GSMA's Internet Value Chain (IVC). About the IVC: "the GSMA commissioned this research to construct a high-level view of the internet economy—the players, economic analysis of different segments and the competitive landscape. We sought a factual assessment, based on available data, of all of the links in the internet value chain to better understand the trends and dynamics [432]". The IVC has gone through three significant iterations: 2010, 2016 and 2022, see Nwana (2022).

The 2022 IVC is shown in Figure 6.3b. I do not dwell much on an expansive description of the IVC here as it is covered in GSMA (2022) and Nwana (2022). In summary, as Figure 6.3 clearly depicts, the IVC has five distinct segments: Content Rights, Online Services, Enabling Technology & Services, Internet Access Connectivity and User Interface. The sub-services in these segments are clearly identified in bold in Figure 6.3a and Figure 6.3b. These segments are replete with digital platforms as shown in Table 6.1.

---

[432] Foreword of paper, by John Giusti, Chief Regulatory Officer, GSMA, May 2016, GSMA | The Internet Value Chain: A study on the economics of the internet | Public Policy - https://www.gsma.com/publicpolicy/resources/internet-value-chain-study-economics-internet

IVC Segment	Sub-Segment	Digital Platform Description	Examples
Content Rights	*Made for Digital*	Users can access news, videos, information collated from two or more types of producers (e.g., citizen journalists, content creators, 3rd party news houses like the BBC, etc). More importantly, access users can interact with journalists, content creators, etc.	X/Twitter Instagram
Online Services	*E-Retail (B2B, B2C)*	Two distinct groups (i.e., buyers and sellers) are matched commercially for products and services. They interact to transact.	Alibaba Amazon Store Google Shopping Facebook marketplace eBay Zalando
	Search	Two distinct groups of users are matched: information query seekers are matched to information provided by other users on websites in a ranked fashion.	Google Bing Baidu Yandex Yahoo!
	Social *Communication & Collaboration*	Two distinct groups of users are matched to connect with, share, collaborate, exchange personal, user-generated information and content - with another set of users (including content and information created by 3rd parties such as media publishers). Interaction is the name of the game.	Facebook Instagram X/Twitter Pinterest Tinder Tencent LinkedIn WeChat WhatsApp Snapchat TikTok
	Gaming *Gambling*	Two distinct groups of users are matched and interact: gamers and game creators and producers (including games created and produced by 3rd parties and uploaded into gaming repository).	Steam Xbox Live King Bet365

		Games can play 'live' against other games. Gamblers are also matched with creators and producers of gambling apps and games (including a variety of 3rd-party games and apps) – and they can bet against other 'live' users.	Betfair
	E-Travel	Two distinct groups (i.e., buyers and sellers) are matched who interact commercially for Personal travel services, bookings and asset sharing	Booking.com Airbnb
	Video *Audio* *Information & Reference*	Two distinct groups are matched – and can interact: Uploaders and/or creators of music, videos, music and miscellaneous other content - e.g. maps, reference information, etc. uploaded into a digital repository & Users (information seekers) who access the repository.	Netflix YouTube Spotify Soundcloud Google Maps Wikipedia Factiva
Enabling Technology & Services	*Payment Platforms*	Matches payers to payees who interact.	Apple Pay Alipay PayPal Google Pay
User Interface	*Software & Systems*	Two distinct groups (i.e., buyers and sellers of apps, operating systems and software licenses) are matched and interact commercially for products and services.	Apple App Store Google Play Store Microsoft McAfee

Table 6.1 – A Typology of Digital Platforms - derived from GSMA's Internet Value Chain – GSMA (2022)'s Figure 6.3a and 6.3b

These digital platforms in Table 6.1 are not meant to be exhaustive of all the digital platforms out there, but they are arguably representative of the typical types of digital platforms across the Internet Value Chain - that are regulated. Some of the platforms are 'free' to use for some users (e.g., Facebook), whilst others are not (e.g., Airbnb). Others provide premium and basic services (e.g., LinkedIn), often using a *'freemium'* business model where basic services are free to users and there is a subscription charge for a premium service. Spotify is another high-profile example of this model.. Some of the digital platforms in Table 6.1 "combine" into a 'constellation of platforms' or 'superplatform' (OECD, 2019), e.g., see Google's 'constellation' of Figure 6.2. As commented above, in regulatory circles superplatforms are most commonly referred to as *'ecosystems'*.

Many of these platforms engage in wide scale user (data) collection activities with sophisticated algorithms, e.g. Google, Bing, Facebook, TikTok, etc. – partly in order to facilitate interactions between groups of platform users. Such interaction-enabling capabilities are the key attribute to them being platforms.

Note that not all the subsegments of the IVC (Figure 6.2) possess digital platforms in Table 6.1. This is because "not all digital products and services provided on the Internet are supplied on a digital platform" (Decker, 2023, p. 457). For example, the 'Cloud Platform & Infrastructure Services' 'sub-segment' services provided by the likes of Azure, Dropbox and AWS are typically *not* digital platforms since they do *not* facilitate interactions between two or more groups of users. They simply provide cloud and infrastructure services to their users. The same applies to 'Design & Hosting Cloud-Based Software Services'.

Likewise, even though BBC News and Bloomberg News users can access news, videos, information collated from two or more types producers (i.e., exclusive content, other content creators, publishers and advertisers) – these platforms do *not* facilitate interactions amongst these user groups. So they are *not* digital platforms. Some argue that my claim here is arguable, e.g. they argue that advertising funded services which are provided free to users do generally involve interaction between different sides of the market indirectly (*indirect network effects*). The interactions have to be more 'direct', but I acknowledge the strength of counterarguments. The largely *physical* 'Internet Access Connectivity' connections (see Figure 6.3) are evidently not digital platforms either.

6.4 Why Regulate Digital Platforms

I hope the Google and Alphabet v EC of Section 6.1 should have already convinced the reader that, at least, the Google mega platform or 'constellation' needs to be regulated.

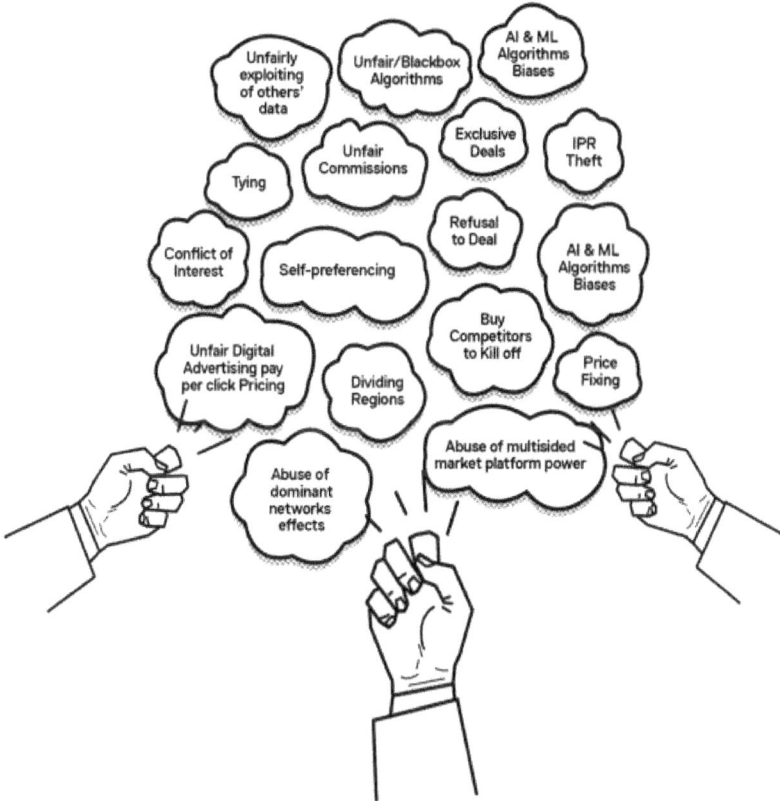

Figure 6.4 – Some Typical Big Tech Competition Harms
Source: Nwana (2022), p. 214

However, I also hope the reader agrees at this juncture that there is nothing quite 'standard' about regulating digital platforms. As Table 6.1 proves, digital platforms come in all shapes, hues and sizes, from search engines like Google to digital payment systems like Paypal, from social network platforms like X/Twitter to online content aggregation video/audio platforms like YouTube, from online marketplaces like eBay/Amazon to information/reference platforms like Wikipedia or Google Maps.

There are good reasons, though, to regulate these platforms anyway. Indeed, there are economic and non-economic reasons for regulating digital platforms.

6.4.1 Economic Reasons for regulating digital platforms

The economic reasons relate to the many theories of harms to both competition and consumers that come with these digital platforms, and their typical Big Tech FANGAM owners.

In Figure 6.4, I capture some of the typical Big Tech theories of harms that I derived from many case studies I cover in Nwana (2022), along with their associated narratives. I want the reader to be able to better appreciate how the harms materialise in reality. The reader will realise these harms are consistent with the characteristics of digital platforms covered in Section 6.2.

- *Conflicts of Interest:* there are typical strong conflict of interests concerns between upstream platform activities and downstream ones when carried out by the same platform owner. For example, Amazon operates in both its upstream intermediation market for businesses (i.e., Amazon's merchants upstream marketplace) and the downstream retail markets, i.e., Amazon runs the platform and also sells its own products on the platform. See EC. vs Amazon case in Chapter 2 of Nwana (2022).

- *Refusal to Deal*: practically all of the Big Tech dominant platforms like Google, Facebook or Amazon have been accused at one time of refusing to deal with rivals in adjacent markets. This is *discrimination*, and it can be anti-competitive because refusal to deal is not always anti-competitive. An example is Google Search's alleged discrimination against Google's vertical rivals. Google Search has clear-cut monopoly power for general-purpose – or horizontal – online search. The allegation here is whether Google is *abusing* this horizontal search market power in specialised – or vertical – search areas? See again the Google constellation of Figure 6.2 to see how easy it can happen or happens.

- *Self-preferencing:* Is it really right that Google Search always prioritises higher its own products and properties? Should this be prohibited? So does Goggle unfairly promote its own vertical properties like Google Maps, Google Local and Google Trips over competitors, i.e. over others like MapQuest, Yelp and Expedia respectively?

- *Tying:* Google has been charged with alleged tying Google Search (which it is clearly most dominant in) with its Google Play app store - bad. Google has also allegedly not only been tying Google Search to its Google Play app store, but also its web browser [Google Chrome] too – even worse. These Google actions allegedly led to the exit of Windows Phone and Symbian devices, which have fallen by the wayside.

- *Unfair commissions:* Apple and Google typically take a commission of up to 30% on digital sales from their apps stores, and for in-app purchases such as subscriptions. In Nwana (2022), I note that South Korean lawmakers see this as anti-competitive and have banned this practice there, and have even fined Apple and Google for breaching these bans[433].

- *Predatory Pricing:* a monopolist that prices its products or services below costs to drive out competitors is engaging in predatory pricing. Amazon, for example, has been accused of this unfair practice during its acquisition attempt of Quidsi, the parent company of online baby-products retailer Diapers.com. After Quidsi refused Amazon's initial offer to purchase it, Amazon allegedly cut its prices for substitute baby products below costs, and this move started impeding Quidsi's growth. Quidsi relented and accepted Amazon's offer, after which Amazon allegedly increased its prices for baby products[434]. This is classic predatory pricing – and it can happen in your market too with these dominant digital platforms.

---

[433] https://en.yna.co.kr/view/AEN20231006005300320 - S. Korea seeks 68 bln won of fines on Google, Apple for in-app billing irregularities | Yonhap News Agency (yna.co.kr)

[434] https://sgp.fas.org/crs/misc/R45910.pdf?utm_source=morning_brew - Antitrust and "Big Tech" (fas.org)

- *Abuse of dominant networks effects:* a digital platform benefits from network effects when its value to its users increases as more online users use it. Mobile operating systems stores like iOS and Android are marketplaces that bring together app developers who list their apps in these marketplaces and app buyers who buy and download the apps. The value of the market to buyers increase as more apps are listed on the marketplace,. Apple iOS and Google Android have been accused of having used dominant network same side effects to accelerate the convergence to just two operating systems. Other smartphone manufacturers can hardly deviate from these two OSs including previous ones like Blackberry.

- *Abuse of multisided market platform power:* in addition to "same side" network effects above, digital platforms typically also benefit from "cross-side" network effects too, wherein the value to users on one side of the market increases as the number of users on the other side of the market increases. In the Google Search/Shopping vs. EC case (of Section 6.1 above), Google allegedly abused its dominant position in Google Search to give advantage to Google Shopping.

- *Dividing regions,* e.g., tacit agreements between two firms not to compete against one another in some geographies or some relevant markets whilst competing in others.

- *Exclusive deals,* e.g. in the Apple Music vs. EC case Apple [EC vs. Apple Music[435]], Apple's rules allegedly prevent app developers from informing users who buy their apps on the Apple App Store that they could have alternative purchasing possibilities outside Apple App store, including from the websites of the apps developers themselves. The apps would be typically cheaper on the developers' websites than from Apple App store. As another example, the European Commission (EC) found Google to be dominant with its Android mobile OS, Google Play Store, and fined the Internet giant €4.34 billion in 2018 for anti-competitive practices[436]. In part, Google is accused of using

---

[435] https://ec.europa.eu/commission/presscorner/detail/en/ip_20_1073 - Antitrust: Commission opens investigations into Apple (europa.eu)

[436] The European Commission, Case numbered 40099 Google Android Decision, 40099_9993_3.pdf (europa.eu) - https://ec.europa.eu/competition/antitrust/cases/dec_docs/40099/40099_9993_3.pdf

its *gateway* dominance in Mobile OS to cement the dominance of its Search engine even further through *exclusive* tying.

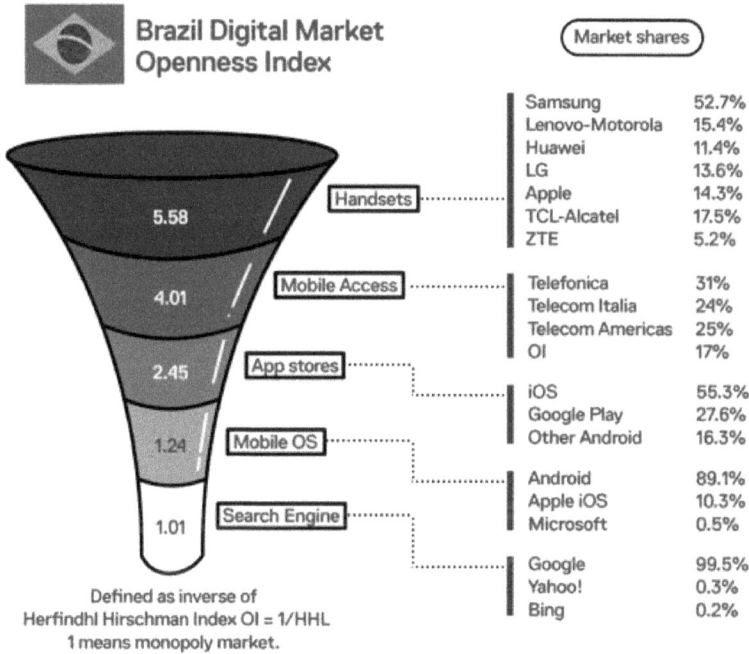

	Market shares
Samsung	52.7%
Lenovo-Motorola	15.4%
Huawei	11.4%
LG	13.6%
Apple	14.3%
TCL-Alcatel	17.5%
ZTE	5.2%
Telefonica	31%
Telecom Italia	24%
Telecom Americas	25%
OI	17%
iOS	55.3%
Google Play	27.6%
Other Android	16.3%
Android	89.1%
Apple iOS	10.3%
Microsoft	0.5%
Google	99.5%
Yahoo!	0.3%
Bing	0.2%

Brazil Digital Market Openness Index

Handsets — 5.58
Mobile Access — 4.01
App stores — 2.45
Mobile OS — 1.24
Search Engine — 1.01

Defined as inverse of Herfindhl Hirschman Index OI = 1/HHL
1 means monopoly market.

Figure 6.5 – The Digital Market Openess Index for Brazil (2018)
Source (Illustrated from Telefonica[437])

- *Buy competitors to kill off*: Big Tech platform owners are typically accused of this. For example, Microsoft (dominant in the desktop productivity market with Office) was scrutinised when it bought task management app Wunderlist and mobile calendar Sunrise in 2015[438]. Both companies were highly regarded by Silicon Valley, but both apps were later scrapped by Microsoft. Indeed, some new research suggests that when a Big Tech acquires a startup or an app, it creates a kill area or kill zone and stifles further innovation

---

[437] https://www.telefonica.com/en/wp-content/uploads/sites/5/2021/06/a_manifiesto_for_a_new_digital_deal.pdf - a_manifiesto_for_a_new_digital_deal.pdf (telefonica.com), page 61

[438] https://www.ft.com/content/39b5c3a8-4e1a-11ea-95a0-43d18ec715f5 - Big Tech's 'buy and kill' tactics come under scrutiny | Financial Times (ft.com)

in the entire area[439]. This speaks to stricter merger control and acquisition rules for Big Tech.

Drawing from the 'real-world' economic examples of economic harms with digital platforms above, one can summarise the rationales for regulating digital platforms as follows.

1. **Natural monopoly rationale**: some large digital platforms clearly exhibit all the characteristics of natural monopoly (see Chapter 2), which – unlike with the network industries chronicled in Chapter 3 – can rapidly "expand to the point where they display 'extreme' or 'hyper' returns to scale and scope" at the global level (Decker, 2023, p. 500). This is because a single operator like Google or Facebook can rapidly expand to serve billions of users worldwide. Consider Figure 6.5 which clearly depicts that. As regards the category of online Search services in Brazil in 2018, Internet users there truly only have a choice of *one* search engine – and that is Google at 99.5%! Such concentrations are monopolistically high – a *de facto hyper monopoly* digital platform – and a similar picture would be the case for most countries. In addition, I note earlier how Google reinforces its economies of scope [and scale] from its extensive data collection activities on users' behaviour across its platform 'constellation' of Google Search, YouTube, Google Maps, Google Shopping, Google News and Gmail (see Figure 6.2). Google Search is indeed a utility for all online users today – but controlled by one operator! Facebook/Meta also experiences panoramic economies of scope by allowing Instagram to use Facebook's advertising infrastructure and ecosystem, not least as it owns Instagram (having acquired it through a merger). Indeed, the USA's FTC has a current open case against Facebook/Meta to this effect – *the Facebook Inc. vs FTC case*[440] in the Federal Court in the District of Columbia. The complaint alleges that Facebook has systematically engaged in an anticompetitive strategy, including its 2012 acquisition of up-and-coming rival Instagram and its 2014 acquisition of the mobile messaging app WhatsApp. The case also alleges the imposition of anticompetitive conditions by

---

[439] https://www.chicagobooth.edu/review/why-big-tech-mergers-stifle-innovation- Why big-tech mergers stifle innovation | Chicago Booth Review

[440] https://www.ftc.gov/legal-library/browse/cases-proceedings/191-0134-facebook-inc-ftc-v - Facebook, Inc., FTC v. | Federal Trade Commission, FTC Matter/File Number 191 0134

Facebook/Meta on software developers in order to eliminate threats to its monopoly. Bottom line, it is nigh impossible to effect price regulation with such platforms. Rather, regulators concentrate on facilitating greater contestability and competition, e.g., such that Bing has a better 'level playing field' to contest and compete against Google Search.

2. **Network Effects & Lock in Rationale**: the networks effects characteristics and others (e.g., extensive use of 'big data') that enable some digital platforms into winner-take-all or winner-take-most positions is very real. It brings with it huge positive externalities for users of the platform, but also comes with huge lock-in risks into a single provider, e.g. Google Shopping, Google Search or WhatsApp. Regulation of digital platforms concern itself with reducing such lock in barriers, because they present huge barriers to new entry.

3. **Regulation to control the exploitation of users and excluding potential competitors**: with a monopoly player benefitting from huge positive network effects – and lock in benefits – comes a huge risk of platform users being exploited by the behaviours of platform owners. These behaviours have been clearly chronicled above in the theory of harms I illustrate in Figure 6.4, in addition to the 'real world' case examples I give at the beginning of this Section 6.4.1. Recall, the harms I describe include 'Buy competitors to kill off' which is just one example of how potential competitors are excluded – in addition to many of the other harms of shown Figure 6.4.

6.4.2 Non-Economic Reasons for regulating digital platforms

There are non-economic reasons to regulate digital platforms too, and they are literally numerous. I borrow Figure 6.6 from Nwana (2022) – which clearly enumerates the numerous harms that come with many digital platforms, and what they are. I do not describe them any further because they read and speak for themselves in Figure 6.6, and Nwana (2022) elaborates on many of them. All I note here is what I wrote in Nwana (2022) – that both Big Tech and the founder of the Internet are *meekly* [in Zuckerberg's below] demanding regulation of digital platforms.

1. The acknowledged creator of the World Wide Web opined in 2018:

> "The changes we've managed to bring have created a better and more connected world. But for all the good we've achieved, the web has evolved into an engine of inequity and division; swayed by powerful forces who use it for their own agendas". Sir Tim Berners-Lee, Creator of the World Wide Web (WWW)[441].

2. Mark Zuckerberg, Founder and CEO of Facebook in an answer at a US Senate hearing:

> "My position is not that there should be no regulation.... I think the real question as the Internet becomes more important in people's lives is 'What is the right regulation, not whether there should be or not[442]". April 10th, 2018.

Note what the Facebook CEO says at the end: "not whether there should be or not". He was then asked by whether he would submit some proposed regulations to the Senate to which he agreed. Eventually, in March 2019, Facebook identified four areas where to start regulating the Internet's digital platforms[443]:

> "Technology is a major part of our lives, and companies such as Facebook have immense responsibilities. Every day, we make decisions about what speech is harmful, what constitutes political advertising, and how to prevent sophisticated cyberattacks. These are important for keeping our community safe. But if we were beginning from nothing, we wouldn't ask companies to make these judgments alone.

---

[441] Sir Tim Berners-Lee, 'One Small Step for the Web...', *Medium* (29 September 2018): https://medium.com/@timberners_lee/one-small-step-for-the-web-87f92217d085

[442] https://www.washingtonpost.com/news/the-switch/wp/2018/04/10/transcript-of-mark-zuckerbergs-senate-hearing/ - 'Marks Zuckerberg's testimony to Congress: Facebook boss admits company working with Mueller's Russia probe' Transcript of Mark Zuckerberg's Senate hearing - The Washington Post

[443] https://www.washingtonpost.com/opinions/mark-zuckerberg-the-internet-needs-new-rules-lets-start-in-these-four-areas/2019/03/29/9e6f0504-521a-11e9-a3f7-78b7525a8d5f_story.html - Opinion | Mark Zuckerberg: The Internet needs new rules. Let's start in these four areas. - The Washington Post

I believe we need a more active role for governments and regulators. By updating the rules for the Internet, we can preserve what's best about it — the freedom for people to express themselves and for entrepreneurs to build new things — while also protecting society from broader harms.

From what I've learned, I believe we need new regulation in four areas: *harmful content, election integrity, privacy and data portability." (the author's emphases)*

Big Tech Meta/Facebook is requesting regulation, and they have suggested some areas to start from.

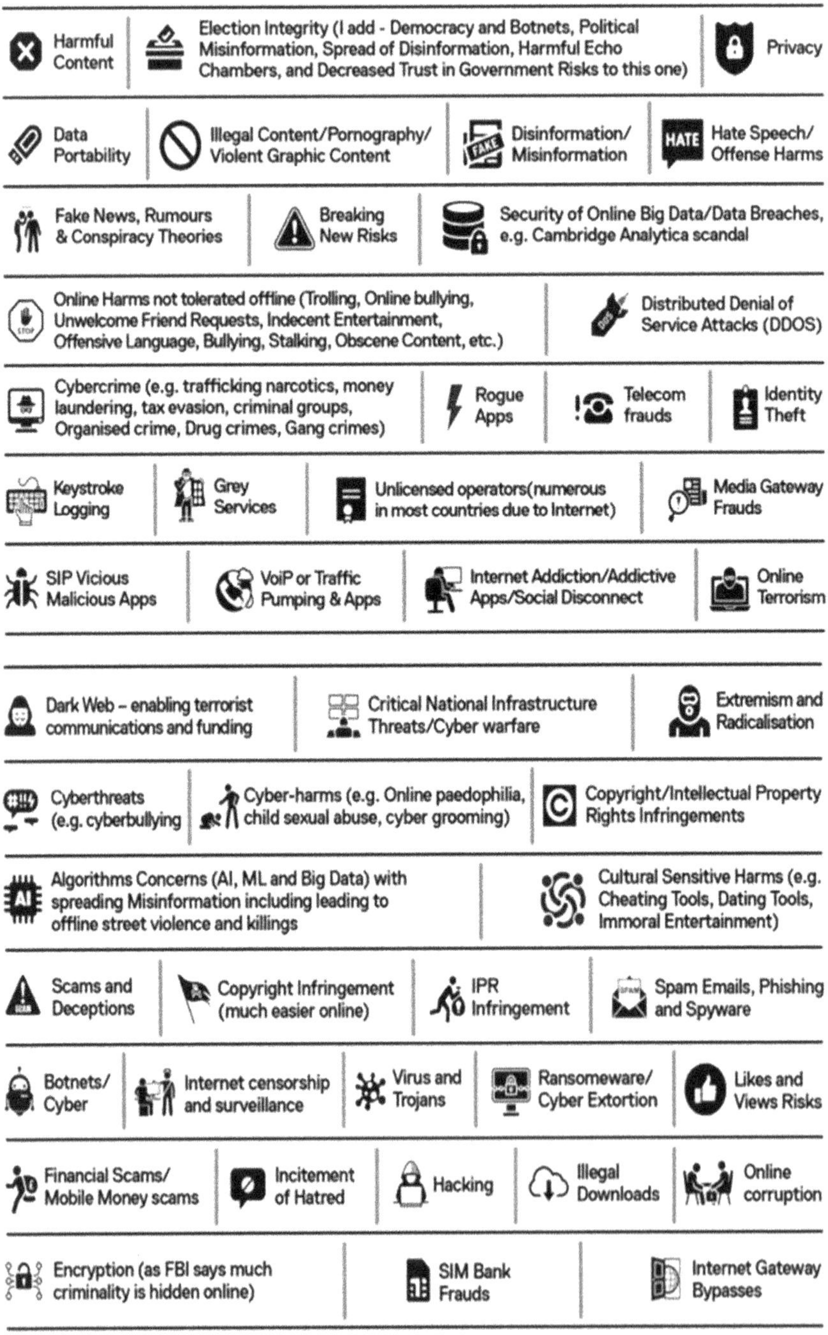

Figure 6.6 – the Numerous Online Harms that come with Digital Platforms *(Source: Nwana, 2022, p.221)*

6.5 Evolving Approaches to Regulating Digital Platforms

Digital platforms regulation is relatively new. Most regulations and rules across the world that have evolved for digital platforms have evolved over the past 5 to 6 years to date as I write in early 2024. I cover just the EU/EC and USA's approaches below – but other jurisdictions are evolving regulations for digital platforms too (see Nwana, 2022).

6.5.1 The EU/EC approach to regulating 'Big Tech' digital platforms

The separate sub-sections of economic and non-economic rationales for regulating digital platforms (of the previous section) *broadly* map, respectively, onto to (i) (*ex-ante* and *ex-post*) economic regulation on the one hand, and (ii) consumer protection-led approaches to their regulation – on the other. Indeed, the EU's European Commission (EC) adopted two pieces of legislation in 2022 – the Digital Markets Act (DMA) and the Digital Services Act (DSA) which broadly cover the following:

- The DMA is concerned with competition and antitrust issues, i.e. competition and economic issues broadly; and
- The DSA is concerned with harmful and illegal goods, services, and content online, i.e. consumer protection concerns broadly, but particular, the growing impacts of disinformation, fake news, political discussions/election integrity in the lead-up to elections, and the societal impact of hate speech (see top of Figure 6.6).

The DMA and the DSA are really aimed at Big Tech digital platforms – not all digital platforms - especially those who enjoy great influence in shaping the digital future of the EU digital market given their market share, or their role as online intermediaries and platforms. The two pieces of legislation are together referred to as the *Digital Services Act* package (DSA package), and collectively, they aim to enable a more competitive, as well as create a safer and more open digital space for businesses and individuals alike. Big Tech (or Tech Giants) is the name given to the four or five most dominant companies in the ICT industry of the USA, namely Amazon, Apple, Google (Alphabet), Facebook/Meta[444] and Microsoft[445].

The EC Digital Markets Act (DMA)[446]: this Act from the EU is narrowly aimed at dealing with competition and antitrust issues (see Figures 6.4 and 6.5) with Big Tech online platforms that the EU denotes as "gatekeepers" in digital markets. This is important because several Big Tech companies have achieved a 'gatekeeper' status by becoming the bottleneck between businesses and customers. The reader just has to look again at the 'bottleneck' Figure 6.5 to see the bottleneck 'gatekeepers' for Search, Mobile Operating Systems (OSs) and App Stores – it is very evident who they are. The DMA originally defined in 2020 "gatekeepers" as those companies that control core services on the Internet and serve more than 45 million monthly active EU users and 10,000 business users. I note "originally" because, on 11 May 2022, the proposal was updated to target companies with more than €7.5 billion in annual revenue turnover or a fair market value of €75 billion.

In effect, the DMA is an extension of the EU competition law regime, ensuring fair practices online among different digital market actors. So, the DMA broadens the range of existing instruments and tools for investigating and correcting anti-competitive market practices through *ex-ante* rules that prohibit certain behaviours. It strives to ensure that these "Big Tech" digital platforms behave in transparent ways online. This Act also gives the Commission wide-ranging investigatory powers as well as the ability to levy fines of up to 10% of global turnover of the preceding financial year, with heavier penalties up to 20% due to repeated non-compliance, and periodic penalty payments of up to 5% of the average daily turnover. To get to such the stage of such latter penalties and more, the Commission has powers to open market investigations and take stronger measures, e.g., stopping and banning acquisitions. This EC Law is a clear move towards *ex-ante* rules with these Big Tech gatekeeper platforms, rather than relying just on *ex-post* investigations and enforcement. The EU would like to see more *contestability* and *fairness*

---

[444] In October 2021, Facebook formally became part of a new parent holding company called Meta.

[445] https://en.wikipedia.org/wiki/Big_Tech - Big Tech - Wikipedia 5th October 2023.

[446] https://commission.europa.eu/strategy-and-policy/priorities-2019-2024/europe-fit-digital-age/digital-markets-act-ensuring-fair-and-open-digital-markets_en - The Digital Markets Act: ensuring fair and open digital markets | European Commission (europa.eu)

with these gatekeeper platforms. The key distinction between contestability and fairness is that contestability is more about promoting competition, while fairness is more about constraining the exercise of market power. This distinction is also reflected in the UK's proposed approach of two types of regulatory measures: Pro-Competitive Interventions and Conduct Requirements[447].

Designated gatekeeper companies to date that fall under the DMA's requirements include: Apple, Amazon, Alphabet (the parent company of Google and Android), Meta (the parent company of Facebook, Instagram and WhatsApp), ByteDance (the parent company of TikTok) and Microsoft. As a designated 'gatekeeper', the Law lists what they are prohibited from doing, e.g., self-preferencing or giving preference to its own goods and services over those of downstream providers using its platforms (see Section 6.1). The examples of the must "do's" include (Source [448]):

- ✓ allow third parties to inter-operate with the gatekeeper's own services in certain specific situations
- ✓ allow their business users to access the data that they generate in their use of the gatekeeper's platform
- ✓ provide companies advertising on their platform with the tools and information necessary for advertisers and publishers to carry out their own independent verification of their advertisements hosted by the gatekeeper
- ✓ allow their business users to promote their offer and conclude contracts with their customers outside the gatekeeper's platform

and example absolute "don'ts" (Source[449]) include

---

[447] see Digital Markets, Competition and Consumers Bill (https://bills.parliament.uk/bills/3453).

[448] https://commission.europa.eu/strategy-and-policy/priorities-2019-2024/europe-fit-digital-age/digital-markets-act-ensuring-fair-and-open-digital-markets_en - The Digital Markets Act: ensuring fair and open digital markets - European Commission (europa.eu)
[449] *Ibid.*

- ✗ treat services and products offered by the gatekeeper itself more favourably in ranking than similar services or products offered by third parties on the gatekeeper's platform
- ✗ prevent consumers from linking up to businesses outside their
- ✗ prevent users from un-installing any pre-installed software or app if they wish so
- ✗ track end users outside of the gatekeepers' core platform service for the purpose of targeted advertising, without effective consent having been granted

The DMA was adopted by the European Parliament on 5 July 2022 and by the Council on 18 July 2022. The DMA came into force at the beginning of May 2023.

The EC Digital Services Act[450] (DSA): was also introduced in December 2020. Whilst the DMA aims to tackle the lack of competition in digital markets by targeting "gatekeepers", the DSA is primarily concerned with harmful and illegal goods, services, online content, transparency, user safety and consumer protection. So, it seeks to address both illegal and harmful content amongst so many other harms as depicted in Figure 6.6.

The DSA targets *digital "intermediaries"* (conduit, caching and hosting providers) and online platforms (e.g., marketplaces, social media, app stores, etc.). It implements special rules for "very large online platforms[451]" (VLOPs) and "very large online search engines[452]" (VLOSEs), in order to address societal risks associated with their operation. The Act addresses the EU's concerns regarding the growing online platforms challenges with political discussions, disinformation campaigns and fake news dissemination in the lead-up to elections, and the general negative societal impact of hate speech. VLOPs and VLOSEs are subject to a list of strict obligations, e.g., rules on how to tackle illegal and harmful content, liability rules to be implemented, reporting obligations and due diligence obligations too.

---

[450] https://commission.europa.eu/strategy-and-policy/priorities-2019-2024/europe-fit-digital-age/digital-services-act_en - The Digital Services Act: ensuring a safe and accountable online environment | European Commission (europa.eu)

[451] which they define as greater than 45 million monthly active EU users (e.g., YouTube)

[452] with 45 million or more monthly active users in the EU.

In summary, the DSA implements new obligations for online platforms, including[453]:

- content moderation
- mechanisms for handling user complaints
- transparency of algorithms
- cooperation with authorities
- measures to prevent spreading illegal content

In broad terms, the DSA aims to protect users' fundamental rights, create a safer digital space, and ensure a level playing field for the EU digital businesses. It is enforced through national regulators supported by a new proposed independent advisory group, a new European Board for Digital Services (EBDS). The European Commission is the primary regulator for them (i.e., VLOPs/VLOSEs) for more effective and collaborative interventions, whilst other service providers are supervised by the EU member states' new Digital Services Coordinators.

Like with the DMA, most would associate the DSA with the regulation of Silicon Valley Big Techs, but they would be wrong. On the 20 December 2023, the EC designated three *new* VLOPs: Pornhub, Stripchat and XVideos – as these adult content websites attract so many visitors each month that they reach the threshold of an average of 45 million users per month. This is the second time the EC designated VLOPs after the first batch on 25 April 2023, when 17 platforms were designated VLOPs and two search engines as so-called "VLOSEs" (i.e., Bing and Google Search). The DSA also covers thousands of smaller European service providers that are affected by the new obligations. The *current VLOP platforms as of early 2024* include: Alibaba AliExpress, Amazon Store, Apple AppStore, Booking.com, Facebook, Google Play, Google Maps, Google Shopping, Instagram, LinkedIn, Pinterest, Snapchat, TikTok, X/Twitter, Wikipedia and YouTube.

The DSA was adopted by the European Parliament on 5 July 2022, and came into force in its entirety on the 17 February 2024. The Act allows for

---

[453] https://usercentrics.com/knowledge-hub/differences-between-digital-markets-act-and-digital-services-act/ - DMA vs DSA - Similarities and Differences - Usercentrics

fines of up to 6% of global turnover and, in extreme cases, restriction of access to platforms.

6.5.2 The USA approach to regulating 'Big Tech' digital platforms

The USA is obviously the 'home market' to most of the firms that come under the EC's DMA, i.e. FANGAM – so what the US eventually does in regulating these companies would truly matter. What I did not spell out in the previous section is that regulating the Big Tech companies is also undoubtedly a *politically-charged* endeavour. You do not believe me? United States Democratic Senator, Elizabeth Warren, strongly advocated and still advocates for breaking up Big Tech - asserting that

> "Today's big tech companies have too much power – too much power over our economy, our society, and our democracy"[454].

If the problem is stated this way, no competition authority can possibly address it, because it is highly political. I have a brief sub-section in Nwana (2022) which I termed 'EC Competition Policy vs. Politics'. I argue in it that any other regulatory body outside the USA trying to break up these Silicon Valley Big Techs inevitably reach that boundary between competition policy and politics. I write, "this is where Politics sets in. The EU will rightly tread very carefully in such a minefield, leaving such a possible move to their US antitrust counterparts such as the Department of Justice (DoJ). The DoJ has already filed its own suit against Google covering similar grounds joined by more than 11 Federal US States[455]". Can any reader truly name another regulator anywhere in the globe best placed to break up the Google ecosystem of Figure 6.2 better that the USA's DoJ?

The above all noted – what is the USA doing about regulating digital platforms? The first obvious answer is nothing close to as comprehensive as the EU/EC's approach of the previous section. The US Congress was/is

---

[454] https://2020.elizabethwarren.com/toolkit/break-up-big-tech - Break Up Big Tech | Elizabeth Warren

[455] https://www.justice.gov/opa/press-release/file/1328941/dl - Justice Department Sues Monopolist Google For Violating Antitrust Laws: Google Complaint

pursuing several different Bills as of June 2021: Congress unveiled 5 bipartisan Bills that mark the biggest steps yet in regulating Big Tech[456]. These Bills emerged after a 16-month investigation into the market power of Amazon, Apple, Facebook and Google. The 5 US Big Tech Bills include:

i. The American Choice and Innovation Online Act - this Bill seeks to stop Big Tech like Google and Amazon from giving preference to their products on their own platforms.

ii. The Platform Competition and Opportunity Act of 2021 - this would prevent Big Tech from buying up early-stage competitors, like the Facebook acquisition of Instagram in 2012. This will also stop buy-to-kill-off.

iii. The Ending Platform Monopolies Act - this bill would address conflict of interest issues by prohibiting Big Tech monopolies from selling products in marketplaces they control, like App Stores.

iv. The Augmenting Compatibility and Competition by Enabling Service Switching (ACCESS) Act of 2021 - this bill aims at the remedy of interoperability, i.e., it makes it easier to leave a social media platform and take your data to a competitor.

v. The Merger Filing Fee Modernization Act of 2021 - this gives the Federal Trade Commission and the Justice Department more monies to take on competition or antitrust cases against Big Tech. It increases the filing fees for tech mergers above $500 million and lowers fees for those under that level.

It is important to note that these bills have a long way to go before they become US Laws. They must pass through the House of Representatives, the Senate, and be signed by President Joe Biden. However as of early 2024, the incredible lobbying power of these firms appear to have succeeded in stalling the five Bills, if not having killed them off at worst[457].

---

[456] https://www.bbc.co.uk/news/technology-57450345 - US lawmakers introduce bills targeting Big Tech - BBC News

[457] https://www.washingtonpost.com/opinions/2023/07/06/congress-facebook-google-amazon-apple-regulation-failure/ - Opinion | How Congress failed to regulate Big Tech - The Washington Post

I cover in Nwana (2022) what other jurisdictions are doing to regulate digital platforms including the UK, Australia, South Korea and China. Other countries like India are getting in on the act too. There is therefore no one-size-fit-all approach to digital platforms regulation.

There are other EC Laws that impact (or would impact) digital platforms too, including the EU Artificial Intelligence (AI) Act[458] (which was adopted/approved by EU MEPs on the 13th of March 2024[459]) and the EU's GDPR Law which has already been used multiple times to fine digital platform companies, e.g., the WhatsApp fine of €225m[460]. The EU AI Act aims to establish a "comprehensive legal framework on AI worldwide" for "foster[ing] trustworthy AI in Europe and beyond, by ensuring that AI systems respect fundamental rights, safety, and ethical principles and by addressing risks of very powerful and impactful AI models.[461]" There is also a less well-known EC digital Law called the Data Governance Act (DGA)[462] that will impact most digital platforms of Table 6.1. The DGA aims at "foster[ing] the availability of data for use by increasing trust in data intermediaries and by strengthening data sharing mechanisms across the EU"[463]. The DGA is applicable as of 24 September 2023. I have scanned this Act, and it looks complex and ambitious because Europe (the EU) appears to want to make data on digital platforms more available. Would this clash with the GDPR? It is still very early days for the DGA as of early May 2024.

---

[458] https://www.europarl.europa.eu/news/en/press-room/20240308IPR19015/artificial-intelligence-act-meps-adopt-landmark-law - https://www.europarl.europa.eu/news/en/press-room/20240308IPR19015/artificial-intelligence-act-meps-adopt-landmark-law

[459] https://www.europarl.europa.eu/news/en/press-room/20231206IPR15699/artificial-intelligence-act-deal-on-comprehensive-rules-for-trustworthy-ai#:~:text=MEPs%20reached%20a%20political%20deal,on%20the%20Artificial%20Intelligence%20Act. - Artificial Intelligence Act: deal on comprehensive rules for trustworthy AI | News | European Parliament (europa.eu)

[460] https://www.bbc.co.uk/news/technology-58422465 - WhatsApp issued second-largest GDPR fine of €225m - BBC News

[461] https://digital-strategy.ec.europa.eu/en/policies/regulatory-framework-ai - AI Act | Shaping Europe's digital future (europa.eu)

[462] https://edri.org/wp-content/uploads/2020/10/Commissions-proposal-on-the-Data-Governance-Ac.pdf - Commissions-proposal-on-the-Data-Governance-Ac.pdf (edri.org)

[463] *Ibid.*

6.6 Challenges to Regulation from the Increasing Digitalisation of most Sectors

So far, this chapter has majored on the evolving regulation of digital platforms, including all of those covered in Table 6.1. However, thanks to the digital platforms (of Section 6.3) and numerous other efforts by tech companies worldwide, digitalisation and digitisation[464] of all sectors is with us today, and it is only accelerating. When you read of e-Government, it is all about *digitisation and digitalisation* of Government. Some estimates suggest that 65% of worldwide GDP would have gone through some form of digitalization by 2022[465] – this is incredulous. This means that practically no sector of the economy is being spared. When Covid19 slowed down of international travels, digitalisation and digitisation soared. These have consequences on regulation too – yes, I mean of current sectors like the network industries on Chapter 3 and more. Why? I argue that there are three types of outcomes, at least, that are emerging:

i.   Some principal sectors are 'birthing' new ones, which necessitate a hybrid regulatory networks approach to their regulation, drawing from the regulators of the 'parent' sectors, e.g. Mobile Financial Service (MFS).

ii.   The business and revenue models of [some] current sectors are being drastically altered by digitalization, necessitating current regulations increasingly not-fit-for-purpose, e.g., traditional advertising revenues model for terrestrial broadcasts (TV and radio) moving online – or the rise and rise of OTT services.

iii.   The unmistakable, emerging Digital Economy – which brings a whole new host of challenges to its regulation, as (partly) covered earlier with the challenges of regulating digital platforms. You may have heard too that many countries say they are also striving towards the 4th Industrial Revolution (4IR)[466] or Industry 4.0. This

---

[464] Digitisation focuses on converting and recording data digitally (including today's paper-only records), whilst digitalisation concerns developing processes and changing workflows to improve manual systems.

[465] https://www.idc.com/getdoc.jsp?containerId=prUS46967420 - IDC Reveals 2021 Worldwide Digital Transformation Predictions; 65% of Global GDP Digitalized by 2022, Driving Over $6.8 Trillion of Direct DX Investments from 2020 to 2023

[466] https://www.mckinsey.com/featured-insights/mckinsey-explainers/what-are-industry-4-0-the-fourth-industrial-revolution-and-4ir - What is industry 4.0 and the Fourth Industrial Revolution? | McKinsey

is yet another buzzword that emerged from the 2016 Davos Summit in Switzerland, coined by Klaus Schwab[467]. It is the next "shiny thing" beyond ICT and Digital Economy, which many developing economies Sector Ministers and Senior Government officials latch on to – and distract themselves from their day-to-day truly-important policy and implementation duties, which would make major differences to both their economies and citizens.

Following, I address several 'contexts' of the evolving regulation pertaining to the increasing digitization across our economies.

6.6.1 Regulating Mobile Financial Services using Regulatory Networks

Some principal sectors are 'birthing' new ones, that necessitate a hybrid regulatory networks approach drawing from the regulators of the 'parent' sectors: a classic example here is the relatively new area of Mobile Financial Services (MFS) – which dominates emerging market countries in Africa and elsewhere. Mobile phones today do not only allow for constant communications. Even to a significant proportion of the world's poorest people, they have also become the conduit for these people to access banking services for the very first time[468]. "MFS include services such as mobile-enabled payment systems and mobile banking with security and convenience for transfers, payments and savings through the concept of a 'mobile wallet' account. MFS are now available in over 70 countries, carrying payment volumes of tens of billions of dollars each month"[469]. Arguably therefore, MFS has been 'birthed' from both the mobile and banking sectors.

---

[467] Founder and Executive Chairman of the World Economic Forum

[468] https://www.itu.int/en/ITU-T/studygroups/2013-2016/03/Pages/mfs.aspx - Mobile Financial Services (itu.int)

[469] *Ibid.*

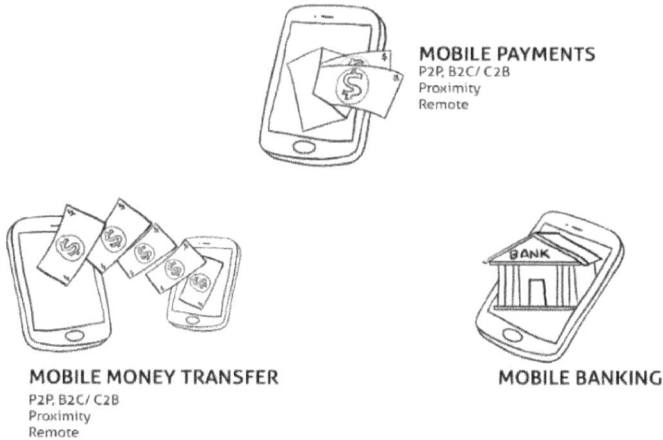

MOBILE PAYMENTS
P2P, B2C/ C2B
Proximity
Remote

MOBILE MONEY TRANSFER
P2P, B2C/ C2B
Proximity
Remote

MOBILE BANKING

Figure 6.7 - Types of Mobile Financial Services
(Source: Adapted from International Telecommunication Union (Source: ITU-T, 2013[470])

'Mobile Financial Services (MFS)' is an umbrella term used to encompass the services provided by financial institutions to be utilised via a mobile device. They fall under the three main subsections of mobile payments, mobile money transfer and mobile banking. The *'mobile payments'* term encompasses proximity payments at the merchant site. This could be on a peer to peer (P2P) basis, or a consumer to business (C2B) basis such as with bill payments or in-store contactless payments, or business to consumer (B2C) such as a customer refund. *Mobile money transfer* is a broad term for the transfer of money from one individual to another or P2P payments, such as remittance services or mobile wallet transfers. *Mobile banking* is a service that allows consumers to access their bank accounts remotely from their mobile devices, conduct financial transactions and view mini statements.

In Kenya - arguably the biggest MFS market in the world - MFS is principally regulated using both the 1998 Kenya Information and Communications Act (KICA) (used to regulate MNOs) and the 2011

---

[470] http://www.itu.int/dms_pub/itu-t/oth/23/01/T23010000200001PDFE.pdf -This report provides an excellent review of the state of the art in near field communications mobile payments.

Kenya National Payment Systems Act [471] (which regulates payment systems and payment service providers). The Central Bank of Kenya (CBK[472]) has adopted:

> "a functional (rather than an institutional) approach to regulation where banks and non-banks – including Mobile Network Operators – are permitted to provide mobile money services. Customer funds must be held in trust with a strong rated *prudentially* regulated bank and no lending or investment of such funds is permitted. *The funds are isolated from the service provider's own funds and safe from claims of its creditors.* Service providers can appoint agents and are responsible for the actions of agents. CBK's oversight, inspection and enforcement duties are formally recognised"[473] (*my emphases*).

So in Kenya, MFS is *hybridlike regulated* by a three-way combination of the CBK (as the prudential banking and payments regulator), the Competition Authority of Kenya[474] (CAK), whilst the Communications Authority [475] (CA) remains as the telecoms regulator. Kenyan MFS services including M-PESA, Airtel Money, and Orange Money, offered by MNOs were originally regulated under an MNO-led approach. However, increased integration of some of these mobile money services with mobile banking services has created hybrid models.

Regulatory Networks are used to implement the Hybrid Cooperation Regulation Framework for MFS: so how does such a hybrid regulatory model work in practice? It works through a cooperation framework amongst the three regulators. As far back a decade ago, the CAK Signed a

---

[471] https://www.gsma.com/mobilefordevelopment/wp-content/uploads/2014/08/NPSRegulationsLegalNoticeNo-2-109.pdf & https://mman.co.ke/content/fintech-regulation-kenya

[472] https://www.centralbank.go.ke

[473] https://www.gsma.com/solutions-and-impact/connectivity-for-good/mobile-for-development/country/kenya/kenyas-new-regulatory-framework-for-e-money-issuers/ - GSMA | Kenya's new regulatory framework for e-money issuers | Mobile for Development

[474] https://cak.go.ke/ - Welcome to Competition Authority Of Kenya | Competition Authority Of Kenya (cak.go.ke)

[475] https://www.ca.go.ke/

MoU[476] with the CBK (Source: [477]), on the 14[th of] July 2014. There is also a MoU between the CAK and Communications Authority of Kenya[478]: '

> 'this MOU will hasten the decision making process and guide the agencies in the extent of consultations to create a harmonious environment for investors''.

So, the regulators are currently working together and sharing information on matters that have both competition, payments and communication dimensions. Any successful cooperation amongst the regulators is dependent on the successful implementation of the MoUs. It is up to the regulators to produce clear arrangements to ensure successful inter-regulators cooperation. Kenya has essentially evolved a ''regulatory networks' approach in regulating MFS – recall from Chapter 3 that underlying theory is that the most optimal regulatory outcomes will typically involve "mixtures" from regulatory institutions and regulatory instruments.

6.6.2 Regulating Evolving OTT Platforms using a combination of Regulatory Models

Regulating Evolving OTT Platforms using a combination of No Regulation, Self-Regulation, Co-Regulation & Statutory Regulation (when truly necessary): many principal sectors are under strain from changing business and revenue models, particularly through the arrival of Over-the-Top Services (OTTs). OTTs are a key approach to modern digitalization, i.e., developing processes and changing workflows to improve manual systems. e-Government is all about digitalizing Government services, and many e-Government services are being implemented as OTT services, through OTT apps which citizens can download and access through their [low cost] smartphones. I proceed to illustrate challenges to regulating new OTT digitization models using the context of telecommunications.

---

[476] Memorandum of Understanding

[477] https://static1.squarespace.com/static/52246331e4b0a46e5f1b8ce5/t/5534a332e4b078b ae80cbaeb/1429513010529/Barnabas+Andiva_Mobile+Money+Kenya.pdf - MOBILE FINANCIAL SERVICES AND REGULATION IN KENYA (squarespace.com)

[478] https://cioafrica.co/ca-cak-sign-pact-on-competition-regulation/ - CA, CAK sign pact on competition regulation | CIO Africa

Big Tech vs. Big Telco 'Fair Share' Debate (the value chain revolutions with revenue shifts from old [digital] platforms to new ones): Let us use a real context from the telecoms sector. The fact is that the rise and rise of OTTs has transformed the functionality and ease of use offered by traditional telecoms services. Just compare a Zoom or Microsoft Teams call or session that many of us are now taking for granted since the Covid-19 pandemic. If you are old enough, compare these experiences to the previous telco-provided conference calls you used to get with your fixed or mobile communications provider.

The previous conference calls were frankly "clunky" and were booked through central telecoms services, and would only support several attendees. Would you return to your old Telco-provided conferencing services anytime soon? Would you swap the apps on your smartphone for the earlier clunky desktop 'fat client' ones the fixed/mobile operators abysmally used to try and provide us?

The telcos woke up to the fact – belatedly – that the Steve Jobs with his iPhone changed the world in 2007 and ushered in the era of the OTTs that dominate our ICT lives today. However, there is something more important at play here. These OTTs are radically changing industry value chains, resulting in significant to drastic revenue shifts from old platforms to new platforms. Advertising revenues are drying up on terrestrial and cable TV platforms and moving online, leading to such broadcast platforms dying on their feet, and needing increasing subsidies. Old PSTN revenues which enriched traditional fixed and mobile/cellular telecoms businesses (like MTN, Verizon, Saudi Telecom, etc.) are moving to OTT revenues because much of the traffic on telecom networks is online Internet traffic as shown in Figure 6.8. As shown from this latter graph, 66% of the exponential growth in Internet traffic in the Caribbean is generated by the top 8 Big Tech platforms, with Facebook/Meta, Google/Alphabet and TikTok dominating markedly. The rest of native traditional telco traffic only constitutes 33%.

MNOs blame OTTs for declining voice and SMS revenues across the telecoms sector. Indeed, some mobile/cellular operators have argued that OTTs have cannibalised voice and SMS revenues, and have warned that the resulting decline of overall revenues leads to lower investment in network infrastructure, sub-standard quality of service, lower tax revenues and lower licensing revenues.

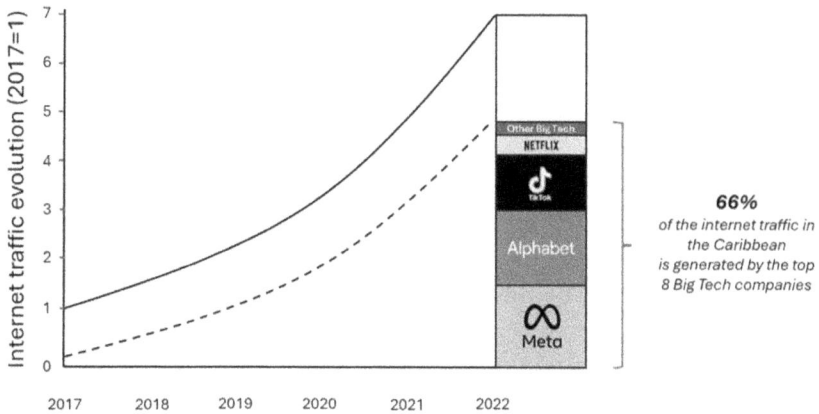

Figure 6.8 – The rise and rise of OTT Traffic on Telco Networks in the
Caribbean between 2017 to 2022
(Source: Based on and adapted from Digicel Group Presentation [479])

We (Stork, Nwana *et al.*, 2020) have investigated these claims by using
publicly available information from mobile operators across Africa in
order to analyse trends in voice, SMS and data revenues. We analysed
three factors impacting revenue trends, namely the changes in usage
patterns across voice, SMS and data, the impact of regulatory interventions
and the choice of business model. We made some important conclusions
(Stork, Nwana *et al.*, 2020).

i.   Revenue from voice and SMS traffic are still on the increase. They
      are just not growing as exponentially as data traffic.

ii.   We concluded that OTTs are now an *integral part* of the telecoms
      business model – and no amount of complaining by
      cellular/mobile operators can change this fact.

iii. We concluded too that the broad digital platforms business model
      is about knowing the customer. The actual battle is not that of
      cannibalisation of one product by another, i.e., replacing voice and
      SMS with data revenues, but one of maintaining data and
      information on subscribers for better monetisation. The
      information that Google, Amazon and Facebook have about me

[479] Source: David Geary of Digicel Group, Presentation at CTO Ministerial Summit,
London, Feb 2023, https://www.cto.int/wp-content/uploads/2023/04/CTO-DW23-Event-
report.pdf

(see Figure 6.2 for Google) is more likely to be economically valuable than the information that an MNO has about me. To enter this market is a business decision, not a regulatory decision.

iv. The impact of OTTs on the financial performance of MNOs depends mostly on the ability of the latter to sell data as seen in Figure 6.8. OTT users and OTT traffic is steadily increasing over time as seen in Figure 6.8 between the years of 2017 to 2022. If OTTs were causing a decline in MNOs' revenues, then we should be able to see a systematic decline in MNO revenues over time, and also for all countries and most operators. We did not find this across the sample of 20+ operators across countries in Africa.

v. Data has become (or is becoming) the primary source of MNO revenues. Indeed, data networks are where the majority of MNO investment of the last 2 decades has gone.

vi. The Internet Value Chain (see again Figure 6.3) is already with us, with each segment of Internet Value chain (e.g., Content Rights, Online Services, Internet Access Connectivity, etc.) subject to own laws, rules and regulations, and implemented by different bodies. Only the Internet access connectivity segment of the value chain is subject to *ex-ante* regulation by the telecommunications regulator. Therefore, asking the telecoms regulator to "do something" about the companies that lie in the Online Services segment is mostly not effective because the TMT regulators typically have the powers *only* to regulate firms that lie in the Internet Access Connectivity segment.

These findings all speak to the telecoms industry growing through drastic revenue and business model shifts due to OTTs becoming an integral part of the value chain. Naturally, Figure 6.8 illustrates the clear revenue and value chain shift to OTT data services. However, these growing or maturing pains has led to a vocal reaction from the Big Telco industry complaining that Big Tech should "find a financing model for the huge investments needed" in the development of next-generation mobile/cellular networks, with emerging technologies like the Metaverse[480]. They argue for this because the graph depicted in Figure 6.8

---

[480] Source: https://builtin.com/media-gaming/what-is-metaverse - Big Tech vs. Big Telco: Top EU official says there's no 'battle' over network funding (cnbc.com) - The metaverse is a network of shared, immersive virtual worlds where people can connect with friends, create and play games, work and shop. You can think of the metaverse as a cyberspace, or an evolved, three-dimensional internet where logging in isn't necessary

would grow worse [for Big Telcos] with new applications like the Metaverse.

This is the conflict that has come to be known as battle over "*fair share*[481]" between Big Telco and Big Tech. This problem is real – but as I argue strongly above - it is mostly about growing pains industry sectors go through with new technologies, business models and new entrants. It is *not* the job of regulators and regulation to protect incumbents.

Three decades ago – circa 1990s – the MNOs with their new mobile technologies and business models displaced fixed operators, and literally sucked all the 'oxygen' (i.e., revenues, traffic and subscribers) away from fixed networks – particularly in developing markets. Regulation and regulators followed suit and fixed much of their attention on mobile operators, and even organisations like the ITU have spent practically all of the last 8 WRCs reallocating spectrum away from satellite to IMT/mobile. The satellite industry has wailed to no avail against national regulators and the ITU – but even they admit that regulators have to 'follow' and protect the interests of consumers where they are going – and they are going mobile/cellular. The e-Commerce sector has similarly impacted the traditional bricks-and-mortar retail sector, with revenues moving online. How has traditional retailers reacted? They have innovated with their own online offerings.

I do not hear any similar Big Retail vs. Big e-Commerce [Big Tech] outcry!

Evolving OTT Platforms should be controlled or regulated using a combination of Regulatory Forbearance, No Regulation, Self-Regulation, Co-Regulation & Statutory Regulation: this is the key logical conclusion from the narrative of this section. Regulators should practice regulatory forbearance before regulating new players who are innovating and disrupting existing industry value chains. Why – the reader may ask? Some brief reasons follow.

---

[481] https://www.cnbc.com/2023/02/28/big-tech-vs-big-telco-top-eu-official-says-theres-no-battle-over-network-funding.html - Big Tech vs. Big Telco: Top EU official says there's no 'battle' over network funding (cnbc.com)

- *Regulatory forbearance/No Regulation*: this can be defined as laxity in regulatory agencies quickly trying to regulate new entrants, new business models, new technologies or new value chains. Do not regulate away some of the potential big Internet companies that may emerge from your country with premature regulation. In Nwana (2022), I make the case that Facebook, Google, X/Twitter, Netflix and many more household Big Tech/Online Businesses grew to what they are today because of favourable regulatory environments. Section 230 is sometimes dubbed the most important law for online speech[482] in the USA. It is a section of Title 47 of the US code enacted in 1996 known as Communications Decency Act – the long version name of 47 US Code 2030. In a section I title *Beware of Regulating Away your next Online Giant* (Nwana, 2022, p. 229), I make the case that without Section 230 - which stipulates that an "interactive computer service" cannot be treated as the publisher or speaker of third-party content - companies like Facebook, Google, Twitter, etc., would have been litigated out of existence – indeed they will all have been still-born – and would not exist today. Think about practicing regulatory forbearance in your country too with new business models and new entrants. I do not make an explicit difference here between regulatory forbearance and no regulation.

  No regulation: as I note in Chapter 3, 'no regulation' does not mean 'no controls'; it essentially means there are no formal rules and regulations laid down by Government or by a Legislature in a particular area of activity. Big Tech has grown without regulation to several USD trillion-dollar and very many USD billion-dollar companies– and it is only latterly as I note in this Chapter - that they are now being caught by regulation for both economic and non-economic reasons (see Section 6.4).

- *Self-Regulation*: rightly or wrongly, many Big Tech companies are still largely self-regulating. i.e., they voluntarily create and adhere to their own rules, codes of conduct and regulations. No regulator – until recent debates - tells Facebook/Meta, Instagram or Twitter what content they should take down. Indeed, there is

---

[482] https://www.theverge.com/21273768/section-230-explained-internet-speech-law-definition-guide-free-moderation - Section 230: everything you need to know about the law protecting internet speech - The Verge

much evidence that they make more monies from hateful and/or controversial content – because they lead people to emote and engage their platforms even more, see Nwana (2022). Self-regulation would still continue with OTT digital platform players in the EU because the heights that companies need to achieve to become designated gatekeeper companies, VLOSEs or VLOPs are very elevated – meaning that thousands or tens of thousands of EU businesses would *not* be caught by these new laws at all, though thousands of others are caught by a subset of the rules. Those not caught would self-regulate themselves for these activities.

- *Co-regulation:* Self-regulation and co-regulatory models are also most relevant. As I note in Chapter 3, co-regulation is really an extension of self-regulation that involves both Industry and the Government (or the Regulator) designing rules/regulations and enforcing them in a variety of combinations for a variety of activities. The rules may be less strict to allow for innovation in business models, value chains and more.

- *Statutory Regulation*: as covered in this chapter, the designated VLOSEs, VLOPs and gatekeeping platforms are now being subjected to statutory regulations like the DMA and DSA in the EU.

My key message in this section is simple. Digitalisation is happening in most sectors of the economy. I have used the telecoms sector in this section to illustrate it. A good example of the digitalization is that ongoing in many sectors through OTT services, and these services tend to disrupt value chains and drastically alter revenue flows. As sectors go through growing pains industry sector with new technologies, new value chains, business models and new entrants - it is not the job of regulators and regulation to protect incumbents. Regulatory forbearance, no regulation, self-regulation or co-regulation may be best to allow for the emergence of future billion-dollar Big Tech companies in South East Asia, Africa or the Middle East.

6.6.3 Regulating the Emerging Digital Economy & Industry 4.0 using Regulatory Sandboxes & Regulatory Networks

One key emerging outcome of digitalization is the unmistakable and emerging Digital Economy and the so-called Industry 4.0. The emerging digital economy [and Industry 4.0] which most countries aspire for their countries brings a whole new host of challenges to their regulation. However, let us start by defining what a digital economy is, and indeed what is Industry 4.0, or the 4th Industrial Revolution (4IR)[483]? Perhaps we should start with Industry 4.0. For a book on Demystifying Economic Regulation written in the 2020s, it is important to point out the risks in future business transformations that would require keen regulating and regulations.

Let me begin with Thomas L. Friedman (2005) who astutely derived that the world has gone through three major historical eras of global business transformations, namely :

i.   Globalisation 1.0 (1492 – 1800):   during this era, the world 'shrank' from Large to Medium. The focus was on Nations creating Empires, comprising places across the globe - and goods could move from one part of the globe to another. The key business focus was to source raw materials for transformation, in order to deliver basic needs, e.g., cotton to shirts, tea leaves to tea, etc. Most workers bar a few were *not* expected to think and/or to be creative, but just to provide mechanical labour and follow orders.

ii.   Globalisation 2.0 (circa 1800 – 2000): the world "shrank" from Medium to Small. The business focus was on integration, with multinational companies identifying raw materials, processing and delivering to markets or to headquarters for final processing or transformation. Unlike with Globalisation 1.0, the numbers of workforce expected to 'think' and make decisions increased significantly, e.g., regional managers and their teams running the show. Regions began competing on who is more profitable.

---

[483] https://www.mckinsey.com/featured-insights/mckinsey-explainers/what-are-industry-4-0-the-fourth-industrial-revolution-and-4ir - What is industry 4.0 and the Fourth Industrial Revolution? | McKinsey

iii.   Globalisation 3.0 (2000 – Present day): the world "shrank" from Small to Tiny, driven by ICT [including Digital Economy and 4IR] revolutions. The business focus is on *innovation* and *creative services*, with every employee invited to be innovative and creative – indeed to create their own businesses. Employee and employer relations is a partnership for mutual growth and benefits, and social influencers play a big role in business decisions. We can see this today around us in the 2020s.

What do these eras have to do with the Digital Economy or with 4IR? Well, the brief answer is the digital economy and 4IR [Industry 4.0] are all part of the evolving ICT evolutions that are powering and *digitalising* business transformation inside Globalisation 3.0. Globalisation 3.0 was (and still is) being powered by ICT, but the core ICT itself is being transformed and revolutionized daily into new areas like 4IR and the digital economy. McKinsey defines Industry 4.0/4IR thus:

> "Industry 4.0—also called the Fourth Industrial Revolution or 4IR—is the next phase in the *digitization* of the manufacturing sector, driven by disruptive trends including the rise of data and connectivity, analytics, human-machine interaction, and improvements in robotics" – *the author's emphasis* (Source: [484]).

McKinsey's 4IR definition emphasizes the digitization of the manufacturing sector. It was the 2016 Davos summit that set the stage for the introduction of this relatively new term "Fourth Industrial Revolution (4IR)" by Klaus Schwab. As Figure 6.9 illustrates (visually), the Fourth Industrial Revolution (4IR) describes the coming of a new era drawing from new technologies, specifically the fusion of the physical, digital and biological spheres (see Fig 6.9). Such a fusion is already envisaged to impact and disrupt industries, education, jobs, government, society and economies. This is real. Consider 3D printing already with us – and the Three-dimensional (3D Printing) of guns! Or the ethical issues involved with bioprinting and synthetic biology[485]?

---

[484] *Ibid.*

[485] Synthetic biology involves the design and construction of novel artificial biological pathways, organisms and devices or the redesign of existing natural biological system (Royal Society, UK).

We may be in Globalisation 3.0, but some of the new evolving ICT tools as shown in Figure 6.9 are truly frightening – and would need much regulation.

As with previous industrial revolutions, 4IR offers great promises and opportunities, but also grave concerns and challenges to regulation and more. Globalisation 3.0 shrank the world from Small to Tiny driven through ICT. However, 4IR provides the tools to a single '"tiny" individual in his/her room or garage to start "manufacturing" (by 3D printing) dangerous weapons.

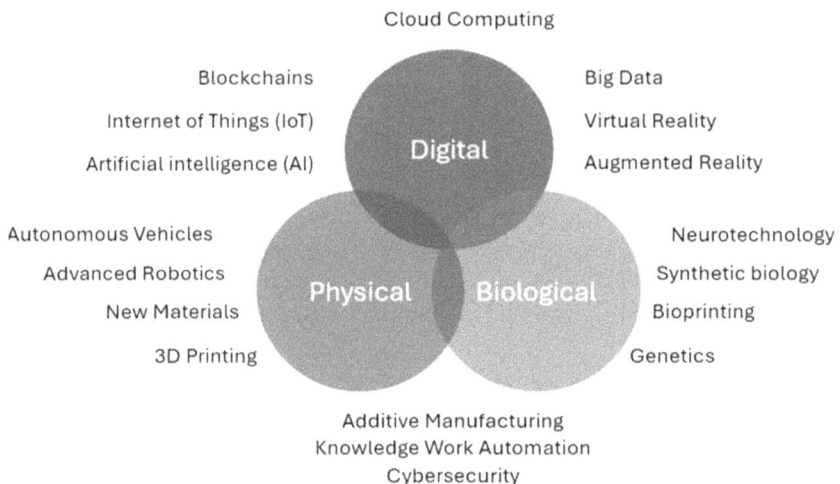

Cloud Computing

Blockchains · Big Data
Internet of Things (IoT) · Virtual Reality
Artificial intelligence (AI) · **Digital** · Augmented Reality

Autonomous Vehicles · Neurotechnology
Advanced Robotics · Synthetic biology
New Materials · **Physical** · **Biological** · Bioprinting
3D Printing · Genetics

Additive Manufacturing
Knowledge Work Automation
Cybersecurity

Figure 6.9 – Defining 4IR or the 4th Industrial Revolution

Source: Based on and adapted from John Grill Centre for Project Leadership and Silicon Valley Innovation Centre[486]

The scale, speed and complexity of 4IR is truly scary. And there are no norms, standards, infrastructure, regulations, and business models that define them. The fusion of 4IR's areas (of digital, physical and biological) may be the source of future technologies that will upend everything else I have covered in this chapter – but also bring with it so many more risks, harms and controversies.

---

[486]https://www.virtualpaper.pro/index.php?route=mag2/article&tracking=5de07f22931bf
&a_id=361 - 4IR: Shaping and Defining New Roles for the
Government   (virtualpaper.pro)

Just consider synthetic biology, bioprinting organs[487488], biotechnology and Genetic Engineering using AI[489], neurotechnology[490] and more. These 4IR areas are hardly uncontroversial. The ethical issues associated with them are numerous.

Returning to Digital Economy, the definition – or more accurately 'categorisation' - I like best is that Bukht & Heeks (2017). Bukht & Heeks categorise digital economy in three concentric circles namely the core circle of digital sector (IT/ICT), the narrow scope of digital economy of digital services and platform economy and broad scope of digitalised economy – as shown in Figure 6.10. The *core* and *narrow scopes* 'digital economies' cover the ICT producing sector as we experience today, including various digital services (e.g. outsourced call centre services, OTTs) and platform economy services (e.g., Facebook/Meta, Google/Alphabet or Amazon).

However, the *broad scope* 'digital economy' includes the exploitation and use of several digital technologies for transformation including 4IR/industry 4.0, e-business, e-commerce, automation, precision agriculture and artificial intelligence (AI) (referred to collectively as the "algorithmic economy"). As shown too, they have "sharing economy" (e.g. Uber and Airbnb) and gig economy on the margins of the second and third concentric circle, i.e. narrow scope and broad scope digital economy.

---

[487] "Biological printing or bioprinting uses living cells, proteins, and nutrients as raw materials and has the potential to produce human tissues for treating injury and disease and to create entire organs for transplants" – NASA

[488] "3D-printed organs may soon be a reality. 'Looking ahead, we'll not need donor hearts" - https://fortune.com/well/2023/02/15/3d-printed-organs-may-soon-be-a-reality/

[489] Biotechnology and Genetic Engineering using AI: A Review | International Journal of Intelligent Systems and Applications in Engineering (ijisae.org) - https://ijisae.org/index.php/IJISAE/article/view/4456

[490] "In its simplest form, neurotechnology is the integration of technical components3 with the nervous system. These components can be computers, electrodes or any other piece of engineering that can be set up to interface with the electric pulses coursing through our bodies" - https://www.technologynetworks.com/neuroscience/articles/neurotechnology-358488#D1

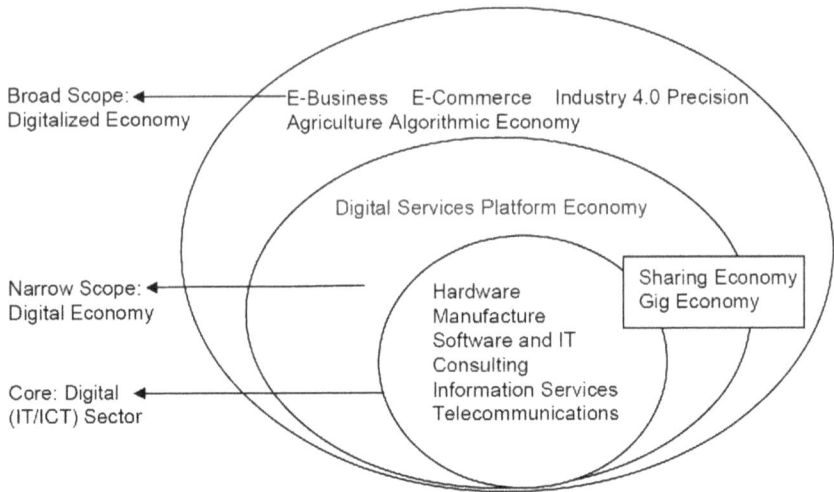

Figure 6.10 – Scoping the Digital Economy[491]

Adapted from Bukht & Heeks (2017)

I like this definition/categorization because – *inter alia* – it clarifies the following:

- Countries can start by setting up and getting their 'Core Digital (IT/ICT) sector right – TMT regulators and standard bodies are already set up in most countries to address this.

- Then, they can start evolving their sectors into addressing the challenges of the *Narrow Scope* digital economy next. This is key to me because I have seen some cases of countries in Africa and South East Asia trying to jump to the *Broad Scope* Digital economy issues like Industry 4.0/4IR without addressing the narrow scope digital services, digital platforms and sharing economy challenges. They inevitably fail. Regulation to realise the narrow scope digital economy is more 'contained'.

- It clarifies that 'Broad Scope' digital economy issues like AI, Industry 4.0, etc., are more advanced – and developed countries and regions

---

[491] https://www.semanticscholar.org/paper/ADBI-Working-Paper-Series-DIGITALIZATION-AND-OF-TWO-Nayak-Behera/f11ac5d538ad694d21bb9b612de700cb08a28182/figure/0 - Figure 1 from ADBI Working Paper Series DIGITALIZATION AND ECONOMIC PERFORMANCE OF TWO FAST-GROWING ASIAN ECONOMIES: INDIA AND THE PEOPLE'S REPUBLIC OF CHINA | Semantic Scholar

like the EU are just enacting regulations for such activities as of 2024, such as the DMA, DSA, DGA and AI Acts. It will take a while for developing economies to get to such laws.

Lastly, what is a 'Regulatory Sandbox' – a term I mention in the heading of this section. Here are some definitions.

- ❖ "A regulatory sandbox is a 'safe space' in which businesses can test innovative products, services, business models and delivery mechanism without immediately incurring all the normal regulatory consequences of engaging in the activity in question.[492]" (UK FCA)
- ❖ "In a nutshell, against the backdrop of whether innovation meets regulatory requirements, a sandbox regime allows entities to test their products, services or solutions in the market under a more relaxed regulatory environment but within a well-defined space and duration agreed with the regulators"[493]. (Baker McKenzie)
- ❖ "A regulatory sandbox is a framework set up by a regulator that allows FinTech startups and other innovators to conduct live experiments in a controlled environment under a regulator's supervision"[494]. (CGAP)

Therefore regulatory sandboxes:

- *Provide for a new approach to the regulatory and supervisory treatment*: of innovative products and services, e.g. 4IR innovations, blockchains, etc. Regulatory sandboxes are just one of several possible measures to promote innovation, not the only one.
- *Regulatory waivers:* waiving away some regulatory rules. Compliance with regulatory requirements and regulations can be most burdensome and overwhelming for companies (especially SMEs), and can hamper growth. In order to promote the

---

[492] https://www.fca.org.uk/firms/innovation/regulatory-sandbox - Regulatory Sandbox | FCA

[493] https://www.bakermckenzie.com/en/-/media/files/insight/publications/2018/12/guide_intlguideregulatorysandboxes_dec2018.pdf Handout_INTP96257_KMaquiling_Manila_11132018.indd (bakermckenzie.com)

[494] https://www.cgap.org/topics/collections/regulatory-sandboxes - Regulatory Sandboxes | CGAP

development of innovations, waivers or modifications to existing rules can be granted to specific applications for products/services that meet pre-defined criteria, i.e., the so-called "regulatory sandboxes".

Many emerging Regulatory Sandbox programmes share two typical common characteristics:

- Genuine innovation: Firms applying for regulatory waivers under regulatory sandboxes are often required to demonstrate that their business idea is a genuine innovation – i.e. use of a new and emerging technology; or the innovative use of an existing technology;
- Identifiable consumer or social benefit: outlining how the proposed innovation can lead to higher quality or lower prices, or how the business model addresses an otherwise unmet demand.

The UK Financial Conduct Authority provides for sandboxing[495], e.g., it seeks to seeks to provide firms with:

- The ability to test products and services in a controlled environment;
- Reduce the time-to-market potentially at a lower cost;
- Support in identifying appropriate consumer protection safeguards to build into new products and services; and to
- Provide better access to finance.

The UK's Financial Conduct Authority (FCA) launched the first regulatory sandbox in 2015 by the UK when it coined the term "regulatory sandbox". The FCA has since generated much interest from regulators and innovators around the world. Since 2015 the concept been applied and gone live across more than 25 countries from UAE to Sierra Leone. Many other countries are in stages of sandbox development: consultation, announcement, in progress, draft bill, agreement to implement sandboxes. Sandboxes have been adopted by many sectors, spreading from FinTech to Health, Transport, Energy and ICT, amongst others.

---

[495] https://www.fca.org.uk/firms/innovation/regulatory-sandbox - Regulatory Sandbox | FCA

Summary of some suggested recommendations to regulate the 'Narrow Scope' and 'Broad Scope' digital economies: the 'Narrow Scope' digital economy should be regulated – depending on the activities - using a combination of Regulatory Forbearance, No Regulation, Self-Regulation, Co-Regulation, Statutory Regulation and Regulatory Networks. The 'Broad Scope' digital economy - as well as tricky areas like 4IR/Industry 4.0 – should/would be regulated through a combination of Statutory, Meta-Regulation and Regulatory Networks, with the support of Regulatory Sandboxes: let me explain some more with some views. These are not necessarily 'hard and fast' rules or recommendations.

- *Statutory regulation for the Core Digital/ICT sector (see Figure 6.10)*: is already being used in most countries to regulate the 'Core Digital (IT/ICT)' sector.

- *Regulatory Networks and more for regulating the 'Narrow Scope' digital economy (see Figure 6.10)*: the narrow scope digital economy should be regulated depending on the activities – as per the previous section - using a combination of Regulatory Forbearance, No Regulation, Self-Regulation, Co-Regulation, Statutory Regulation and Regulatory Networks. Why you – the eagled eye -may wonder have I included Regulatory Networks which I did not have in the last section at all? The answer is that in many economies – even including developing economies – the narrow scope digital economy is already evolving and emerging. This has resulted in a plethora of regulators emerging in addition to the TMT/telecoms regulator. They include a Cybersecurity regulator, a Data Protection Office or regulator, a Digital Government agency, a broadcasting regulator[496], a Payments Services regulator, etc.

These regulators would have to find a coherent and harmonious way of working together and sharing information on matters that have both competition, data protection, Government, payments and communication dimensions. It is up to the regulators to produce clear arrangements to ensure successful inter-regulators cooperation – as Kenya has essentially evolved in regulating MFS. Recall from Chapter 3 that the underlying theory of Regulatory Networks is that the most

---

[496] Some countries still have broadcast regulators in this era of total convergence. Do not ask me why.

optimal regulatory outcomes will typically involve "mixtures" from regulatory institutions and regulatory instruments.

- *Regulatory Sandboxes for both narrow and broad scope digital economies (see Figure 6.10)*: many, if not most of the activities, in the narrow scope, and certainly the broad scope digital economy, are amenable to regulatory sandboxing as described above.

- *Statutory Regulation, Meta-Regulation and Regulatory Networks (with support of Regulatory Sandboxes) to regulate the 'Broad Scope' digital economy (see Figure 6.10):* the use of statutory (*ex-ante* and *ex-post*) regulation is already being used in the EC – as covered earlier in this chapter – to regulate narrow and broad scope digital economy issues as is evidenced by the swathe of new EC laws like the DSA, DMA, DGA and AI Acts. The role of Regulatory Networks is already covered in the previous bullet. Why meta-regulation too? Recall from Chapter 3 that term 'meta-regulation' refers to "processes in which the regulatory authority oversees a control or risk management system, rather than conducts regulation directly – it 'steers rather than rows'". I would argue the EC is a meta-regulator who 'steers' other national regulatory authorities (NRAs), rather than 'row' – at least for the *telecoms sector*. I think with the plethora of regulators that are already emerging, the role for meta-regulation nationally is becoming stronger and stronger. However, it is true that the DSA, DMA, DGA and AI Acts are principally being implemented centrally by the EC, not the EU's NRAs

- *Informal Networks of Regulators*: many, if not most of the activities, in the narrow scope, and certainly the broad scope digital economy, are amenable to regulatory sandboxing as described above. However, informal networks of established regulators are also emerging.

For example, the UK has a network of regulators called UKRN[497], or UK Regulators Networks. The UKRN describes itself as:

> "The UKRN brings together regulators from the UK's utility, financial, transport and housing sectors, for the benefit of

---

[497]https://ukrn.org.uk/about/ - About | UKRN: the UK Regulators Network

consumers and the economy. We were *established by our members* in 2014 and *have developed strong relationships and a culture of collaboration and learning.* We work together *to share knowledge and innovation, explore cross-cutting issues and build better ways of working".* *The authors emphases* - (Source: [498])

I think the above quote speaks for itself, and the UKRN is arguably not only a Regulatory Network in the UK, but a Meta-Regulator which could/would 'steer' its members. I (re)emphasize that my views above are not that 'hard and fast'. I want the reader to reflect on the logic I use to justify them more.

- *Digital Regulation Cooperation Forum (DRCF) – Non Statutory*: Since this chapter is about digital regulation, I conclude by referring to the interesting regulatory network model in the form of the non-statutory Digital Regulation Cooperation Forum [499], between the CMA, FCA, ICO and Ofcom. Its CEO states that:

> "Working together as the DRCF enables our four member regulators to achieve better outcomes for industry and consumers. The DRCF creates coherence to resolve potential tensions between our members' regulatory regimes; collaboration to work together on complex challenges; and capabilities for the future, with the right people, skills and critical functions to navigate the rapidly developing digital economy."[500]

I believe the goals of the DRCF are both very sensible and laudable, and ones that other countries would (or should) consider as 'best practice' – as pertains to the regulation of digital activities in their countries. It is inconceivable that such cooperation would not be indispensable.

---

[498] *Ibid.*

[499] https://www.drcf.org.uk/home

[500] *Ibid.*

6.6.4 Regulating the increasing use of Artificial Intelligence using Statutory Regulation, Self-Regulation, Guidelines & Regulatory Sandboxes

Increasing digitization and digitalization of sectors of our economies brings with them the increasing employment of Artificial Intelligence (A) and Machine Learning. AI is a branch of computer science dealing with the simulation of intelligent behaviour in computers and electronic communication systems.

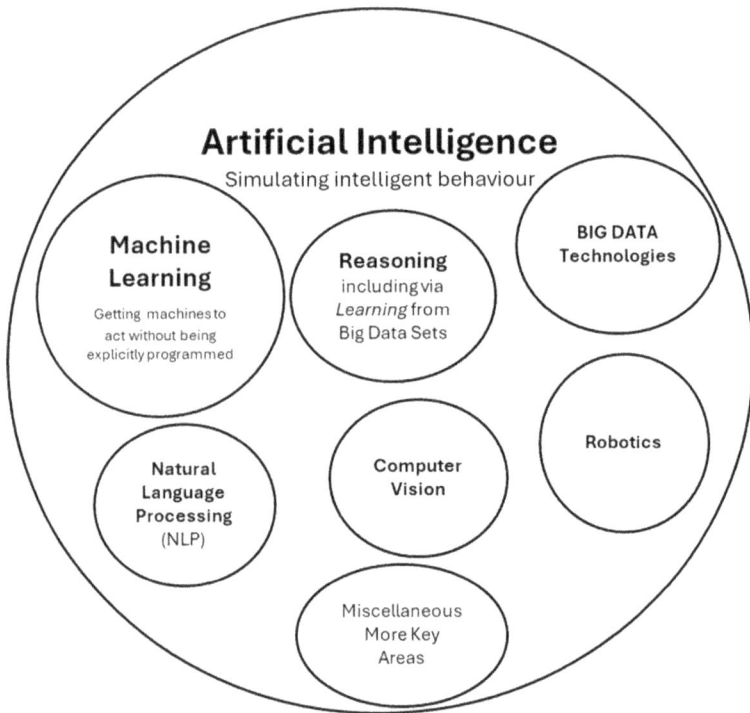

Figure 6.11 – The 'Umbrella' called Artificial Intelligence (AI)

As shown in Figure 6.11, AI is today an 'umbrella' term that refers to computer systems capable of performing complex tasks that historically only humans could do, such as reasoning, solving truly complex problems and making decisions from big data sets, such as recognising speech, 'recognising' and identifying people's faces through computer vision, complex translations between languages and more. AI encompasses and uses a wide variety of technologies, including machine learning, big data technologies, computer vision, robotics, natural language processing (NLP), cognitive networks and much more not shown in Figure 6.11. In particular, machine learning (ML) and big data technologies are two key components of AI. The former – ML - describes the science of getting computers to act without being explicitly programmed. Today, complex AI algorithms learn from the biggest 'Big Data' data sets imaginable: just consider that 2.5 quintillion[501] data bytes of data was created daily in 2020 (Source, Domo[502]).

This is why my favourite definition of "Big data technologies" is the following: big data technologies describe a new generation of technologies and architectures, designed to economically extract *value* from very large *volumes* of a wide *variety* of data, by enabling high-*velocity* capture, discovery, and/or analysis[503]. AI and Big Data have now evolved to be two sides of the same coin. This is because AI – which has been around since the 1950s – has come into its element as it is increasingly used to extract value from high-velocity big data. Today, with (i) huge amounts of data (Big Data), (ii) advanced algorithms, (iii) oodles of storage and (iv) high end computing power. As I wrote in 2022, AI has been put on steroids (Nwana, 2022).

Artificial intelligence (AI) and Machine Learning are expanding into more industries (often in surprising ways), and in many cases catching regulators unaware. A mixture of regulatory models are being evolved and adopted worldwide on the increasing use of AI: no regulation, statutory regulation, self-regulation, self-regulation with official guidelines, regulatory sandboxes and Trustworthy AI.

6.6.4.1 Trustworthy AI – towards a more Ethical AI

AI and ML are at the core of some emerging Digital Economy harms. For example, Meta/Facebook's Founder and CEO Mark Zuckerberg allegedly fully acknowledges the problem of Facebook's AI-based ranking models

---

[501] A quintillion is 1 followed by 18 zeroes.

[502] Press Release - Domo Releases Annual "Data Never Sleeps" Infographic | Domo - https://www.domo.com/news/press/domo-releases-annual-data-never-sleeps-infographic

[503] https://journalofbigdata.springeropen.com/articles/10.1186/s40537-016-0059-y

favouring controversy, misinformation and extremism (Nwana, 2022, see Figure 24). In plain English, this means the more a post approaches the Facebook prohibited content policy line, the greater the user engagement. Even more plainly, the Facebook platform's algorithms were shown to have maximised engagement by rewarding more inflammatory, controversial and/or extremist content. This had real world consequences. Facebook has since admitted its AI and Machine Learning-based ranking algorithms helped to "incite offline violence" in Myanmar[504] with the Rohingya Muslim crisis. Therefore, the harms[505] that AI and ML are enabling are not only offline, but also *ethically* very difficult.

Lest you think that such AI/ML harms only apply to Big Tech companies, you will be wrong. Consider the following. AI and Machine-Learning based Facial Recognition software *wrongly* matched 2000 people as possible criminals in the Cardiff, Wales in 2018[506]. Civil Liberty groups were incensed, rightly citing lack of regulation and human rights concerns:

> It is a far more powerful policing tool than traditional CCTV - as the cameras take a biometric map, creating a numerical code of the faces of each person who passes the camera. These biometric maps are uniquely identifiable to the individual." It is just like taking people's DNA or fingerprints, without their knowledge or their consent," said Megan Goulding, a lawyer from the civil liberties group Liberty which is supporting Mr Bridges. However, unlike DNA or fingerprints, there is no specific regulation governing how police use facial recognition or manage the data gathered. Liberty argues that even if there were regulations, facial recognition breaches human rights and should not be used.
>
> (Source: BBC[507])

---

[504] Facebook admits it was used to 'incite offline violence' in Myanmar - BBC News - https://www.bbc.co.uk/news/world-asia-46105934

[505] E.g., joining Facebook terrorism groups (see Nwana, 2022).

[506] 2,000 wrongly matched with possible criminals at Champions League - BBC News - https://www.bbc.co.uk/news/uk-wales-south-west-wales-44007872

[507] Police facial recognition surveillance court case starts - BBC News - https://www.bbc.co.uk/news/uk-48315979

What about this further example. "Artificial Intelligence has a problem with Gender and Racial Bias…[508]". These are the words of MIT graduate Joy Buolamwini who has since founded an organisation called the Algorithmic Justice League[509].

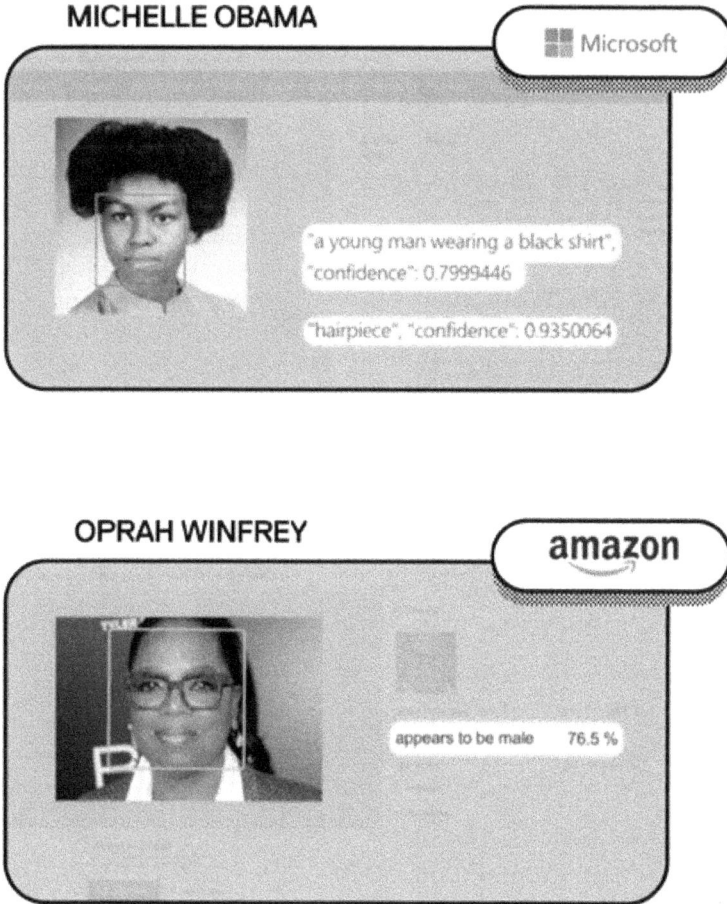

Image 6.1 – AI & Machine Learning Software getting it badly wrong
(Adapted from Source: Joy Buolamwini[510])

Artificial Intelligence Has a Racial and Gender Bias Problem | Time - https://time.com/5520558/artificial-intelligence-racial-gender-bias/
Research - The Algorithmic Justice League (ajl.org) - https://www.ajl.org/library/research
Ibid.

Her research found that some facial analysis software [from IBM, Microsoft and Amazon] could not detect her *dark-skinned* face until she put on a white mask, because the systems were trained on predominantly *light-skinned men.*

> The companies I evaluated had error rates of no more than 1% for lighter-skinned men. For darker-skinned women, the errors soared to 35%. AI systems from leading companies have failed to correctly classify the faces of Oprah Winfrey, Michelle Obama, and Serena Williams. When technology denigrates even these iconic women, it is time to re-examine how these systems are built and who they truly serve.
>
> Joy Buolamwini[511]

According to her [Joy Buolamwini's] research – as depicted in Image 6.1 – the American icon Oprah Winfrey "appears to male 76.5%" using some Amazon's image recognition software and former USA First Lady Michelle Obama was "a young man wearing a black shirt, confidence: 0.7999446" according to another Microsoft facial recognition system. China's Face++ system simply classified tennis legend Serena Williams as male. Buolamwini is making recommendations on how to get such systems to address such *obvious biases and discriminations* in them. Is the reader surprised then that 2000 people were *wrongly* matched as possible criminals in the Cardiff, Wales in 2018?

Algorithmic Transparency and Trust issues are emerging as key issues with AI Algorithms. They cover (not exhaustive):

- Rankings mechanisms (e.g. with Search engines)
- Recommendation mechanisms like Buy Boxes (e.g. Amazon)
- Dominant platforms (e.g. Google and Amazon) "prescribe" and recommend using their "black box" algorithms
- How do we *ethically balance* Personalisation benefits (for the benefit of the online user) vs. the Supplier benefit (i.e., the digital platform maximising its revenues and profits)?

---

[511] Artificial Intelligence Has a Racial and Gender Bias Problem | Time - https://time.com/5520558/artificial-intelligence-racial-gender-bias/

- What about the ethics of "free" advertising business models encouraging online users to part away with most sensitive data about themselves?
- AI algorithms carrying out credit scoring, recruitment, image identification, age identification, etc. How fair is it?

These ethical issues here truly abound, but *trust* seems to be a major issue. Most ML algorithms, particularly neural networks, cannot be "understood" by humans easily, and perhaps even by their creators. The reputational damage with black-box solutions when things go wrong are just humongous as the examples above attest. What about the EU's GDPR core principle requirement for the "explain-ability" of decisions? Where does this sit with such AI and ML algorithms?

The reality is that Artificial Intelligence (AI) and Machine Learning crystallise two key challenges in how society traditionally operates today.

- Lack of legal precedents for dealing with harms originated by algorithms and machines (trading-off with efficiency gains);
- And that the tech sector that is still mostly unregulated in most jurisdictions.

These are two huge issues to deal with pertaining to controlling AI and its "ethics". So, the terminology Trustworthy AI[512] has emerged to start addressing such challenges with AI and ML systems. However, it is still very early days.

For the time being the EU (as part of its Artificial Intelligence Act[513]) has pioneered some key ethical principles and guidelines which I believe are sensible for most countries[514].

The 4 ethical AI principles they recommend include:

(i) Respect for human autonomy
(ii) Prevention of harm

---

[512] https://digital-strategy.ec.europa.eu/en/library/ethics-guidelines-trustworthy-ai

[513] https://www.europarl.europa.eu/news/en/press-room/20240308IPR19015/artificial-intelligence-act-meps-adopt-landmark-law - https://www.europarl.europa.eu/news/en/press-room/20240308IPR19015/artificial-intelligence-act-meps-adopt-landmark-law

[514] https://ec.europa.eu/futurium/en/ai-alliance-consultation/guidelines

(iii) Fairness

(iv) Explicability

Their 7 core AI requirements include:

i. Human agency and oversight

ii. Technical robustness and safety

iii. Privacy and Data Governance

iv. Transparency

v. Diversity, non-discrimination and fairness

vi. Societal and environmental wellbeing

vii. Accountability

As I note earlier, a mixture of regulatory models are being evolved and adopted worldwide on the increasing use of AI: no regulation, statutory regulation, self-regulation, self-regulation with official guidelines and regulatory sandboxes. I cover them next.

6.6.4.2 Statutory Regulation of AI

In the previous main section (Section 6.5), I briefly mention the EU Artificial Intelligence (AI) Act[515] (which was adopted/approved by EU MEPs on the 13th of March 2024[516]) which aims at establishing a "comprehensive legal framework on AI worldwide" for "foster[ing] trustworthy AI in Europe and beyond, by ensuring that AI systems respect fundamental rights, safety, and ethical principles and by addressing risks of very powerful and impactful AI models"[517].

---

[515] https://www.europarl.europa.eu/news/en/press-room/20240308IPR19015/artificial-intelligence-act-meps-adopt-landmark-law - https://www.europarl.europa.eu/news/en/press-room/20240308IPR19015/artificial-intelligence-act-meps-adopt-landmark-law

[516] https://www.europarl.europa.eu/news/en/press-room/20231206IPR15699/artificial-intelligence-act-deal-on-comprehensive-rules-for-trustworthy-ai#:~:text=MEPs%20reached%20a%20political%20deal,on%20the%20Artificial%20Intelligence%20Act. - Artificial Intelligence Act: deal on comprehensive rules for trustworthy AI | News | European Parliament (europa.eu)

[517] https://digital-strategy.ec.europa.eu/en/policies/regulatory-framework-ai - AI Act | Shaping Europe's digital future (europa.eu)

This EU AI Act is mainly enforced at national level by EU Member States, with the exception of general-purpose (GP) AI models, which are enforced by the European AI Office. The AI Office has the power in the Act to conduct evaluations of GP AI models, and the Office may also assist and support national authorities in relation to market surveillance of high-risk AI systems. The EU AI Act is clearly *statutory* and is considered to be the world's first comprehensive horizontal legal framework for AI based on a risk-based approach. The risk-based approach to AI Regulation adopts a philosophy where the obligations on an AI system are proportionate to the level of risk that the system poses. Specifically, the EU AI Act outlines four levels of risk[518]: (i) low risk systems, (ii) limited or minimal risk systems, (iii) high-risk systems and (iv) systems with unacceptable risk.

- **Low-risk AI systems**: are the majority and includes spam filters for example powered by AI. Low-risk AI systems are practically subject to no statutory rules.

- **Limited or minimal risk AI systems**: include chatbots and they refer to AI systems that interact with humans, detect humans based on biometrics like their voice and manipulate content. Such systems can be used to produce deep fakes – and therefore such limited or minimal risk systems are subject to *transparency* obligations in the EU AI Act.

- **High-risk AI systems**: refer to those which the EU deems can impact the life chances of user, e.g. their health, safety or their fundamental rights. There are eight such systems identified and categorised: (i) biometric identification systems, (ii) systems employing AI used in employment, (iii) systems for education and vocational training employing AI, (iv) systems for critical infrastructure and protection of the environment employing AI, (v) systems for talent management and access to self-employment employing AI, (vi) systems controlling access and use of private and public services and benefits which employ AI, including AI-based insurance systems, (vii) law enforcement systems employing AI, and (viii) systems used to manage asylum, border control, migration, and systems used in the administration of justice and democratic processes. The Commission is tasked with maintaining an EU database for the high-risk AI systems

---

[518] https://www.europarl.europa.eu/RegData/etudes/BRIE/2021/698792/EPRS_B RI(2021)698792_EN.pdf

listed in this annex[519]. These high-risk AI systems are subject to stringent obligations under the EU AI Act and must undergo "conformity assessment procedures" before their products can be sold and used in the EU.

- **AI Systems with 'unacceptable' risks**: are simply prohibited in the EU under the Act. Such systems include "AI systems that deploy harmful manipulative 'subliminal techniques'; AI systems that exploit specific vulnerable groups (physical or mental disability); AI systems used by public authorities, or on their behalf, for social scoring purposes; 'Real-time' remote biometric identification systems in publicly accessible spaces for law enforcement purposes, except in a limited number of cases"[520].

6.6.4.3 No Regulation of AI

Many countries and regions are still adopting a 'wait and see' approach to the regulation on AI, choosing regulatory forbearance as their preferred approach. In many developing countries in South East Asia, Africa, Caribbean and elsewhere, no regulation of AI is more of a 'default' approach, i.e. not a conscious choice. This is because they are typically nowhere near mature and ready to set up the sort of sophisticated AI laws and their enforcement like the EU AI Act and the European AI Office.

6.6.4.4 Self-Regulation of AI (with regulation to come)

I would argue that the USA – at the federal level - as of May 2024 has allowed companies themselves to self-regulate in relation to the increasing adoption of AI. As I note in Section 6.4, even Big Tech in America (e.g. Meta/Facebook) is requesting some federal regulation, and they have suggested some areas to start from. To date in May 2024, due to no federal AI laws, they are largely self-regulating. I argue in Nwana (2022, p. 191) that this leads to disastrous consequences in some cases, e.g. AI amplification algorithms that even Meta/Facebook concedes was used to "incite offline violence" in Myanmar[521] through viral fake news and hate

---

[519] *Ibid.*

[520] *Ibid.*

[521] https://www.bbc.co.uk/news/world-asia-46105934

speech about the Rohingya Muslim minority [instigated by the ruling military junta]. So, the USA authorities have in my opinion made a conscious choice not to regulate AI.

However, some US States have started making inroads into regulating AI at their States-level for specific problematic use cases, e.g. the use of AI in recruitment and employment: "for example, New York joined a number of states, including Illinois and Maryland, in regulating Automated Employment Decision Tools (AEDTs) that leverage AI to make, or substantially assist, candidate screening or employment decisions. Under New York's law, AEDTs must undergo an annual "bias audit," and results of this audit need to be made publicly available" (Source[522]). In this vein, in 2021, the US Equal Opportunity Employment Commission (EEOC[523]) – a clear federal agency - launched an initiative on "algorithmic fairness" in employment. Jointly with the US Federal Department of Justice, they issued guidance on the use of AI tools in employee hiring[524], with the guidance focusing on AI that can, even if inadvertently or unintentionally, violate laws through screening out employees with disabilities. Is this beginning of the federal regulation of AI in the USA?

6.6.4.5 Guidelines-Based Regulation of AI

Some regions like ASEAN[525] have issued *non-binding* guidelines in February 2024 on AI Governance and Ethics: "the ASEAN Guide on AI Governance and Ethics aims to empower organisations and governments in the region to design, develop, and deploy traditional AI systems responsibly and increase users' trust in AI"[526]. It promotes key guiding principles including (i) transparency and explainability, (ii) fairness and equity, (iii) security and safety, (iv) robustness and reliability, (v) human-

---

[522]   https://www.alston.com/en/insights/publications/2022/12/ai-regulation-in-the-us - AI Regulation in the U.S.: What's Coming, and What Companies Need to Do in 2023 | News & Insights | Alston & Bird

[523] https://www.eeoc.gov/

[524] https://www.eeoc.gov/ai

[525] ASEAN is political and economic union of 10 states in Southeast Asia, representing a population of over 600 million people.

[526]https://asean.org/wp-content/uploads/2024/02/ASEAN-Guide-on-AI-Governance-and-Ethics_beautified_201223_v2.pdf

centricity, (vi) privacy and data governance and (vii) accountability and integrity.

The ASEAN AI framework's key components cover (a) internal governance structures and measures for regulating AI such as an AI Ethics Advisory Board, to oversee AI governance efforts, (b) determining the level of human involvement in AI-augmented decision-making, (c) operations management including how to conduct risk-based assessments and (d) stakeholder and communications to develop trust with stakeholders.

These ASEAN guidelines are well-thought through and come with national level recommendations too including nurturing AI talent/upskilling workforce and promoting adoption of useful tools by businesses to implement the ASEAN Guide on AI Governance and Ethics. The ASEAN AI framework's core components and recommendations – somewhat similar to the EU AI Act - emphasise the importance of a *risk-based approach to AI* Governance and Ethics whereby the impact of AI on its users and stakeholders dictates the level of human oversight over AI technology. Unlike with the EU AI Act, these ASEAN AI guidelines are non-binding on ASEAN member states, but offers a flexible framework for the harmonization of AI Policy among the 10 member states of ASEAN. Since the guidelines are non-binding on ASEAN States, leading AI firms in many ASEAN states are *de facto* practicing self-regulation of AI, using the guidelines as necessary. It is still early days since these guidelines were published in February 2024 as I write these sentences in May 2024.

6.6.4.6 Additional AI Guidelines to Supplement Statutory Regulations

Even with the statutory EU AI Act which the Dutch Government is subject to, the latter has issued additional specific AI guidelines on the use of AI in public service use. To be fair, the origins of the Dutch-specific national AI requirements preceded the final enactment of the EU AI Act in March 2024 – however, these guidelines still stand after the EU AI Act came into force. As Marcus Grazette writes:

> "The Dutch approach is shaped by the scandal around a biased algorithm that their tax office used to assess benefits claims. The tax office implemented the system in 2013 and, after civil society raised concerns, two formal investigations in 2020 and 2021 uncovered

systematic bias affecting 1.4 million people. Amnesty International's report on the scandal documents the harms people suffered as a result; some lost their homes, life savings and suffered ill health due to stress. In 2021, then Prime Minister Mark Rutte issued a formal apology and his entire Cabinet resigned over the scandal"[527].

I include the above citation to provide a real-world example of the potential harms of the unconstrained use of AI in public systems.

6.6.4.7 Regulatory Sandboxes for Generative AI Systems

As I noted earlier citing the UK's FCA, a regulatory sandbox is "a 'safe space' in which businesses can test innovative products, services, business models and delivery mechanism without immediately incurring all the normal regulatory consequences of engaging in the activity in question[528]".

Some Authorities are employing the Regulatory Sandbox model for regulating certain AI systems. For example, Singapore is developing a generative AI sandbox[529] overseen by the Infocomm Media Development Authority[530] (IMDA) and AI Verify Foundation[531]. "The Sandbox will bring global ecosystem players together through concrete use cases, to enable the evaluation of trusted AI products. The Sandbox will make use of a new Evaluation Catalogue, as a shared resource, which sets out common baseline methods and recommendations for Large Language Models (LLM)".[532]

---

[527] https://www.holisticai.com/blog/the-netherlands-ai-regulation - AI Regulation Around the World: The Netherlands (holisticai.com)

[528] https://www.fca.org.uk/firms/innovation/regulatory-sandbox - Regulatory Sandbox | FCA

[529] https://www.imda.gov.sg/resources/press-releases-factsheets-and-speeches/press-releases/2023/generative-ai-evaluation-sandbox - Generative AI Evaluation Sandbox | IMDA - Infocomm Media Development Authority

[530] https://www.imda.gov.sg/

[531] https://aiverifyfoundation.sg/what-is-ai-verify/

[532] https://www.imda.gov.sg/resources/press-releases-factsheets-and-speeches/press-releases/2023/generative-ai-evaluation-sandbox

This is Singapore's approach to have a common standard approach to assess generative AI. The IMDA claims that over 10 global players have joined the Sandbox to develop evaluation benchmarks for trusted Generative AI including key model developers like Google, Microsoft, Anthropic, IBM, NVIDIA, Stability.AI and Amazon Web Servies (AWS). A Generative AI Evaluation Sandbox makes much sense to me not only in forging a harmonized and responsible use of generative AI technologies including machine learning applications, but it also encourages developers to evaluate their applications for adherence to common standards. This approach also encourages a shared trusted ecosystem approach of independent, open source, and third-party model evaluations that are critical to building safe and trustworthy AI. This is achieved through the use of the Evaluation Catalogue for large language models which caters for countries like Singapore because of its cultural and language specificities. As the IMDA promises, "the Catalogue provides an anchor by (a) compiling the existing commonly used technical testing tools and organising these tests according to what they test for and their methods; and (b) recommending a baseline set of evaluation tests for use in Gen AI products"[533]. This approach is both very innovative and would scale widely beyond the shores of the tiny city state of Singapore.

To conclude this subsection, the increasing digitization and digitalization of sectors of our economies is increasingly employing AI and Machine Learning algorithms. Artificial intelligence (AI) and Machine Learning are expanding into more and more industries. However, some of the transformations are very profound for society, necessitating controls and regulations for AI for consumers and citizens' interests. As covered in this section, many of them entail major ethical, societal and political decisions. The risk-based and sandboxing approaches to AI regulation digitization make much sense at this stage, but more countries better take the regulation of AI seriously.

---

[533] *Ibid.*

6.6.5 Regulating Cloud Computing – another emerging new area of digital regulation

Whether we like it or not, most of us engaged in the digital world are *de facto* engaged in Cloud Computing. What is cloud computing? Investopedia defines cloud computing as

> "the on-demand delivery of computing services such as servers, storage, databases, networking, software, and analytics. Rather than keeping files on a proprietary hard drive or local storage device, cloud-based storage makes it possible to save remotely. Cloud computing is a popular option for people and businesses, allowing for cost savings, increased productivity, speed and efficiency, performance, and security"[534].

With the Internet Value Chain (IVC), see Figures 6.3a and 6.3b, numerous services are delivered through the Internet which includes tools and applications like servers, databases, data storage, software and networking – as the Investopedia definition above describes.

Indeed, most – if not all - of the services in the 'Online Services' segment of the IVC are enabled by *cloud computing* services of the 'Enabling Technology and Services' segment. These include design and hosting, payment platforms, cloud platform & infrastructure services, IoT platforms, analytics, online advertising services and content delivery services (see Figure 6.3b). Cloud computing is therefore an integral part of digital lives. Checking your Yahoo! Email or Gmail messages, or using search engines like Google or Bing, attending virtual meetings on Zoom and Microsoft Teams, using Google Maps, or using your favourite social media apps (X/Twitter, Facebook, Instagram, TikTok, etc.), purchasing goods on Amazon and eBay – these services are all enabled by background cloud computing services. Using these digital services feel so 'natural' and 'native' that you may think there is no need for regulation of cloud computing. Sadly, you will be wrong to think this way.

The regulatory challenges are many, and they stem from our widespread dependence on [cloud] computing 'as a service' (as is evidenced by all the

---

[534] https://www.investopedia.com/terms/c/cloud-computing.asp

categories of examples in the 'Online Services' segment of the Internet Value Chain, see Figure 6.3b). Drawing from Levite & Kalwani (2020) and from our Cenerva[535] training lectures, cloud computing regulatory challenges include:

Consumer and Data Protection Concerns

(i)   Who can access our (consumers/citizens) data?

(ii)   What rights do cloud consumers have regarding their data and the increasing 'utility' services, with many provided 'for free'?

(iii)   How transparent are the cloud service providers (CSPs) about their terms of service, data handling practices, and privacy policies?

(iv)   In the byzantine network of cloud service arrangements, who is truly responsible for understanding the contents of consumers' rights and complying with them? Their right to be informed, right to access, right to rectification, right to be forgotten, right to object, right to understand automated decision making and profiling about them, etc. – concisely, their rights to their *personal data*?

Resilience and Business Continuity Concerns

(i)   What happens if a service fails? Earlier in this chapter, I note this headline from the 23rd of January 2024: *Safaricom Faces Backlash As M-PESA Outage Hits Kenya: Poor Communication Raises Concerns*[536]. Just like M-pesa is now clearly a Critical National Infrastructure (CNI) utility mobile financial services platform in Kenya – so are many of the top-used services in the 'Online Services' segment of the Internet Value Chain. Just consider outages of services like GPS, Google Search, Google Maps, Facebook, YouTube, etc. – this is unfathomable to most consumers today.

(ii)   What are the backup and redundancy strategies to assure and ensure continuous availability to these 'utility' services like Google Search? Should a private company like Google/Alphabet be controlled or regulated to ensure Google Search 'outages' do not occur? Particularly, when we do not explicitly pay for such search services – but rather through 'giving away' data about ourselves?

---

[535] www.cenerva.com

[536] https://www.wazoplus.com/article/-safaricom-faces-backlash-as-m-pesa-outage-hits-kenya-poor-communication-raises-concerns--efd771c1 - Safaricom Faces Backlash As M-PESA Outage Hits Kenya: Poor Communication Raises Concerns

Human and Civil Rights Concerns

(i)   Article 12 of the UN 1948 Universal Declaration of Human Rights (UDHR) speaks to the right of protection to any individual, his/her family or home against "arbitrary interference", "nor any attacks upon his honour and reputation. Everyone has the right to the protection of the law against such interference or attacks"[537]. Article 7 of the EU Charter of Fundamental Rights stipulates "- "Everyone has the right to respect for his or her private and family life, home and correspondence"[538]. How does the use of cloud computing impact such individual privacy and data protection human rights?

(ii)   Internet Censorship and Surveillance is arguably already with us today as Nwana (2022. P.163-165) paints a likely trend towards a 'bifurcated' Internet, i.e., either a more Open Internet or a more censored one. For the latter, consider an Internet connected to a DNA database of millions of people "to help solve crimes"[539] as cited in the respected Nature journal. Or using advanced AI facial recognition technology, online systems, or allegedly collecting voice recognition samples to boost Internet surveillance[540]. Cloud computing services make these feasible. However, where does this leave – not only consumers and citizens' privacy and data protection human rights - but also their liberty and freedom of expression?

(iii)   What safeguards should then be put in place to prevent the misuse of cloud services for surveillance or censorship, and how would they be enforced?

Cybersecurity, Robustness and Data Governance Concerns

(i)   How can CSPs ensure the security and robustness of their cloud-based systems' infrastructures and services with byzantine cloud arrangements amongst several players across several continents?

(ii)   How do they ensure against the key 3 'Ds' Cybersecurity threats of *Disruption, Distortion* and *Deterioration?* Disruption would happen with fragile connectivity. Distortion happens due to loss of trust in information integrity. Deterioration happens when controls

---

[537]   Universal Declaration of Human Rights | United Nations - https://www.un.org/en/about-us/universal-declaration-of-human-rights

[538]   text_en.pdf (europa.eu) - https://www.europarl.europa.eu/charter/pdf/text_en.pdf

[539]China's massive effort to collect its people's DNA concerns scientists (nature.com) - China's massive effort to collect its people's DNA concerns scientists (nature.com)

[540]   China: Voice Biometric Collection Threatens Privacy | Human Rights Watch (hrw.org) - https://www.hrw.org/news/2017/10/22/china-voice-biometric-collection-threatens-privacy

are eroded either through technology, regulation or other. These threats are on the rise with attacks on critical national infrastructure, ransomware attacks, insider attacks (i.e. disruptions); fake news or subverted blockchains (i.e. distortions); and exposing private data, privacy breaches, data poisoning, etc., i.e. deterioration.

(iii)   What measures should be put in place with cloud-based services in order to protect against such data breaches, unauthorized access, and other cyber threats?

(iv)   Cybersecurity and Data Governance are much interrelated. What data governance laws and arrangements should be put in place to regulate byzantine cloud arrangements?

(v)   What data sovereignty and localization standards are in play? The reality is that such policies and standards are aimed at promoting local country/region economic and social interests, and particularly to boost the growth of innovative data-driven domestic industries and services. However, they are typically couched in terms of addressing security and privacy concerns.

(vi)   Should regulation delineate the burden sharing, and codify of the "shared responsibility" for security and robustness between CSPs and their clients, and in some cases also the operators of supporting telecommunications networks[541]?

(vii)   Who drives regulatory actions around the need for standards and adequate levels of transparency in CSP cybersecurity and risk management controls? This should include both systemic controls and operational defensive measures. "This includes not only cybersecurity and safety measures and practices, but also physical protections and back-up arrangements pertaining to both data centers and their supply chains as well as underlying infrastructure, especially telecommunications channels" (Levite & Kalwani, 2020).

---

[541] As recommended in Levite & Kalwani (2020), See examples of such agreements from two of the largest CSPs: "Shared Responsibility Model," Amazon Web Services, https://aws.amazon.com/compliance/shared-responsibility-model/; "Shared Responsibility in the Cloud," Microsoft Azure, https://docs.microsoft.com/en-us/azure/security/fundamentals/shared-responsibility

Competition Concerns

(i)   Many Cloud Service Providers (CSPs) including FANGAM are significant, if not dominant, market players in their markets or sub-segments (see Figure 6.3b), e.g. Google in Search, Facebook in Social Media, WhatsApp in Communication & Collaboration, Azure and AWS in Cloud Platform & Infrastructure Services. How do you ensure that dominant Cloud-based market players do not crowd out and kill off newer competitors? The competition concerns with the big digital behemoths are already acute, see Figures 6.2 and 6.5. The EU is regulating some key cloud service providers through its DMA, DSA, DGA and Artificial Intelligence Acts.

(ii)   What concentration of market power in the cloud services industry would lead to operational and cost efficiencies, albeit coming at the expense of consumer protection, security and resilience/single point of failure concerns.

(iii)   Should key 'utility' cloud services be subject to designation as critical infrastructure, and CSPs as critical service providers? Who should do any such designations? US Authorities like Cybersecurity Infrastructure Security Agency (CISA[542]) have commenced doing this across sectors of the economy[543]. Levite & Kalwani (2020) note that U.S. lawmakers had requested that the Financial Stability Oversight Council (FSOC) analyse and regulate some CSPs as examples of systemically important financial market *utilities*.

Economic Growth & Sustainability Concerns

(i)   How can CSPs along with their cloud adoption truly drive innovation and economic growth?

(ii)   What policies and their implementation should be put in place to encourage responsible cloud usage while minimizing negative environmental impact? Consider the fact that there are already around 600 *hyperscale data centres* – i.e., ones with over 5,000 servers – in the world. Around 39% of them are in the US, while China, Japan, UK, Germany and Australia account for about 30%

---

[542] Cybersecurity Infrastructure Security Agency - https://www.cisa.gov/

[543] "Critical Infrastructure Sectors," Cybersecurity and Infrastructure Security Agency, last updated March 24, 2020, https://www.cisa.gov/critical-infrastructure-sectors

of the total[544]. The largest data centres in the world are China Telecom's Data Centre, in Hohhot, China, which occupies 10.7 million square feet and the Citadel in Tahoe Reno, Nevada, which occupies 7.2 million square feet and uses 815 megawatts of power. More than half a dozen countries in Africa including Mali do *not* have on-grid installed generation capacity to serve their populations anywhere near 815 megawatts in 2024.

(iii) How is cloud computing regulated for environmental sustainability and Net Zero needs, i.e., achieving an overall balance between emissions produced [by data centres and their hundreds or thousands of servers] and emissions taken out of the atmosphere of the earth through carbon sinks, for example (see Section 4.8.2)?

Drawing from these challenges, the regulation of [increasing] cloud computing should take into account and *balance* factors like economic growth, consumer and data protection, cybersecurity, data governance, resilience and business continuity, sustainability, outsourcing/vendor management, recordkeeping and human/civil rights. These make the regulatory landscape and context of cloud computing to be extraordinarily complex. Understanding and regulating the many issues emerging from this context is critical to unlocking the potential of cloud services for society in a responsible way. The increasing importance of cloud services and cloud service providers (CSPs) in society with increasing digitization and digitalization has therefore caught the attention of policymakers and regulators seeking to maximise the benefits of the technology to society while managing its attendant risks – this is the nub of Cloud regulation.

To truly regulate Cloud Computing, one needs to have regard to the context(s) at hand, i.e., one needs to start by demystifying the cloud service arrangements for the specific context(s). Then, using Chapter 5's Formula I/the TPI Formula, one would have to start with the Law, i.e. by defining some clear legal frameworks in order to provide appropriate safeguards.

Queen Mary, University of London, set up the first worldwide Cloud Legal Project[545] (CLP) in 2009 which has been influential in this regard. As the

---

[544]   https://theconversation.com/the-worlds-data-explained-how-much-were-producing-and-where-its-all-stored-159964

[545] https://www.qmul.ac.uk/research/featured-research/cloud-computing--how-should-it-be-regulated/

founders of the CLP Project led by Professor Christopher Millard[546] note and write:

> "Cloud supply chains can be complex, with providers of important cloud services often relying on other cloud providers to deliver the services we use. For example, your Zoom meetings and recordings might be hosted by Amazon Web Services (AWS) or Oracle. Such 'layered arrangements' are extremely common, and there is often a lack of transparency as to where, and by whom, data are being processed. Indeed, most people who use Apple's iCloud to store their photos probably don't know that their data might actually be stored in facilities operated by other cloud providers such as AWS and Google Cloud… In 2010 the CLP was the first research team to publish a large-scale analysis of the standard form cloud contracts which people typically 'click to accept' without reading. The research showed how one-sided such contracts could be, and that many contained provisions that appeared to be unfair, or even unlawful"[547].

Professor Christopher Millard has since edited a book on the most comprehensive study of the legal issues pertaining to cloud computing (Millard, 2021).

As noted earlier, to regulate a cloud context would first benefit from an understanding and demystification of the cloud services context and arrangement, along with having a defined set of legal frameworks to provide appropriate safeguards. Several relevant existing legal frameworks already exist in most jurisdictions and regions (e.g. the EU).

To regulate many cloud [computing] contexts would typically include *data protection challenges* (requiring the employment of wide territorial/international data protection laws like the GDPR), *cybersecurity challenges* (requiring a cross jurisdictional cybersecurity law like the EU's

---

[546] Professor Chrisopher Millard, Professor Ian Walden and Professor Chris Reed -all of Queen Mary, University of London,

[547] https://www.qmul.ac.uk/research/featured-research/cloud-computing--how-should-it-be-regulated/

433

NIS2 Directive [548]), perhaps *cybercrime challenges* (requiring cross jurisdictional cybercrime laws), *competition challenges* and *consumer protection challenges* (preferably requiring a cross jurisdictional antitrust and consumer law like the EU's EECC code/directive established by Directive 2018/1972[549]), *human/civil rights* challenges (requiring the use of laws like the UNHR and the EU's Charter of Fundamental Rights), *Big Tech competition and antitrust challenges* (see Figure 6.4) covering Big Tech online (cloud) platforms that the EU denotes as "gatekeepers" (using the EC Digital Markets Act (DMA)[550], EU *consumer protection challenges pertaining to online content and services* (requiring the use of the EC Digital Services Act[551] (DSA)), etc.

Regulation	Scope
GDPR[552]	Processing personal data
NIS2 Directive[553]	Critical Infrastructure
EECC Directive[554]	Telecoms (incl. OTT services)
DORA[555]	Financial Institutions
PSD2 Directive[556]	Payment Services

---

[548] The EU's NIS2 Directive (Directive on security of network and information systems) is the EU-wide legislation on cybersecurity. It provides legal measures to boost the overall level of cybersecurity in the EU. It aims to achieve a high common level of network and information system (NIS) security across the EU's *critical infrastructure*. https://digital-strategy.ec.europa.eu/en/policies/nis2-directive

[549] https://eur-lex.europa.eu/eli/dir/2018/1972/oj

[550] https://commission.europa.eu/strategy-and-policy/priorities-2019-2024/europe-fit-digital-age/digital-markets-act-ensuring-fair-and-open-digital-markets_en - The Digital Markets Act: ensuring fair and open digital markets | European Commission (europa.eu)

[551] https://commission.europa.eu/strategy-and-policy/priorities-2019-2024/europe-fit-digital-age/digital-services-act_en - The Digital Services Act: ensuring a safe and accountable online environment | European Commission (europa.eu)

[552] General Data Protection Regulation - https://gdpr.eu/what-is-gdpr/

[553] https://digital-strategy.ec.europa.eu/en/policies/nis2-directive

[554] https://eur-lex.europa.eu/eli/dir/2018/1972/oj

[555] The Digital Operational Resilience Act (DORA) is an EU regulation that aims to strengthen the operational resilience of the financial sector and ensure continuity of critical services - https://regulation-dora.eu/

[556] https://eur-lex.europa.eu/eli/dir/2015/2366/oj

eIDAS Directive[557]	Electronic Trust services
Cybersecurity Act[558]	Certification framework for ICT

Table 6.2 – Patchwork of Different Regulations that apply to
'Cybersecurity' Regulation in the EU (non-exhaustive)
Source: David Michels, Cenerva Ltd Regulatory Training on Cybersecurity

So, cloud regulation requires the employment of several, if not many, legal frameworks in many jurisdictions. For example, the cybersecurity regulatory framework in the EU – *just by itself,* let alone other legal frameworks I note in the prior paragraph like the DMA, DSA or the UNHR – is *not* governed by a single EU directive on 'cybersecurity'. It is governed by a patchwork of different regulations that apply by sector and by activity as shown in Table 6.2. This is complicated.

For a complex EC/EU *cloud computing scenario context* involving cloud arrangements that cover cybersecurity, consumer protection, cybercrime, data protection, artificial intelligence, Big Tech cloud players, etc. – there may be twenty or more EU regulations 'in play'. This is why cloud regulation is extraordinarily complex, and still an evolving field of regulation.

Therefore, I surmise that even though Cloud Computing regulation is still emerging, it would employ statutory regulators (like data protection, cybersecurity, competition, consumer and cybercrime regulators), Regulatory Networks of such aforementioned statutory regulators and others, Meta-regulation, and other Regulatory Guidelines and Regulatory Sandboxes for some cloud [computing] contexts.

---

[557] https://eidas.ec.europa.eu/ - EU regulation on electronic identification and trust services for electronic transactions in the internal market, which provides a regulatory environment for electronic identification of natural and legal persons and for trust services.

[558] https://digital-strategy.ec.europa.eu/en/policies/cybersecurity-act -

the Cybersecurity Act strengthens the EU Agency for cybersecurity (ENISA) and establishes a cybersecurity certification framework for products and services.

6.7 Summary

This chapter on the challenges of regulating digital platforms (including the challenges of AI, Machine Learning and Cloud Computing) and the increasing digitalisation happening in our economies brings us to the end of the core chapters and narrative story of this book (see the Preface again). It is critical that such complex decisions about the future of our economies, political systems, and societies are widely consulted upon and deliberated amongst all the relevant stakeholders, including Governments, industries, and interest groups.

Much of this chapter – just like the last too (Chapter 5) – draws on my experiences, and the reader is encouraged to challenge my views expressed in the chapter. It is good for scholarship.

For readers who desire a deeper understanding on digital platforms regulation and the digital economy, Chapter 13 of Decker (2023) and Nwana (2022) are two excellent sources, respectively, to start from. A useful overview of different approaches to digital competition regulation is in Fletcher & Amelia (2023). For readers who desire a deeper understanding on the legal issues surrounding cloud computing, Millard (2021) is a truly excellent recommendation. As for the policy and regulatory issues pertaining to cloud computing, Levite & Kalwani (2020) is a genuinely good paper to start from.

Chapter 7

Conclusions

Even though, I title this chapter 'Conclusions', perhaps 'Reflections' or 'Postscript' (or all three) is (are) more apt. I make the following conclusions or reflections/postscript on the journey of this book.

First, I state in the Preface of this book that my goal for this book is rather bold: *to demystify economic regulation*, even though I assert that regulation is both complex and nuanced. I provide a 'Graphical Summary Narrative of Book' after my Preface, and it attempts to summarise – graphically - my entire logic narrative of this book. Much considerable ground has been covered in the last 6 chapters. I believe I have given it my best shot at Demystifying Economic Regulation, knowing fully well that it may have fallen short of my ambition. I take comfort the fact that I tried. The several academic practitioner reviewers of the book *concluded* that I have broadly succeeded in my goal.

Second, I wrote it because I have had the honour to have engaged and still engage several dozen to circa a hundred *practicing* senior regulators, policy makers, operators and others annually (for a decade now), as trainees interested in the principles and practice of [economic] regulation. Many a time, they ask me to recommend a 'textbook' or an 'accessible' reference book. I would typically provide recommendations like the edited volume, *Oxford Handbook on Regulation* (Baldwin *et. al*, 2010), the equally good *Understanding Regulation: Theory, Strategy and Practice* (Baldwin *et. al*, 2012) or the truly excellent *Modern Economic Regulation: an Introduction to Theory and Practice* (Decker, 2015, 2023). However, most of those who looked at these books, if not all of them, would typically revert telling me that the books were written by academics for academics, and that they assumed much multi-disciplinary knowledge that they do not have. I do not fully agree with them because I believe the Baldwin *et al.* (2012) and Decker (2023) books are quite 'accessible' – but, again, I may have the assumed multi-disciplinary and academic backgrounds that they [the trainees] do *not* possess. Indeed to support their [my trainees] case, (Baldwin *et. al*, 2010) themselves write about their handbook (p. 625):

"Handbooks are "expressions of the state-of-the-art of a particular area of study … motivated by three rationales. One is to state the 'latest' thinking within a predefined discipline… A second is to use the handbook as a tool to encourage cross-cutting discussions across disciplines that previously have remained distinct and unconnected. A third rationale … is for bringing together a defined field of study that draws on different disciplines and therefore contributes to a greater cross-disciplinary understanding of the field".

It is clear that practitioner regulators and policy makers are *not* the audience for the Handbook – though I have drawn much from it. This is why I have taken an approach of *A Practitioner's Guide: Theory, Methods and Practice* to my attempt to demystify economic regulation in this book. I only hope the reader *concludes* that this book adds to the body of practitioner knowledge on economic regulation.

Third, regulation is truly a fascinating area, but – as alluded above – it is inherently multi-disciplinary (across social sciences, business, politics, law, economics, technology, etc.) - and it is both an art and a science. I hope the reader agrees with this assertion, because this is a key conclusion of the journey of this book. I started the book thinking – because of my science and engineering background – that regulation is *much* more science than art. I ended the book concluding that the art in regulation is quite more significant than I thought. The reader may choose to contest this conclusion of course. Take the two 'two 'simplistic' formulae that I posit in Chapter 5 for Regulation:

Practical Regulation = Law + Economics + Technology/Engineering [Networks] + Key Supporting Evidence Base + Good Practice Principles (consistent, predictable and rational) + Soft Power + Much Commonsense [+ Hard Power, e.g., Fines, Sanctions, Penalties]   **Formula I**

Good Regulation = Addressing Market Failures + Checking Market Power of Dominant Firms + Application of best practice methods of regulation to do the formers **Formula II**

Frankly, both these formulae are works of 'art'. They are a distillation of my years of experience as a practitioner regulator. Both equations can arguably be seen as *heuristics*. I did a doctorate in AI at the tail end of the 1980s when expert systems with their heuristics were immensely popular. Investopedia defines a heuristic as "a mental shortcut commonly used to simplify problems and avoid cognitive overload. Heuristics are part of how the human brain evolved and is wired, allowing individuals to quickly reach reasonable conclusions or solutions to complex problems"[559]. The two 'formulae' I posit above are heuristics as they are arguably 'mental shortcuts to minimise cognitive overload, allowing regulation practitioners to quickly reach reasonable conclusions or solutions to complex regulatory problems'. These heuristic formulae were 'constructed' by me singularly – *not* derived from a survey of dozens of regulatory practitioners. This makes it an art because it is replete with all my personal biases, which a bigger sample would avoid. The 'use' of the heuristic formulae as I do in Chapter 5 also takes further 'art', as I realised towards the end of the book.

Frankly, had I taken the view that regulation was all or mostly art, I do not think I would have ever started a book of this nature in the first place! The reader may want to refer (again) to my 'Graphical Summary Narrative of Book' after the Preface of this book. That was my plan as I started the book, assuming regulation is much more of a science. However as I conclude, regulators have to 'balance' so many interests daily, from consumers, suppliers, Government, standard bodies, international partners, investors, the various drivers and evidence of the local economy (see Chapter 1), Government policy [and politicians], uncertainty, balance rationales, theories and hypotheses of regulation, and more. We all should know, then, that there is genuinely no 'right answer' to a complex regulatory challenge, but good regulators must derive 'acceptable' solutions that are defensible (legally, economically, socially, technologically, politically, locally-relevant) and more, despite the inevitable trade-offs. Regulation is genuinely politically-contentious in most countries. Clearly, there is much art to all these balances.

Fourth, regulation is arguably getting harder by the day as sectors digitalise: It is hard enough regulating the network industries (with local licensees of Chapter 3) *ex-ante*; it is so much harder regulating Big Tech behemoths with HQs in Silicon Valley (USA), Shanghai (China) and elsewhere. As we see in Chapter 6, the harms (i.e., negative externalities)

---

[559]https://www.investopedia.com/terms/h/heuristics.asp#:~:text=A%20heuristic%20is%20a%20mental,or%20solutions%20to%20complex%20problems. - Heuristics Definition (investopedia.com) – March 2024

that come with the digital economy, the Internet Value Chain and increasing digitization and digitalization are so numerous (see Figure 6.6), that you may want to admit defeat and not have these innovations in your country at all. Yet the positive externalities are equally humongous. Regulators should *not* regulate away their future Big Tech or other businesses in their countries - which may just upend some of current billion-dollar Silicon Valley behemoths. Afterall, these latter companies upended the Big Telcos and Big Oil companies to become the biggest companies in the world by market valuation. Please revisit Image 1.2 in Chapter 1 of the biggest companies in the world in 2010 compared to those in 2020 to confirm this fact. With the sort of technologies that 4IR promises (see Figure 6.9), who is to say some "sandboxed" new businesses in your country (with incredible new "fused" physical, digital and biological characteristics) may not be a company that upends some of the biggest Digital Platforms out there today? Why do you think Facebook/Meta is betting on Metaverse which – at the very least – fuses the digital and the physical? Though, I conclude regulation is getting harder, I also conclude it is getting ever exciting too. The new regulatory challenges are truly intellectually stimulating.

Fifth, regulatory failures can be very costly. Recall that according to Investopedia[560], the 2008 Financial Crisis sent the world into a great recession with 8.8 million jobs lost, unemployment spiking by 10% by October 2009, 8 million home foreclosures, USD 19.2 Trillion household wealth wiped out and much more. This was no little regulatory failure, arguably due to excessive deregulation of the finance sector during the Ronald Reagan/Margaret Thatcher years. It is the job of regulators to minimise such failures. The opportunity costs – too - of poor regulation (or stifling regulation) that I see in many countries are incalculable. One can only guess the magnitude of the value forgone by positing a counterfactual. For example, consider that the Mobile Financial Services (MFS) platform (M-pesa) owned by MNO Safaricom in Kenya had a turnover in 2019/20 of 50% of [Kenyan] GDP. Also consider this headline from the 23rd of January 2024: *Safaricom Faces Backlash As M-PESA Outage Hits Kenya: Poor Communication Raises Concerns*[561]. Clearly, M-pesa is now Critical National Infrastructure (CNI) – indeed an everyday

---

[560] https://www.investopedia.com/news/10-years-later-lessons-financial-crisis/ - Over 10 Years Later, Lessons From the Financial Crisis (investopedia.com)

[561] https://www.wazoplus.com/article/-safaricom-faces-backlash-as-m-pesa-outage-hits-kenya-poor-communication-raises-concerns--efd771c1 - Safaricom Faces Backlash As M-PESA Outage Hits Kenya: Poor Communication Raises Concerns

utility platform in Kenya. Imagine the opportunity costs had Kenyan Regulators wrongly stopped M-pesa in its tracks at birth by archaic regulations. This is a reasonable counterfactual. Today in 2024, Safaricom in Kenya provides more connectivity and financial inclusion than any other equivalent Industry company in other African countries. Regulatory forbearance, 'smart' and agile regulation enabled M-pesa to happen. Today, Safaricom is so dominant - M-PESA has a 97% share of m-money subscriptions in Kenya[562] - that the Central Bank of Kenya is forcing a structural (legal) separation (see Chapter 4) of the company's MFS/mobile money business from its telecoms business, in order to "improve regulation and customer protection".[563] However, a split can only occur if Kenya's Information and Communications (Amendment) Bill 2022 ends up being passed. As of June 2024, it has still not been passed into Law.

Sixth, statutory regulation is 'no longer the only show in town' and the future of regulation is increasingly collaborative amongst several established regulators. In Chapter 6, I introduce the UK network of regulators called UKRN, or UK Regulators Networks which describes itself as working "together to share knowledge and innovation, explore cross-cutting issues and build better ways of working"[564]. Indeed, the UKRN, established in 2014, brings together regulators from the UK's utility, financial, transport and housing sectors. These regulators have developed "strong relationships and a culture of collaboration and learning" for the benefit of consumers and the economy. Furthermore, as also seen in Chapter 6, there is an increasingly emerging role for several other models of regulation. For example, I conclude that the 'Narrow Scope' digital economy (see Figure 6.10) should be regulated – depending on the activities - using a combination of Regulatory Forbearance, No Regulation, Self-Regulation, Co-Regulation, Statutory Regulation and Regulatory Networks. The 'Broad Scope' digital economy - as well as tricky areas like 4IR/Industry 4.0 including Artificial Intelligence and Machine Learning – should/would be regulated through a combination of Statutory, Meta-Regulation, Guidelines and Regulatory Networks, with the support of Regulatory Sandboxes – in some combination. Policy makers and regulators should value the roles of other regulatory models beyond statutory regulations. Meta-Regulation, Regulatory Networks (see

---

[562] https://www.telcotitans.com/vodafonewatch/rumours-linking-safaricoms-m-pesa-outage-to-kenyan-tax-agency-denied/7651.article - Rumours linking Safaricom's M-PESA outage to Kenyan tax agency denied | Public Affairs | TelcoTitans.com

[563] *Ibid.* and https://techweez.com/2022/09/26/safaricom-split-to-be-done-by-jan-2023/

[564]https://ukrn.org.uk/about/ - About | UKRN: the UK Regulators Network

Section 3.1) and more collaboration amongst regulators are increasingly and necessarily the norm with increasing digitization and digitalization of sectors of our economies, not least as vertical sector regulators have to deal with horizontal (cross-sectors) issues like E-Commerce, the Internet, Cybercrime, Online Regulation, Artificial Intelligence and Big Data.

Seventh, understanding the objectives, theories and rationales for [economic] regulation of an industry truly matter. The economics concepts matter too. They are crucial to the design of any 'acceptable' regulatory policy, rules and regulations, preferably coupled with Impact Assessments (IAs). It may (or typically would) *not* be 'acceptable' for a monopoly firm to manufacture *less* output Q1 (see Figure 2.1 in Chapter 2) in order to maximise its profits, even if Q1 is much less than the demand needed by society. Regulation to the socially Optimal Quantity (achieving allocative efficiency) may/would be necessary. Most good regulators will want higher quantities and lower prices. So, the regulator may force the private natural monopoly to change production to the socially optimum point, to be 'acceptable' to society as Figure 2.1 shows. These economic concepts are important. Concepts like allocative efficiency, productive efficiency and dynamic efficiency (see Chapter 5) really matter, particularly in the regulation of scarce resources like radiofrequency spectrum, fossil fuels or minerals. Similarly, understanding typical regulatory risks and failures to well-functioning regulatory regimes would also help pre-empt them. These economics matters are the subject of Chapter 2. I urge the non-Economics readers of this book not to be put off by these concepts. They appear scarier than they actually are.

Eighth, with the regulation of [network] industries, statutory regulators draw from two broad toolboxes as shown in Figure 3.10 (Chapter 3). As Figure 3.10 diagrammatically overviews, on the one hand, statutory regulators possess tools (or methods) which are mainly "regulatory" in nature (like SMP regulation, access regulation, price regulation, universal service regulation, etc). On the other hand, there are tools under "competition law" (e.g. essential facilities, margin squeezes, etc.). There is this key 'interplay' of competition vs. regulation which is at the core of the market failure theory, which is especially important to economic regulation in general, particularly for network industries. If competition is working fine in some 'unbundled' component of the value chain of the industry, there is no need (or less need) for regulation. If it is *not* working fine – and there is some scope for competition judged possible for some component of the value chain – then regulation may force some competition in that component. I hope the reader concludes that there is much repeatable *science* in analysing this competition vs. regulation dynamic in network industries as is evident in all the seven network industries [case studies] overviewed in Chapter 3. Using basic tools like network theory, the characterising (through 'unbundling') the value chain of the said network industry, and analysing the scope for competition in each unbundled component – these would allow for making regulation vs. competition decisions across the value chain. I believe that the network industries case studies of Chapter 3 demystify much of how these industries are statutorily regulated today.

Ninth, many of our trainees are fazed and dazed with many methods of regulation like Price regulation, Access regulation and more. They do not understand their 'mechanics' and *when, where* and *why* they are used. I hope they understand the when, where and why questions from the Chapter 3 case studies. I also hope they would conclude from the details of the methods of regulation in Chapter 4 that they broadly allow for much repeatable *science* in their use. For example, the mechanics of Rate of Return and Price cap regulation described in Chapter 4 can be repeated in their countries. Ditto the DREAM framework to Enforcement regulation, the use of the World Bank "Gaps Model" in the implementation of Universal Services regulation, and the OECD tool on Risk-based regulation. The details of these methods of regulation of Chapter 4 – collated in one place - should hopefully demystify much of their use.

Tenth, I claim that regulation is capable of being demystified; indeed, I 'conclude' earlier in this chapter that I believe that I have done so in this book, at least to some significant degree. I am glad the esteemed reviewers of this book agree. The logic of my demystification is captured in the 'Graphical Summary Narrative of Book', just after my Preface.

Demystification – hopefully - happens because of the splitting of regulation into its 'unbundled' constituent 'components', further explaining the details of the 'components' (as I try and do in Chapters 2, 3 and 4). Chapter 5 uses heuristic 'formulae' and provides examples of their use. I believe Figure 5.10 on a 'More Detailed Inputs-Outputs Anatomy Model of the Art & Science of Regulation (drawing from the rest of this book)' is an important contribution to the demystification of regulation too – and there is more science than art to it, compared to my earlier two heuristic formulae of Chapter 5. I truly encourage practitioner regulators to try out the concepts I posit in Chapter 5, adapt them as they see fit and hopefully publish their own approaches to the demystification of regulation.

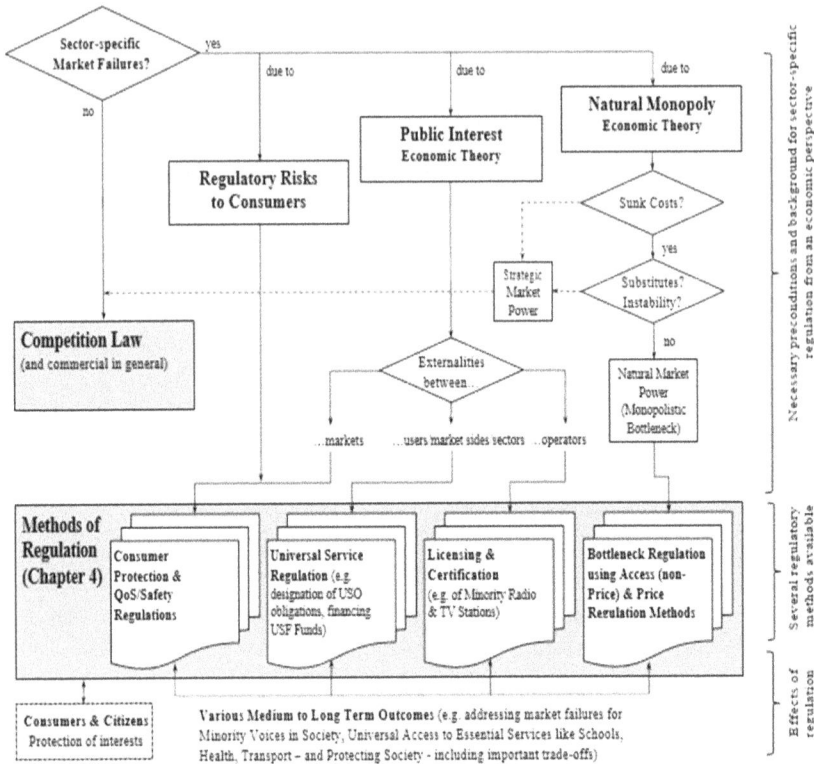

Figure 5.13 – A more general use of the Application of the detailed Anatomy Model of Regulation (i.e., Figure 5.10) to Network Industries

(Original Source of Diagram: Jaag & Trinkner, 2009[565] - with some updates by the Author; nevertheless, updated diagram printed with written permission of the original authors, Jaag & Trinkner)

Eleventh, I am a big fan of linking theory to practice of everything I do. I begin Chapter 3 with Karl Marx's (1819-1883) famous quote: he is famously reputed to have said: "Practice without Theory is blind; Theory without Practice is sterile." In my demystification efforts in this book, I have tried to 'fuse' theory and practice as much as possible. I encourage regulatory practitioners to do ditto. As I hope this book demonstrates, 'theories' of regulation are not marginal – at all – to practice. Chapter 3 should have expunged this view. Figure 5.13 (in Chapter 5) illustrates the

---

[565] https://www.swiss-economics.ch/RePEc/files/0016JaagTrinkner.pdf

use of theory in practice – showing the use of 'Natural Monopoly' theory, 'Public Interest' Theory and 'Regulatory Risks' theory.

Twelfth, regulation is by definition truly and necessarily *technocratic*. I hope this is truly clear from this book. This means that regulators must really keep up their skills through regular capacity building – and take the job of updating their knowledge most seriously.

Thirteenth, I am guilty (before you ask) of positing – as I do in Chapter 6 - that the 'Future of Regulation' would largely be concerned with the challenges of 'Digital Platforms' and the increasing 'digitalization' of most sectors of our economy, as well as the increasing challenge of regulating Artificial Intelligence (AI) and Cloud Computing technologies. My justification is simple – regulation must also follow where consumers spend most of their time – and it is online and with cloud-based services. In the UK, regulator Ofcom reported in 2023 that '*We're spending an extra two days each year online*'[566]. Ofcom reported that

> "the average amount of daily time spent online has seen a modest increase of eight minutes, to *3 hours and 41 minutes* a day in May 2023. This means the average online adult now spends around *56 days each year online* – two more days than in 2022". Young online adults aged 18–24-spend the most time online, at *4 hours 36 minutes each day in* May 2023".
>
> *The author's emphasis* – Source: [567]

The average UK adult spends 56 days online each year! Young adults spend – by my math – almost 70 days a year online in the UK. I do not know about you, but I find this incredulous. Digital platforms are increasingly dominating our lives, and increasing digitization and digitalization is birthing new sectors (e.g.., MFS), ushering in increased OTT services across all sectors of the economy and bringing in the narrow scope and broad scope digital economies. I hope the reader agrees with me that regulating Digital Platforms and Online Services would be the main

---

[566] https://www.ofcom.org.uk/news-centre/2023/top-trends-from-our-latest-look-at-peoples-online-lives#:~:text=The%20average%20amount%20of%20daily,more%20days%20than%20in%202022 - Top trends from our latest look at people's online lives - Ofcom

[567] *Ibid.*

key challenges of regulation for the near future, (i.e., at least for the next decade). The use of Artificial Intelligence (AI), Machine Learning and Big Data in many parts of our economies is accelerating.

Recall the Dutch example of Chapter 6 which led then-Dutch Prime Minister Mark Rutte's entire cabinet to resign in 2021 after two formal investigations in 2020 and 2021 uncovered systematic bias around a *biased algorithm* (employing AI) that the Dutch tax office used to assess benefits claims, affecting 1.4 million people. This is AI negatively impacting more than a million real people. Regulating Digital platforms, the digital economy, Online (OTT) Services, Cloud Computing and algorithms increasingly employing AI are the reasons why Chapter 6 of the book was written. Regulating Cloud Computing is truly another new and complex emerging area of digital regulation – which is why I also overview it in [at the end of] Chapter 6. The cloud is an essential aspect of our digital lives with FANGAM companies offering cloud computing as utility services, e.g. Google Search or Google Maps. The nebulous 'cloud' which are usually located at remote data centres and operated by major cloud service providers (CSPs) increasingly need regulation across several dimensions covered in Chapter 6,

Fourteenth, just as I was concluding this book, I heard and read about how '*Mexico's president vows to eliminate regulatory, oversight agencies, claiming they are 'useless'* [568], and that they cost too much. This is the real 'future of regulation' I dread the most that could start happening across developing and emerging market countries.

> "There are a lot of wasteful agencies that do not serve any purpose," President Andrés Manuel López Obrador said. "All of these supposedly autonomous agencies have to disappear.[569]"

During early 2024, the Mexican President vowed to send a bill to Congress to *eliminate the federal anti-monopoly commission and agencies regulating telecommunications, the energy market and access to Government information.* President Andrés Manuel López Obrador's only

---

[568] https://apnews.com/article/mexico-president-regulatory-agencies-government-e68011d7be18ba4156d17ef6f2c2eaaa - Mexico's president vows to eliminate regulatory, oversight agencies, claiming they are 'useless' | AP News

[569] *Ibid.*

6-year term concludes in 2024, and I genuinely hope his successor does not adopt a similar viewpoint.

I personally find this President López Obrador's view truly frightening. He is very wrong and mistaken on his views and intentions which I hope do not materialize. As I pen this paragraph in May 2024, his term of office is coming to an end as Mexico elected its first ever woman president in President-elect Claudia Sheinbaum [570] who takes over from President López Obrador on the 1st of October 2024. My key point here is that I can see other Presidents adopting similar stances like President López Obrador's. In my Preface of this book, I observe that the political class we observe in many of developing and emerging countries do *not* appreciate why regulators need to be left *independent*. I warn against our [Cenerva[571]] observations that the regulator class have become truly lazy to the task of regulation because it is hard, nuanced and complex, and in many cases caught in webs spun by dominant sector players. My point is if the regulator classes in such developing and emerging market countries become lazy and deliver zero positive outcomes from regulation, opportunistic politicians like President Andrés Manuel López Obrador [of Mexico] may/would have more than plausible reasons to eliminate regulatory agencies. Regulators must never take their statutorily elevated roles in society for granted. They must earn it every day, with demonstrable *outcomes* – not just outputs – to consumers and citizens *which would not come about absent regulation*. Lazy regulators may be sowing the seeds of their own elimination by politicians – and they would have only themselves to blame.

Fifteenth and lastly, [economic] regulation truly matters. This is at the heart of why I became a fulltime regulator for 5 years, and why I continue to work with regulators and policy makers. I want others to truly believe this too – and if just one reader of this book is 'converted' - it would have been worth the effort of me writing this tome. Thank you for indulging me and my views espoused in this book.

"Never tire to study – and to teach others." – Confucius.

---

[570] Mexico elects Sheinbaum as first woman president - BBC News - https://www.bbc.co.uk/news/articles/cp4475gwny1o

[571] www.cenerva.com

Selected References & Bibliography

Aldous, J. M. & Wilson, R. J. (2000), *Graphs and Applications: An Introductory Approach*, London: Springer Verlag.

Avrerch, M. & Johnson, L. (1962), "Behaviour of the Firm under Regulatory Constraint", *American Economic Review* **92**, pp. 1052-69

Ayres, I. & Braithwaite, J. (1992), *Responsive Regulation*, Oxford: Oxford University Press.

Baldwin, R., Cave, M & Lodge, M. (2010), *The Oxford Handbook of Regulation*, Oxford: Oxford University Press.

Baldwin, R., Cave, M & Lodge, M. (2012), *Understanding Regulation: Theory, Strategy, and Practice*, Second Edition, Oxford: Oxford University Press.

Baumol, W. J. (1977), "On the Proper Cost Tests for Natural Monopoly in a Multiproduct Industry", *American Economic Review* **809**.

Baumol, W. J. & Sidak, J. G. (1994), "The Pricing of Inputs Sold to Competitors", *Yale Journal of Regulation* **12**, pp. 177-186.

Becker, G. (1983), "A theory of competition among pressure groups for political influence", *Quarterly Journal of Economics* **98**: 371-400.

Brynjolfsson, E., McAfee, A., Sorell, M. & Zhu, F. (2008), "Scale Without Mass: Business Process Replication and Industry Dynamics", *Harvard Business School Technology & Operations Mgt. Unit Research Paper* No. **07-016**. Available at SSRN: https://ssrn.com/abstract=980568 or http://dx.doi.org/10.2139/ssrn.980568

Bukht R & Heeks R (2017). Defining, conceptualizing and measuring the digital economy. Development Informatics, Working Paper No. 68. Centre for Development Informatics, University of Manchester, Manchester

Decker, C. (2023), *Modern Economic Regulation: An Introduction to Theory and Practice*, 2nd Edition, Cambridge: Cambridge University Press.

Demsetz, Harold (1968), "Why Regulate Utilities?," *Journal of Law and Economics* 11(1), Article 6., Available at: https://chicagounbound.uchicago.edu/jle/vol11/iss1/6

Derthick, M. & Quirk, P. J. (1985), The Politics of Deregulation, Washington D.C.: Brookings Institution Press, September 1, The Politics of Deregulation | Brookings - https://www.brookings.edu/books/the-politics-of-deregulation/

CAA (2023), Economic regulation of Gatwick Airport Limited: consultation on proposal to extend the current commitments CAP2554 https://publicapps.caa.co.uk/docs/33/CAA%20Economic%20regulation%20of%20GAL%20(CAP2554).pdf

EC (2020), "Commission Recommendation (EU) 2020/2245 of 18 December 2020 on relevant product and service markets within the electronic communications sector susceptible to ex-ante regulation in accordance with Directive (EU) 2018/1972 of the European Parliament and of the Council establishing the European Electronic Communications Code (notified under document C(2020) 8750)", https://eur-lex.europa.eu/legal-content/EN/TXT/?uri=CELEX%3A32020H2245 - EUR-Lex - 32020H2245 - EN - EUR-Lex (europa.eu)

Esselaar, S. and Stork, C. (2018). ICT Sector Taxes in Uganda, RIS Policy Brief, 22 August 2018, https://researchictsolutions.com/home/wp-content/uploads/2019/01/Unleash-not-squeeze-the-ICT-sector-in-Uganda.pdf.

FCC (2017), Business Data Services in an Internet Protocol Environment et al. - Report and Order – WC Docket No. 16-143 et al., DOC-344162A1.pdf (fcc.gov) - https://transition.fcc.gov/Daily_Releases/Daily_Business/2017/db0330/DOC-344162A1.pdf

FCC (2018), *Eighth Measuring Broadband America Fixed Broadband Report, Raw Data - Measuring Broadband America - Eighth Report | Federal Communications Commission (fcc.gov)*

Fletcher, A (2020) 'Engaging the disengaged: why does it matter, and why is it hard?' Agenda (Oxera), June, https://www.oxera.com/wp-content/uploads/2020/06/Engaging-the-disengaged-why-does-it-matter-and-why-is-it-hard.pdf

Fletcher & Amelia (2023) 'International pro-competition regulation of digital platforms: healthy experimentation or dangerous fragmentation?' *Oxford Review of Economic Policy*, **39**(1): 12–33, https://doi.org/10.1093/oxrep/grac047

Friedman, T. L. (2005), "It's a Flat World, After All", *New York Times Magazine*, Apr 3, 2005.

GSMA (2022), The Internet Value Chain 2022, May, Available at https://www.gsma.com/publicpolicy/wp-content/uploads/2022/05/Internet-Value-Chain-2022-1.pdf

Gunningham, N. & Grabosky, P. (1998), *Smart Regulation: Designing Environmental Policy*, Oxford: Oxford University Press, p.422-453.

ICAO (2019), *Aviation Benefits Report*, Published through the cooperation and agreement of the global aviation Industry High-level Group, https://www.icao.int/sustainability/Documents/AVIATION-BENEFITS-2019-web.pdf

ITU-T (2013), The Mobile Money Revolution, Part 1: NFC Mobile Payments, ITU-T Technology Watch Report, May 2013, http://www.itu.int/dms_pub/itu-t/oth/23/01/T23010000200001PDFE.pdf

Jaag, C. & Trinkner, U. (2009), "A General Framework for Regulation and Liberalization in Network Industries", Swiss Economics Working Paper 0016,

December, Address: Swiss Economics SE AG, Abeggweg 15, CH - 8057 Zürich, Switzerland.

Jaag, C. & Trinkner, U. (2011), "A General Framework for Regulation and Liberalization in Network Industries" (2011). In Finger, M. and Künneke, R. (Eds.), *International Handbook of Network Industries*, pp. 26-53.

Koop, Christel & Lodge, Martin (2017) 'What is regulation? *An interdisciplinary concept analysis',* Regulation & Governance **11**(1): 95-108: https://doi.org/10.1111/rego.12094

KSA Bylaws (2002), *Telecom Act Bylaws*, Issued by the of the Minister of Post, Telegraph and Telephone resolution No. (11) dated 17/05/1423H (corresponding to 27/07/2002

Leinyuy, J (2013), *Unpublished Lecture Slides on Economics of Regulation*, City University, University of London.

Levite, A. E. & Kalwani, G. (2020), "Cloud Governance Challenges: A Survey of Policy and Regulatory Issues", Working Paper, Carnegie Endowment for International Peace, Publications Department, 1779 Massachusetts Avenue NW, Washington, DC 20036, https://carnegie-production-assets.s3.amazonaws.com/static/files/Levite_Kalwani_Cloud_Governance.pdf

Levy, B & Spiller, PT (1996), *Regulations, Institutions, and Commitment: Comparative Studies of Telecommunications*, Cambridge, Cambridge University Press.

Littlechild, S. C. (1983), Regulation of British Telecommunications' Profitability, Report to the Secretary of State, February 1983, https://www.eprg.group.cam.ac.uk/wp-content/uploads/2019/10/S.-Littlechild_1983-report.pdf

Littlechild, S. C. (1983), "Economic Regulation of Privatised Water Authorities and Some Further Reflections", *Oxford Review of Economic Policy* **4**: 40-68.

Lodge, M. & Stirton, L. (2010), "Accountability in a Regulatory State", in Baldwin, Cave & Lodge (Eds.), *Handbook of Regulation,* Oxford: Oxford University Press.

Meister, Urs (2006), "Franchise Bidding in the Water Industry — Auction Schemes and Investment Incentives", Chapter 5, In *Introducing Competition into the Piped Water Market*, pp 89–123, DUV. https://doi.org/10.1007/978-3-8350-9231-0_6

Millard, C. (2021) Editor., Cloud Computing Law, 2nd Edition, Oxford: Oxford University Press.

Moloney, N. (2010), "Financial Services and Market", in Baldwin, R., Cave, M & Lodge, M. (Eds.), *The Oxford Handbook of Regulation*, Oxford: Oxford University Press, pp.437-461.

Morenno Bolleso, N. (2021), *Google v Commission (Google Shopping): A Case Summary*, Available at SSRN: https://ssrn.com/abstract=3965639 or http://dx.doi.org/10.2139/ssrn.3965639, November 17, 2021.

451

Muente-Kunigami & Navas-Sabater, J. (2010), "Options to Increase Access to Telecommunications Services in Rural and Low-Income Areas", World Bank Working Paper No 178, Washington DC: The World Bank, https://openknowledge.worldbank.org/server/api/core/bitstreams/b879e8ed-410a-53bd-8a04-ee3ddd6c3829/content

Myers, Geoffrey (2023), *Spectrum Auctions: Designing markets to benefit the public, industry and the economy*, London: LSE Press, https://doi.org/10.31389/lsepress.spa

Navas-Sabater, Juan, Dymond, S.& Juntunen, N. (2002), "Telecommunication an Information Services for the Poor", The World Bank, Washington, D.C.

Nwana, H. S. (2014), *Telecommunications, Media & Technology (TMT) for Developing Economies: How TMT can Improve Developing Economies in Asia and Elsewhere for the 2020s*, London: Gigalen Press, http://www.amazon.co.uk/Telecommunications-Media-Technology-Developing-Economies/dp/099282110X.

Nwana, H. S. (2022), *The Internet Value Chain and The Digital Economy: Insight and Guidance on Digital Economy Policy and Regulation*, London: Pita Press, The Internet Value Chain and The Digital Economy: Insight and Guidance on Digital Economy Policy and Regulation (Telecoms, Media & Technology - Digital Economy): Amazon.co.uk: Nwana, H Sama: 9798800751444: Books

OECD (2019), *An Introduction to Online Platforms and Their Role in the Digital Transformation*, OECD Publishing, Paris, https://doi.org/10.1787/53e5f593-en

Peacock, M. C., Miller, S. E. & Perez, D. R. (2018), "A Proposed Framework for Evidence-Based Regulation", George Washington University Regulatory Studies Center Working Paper, Feb 22, 2018, https://regulatorystudies.columbian.gwu.edu/proposed-framework-evidence-based-regulation

Peltzman, S. & Keeler, T. (1984), "Theories of Regulation and the Deregulation Movement", *Public Choice* **44**: pp. 103-145.

Peltzman, S. (1989), "The Economic Theory of Regulation after a Decade of Regulation", Washington D.C.: Brookings Papers: *Microeconomics*, 52 pages, https://www.brookings.edu/wp-content/uploads/1989/01/1989_bpeamicro_peltzman.pdf

Starks, Michael (2004), Report of the Digital Project, Version 6, November 2004, http://www.kigeit.org.pl/FTP/kl/DICE/Report_of_the_Digital_Television_P roject_UK.pdf

Stern, Jon (1997) "What Makes an Independent Regulator Independent?" *Business Strategy Review* **8**(2): 67-74, https://doi.org/10.1111/1467-8616.00027

Stern, Jon (2007) *Infrastructure Regulatory Institutions and their Impact,* Papers from CCRP, City University Workshop 2006, https://www.city.ac.uk/__data/assets/pdf_file/0013/81031/stern_regulatory_ institutions.pdf - also published in *Utilities Policy*, **15**(3): 161-164, https://doi.org/10.1016/j.jup.2007.05.003

Stigler, G, J. (1971), "The Theory of Economic Regulation", *The Bell Journal of Economics and Management Science*, Vol. 2, No. 1 (Spring 1971), pp. 3-21, RAND Corporation Press.

Stork, C., Nwana, H. S, Esselaar, S. & Koyabe, M (2020), *Over The Top (OTT) Applications and the Internet Value Chain: Recommendations to Regulators, Policy Makers and Tax Authorities*, Commonwealth Telecommunications Organisation Paper, May 2020 – a follow up to the 2018 CTO Report into OTTs. CTO-OTT-Final-Report-for-Publication-Web_Online-22-May-2020 - https://cto.int/wp-content/uploads/2020/05/CTO-OTT-REPORT-2020.pdf

Taylor, G. & Middleton, C. (2020) Eds., *Frequencies: International Spectrum Policy Paperback* – Illustrated, Canada: McGill-Queen's University Press, https://www.mqup.ca/frequencies-products-9780228001782.php.

Taylor, Chris (2023), *Consumer Policy and Consumer Protection Regulatory Training Slides*, Cenerva Ltd, UK (www.cenerva.com)

Towse, A. & Danzon, P. (2010), "The Regulation of the Pharmaceutical Industry", in Baldwin, R., Cave, M & Lodge, M. (Eds.), *The Oxford Handbook of Regulation*, Oxford: Oxford University Press, pp.548-571.

UN-Water (2019), "Leaving No One Behind: Facts and Figures", *The United Nations World Water Development Report*, https://unesdoc.unesco.org/ark:/48223/pf0000367276

Vietor, R/ H. K. (1994), *Contrived Competition: regulation and Deregulation in America*, Boston: Harvard University Press (HUP).

Wasserman, S. & Faust, K. (2008), *Social Network Analysis*, Cambridge: Cambridge University Press.

WHO (2022a), Drinking-water: Key Facts, Drinking-water (who.int), 21st March

WHO (2022b), Sanitation: Key Facts, https://www.who.int/news-room/fact-sheets/detail/sanitation, 21st March

World Bank (2009), "Protecting Progress: The Challenge Facing Low-Income Countries in the Global Recession" (September), Background paper prepared by World Bank Group staff for the G-20 Leaders' Meeting, Pittsburgh, USA, September 24-25, 2009. Washington, DC: World Bank.

Index

CISA (USA), xxiii, 431

G

H

Investopedia, 72, 264, 301, 439, 440
Iphone, 13, 19
Islam, 35
ISO, 279

N

O

P

X

Y

Z